D1760302

University Centre at Blackburn College

Telephone: 01254 292165

Please return this book on or before the last date shown

Maria Mellins · Sarah Moore
Editors

Critiquing Violent
Crime in the Media

Editors
Maria Mellins
St Mary's University
Twickenham, UK

Sarah Moore
University of Bath
Bath, UK

ISBN 978-3-030-83757-0   ISBN 978-3-030-83758-7   (eBook)
https://doi.org/10.1007/978-3-030-83758-7

This Palgrave Macmillan imprint is published by the registered company Springer Nature Switzerland AG
The registered company address is: Gewerbestrasse 11, 6330 Cham, Switzerland

Acknowledgements

This book started life as a symposium that never quite happened, because of the COVID-19 pandemic. The scheduled speakers redirected their energies towards writing book chapters, instead of paper presentations, and they did so during a time of unprecedented uncertainty and upheaval. Our first thanks, then, go to our authors—for sticking with it and muddling through, and managing, somehow, to weave gold during these exceptionally hard times. Although they never had the chance to share their work in-person, we hope that this collection serves as an alternative means of bringing their ideas and thoughts together. We're very proud of what they—we—have achieved, and it feels very much a collective effort, made all the more extraordinary by the constraints of social distance.

We'd like to thank, too, the various cohorts of students who have taken our classes on 'Crime and the Media' over the years. They have been amongst the most astute viewers, thoughtful readers, and earnest critics—and for that we feel both grateful and hopeful.

Finally, we'd like to thank our families—our partners in particular—for putting up with so much dinner table chat about season finales, podcast twists, 'true crime' specials and 'must watch' docu-series.

Contents

Notes on Contributors

Brigid Cherry is an independent scholar, retired from the post of Research Fellow in Screen Media at St Mary's University, Twickenham. Her research is focussed on the horror genre, and fan cultures. Recent publications include work on *Twin Peaks* fan memes, graphic novel adaptations of *Alice in Wonderland*, and Gothic aesthetics in the films of Tobe Hooper. She is the author of the books *Cult Media, Fandom and Textiles* (2018), and *Lost* (2021). She is also a co-editor of *Doctor Who—New Dawn: Essays on the Jodie Whittaker Era* (2021).

Ian Cummins is a Senior Lecturer in the School of Health and Society at Salford University. His research interests include mental health and the CJS and cultural representations of crime and punishment.

Marian Foley is a former Senior Lecturer at Manchester Metropolitan University, UK. Her research focuses on the impact of sexual violence on women and children. She is currently a practising social worker working with children and families.

Simon Hobbs is a Senior Lecturer in Visual Culture at the University of Portsmouth. His research areas include extreme art cinema, fandom, material culture, paratextual studies and true crime. His work has been published in several edited collections and journals, including *Transnational Cinemas* (Taylor & Francis, 2015), *Popular Media Cultures: Fans, Audiences and Paratexts* (Palgrave Macmillan, 2015), *Snuff: Real Death and Screen Media* (Bloomsbury, 2016), and *Grease Is the Word: Exploring a Cultural Phenomenon* (Anthem Press, 2019). He is the author of *Cultivating Extreme Art Cinema: Text, Paratext and Home Video Culture* (Edinburgh University Press, 2018).

Megan Hoffman is an independent scholar. Her research interests include crime fiction, true crime, popular culture and gender studies. She is the author of *Gender and Representation in British 'Golden Age' Crime Fiction: Women Writing Women* (Palgrave Macmillan, 2016). Her work has also been published in several edited collections including *100 British Crime Writers* (Palgrave Macmillan, 2021), *100 American Crime Writers* (Palgrave Macmillan, 2012) and *Murdering Miss Marple: Essays on Gender and Sexuality in the New Golden Age of Women's Crime Fiction* (McFarland & Co., 2012).

Farhana Irshad is a Ph.D. candidate at St Mary's University in London. Her research focuses on horror and true crime genres and their evolvement to suit the digital streaming and exhibition practises within the current digital climate. Her broader research areas include binge-watching, narrative transportation and audience behaviour.

Martin King is a former Principal Lecturer at Manchester Metropolitan University, UK. His research focuses on masculinity, celebrity, fandom and popular culture.

George S. Larke-Walsh is a faculty member in Arts and Creative Industries at the University of Sunderland. Her current research focuses on audience engagement with discourses of crime in both factual and fictional films and TV. Her recent publications include a collection of new scholarship on the gangster genre as it appears in the global film (*A Companion to the Gangster Film*, Wiley-Blackwell, 2018). She also has various journal articles and book chapters on the social purpose of injustice narratives in true crime documentary, compassion in verité documentary filmmaking, and the complex appeal of retributive masculinities in contemporary British crime dramas.

Maria Mellins is an Associate Professor in Criminology and Sociology at St Mary's University. Maria is also a trained Independent Stalking Advocacy Caseworker (ISAC) with Paladin National Stalking Advocacy Service, which underpins her undergraduate and postgraduate teaching in the area of gender-based violence. Together with the Alice Ruggles Trust, where she holds the position of Trustee, Maria has written a suite of stalking awareness qualifications (SAfEE) that are Ofqual accredited and offered to education providers throughout the UK. In terms of research, Maria has a research podcast, *Murder and Society*, which covers issues concerning the representation of sexual violence and homicide victims in the press, the so-called 'ideal' victim, victim blaming, and tales of caution in Drug Facilitated Sexual Assault (DFSA) cases. Previously, Maria has written sociological monographs, novels, research papers, and articles including *Vampire Culture* (Bloomsbury, 2013) a non-fiction book that draws on Maria's Ph.D. in the area of subcultures: gender and crime.

Susanna Menis is a Lecturer in Law at Birkbeck London University, School of Law. She has worked with several criminal justice organisations and charities; her most recent engagement was with the Independent Monitoring Board of Prisons. She writes and publishes on the historical development of prisons; she has carried out several projects addressing criminal law doctrine within the context of social history, legal history, emotions, psychology and literature.

Sarah Moore is a Senior Lecturer in the Department of Social and Policy Sciences at the University of Bath. She has published four books, including *Crime and the Media* (2014) and *Detecting the Social: Post-1970s Detective Fiction* (2018). She is especially interested in socio-cultural processes of blame and responsibility. Her research is concerned with two questions. How and why are certain social groups made to feel responsible for their personal safety and wellbeing? And how do late modern social institutions make themselves accessible and accountable to the public? These questions have guided her research on a range of phenomenon, including courtroom broadcasting, the rise of the 'virtual' court, transparent justice initiatives, the cultural treatment of sexual violence, cultural amnesia in 'real life' crime drama, and post-1970s detective fiction as a form of critical sociological enquiry.

Carole Murphy is Associate Professor in Criminology and Sociology and M.A. Human Trafficking, Migration and Organised Crime. She played a key role in establishing the Bakhita Centre for Research on Slavery Exploitation and Abuse (formerly the Centre for the Study of Modern Slavery) at St Mary's University in 2015 and is currently Acting Director and research lead for the Centre. Her main research interests are in human trafficking and modern slavery and intersections with social problems, inequalities, addiction and health/mental health issues. Carole has published on the challenges faced by asylum seeking survivors in the UK (2020). Her report, *A Game of Chance?: Long-term support for Survivors of Modern Slavery* (2018), a study based on interviews with first responders in the UK including police and NGOs, evaluated the impact of gaps in long-term support for survivors of modern slavery. She has also published on the performance of identity in recovery from addiction and on media representations and political discourses about migration, smuggling and human trafficking. She is currently examining the experiences of survivors of modern slavery outside the NRM.

Alexa Neale is Leverhulme Early Career Research Fellow in Historical Criminology at the University of Sussex where her current research project concerns narratives of murder and mercy in the institutional memory of capital punishment at the UK Home Office. She also researches and writes about forensic photography and other visual representations of crime narratives. Her first monograph, *Photographing Crime Scenes in Twentieth-Century London: Microhistories of Domestic Murder* will be published by Bloomsbury later this year.

Hannah Thurston is a Senior Lecturer in Criminology at the University of Brighton. Hannah's research interests include prison and punishment tourism; qualitative and interpretative methodologies with a focus on narrative analysis; and the use of museums as research sites. In the last few years Hannah has published a book about Texan punishment museums, a chapter about the narratives at work within these museums and an article about evoking the ethnographic tradition in tourist sites. Within this context the cell often becomes a storied space and for a brief time we (the 'free') become part of that story. More recently though, Hannah has turned attention to tourist sites which tell supposedly 'true' stories about crime and punishment. These include policing museums, jails cell tours, and the focus of her chapter for this collection—*True Crime Museum* in Hastings, England. These attempts to capitalise on the sites and stories of crime and punishment may seem somewhat inconsequential, however, Hannah believes in an era of mass incarceration and penal populism, such developments warrant critical attention.

Gregor Urbas is an Australian lawyer and academic specialising in cybercrime, criminal law and evidence, with recent publications including *Cybercrime: Legislation, Cases and Commentary* (LexisNexis, 2nd edition 2020), *Biometrics, Crime and Security* (CRC Press, 2018) and *Technology Law* (Cambridge University Press, 2020). He has been a researcher at the Australian Institute of Criminology, the Law Council of Australia and IP Australia, has chaired a crime victims' advocacy group and worked as a barrister in the Australian Capital Territory. Dr. Urbas is currently an Adjunct Associate Professor at the Australian National University, teaching Criminal Law and Procedure, and also teaches online courses at Charles Sturt University and the University of New Hampshire.

Louise Wattis is a Senior Lecturer in Criminology at Teesside University. Her research and writing interests focus on crime, gender, and violence with a specific focus on the representation of female victims of male violence. She has published extensively around the gendered nature of serial murder and the framing of victims in popular culture and news media.

List of Figures

1

Introduction

Sarah Moore and Maria Mellins

Introduction

The early twenty-first century is a period of significant unrest, characterised by fractured publics, populist politics, emotion-laden debate, and social justice activism. Media treatments of violent crime bring these schisms, contestations, and injuries into sharper focus. We're thinking here, amongst other things, of the role of 'true crime' television series in opening up fierce debate about miscarriages of justice, the importance of news coverage of police brutality in galvanising support for the Black Lives Matters movement, and the trend towards deeply visceral, graphic

S. Moore (✉)
University of Bath, Bath, UK
e-mail: sm2315@bath.ac.uk

M. Mellins
St Mary's University, Twickenham, UK
e-mail: maria.mellins@stmarys.ac.uk

© The Author(s), under exclusive license to Springer Nature
Switzerland AG 2021
M. Mellins and S. Moore (eds.), *Critiquing Violent Crime in the Media*,
https://doi.org/10.1007/978-3-030-83758-7_1

1

accounts of violence in forensic police procedural fiction. These media portrayals do more than distil the cultural and social tensions that shape our public realm; they tell us much about how we might make sense of, and perhaps even respond to them.

This is the book's point of departure. It seeks to dissect, discuss, and critique cultural treatments of violent crime, and provide space to consider today's most significant cultural problems and dilemmas. It does so by returning throughout to a set of core themes: the failure of formal routes to justice, the educative role of the media, the commodification of suffering and victimhood, the unsettled bases of 'truth' and 'reality', and the jurification of media audiences. The book maps out the distinctive terrain of media coverage of crime in the twenty-first century—from the resurgence of interest in 'true crime' to the problem of ubiquitous as-live coverage, from increased interest in the serial killer to the creation of new spaces (some physical, others virtual) designed to deepen our vicarious experience of violent crime. And we discuss, too, the ongoing influence of more long-standing formats, conventions, and genres, including the Gothic, the monstrous Other, norms around 'ideal' victimhood, and serialisation.

In addressing these themes and ideas, the book brings together contributions from academics working in a wide range of disciplines, including sociology, criminology, psychology, law, film studies, history, literary studies, and cultural studies. This eclecticism has helped us, as editors, to think again about the role and meaning of crime stories, and we hope that readers find in the book a spur to open-minded, critical thinking about some especially thorny cultural debates. The book is novel, too, in its focus on critiques of crime—and here we have in mind the possibility that media texts can be both the object of critique and a spur to critique. Eagle-eyed readers will have noticed that we're interested, specifically, in critiquing *violent* crime in the media. The next section explains that focus, and considers some of the perils in studying media treatments of violent crime. From there, by way of contextualising the chapters that follow, this introductory chapter outlines a set of key developments and trends in early twenty-first-century media treatments of crime, including the vogue for 'true' crime, the proliferation of media platforms, and the global flow of images. The chapter ends with an overview of the book and an introductory study task.

The Media Construction of Violent Crime

This book focuses on violent crime in the media, and specifically the sort of coverage and depictions that make headline news, go viral, and become the basis for best-selling novels and most-watched television shows. We're interested, in other words, in the popular. We do so, as noted above, with a view to critiquing the popular—and revealing how popular renderings of crime might serve as critiques. Still, in focussing on the dominant media treatments of violent crime, we run the risk of replicating the omissions and distortions of popular culture, and so here, by way of introduction to the collection, we want to explore the media's role in shaping our understanding of violent crime.

Criminologists and Media Studies academics have long pointed to a fundamental disjuncture between the media-created view of violence and its empirical reality (see, amongst others, Surette, 2014). Violent crime, as it is depicted by today's mainstream media producers, tends to be sensational and dramatic, random and one-off. Think about your favourite detective novel or crime drama, the last 'true crime' documentary you watched, and a recent viral crime story. It's likely that most of these focussed on seemingly sporadic acts of violence, in most cases murder carried out by someone barely known to the victim. What this obscures is the fact that most acts of interpersonal violence are carried out by people that we know, and often by people we live with and who claim to love and protect us.[1] This is the complicated, messy, disturbing reality of violence: for many, it's a regular occurrence, hidden, and difficult

---

[1] According to Crime Survey for England and Wales (CSEW) data, acquaintances are most common perpetrators of violent crime (accounting, in 2019/20, for 43% of the offences reported). In this same report, 16% of the incidents were categorised as domestic violence. We know, though, that the CSEW routinely under-reports domestic violence and doesn't include sexual violence, so the proportion of violence that is perpetrated by intimate partners is likely to be far higher than suggested by CSEW data (see, for a really useful discussion of this—Cooper & Obolenskaya, 2021).

to escape. This might seem like a less drama-ready type of violence—everyday violence removes the settled 'before' and cathartic 'after' a crime—but we should resist the idea that there's anything inevitable about which forms of violence become the basis for media depictions.

A brief look at the changes in media depictions of crime and criminal justice in the post second world-war period alerts us to the fact that the media focus on spectacular violence is a relatively new phenomenon (Reiner et al., 2003). Far from there being a timeless logic to cultural treatments of crime—the idea that 'blood and guts' has always topped the news agenda—what we see is an evident shift in the second half of the twentieth century. From herein, we find, in greater occurrence, more gory and sexually explicit crime stories, more sensationalism, and a greater reliance on simplistic explanations for crime.[2] There are many reasons for this, including (in the UK) the growth and market repositioning of a tabloid press, the new capacity for computer-enhanced images, and a culture that is more open in discussing sex (which isn't to say it's inevitably less censorious). There is, too, a broader set of socio-cultural trends at work here. In the post-1970s period—and with a marked acceleration from the mid-1990s—late capitalist countries around the world embraced a 'tough on crime' agenda, one outcome of which has been a huge, unprecedented expansion in prison numbers. We are living in what criminologists call the era of mass incarceration, the effects of which have not been evenly felt: the prison population, in both the USA and the UK, is disproportionately made up of young black men from economically disadvantaged, urban areas.[3]

The mainstream media construction of violent crime serves, in many instances, to justify and naturalise the project of mass incarceration. It confirms to us that the world is a very bad and dangerous place—out there, on the streets, that is—and that prison and military-style policing are necessary solutions. None of this is to suggest an easy and straightforward relationship between political decisions and cultural treatments. We should avoid the idea that where politics leads, the media simply

---

[2] For more on this set of trends, see Moore (2021).

[3] See Christie (2016) for a very readable, critical criminological account of this trend in the USA, the UK, and beyond.

follows. After all, in precisely this same post-1970s time frame, there has been an evident growth in media accounts that are critical of the criminal justice system, whether that's at a local level of police action or at an institutional level of policy, organisational practice, and law. This too is a response to those socio-political conditions of punitive crime control outlined above, and this book is interested in what such accounts have to tell us about the construction and treatment of violent crime in the twenty-first century.

Still, these more critical cultural offerings run against the grain. The reaction to the final episode of the seventh (and, sorry fans, most likely final) series of *Line of Duty*, the BBC hit television police drama, is revealing in this respect. This hugely popular television series follows the work of AC-12, a fictional anti-corruption police unit, in identifying—we can't resist writing it—bent coppers. Across seven series, the AC-12 team has been tracking the kingpin (codename: 'H'), a corrupt police officer who facilitates the work of organised crime groups and facilitates police violence. Series seven culminates in the 'big reveal', and 'H' turns out to be—spoiler alert—an unremarkable, bumbling, inept, promoted-above-his-abilities Detective Superintendent. Institutional corruption, even where it takes murderous form, ends up being really rather mundane in *Line of Duty*. It is the product of a work culture that continually lets things slide, nepotistic in-groups that promote their own, and self-serving accountability procedures. This is what makes corruption an institutional problem, rather than—the more culturally dominant narrative—a problem of a few 'bad apples' driven by blood lust and evil intent.

The immediate social media response to *Line of Duty*'s ending, as well as the response in the mainstream news the following day, was generally scathing, with viewers bemoaning the absence of a proper villain and sensational denouement. The problem, for most of those posting on social media, was not that the ending was unbelievable; it was that it was *too believable*, too much of the real world. Don't we have enough of *that* in our lives already? It's a perspective that takes the goal of fiction to be, straightforwardly, to entertain. Yet, on its own terms, *Line of Duty* tries to do something more (even as it is resolutely popular in its appeal). It asks us to think differently about crime and criminal justice. We might all know, deep down, that institutional corruption works like this, but how many of us, when asked to think about crime, and violence, in particular, think first-and-foremost of the harm inflicted by organisations and institutions? Looked at in this way, our fascination with lone, bad apple perpetrators—whether it's an 'H' or a serial killer—reflects a deeper cultural fiction: that crime, and violence, in particular, is mainly a problem of individuals harming other individuals. Yet, as social harm theorists point out, if we were to focus our attention on the acts and omissions that cause the most harm—in terms of the number of people killed or hurt—we'd soon realise that corporations, governments, and work-places are responsible for most of the violence in our societies.[4] Most activists and academics concerned with interpersonal violence, too, see gender norms, institutional responses, and social structures of inequality as fundamentally violent in their effects. For such critical theorists, the official and cultural understanding of violent crime is part of this problem, in that it obscures and misleads, distracts and distorts. We share those concerns about the impact of dominant cultural narratives, even as we believe that there is room for specific media treatments to engage in and prompt more thoughtful and critical consideration of violence.

Twenty-First Century Media: Key Trends and Cultural Currents

Above, we noted that the book has a focus on popular depictions of violent crime. It also has a particular focus on the 'new'. Most chapters attend to media treatments of violent crime in the twenty-first century, and a brief glance at the contents list shows a recurring interest in recent media trends and cultural currents—amongst other things, 'real life' and 'true' crime, the image-driven nature of media coverage, and the role of the media in raising awareness about social harms and injustices. By way of introduction, this chapter turns now to consider the broader social

---

[4] We'd like to recommend, here, as additional reading, Canning and Tombs' (2021) introduction to the social harm perspective.

context for these trends, and the technological, cultural, and economic factors that have shaped them.

Chief amongst these factors is the emergence of digital media, and with it, the ability to produce and circulate text, images, and audio-visual material in real time, and with near global reach. We're so used to this set of socio-technological developments, that their novelty and impact often escape us. When the World Trade Center in New York City was attacked in 2001, news channels around the world abruptly switched their coverage to the 'breaking news' story. People round the world watched those events unfold in real time, and that was made possible by the ability, from the mid-twentieth century onwards, to instantaneously transmit and receive images from around the world via satellite and, since the advent of digital television systems, for us to watch those images in high definition. From the 1990s, as the Internet became widely available and streaming services emerged, the distribution of digital content has become part of our everyday lives. It has given us the ability to send videos and images—taken using our own mobile phones, often equipped with professional-grade cameras—to almost anywhere in the world, in the blink of an eye, as well as the ability to watch (and re-watch) almost any digital content that has been previously transmitted.

This set of developments has had a huge impact on the organisation of the media industry. Where, once, a handful of powerful sources—news agencies, as well as newspapers—had exclusive control over a news story, now, we expect to have access to major events as they happen and to hear from those 'on the ground'. We've seen a radical expansion in the media, with the proliferation of commercial channels as well as lay people taking on a new role in circulating their own content (so-called citizen journalists). We are now potential media producers, as well as media consumers. And even if we don't produce our own footage, we can contribute to debates about media treatments and coverage, again, in real time, as those stories are unfolding or being broadcast or released, via social media or the comments feeds of online news articles (all readily accessible on our mobile phones).

The interactive nature of today's media coverage puts us into a new relationship with the media we consume. For one thing, we might now expect that crime stories will have a spill-over effect, and be discussed and dissected in other media formats and platforms. On occasion, as in the case of the social media reaction to *Line of Duty*, those spill-over media effects themselves become part of the formal news agenda. More generally, there is a new porosity to media accounts, a tendency for stories that emerge in one format or medium to move to others, and even be produced with that in mind (something that Media Studies researchers call 'transmediality'). There is a restlessness to today's crime stories, and this, combined with the democratisation of media production alluded to above, offers up the possibility for previously unheard voices and accounts to come to the fore and circulate widely. Take, for example, Chanel Miller, a Stanford University student who was raped by a fellow student and then had to endure a trial in which she was effectively made into a silent bystander in the courtroom, listening to salacious re-tellings of 'what happened'. Miller re-inserted herself into the story by writing her own, incredibly powerful account and circulated it, first as a blog which quickly went viral, and then as a best-selling book (Miller, 2019). Such cases suggest the potentially radical and liberating effects of the new media landscape, particularly, as explored in Hoffman and Hobbs's chapter, for female-led stories to come to the fore. There is the possibility, here, for the media to play an educative and campaigning role, an idea taken up in chapters by Mellins and Murphy. And, as Irshad explores in her chapter on 'digital detectives', there are all sorts of opportunities for community-building, too, in the new online worlds that have sprung up to share thoughts and observations about 'real life' cases of violent crime.

There is a darker side to these developments. Urbas, in his chapter on live-streamed murder, details the challenges that arise when anyone has the ability to produce media content and media providers are poorly regulated. There is the possibility, too, that personal accounts or responses can be co-opted by media outlets, repackaged and featured as tomorrow's news. Commodification is a key driver here, and it's a factor that several of the contributions to this collection point to as a fundamental feature of media treatments of violent crime. This might give us pause to think again about the socio-technological developments outlined above. They have occurred in the particular political-economic context of late capitalism. Looked at in this way, media ubiquity is the consequence of the inexorable push to find new markets, create new wants, and produce new commodities. That social media debate might itself become part of the news cycle is an example of this. So, too, is the tendency for mainstream media producers to appropriate victims' and survivors' experiences and transform them into easily digestible, sensational stories. This is the focus for Menis and Neale's chapters in this collection, and both point to the tendency for co-opted victim-survivor stories to be highly reductive and pernicious in their reliance on ideas about cultural ideals about victimhood. Along similar lines, Cummins, Foley and King's chapter points to the role of 'that' photograph of Myra Hindley in media coverage of the Moors Murders in conveying the simplistic and rhetorical notion that she was 'pure evil'. The mass reproduction and circulation of Hindley's photographic image is at once a consequence of what's technologically possible and a product of, again, the drive to commodify the core elements of crime stories.

A similar set of observations might be made about another key trend in twenty-first- century media depictions of violent crime: the popularity of 'true' or 'real life' crime stories. We have in mind here the proliferation of television programmes that allow us to 'see under the bonnet' of criminal justice processes and practices—whether that's the police on the beat, courts in session, or the everyday degradations of prison life—as well as documentaries that allow audiences to follow investigatory work as it unfolds or re-examine cold cases. Many of the chapters in this collection speak to the peculiar interest in, as well as the distortions of and possibilities afforded by, these relatively new media formats. These crime stories are at once a product of those technological trends noted above—the sheer proliferation and availability of as-live and in-situ footage—and the endless drive to stimulate consumer interest. They reflect, too, an important set of cultural shifts in the late twentieth, early twenty-first centuries. Thompson (2005), in his account of the historical role of visibility in delimiting political power in European liberal democracies, points out that the technological changes in mass communication map onto and are intimately connected to changing ideas about power. He points to the rise of electronic media—first radio, and then, into the twentieth century, television—as allowing for what he calls 'de-spatialized simultaneity', whereby '[d]istant others could be rendered visible in virtually the same time frame, could be heard at the very moment they spoke and seen at the very moment they acted' (Thompson, 2005, p. 37). Thompson (2005) links this shift to the emergence of a more intimate mode of politics, whereby television, and the possibility for as-live transmission, creates an *expectation* of seeing an unvarnished, unscripted, more emotionally authentic side to political leaders. We might extend Thompson's (2005) thesis to think about our interest in 'real' and 'true' crime. Here, too, there is a new expectation and desire to be able to see what *really* happened, and this is twinned with an assumption that the 'truth' of the situation lies in the work-a-day practices of police officers, the unguarded remarks of a suspect, and newly unearthed 'facts'.

Into the twenty-first century, the fascination with such crime stories is frequently—though by no means always—combined with a sense of unease about accounts that claim to show us a new, complete reality. We know, for example, that the photographic image—that seemingly objective, non-representational form—is subject to editorial manipulation, gloss, and now, with new fears about deep-fakes, outright forgery and fabrication. Bruzzi (2016), in her writing on the 'true crime' documentary, draws attention to film-makers' understanding that twenty-first century audiences have a deep-seated scepticism concerning claims to objectivity. This combines with another important cultural current: widespread distrust in criminal justice agencies and actors. It is no coincidence that many of the 'true crime' documentaries that have gained widespread popularity over the last two decades are, to borrow a phrase Larke-Walsh uses in her chapter, 'injustice narratives'. They tap into and deepen a sense of deep dissatisfaction with official versions of 'what happened', in some instances in such a way as to assert the validity of their counter-narrative, and at other times to cast doubt on the possibility that we can ever know for sure.

The chapters in this collection circle round the achievements and limitations of 'true crime' injustice narratives. For Neale, there is a risk that such stories repurpose narratives concocted for the singular purpose of legal defence, and in such a way as to distort and obscure. Moore finds a similar set of biases at work, but is interested, too, in what the format of 'true crime' documentaries—and particularly their tendency to repeat and re-enact—tell us about the dangers of domestic routine and our collective fears about missing what's in plain sight. And for Larke-Walsh, the 'true crime' format issues an open invitation to audiences to get to know the protagonists and make up their own minds about 'what happened'.

For all of these authors, there is at once something modern—perhaps, late modern—about such media treatments of violent crime, and much more long-standing myths, formats, and themes at work. These include crime stories' historic reliance on serialisation (Moore), long-standing narrative techniques of characterisation (Larke-Walsh), and deeply embedded gender norms concerning female freedom and blameworthiness (Neale). This interest in the more enduring elements of crime stories is evident elsewhere in the collection. Wattis, for example, is concerned with the ongoing appeal of masculine violence, and considers the various forms this takes today across serial killer and gangster stories. Cummins, Foley and King, as well as Cherry, in her vivid account of the cultural bases of serial killer stories, and Thurston, in her fascinating analysis of a 'true crime' museum, point to the connection between today's horror-inducing depictions of violent crime and the gothic. They remind us that today's culture—however 'new' it might seem—relies, perhaps in renewed fashion, on the demonisation of those individuals who cross cherished cultural boundaries.

Overview of the Book

The book is organised into four parts. The first of these explores 'trials' in the popular culture, with a particular focus on 'true crime' documentaries, podcasts, and books. Chapter 2 examines the television documentaries that revealed the crimes of Jimmy Savile, the UK popular entertainer. Released following Savile's death, the documentaries enacted a 'trial by media' of the deceased-accused, and in doing so, Susanna Menis argues, transformed Savile's violence into entertainment. The focus of her critique is the documentaries' appropriation of victim-survivor testimony, and specifically their repackaging of these accounts as sensational stories of 'ideal victimhood'. What's obscured, Menis forcefully argues, is the institutional and societal bases for Savile's abuse, as well as the more emotionally complex aspects of victim-survivors' experiences.

Chapter 3 shifts our focus towards a more usual variant of the crime-based documentary: the true crime 'injustice narrative'. George Larke-Walsh's chapter explores the techniques used by hit US documentary, *Making a Murderer* (Demos & Ricciardi, 2015, 2018) to cultivate viewers' emotional engagement with the convicted felons, Stephen Avery and Brendan Dassey. Carefully weighing the criticism levelled at 'injustice narratives', Larke-Walsh points to the need to resist easy ideas about audience engagement (that 'Netflix tells us what to think', to borrow from her chapter title). Instead, in a fine-graded analysis of techniques of characterisation, she explores how the documentary series encourages us to 'get to know' the convicted, and in such a way as to prompt us to engage our critical faculties.

If, in some instances, media treatments of violent crime encourage an open re-appraisal of 'the facts', on other occasions they provide decidedly closed and partial accounts of 'what happened'. Chapter 4 provides one such case study. Here, Alexa Neale provides a detailed account of the murder of Gay Gibson in 1947 and its reimagining in twenty-first-century media as a 'cold case', with until-now hidden 'facts' revealed by new methods of forensic science. Neale's careful analysis demonstrates that this revisionist account is deeply one-sided, relying entirely on the narrative concocted by the legal defence in the original criminal trial and neglecting the ample evidence that led to the original conviction of Gibson's murderer. There are, Neale points out, decidedly retrograde patterns of cultural representation at work in the media rehashing of the Gibson case, not least of all the reliance on gender norms in the repeated interrogations of Gibson's credibility as a victim.

The opening three chapters tackle—albeit in different ways—the question of how documentary accounts of violent crime repackage reality, and the effects of that on audiences and the culture more broadly. Chapter 5 changes tack, and focuses on another key feature of 'true crime' documentary series: their serial format and use of repetition. Based on an in-depth reading of the television documentary series *The Staircase* (de Lestrade, 2004) and Season One of the podcast series *Serial* (Koenig, 2014), Sarah Moore explores the function of re-enactment, doubling, and revelation in these crime stories. She argues that these tell us something about the collective, cultural problems of remembering, reliving, and re-seeing that are especially pertinent in the early twenty-first century, as we are forced to address historic abuses that have been there all along in plain sight.

Part II of the book focusses on representations of victim-survivors. Chapter 6 considers the impact of the #MeToo movement on 'true crime' stories, and specifically the greater focus on victim-survivors' accounts and lives. Here, Megan Hoffman and Simon Hobbs point to the rise of female-led 'true crime' stories, and consider the more radical possibilities afforded by the 'true crime' genre for dislodging dominant accounts of crime and giving voice to those who have been historically side-lined. In a wide-ranging discussion—of, amongst other formats, television series, podcasts, and books—Hoffman and Hobbs explore how 'true crime' accounts can work towards reclaiming stories of violence and restituting victims' voices.

Chapters 7 and 8 shift our focus towards the possible role of the media in campaigning, educating, and raising awareness about the risks and experience of victimisation. Maria Mellins, in Chapter 7, focuses on the case of Alice Ruggles, who was murdered by her stalker in 2016. Mellins forensically details Alice's experiences, and through this explains the key dimensions of stalking behaviour. She identifies and critiques a cultural tendency to trivialise stalking, not least of all by linking it to norms of romantic love. Mellins balances these problems against the potential of certain media formats (such as podcasts and documentaries) to provide a much-needed insight into victims' experiences of stalking.

Chapter 8 continues this critical focus on the question of what the media can and should tell us about violent crime. Carole Murphy's concern here lies with the media depiction of coercive control, and her analysis takes in two very different contexts: domestic abuse and intimate partner violence on the one hand, and modern slavery and human trafficking on the other. She points out that both categories of crime are hidden from public view, and so the media plays an especially crucial role in raising public awareness. In her thorough analysis of media coverage—ranging across news items, as well as fictional treatments of coercive control—Murphy points to consistent distortions in media coverage, including a lack of concern for the psychological mechanisms of controlling behaviour. She points out that this is mirrored in the limited public and professional understanding of the meaning and techniques of coercive control.

The third part of the book, titled 'Consuming Homicide Narratives', considers the sickening allure of violent crime stories, with a particular focus on serial killer narratives. In Chapter 9, Ian Cummins, Marian Foley and Martin King draw upon their extensive research on the Moors Murders to explore the role of the photographic image—in particular, the infamous police mug-shot of Myra Hindley ('*that photograph*', as Cummins, Foley and King put it)—in sustaining salacious interest in this notorious crime. For Cummins, Foley and King, the commodification of the image—its perpetual reproduction and re-circulation—is key to this, as is the association of serial killers with the celebrity culture of the post-1960s period. They note, too, the influence of a much more long-standing artistic tradition, the Gothic, in the depiction of the Moors Murderers.

This proposition—that popular culture's treatment of serial killers betrays the continued influence of the Gothic—is more roundly explored in Chapter 10. Based on an in-depth analysis of three US hit television drama series from the 2010s—*Aquarius* (NBC, 2015–16), *I Am the Night* (TNT, 2019), and *Mindhunter* (Netflix, 2017–19)—Brigid Cherry sketches out the connection between these twenty-first-century serial killer stories and their non-fictional antecedent texts, as well as the Gothic. She explores the depiction of their protagonists as supernatural Gothic monsters, by turns vampiric, devilish, and spectral. There are other forms of Othering at work in these US television shows, not least of all, Cherry observes, that which springs from the US history of racial segregation and prejudice. She ends her chapter by considering these shows as examples of an African American Gothic genre, concerned with the long-buried stories of abuse and collective trauma experienced by African American communities.

Chapter 11, the last in this trio of chapters, takes an expansive look at cultural depictions of the serial killer across fact-based and fictional media treatments, taking in discussions of, amongst other things, the podcast series *My Favorite Murder* (2016—Kilgariff & Hardstark), the novels of Thomas Harris, and the television series *Dexter* (Showtime, 2006–2013). Louise Wattis's concern here is with what she calls the 'enduring fascination with troubled violent subjects'. She calls for a broader appreciation of media depictions in this area, and neatly extends her analysis of serial killer narratives to consider depictions of the gangster as a figure in popular culture. In comparing popular representations of these two figures, Wattis explores what they tell us about the cultural construction and consumer appeal of masculine violence.

Where the chapters in the third part of the book are in different ways interested in the appeal of violent crime stories (and, by extension, the question of why we consume them), the fourth and final part of the book turns our attention to the spaces—physical and virtual—in which we consume images and stories of violent crime. In Chapter 12, Hannah Thurston throws open the doors of the 'true crime' museum. She starts by offering a typology of these dark tourism sites and then takes us on a guided tour of one particular 'true crime' museum dedicated to the crimes of serial killers. Thurston's reflective, thoughtful critique considers, amongst other things, the role of gamification and humour in encouraging particular forms of consumer engagement, as well as the differences between US and UK 'true crime' museum spaces (and here the discussion picks up on themes discussed elsewhere in the collection, namely the role of celebrity culture and the influence of the Gothic).

Chapter 13 conjures up an altogether different set of spaces for violent crime-enthusiasts. Here, Farhana Irshad considers the rise of the 'digital detective', that is, amateur sleuths who carry out online research to solve violent crime. Her chapter ranges across discussions of specific online sites that facilitate this research, such as the BuzzFeed Unsolved Network, as well as television shows documenting the extensive work of 'digital detectives'. In an extended analysis of the hit Netflix series, *Don't Fuck with Cats: Hunting an Internet Killer*, Irshad explores how the activity of digital detection creates distinctive online spaces and communities that offer safety and a sense of belonging. She extends this analysis to consider how 'true crime' podcasts urge a form of audience engagement akin to detective-work and offer new forms of narrative-immersion.

Where Chapter 13 provides an insight into the new forms of sociability that might emerge in online worlds where information is widely and readily available, Chapter 14 focuses our attention on the darker side of these developments: namely, a lack of control and regulation over what is transmitted. Gregor Urbas assesses the challenges involved in tackling the live streaming of murder, provides an overview of key cases, and reviews the legislation introduced in an Australian context. He explores, amongst other things, the role of social media sites in spotting and removing such content (and the challenges therein), as well as the problematic vagueness of legal definitions of 'abhorrent violent material'.

The final chapter in this collection—Chapter 14—seeks to draw together the insights from across the collection to identify and discuss a set of key themes: the commodification of victims, spatial transformation and digital crime, nostalgic aesthetics, and the educative role of the media.

Introductory Study Questions

Think of three stories (or series of stories) that you've come across in the last year that focus on violent crime. Your examples might include notable news stories, television series, podcast series, films, novels, etc.

- What sort of crime is depicted?
- Did they have a spill-over effect, and receive coverage or attention in other media and media formats?
- How are alleged perpetrators and victims-survivors represented? What are the key themes and story-elements?
- Do they reflect any of the media trends and cultural currents noted above? If so, do they tell us anything about the impact and meaning of these trends and currents?

Now think: how do these crime stories ask us to think about violent crime? Does this run counter to or confirm dominant ideas about violent crime?

Bibliography

Bruzzi, S. (2016). Making a genre: The case of the contemporary true crime documentary. *Law and Humanities, 10,* 249–280.

Canning, V., & Tombs, S. (2021). *From social harm to Zemiology: A critical introduction.* Routledge.

Christie, N. (2016). *Crime control as industry: Towards gulags, Western style.* Routledge.

Cooper, K., & Obolenskaya, P. (2021). Hidden victims: The gendered data gap of violent crime. *British Journal of Criminology, 61*(4), 905–925 (Online-First).

Miller, C. (2019). *Know my name: The survivor of the Stanford sexual assault case tells her story.* Penguin, Viking.

Moore, S. (2021). Crime and the media. In. P. Davies & M. Rowe, *Criminology: An introduction.* Sage.

ONS. (2021). *The nature of violent crime in England and Wales: Year ending March 2020.* https://www.ons.gov.uk/peoplepopulationandcommunity/crimeandjustice/articles/thenatureofviolentcrimeinenglandandwales/yearendingmarch2020

Reiner, R., Livingstone, S., & Allen, J. (2003). From law and order to Lynch Mobs: Crime news since the Second World War. In P. Mason (Ed.), *Criminal visions: Media representations of crime and justice* (pp. 13–32). Willan.

Surette, R. (2014). *Media, crime, and criminal justice: Images and realities* (5th ed.). Wadsworth Press.

Thompson, J. B. (2005). The new visibility. *Theory, Culture, and Society, 22*(6), 31–51.

Part I

Popular Culture 'Trials'

2

The Deceased-Accused and the Victim as a Commodity: Jimmy Savile as a Case Study to Examine the Role of Real-Crime Documentary in Reproducing Violence as Entertainment

Susanna Menis

Introduction

On the 3 October 2012 the documentary *Exposure: The Other Side of Jimmy Savile* led to a cultural transformation of Savile's place within British entertainment, and over time a more wholesale change to the historical narrative concerning sexual predation in this key UK institution. This Independent Television (ITV) documentary, in which shaky and shy victims revealed the unsettling reality that the philanthropist, TV and radio presenter Jimmy Savile was, rather than a national treasure, a sexual predator, broke decades of silence. These alleged sex crimes took place in the 1960s and 1970s; most victims were girls and boys in their early teens. Several other documentaries on this subject were aired between 2012 and 2016, one of the last being *Abused: The Untold Story* by the British Broadcasting Company (BBC), broadcast on 11 April

S. Menis (✉)
School of Law, Birkbeck London University, London, UK
e-mail: s.menis@bbk.ac.uk

© The Author(s), under exclusive license to Springer Nature
Switzerland AG 2021
M. Mellins and S. Moore (eds.), *Critiquing Violent Crime in the Media*,
https://doi.org/10.1007/978-3-030-83758-7_2

2016.[1] Savile was by no means the first UK celebrity to be subject to such revelations, but what did make this case unique was the fact that the first documentary was aired almost a year after Savile's death.

This chapter is concerned with the role of the media in reproducing violence as entertainment. It aims to demonstrate that the documentaries revealing Savile's crimes were responsible for a problematic culturalisation and construction of the victims as ideal. Certain victims of sex crimes—those whose behaviour and attitudes are not perceived to be socially desirable—have historically been denied recognition as genuine victims, and as such have been routinely treated as undeserving of public attention and protection. The ripple effect triggered by these documentaries in relation to the need for a better protection of victims of sex crimes is evident in the mobilisation of several other public agencies; however, it is argued here, that this has created the misconception that the situation is about to change for the better. By capitalising on what will be referred to here as the real-crime-*victim* documentary, the media has been a participant in the commodification of the victim; in other words, Savile's victims became objects of entertainment. This chapter does not aim to dispute or challenge these victims' stories; their participation in these documentaries is not judged. The focus of attention here is on the moral, social, cultural and legal detriments caused by partial, commercially driven, media attention.

The chapter has four sections: (1) The real-crime documentary and Jimmy Savile; (2) The Ideal Victim; (3) Victim as commodity; (4) Implications: reproducing violence. Section "The Real-Crime Documentary and Jimmy Savile" provides a context to the events; it explains who Jimmy Savile was and the place he had within British society. It then moves on to examine some of the characteristics of the real-crime documentary. Finally, it explains how the Savile documentaries are different from mainstream crime documentaries and the implications of that.

---

[1] The broadcasts have been as follows: *Exposure: The Other Side of Jimmy Savile* (ITV1, 3 October 2020); *Jimmy Savile—What the BBC Knew: A Panorama Special* (BBC1, 22 October 2012); *Exposure Update: The Jimmy Savile Investigation* (ITV, 21 November 2012); *Panorama—After Savile: No More Secrets?* (BBC1, 4 November 2013); *Panorama—Savile: The Power to Abuse* (BBC1, 2 June 2014); *Britain's Worst Crimes: Jimmy Savile* (Channel 5, 18 November 2015); *Abused: The Untold Story* (BBC1, 11 April 2016); *Louis Theroux: Savile* (BBC2, 2 October 2016).

Section "The Ideal Victim" starts with a discussion of the changing role of victims in the criminal justice landscape; then, the chapter considers how this has affected the attention paid to sex crime victims. Section "Victim as Commodity" examines extensively the role of the media as a conduit for culturalisation, its commercial drive and its responsibility for the commodification of the victim. Finally, section "Implications: Reproducing Violence" brings the discussion to an end with critical considerations on the moral, social and legal implications of what is considered here to be socially dangerous media attention.

The Real-Crime Documentary and Jimmy Savile

Jimmy Savile died on 29 October 2011 at the age of 84. Up to this point and for perhaps a year thereafter, Savile was known and remembered as a national icon (Leyshon, 2012). News tributes at the time remembered him as, for example, a 'flamboyant disc jockey with a flair for good works' (Sweeting, 2011), an 'eccentric adornment to British public life' (*The Telegraph*, 2011), and '[a] proper British eccentric' (Bull, 2011). He was a media personality: a DJ, television and radio presenter. However, he stood out. He certainly benefited from the cultural effects of pop music (Collie & Irwin, 2013), being the presenter of the music chart show *Top of the Pops* during its peak time (1960s–1980s).[2] A reviewer commented, for example, that 'I don't know what it was like in the 60s and 70s but you can't argue with audience figures of 15–16 million, while [*Top of the Pops*] now gets 2 million if it's lucky'. Another mentioned that 'I was born in 1967 so I can remember watching *Top of the Pops* from the early seventies to its peak which was the early 1980s. Beyond that I think it has gone downhill' (*Top of the Pops* IMDb, 2003–2019). Savile's eccentric style accompanied by his generous charity-work, made him not only a

---

[2] The show was first aired in 1964 on the British Broadcasting Corporation (BBC) (Top of the Pops [TV Series 1964–2019])—IMDb https://www.imdb.com/title/tt0139803/. Accessed 28 Apr 2020.

70s and 80s VIP, but also an officer of the Order of the British Empire in 1972 and a knight in 1990.

This idyllic picture was occasionally at risk of being spoiled. Several allegations of sexual misconduct and suggestions of child abuse were made throughout Savile's career. Sporadic police investigations came to a halt through lack of evidence. At least twice during this period, Savile sued tabloid newspapers for defamation (Casciani, 2013). Journalist Lynn Barber confronted him in an interview in 1990: 'What people say is that you like little girls'. Savile replied that this impression was due to the fact that he was in the pop industry, and 'when I go anywhere it's the young ones that come round me' (Barber, 2020). To Barber, this made sense: 'this seems a perfectly credible explanation of why rumour links him to young girls' (Barber, 2020). In 1994, in an interview for *The Times*, Julia Llewellyn Smith reflected on the fact that 'countless rumours circulate about his sex life, but no tabloid paper has ever dredged up any evidence of any liaison and whatever the truth may be'. She concluded that 'Sir Jimmy's motivations may not then be saintly, but it seems ungracious to quibble. After all, a lot of people have a bit of fun and nobody, it seems, gets hurt' (Llewellyn-Smith, 1994). In a documentary aired in 2000 by the BBC, Louis Theroux teased out paedophile allegations; to these, Savile replied that 'it's easier for me as a single man to say I don't like children because it puts a lot of salacious tabloid people off the hunt [...] and it worked a dream' (When Louis Met...Jimmy, 2000). Despite these earlier signs of a problem, it was only in 2012, a year following his death, that Savile was declared by the media as a predatory sex offender; they were allegations to which Savile could make no reply.

Before discussing the two documentaries concerning Jimmy Savile, it is helpful to briefly explain the real-crime documentary paradigm. Illustrating its recent 'explosion in number' (Bruzzi, 2016, p. 249), the British audience only needs to skim through the BBC, ITV, Channel 4 and Netflix, for example, to gain an understanding of the magnitude of the real-crime documentary phenomenon. Usually, the documentary will follow an accused during their pre- and/or post-trial journey; hence, fostering a sense of empathy towards the subject. Bruzzi explains that such documentaries have gained 'cultural prominence and resonance'

(2016, p. 251); they have opened a channel for public debate on questions of social and legal justice (Fuhs, 2014). Scholars have grappled with the idea of what they term real-life crime documentary's 'activist goals'. On the one hand, Fuhs, for example, argues that such documentaries tease out the 'structural imbalance of power between the state and its subjects' (2014, p. 783). It allows for an alternative, and perhaps more 'just' (as suggested by the documentary itself) public trial; while at the same time, it facilitates another judgement—the one 'on the legitimacy of the actual trial', that is, the flaws in the law (Fuhs, 2014, p. 784). On the other hand, while it might appear that the documentary is critical of the criminal justice system (in whichever jurisdiction the story lies), it also reinforces the place and authority of the law and its cultural value as a social institution (Fuhs, 2014; Silbey, 2010). For example, the documentary's narrative might emphasise how the trial's adversarial principles allow for a cross examination that leads to the revealing of the police's malpractice; or alternatively, how the acceptance of new evidence and subsequent appeal is, after all, facilitated by the law. Furthermore, Silbey explains that originally, the documentary genre was used by the state to facilitate 'nation building, public education, and advocacy'; it has 'consistently been harnessed to the manufacture of social consent' (2005, p. 153).

Overall, for Bruzzi (2016), real-crime documentaries have helped shape perceptions about the law, justice, legal narratives and evidence; yet, it is the question of 'truth' that is of great concern. Tracing the history of 'filmmaking realism', Silbey explains that documentaries bring a constructed reality, and that 'the perception of film's capacity to wholly and truthfully reveal the world is and was always a myth' (2005, p. 144). Although its aim might be to objectively depict real life, according to Silbey, this is still a 'form of artistic and politicized expression' (2005, p. 144). In other words, as put by Renov, this is an 'artful rephrasing of the historical world' (1993, cited by Fuhs, 2014, p. 782). The one-sided narrative approach taken by the real-crime documentary is complex. It reflects only one version of an historical event (Silbey, 2005); Nichols suggests that 'it introduces the moralizing perspectives or social belief of an author' (2001, cited in Silbey, 2005, p. 152). Also, the constructed truth depends on the 'viewers' interaction' with the narrative (Winston,

1995, cited in Fuhs, 2014, p. 800). Silbey reminds us that the documentary's 'voices' have been specifically chosen, to persuade the audience of a particular point of view (Silbey, 2005, 2010). Narrative, montage and their juxtaposition are used to shape and lead the viewers towards a desired conclusion (Fuhs, 2014; Silbey, 2005). To build integrity and credibility, the story-line is further strengthened with cinematic techniques such as re-enactment, archival footage, interviews and music. Bruzzi explains that returning to the site of crime is also a potent feature in helping to make the audience active spectators, investigators and adjudicators of the subject's case (Bruzzi, 2016).[3]

The Savile documentaries, however, present other and different characteristics than the classic real-crime documentary. The two Savile crime documentaries discussed here were aired four years apart. The first documentary, *Exposed: The Other Side of Jimmy Savile*, was aired by the British commercial channel Independent Television service (ITV) on 3 October 2020. The second documentary, *Abused: The Untold Story*, was broadcast by the BBC on 11 April 2016. Although the BBC documentary was more sophisticated in style and presentation, both documentaries were constructed around witnesses' and victims' narratives; in both there was a sense that the BBC, as an institution, was responsible for ignoring decades of Savile's sexual exploitation of teenage girls. A police investigation was carried out alongside an independent review of the historical sex abuse by the former High Court Judge Dame Janet Smith in 2016; this confirmed the allegations, at least as far as it was feasible by only drawing on victims' statements (Smith, 2016). These documentaries have triggered a variety of academic debates. For example, recent research has grappled with the question of physically removing Jimmy Savile from the national memory by tampering with the BBC archives (Aust & Holdsworth, 2017). Another study, on behalf of the Secretary of State for Health, went as far as attempting to draw 'lessons' from what was identified as poor security measures to prevent uncontrolled visits to patients under the care of the National Health Service (NHS) during Savile's time and thereafter (Lampard & Marsden, 2015). In an article in *Celebrity*

---

[3] Moore et al. (2019) make similar observations in relation to what they argue is a questionable transparency of video transmissions of (real) courts' proceedings.

2 The Deceased-Accused and the Victim ...

Studies one scholar reflected on the possibility that the media culture generated by cases of historical sex abuse scandals[4] can facilitate a therapeutic catharsis for the public (Bainbridge, 2020). Other academic work has drawn attention to what has been identified as the BBC's institutional denial of sex abuse (e.g. Greer & McLaughlin, 2012, 2013, 2015).

However, the role of the media as adjudicator, its 'use' of the victims for filmmaking purposes and the fact that the alleged offender was dead before his crimes were verified by law—all these elements have received little or no attention; in turn, these form the focal point of this chapter. The Savile documentaries are an example of a sub-genre of real-crime documentaries where the alleged offences are exposed only after the culprit has died, and thus the narrative only focuses on the victims' stories. The documentaries about the legendary Michael Jackson in the United States and the Israeli national hero Rehavam Ze'evi[5] are other examples of such a sub-genre. Their alleged sexual deviance was exposed post-mortem via 'glossy' TV documentaries; and these programmes also told the stories of those identified by the documentaries' authors as victims (Channel 2 Keshet, Israel, 2016; Channel 4, UK 2019). Scholars have argued that the criminal trial 'shapes conventional meanings and social behaviour' (Fuhs, 2014, p. 783); yet in the absence of the alleged offender and any subsequent legal trial, this sort of documentary acquires a questionable power in the shaping of cultural meanings. Significantly, unlike more mainstream examples of the real-crime documentary mentioned above, where the trial becomes a focal point, in this sub-genre—where victim stories become the focus —the public 'trial' cannot be matched by a legal trial. The accused-centred real-crime documentary allows a level of flexibility in building up empathy—the closure brought about by the trial or by the sentence allows the audience to make up its

---

[4] The author refers also the case of Harvey Weinstein in the US.

[5] Rehavam Ze'evi (1926–2001), was a well-known public figure. Nicknamed 'gandhi', Ze'evi was a general in the Israel Defence Forces, a politician and cabinet minister. He was born in Jerusalem under what was then the British Palestine Mandate, and later joined the Palmach organisation which played a central role in the fight for Israeli independence. His extreme political approach to the Gaza question was cut short when in 2001 he was killed by members of the Popular Front for the Liberation of Palestine (Knesset.gov.il, 2009). After his death and despite his controversial political views, Ze'evi became an Israeli historical hero, where his life was integrated into the school curriculum and roads were named after him.

mind as to whether it might agree or disagree with the legal decisions and penal outcomes. In the case of the victim-centred real-crime documentary, this is not possible; the narrative and montage are wholly geared towards validating one truth.

The Ideal Victim

The fact that the accusations against Savile were made after his death, hence eliminating the possibility for a legal trial, generates the need to reflect on the victims' place within this new context. First, it is helpful to briefly trace the changing role of victims, more generally, within the criminal landscape.[6] Walklate (2017) explains that up to the mid-nineteenth century it was the victim who triggered a criminal prosecution. In other words, the majority of the prosecutions were private rather than state driven. The victim's role included all those aspects which today are performed by, in a UK context, the Crown Prosecution Service, i.e. choosing the charge, identifying witnesses and even challenging the sentence.[7] Allowing the victims to own their harm and control its reparation meant that they could utilise a wider range of resolutions. For example, along with actions of retribution, retaliation and vigilantism (sometimes aided by the community itself), Kearon and Godfrey clarify that 'a vast number of "crimes" disappeared with a handshake' (2007, p. 22). From the mid-nineteenth century, however, a much more state-regulated police body took over as the key agency involved in investigating and preventing crime.[8] Finally, the Prosecution of Offences Act 1985 centralised and generalised the state's responsibility for and control over social (rather than individual) protection (Kearon & Godfrey, 2007). Kirchengast takes this further, suggesting that the 'genealogy of the victim is therefore the gradual divestment of

---

[6] The historiography of the development of the English criminal justice which also critically debates the victims' roles includes writing by John H. Langbein (1983) and Hay et al. (1975).

[7] See also detailed historical discussion in Kirchengast (2006).

[8] See also a critical historical discussion in Hay and Snyder (1989).

the ownership of rights and powers constitutive of the criminal conflict at law' (2006, p. 6).

The centrality of the victim within the administration of justice shifted, although it never really disappeared from the criminal landscape. Over time the word 'victim' became a label used to justify criminal justice policy, while its use by the media made this an increasingly culturally laden term. Kearon and Godfrey explain that legal and social reforms from the second half of the nineteenth century started to 'evoke images of vulnerable and innocent' potential victims (2007, p. 24). Fostered by this new discourse[9] the 1960s and 1970s brought renewed awareness of the need to be mindful of victims' needs.[10] Furthermore, Kirchengast (2006) argues that questions concerning human rights and access to justice have helped twenty-first-century victims to reclaim their presence.[11] It appears, however, that this presence does not come without critique nor costs.[12] Indeed, it remains questionable whether the crime victim can be considered an active participant in the administration of justice.[13] Rather, scholars have argued that the emphasis on victims' rights has enhanced the perception of victims' passivity, vulnerability and helplessness; in turn, this has further emphasised the distinction between types of victims, hence leading to differential protection through, for example, measures designed for 'vulnerable' victims.[14] Moreover, Gewirtz suggests that the intricate nature of the criminal trial process means that victims might be kept in the dark for much of the proceedings; thus, the 'victim

---

[9] See discussion on the problematics of this discourse in Kirchengast (2006).

[10] Kearon and Godfrey (2007) mention several examples such as the Criminal Injuries Compensation; they also place this discussion within the context of academic research carried out during 1960s–1990s.

[11] Kirchengast (2006) gives examples such as: victim impact statement; measuring impact of harm; alternative ways of testifying; and measures of restorative justice.

[12] Fattah (1986) gives a thorough overview on issues concerning the 'victim movements' as experiences in the 1980s.

[13] Gewirtz argues that the 'victims' rights' movement indeed reflect 'the sense of many that the law had evolved too far in the direction of protecting the rights of defendants and had slighted the interests of victims' (1996, p. 868).

[14] For example, Rock (1990), Godfrey et al. (2007), Walklate (1992), Fattah (1999), cited in Kearon and Godfrey (2007, p. 29). Even newer interventions such as restorative justice, have been criticised for deceivingly promoting victims' interest where it predominantly focuses on the rehabilitation of the offender (Ashworth, 2000, cited in Kearon & Godfrey, 2007, p. 29).

loses control of how his or her story is presented' in the courtroom, leading to a second 'victimisation' (Gewirtz, 1996, p. 866).[15] Empirical research carried out by Orth (2002) confirms the negative effects criminal proceedings have on the victims of crime. These could range from severe psychological implications to mere negative 'justice appraisals of outcomes and procedure' (Orth, 2002, p. 322).

Savile's victims might not have been so-positioned by trial procedures, but in their media representation there was an evident attempt to frame them as 'ideal victims'. Scholars have attached the label of 'ideal victim' to those victims perceived, by the government and society, as deserving particular social empathy and recognition. Christie clearly defined ideal victims as the 'individuals who – when hit by crime – most readily are given the complete and legitimate status of being a victim' (1986, p. 18). Identifying the social construct of the 'victim' helps to draw attention to the partiality of treatment and support. Take, for example, the typical cultural construction of the young antisocial drug user who is harassed and attacked in a city-centre and the elderly lady attacked in her home. The former tends to be framed in media accounts as a less deserving victim, despite the likelihood that they have experienced a life-time of victimisation.

Christie (1986) identified several personal attributes which might make the victim 'ideal' in cultural terms; these could be vulnerability, weakness (in comparison to the offender), combined with a more general sense that the victim was not in the wrong (in contrast to this, we find all sorts of imputed deviance in media representations and court hearings, such as mention of what the female victim was wearing and doing prior to attack).[16] Indeed, generally, children, the elderly and women who appear to conform to the attributes of western stereotypical femininity, will be more easily constructed in the culture as deserving victims (Green, 2011). However, a personal attribute approach cannot explain why perceptions have changed in relation to who and what is considered 'ideal'. Indeed, scholars have developed Christie's perspective, placing

---

[15] More on the mediated process of victims' narrative in Serisier (2018).

[16] See also a critique on that in Green (2011). See a helpful summary of critique in Newburn (2017).

greater emphasis on its social construction.[17] To put it simply, the social construction of an individual as an ideal victim awards her a particular 'social status'; hence, it is this which legitimises her 'idealness'.

However, the 'idealness' of Savile's victims should not be taken as obvious. True, the social, or rather, media construction of Savile's victims as 'deserving' was subsequently and successfully endorsed by the Operation Yewtree report (Gray & Watt, 2013) and Dame Janet Smith's Review (2016). Dame Janet Smith established that 'it is obvious that some of the young girls in the participating audience were at risk of moral danger' (2016, pp. 46, 61). Also, it was confirmed that out of the 214 formally recorded sexually related offences with Savile named as perpetrator, 82% of the victims were females, many in their early teens at the time when the crimes occurred (2016, pp. 46, 61). However, although this data might arouse in current contemporary society a sense of great concern, historically, victims of sexual abuse and rape have rarely received the 'status' of a deserving victim. The cultural tolerance and media appeal of sexually related offences has changed over time (Moore, 2014). This is not to say that sexual offences against children and young people were not officially recognised as crimes in the 1960s, at the time of Savile's predation[18]; however, these were seldom reported, or if reported, dismissed and at best, cases were dealt with outside of the criminal justice system (Harris & Grace, 1999).[19] Moreover, Weis and Borges (1973) explain that maintaining secrecy was important in order to avoid the victim's stigmatisation. In the worst cases though, the victim might have been perceived as complicit or to be blamed for the consequences (Moore, 2009).[20] In the case of Saville, a mixture of self-blame and awe towards the perpetrator might have been another reason for not reporting. For example, a victim who said to have been abused by Savile over a period of eighteen months while working as a nurse at Stoke

---

[17] Quinney (1972) drew attention to the social construct of the victim already in the 1970s; also see discussion on the social construct of the victim providing wider literature in: Walklate (2012), Strobl (2004). A recent examination is available in Duggan (2018).

[18] Sexual Offences Act (1956).

[19] More on victims rape stories and accounts in, for example, Brownmiller (1976); a critical analysis concerning rape narrative is available in Serisier (2018).

[20] Moore (2009) also cites Benedict (1992) and Meyers (1997) to further illustrate that point.

Mandeville Hospital at the age of 17, asked her mother not to make a fuss, explaining that she 'was too embarrassed because he was Jimmy Savile. You don't want to get him into trouble. He was Jimmy Savile and I couldn't say a bad word against him' (BBC News, 26 February 2015).

Differences in cultural attitudes towards victims of sexual abuse in the 1960s and 1970s[21] do not justify unlawful behaviour. Rather, the point made here is that cultural attitudes contributed to a situation where Savile's victims were denied recognition. Dame Janet Smith's report is evidence that people were aware at the time of Savile's transgressions; although, only a few complaints were made officially, and none were dealt with. An anecdote, which was only brought to public attention following the unfolding of the case, well illustrates this blasé attitude. In 1976 fans of the *Top of the Pops* witnessed a person in the audience, 18 years old at the time, leaping off her chair. Apparently, Savile grabbed her backside; when expressing her concern, she was told 'don't be stupid, this is just Jimmy Savile' (YouTube, 2012). Another example is given by Dame Janet Smith. In 1969 a young woman complained to her female and male managers about Savile grabbing her breasts with both hands; she said that she was told that it would have been more surprising if Savile had not tried to touch her. For Dame Janet Smith the reaction of the managers was inappropriate, but she recognised that it was 'not surprising given the culture of the times' (2016, p. 3). However, comments made by the press, such as 'how did Savile get away with it?' and 'how could this be allowed to happen?' (Easton, 2015; Sillto, 2016) have boosted our current sense of social righteousness, helping us to shift responsibility for the events from the social to the institutional (the BBC and the government, including the NHS). For example, Barford and Westcott's complaint that 'in an age of criminal records checks and children's rights, it seems almost inconceivable that someone would be allowed such unfettered access' (2012, n.p.)—reflects an observation that locates blame squarely with organisations, rather than with the broader culture.

---

[21] See research touching that period by Harris and Grace (1999), and Du Mont et al. (2003), Jordan's (2001) reference list provides research from the 1970s and 1980s.

Victim as Commodity

The media's role as a conduit for culturalisation should not be underestimated. Presdee (2000) suggests that in our neoliberal culture the way we perceive our moral-social environment has much to do with the way the media contextualises and assimilates popular knowledge into culture. The culturalisation of the victim is significant, because it is this process, according to Presdee which 'define[s] and shape[s] dominant forms of social life' (2000, p. 17). In other words, the media helps to enhance what Greer (2007) calls a hierarchy of victimisation; hence, aided by the media's visual tricks, some victims will be literally described and judged as more deserving than others. This dynamic is facilitated by the media's understanding of the processes of commodification and the marketplace of communications (Presdee, 2000). Hence, the ideal victim is transformed into what Green (2011) defines as a type of currency; the greater the perceived level of vulnerability and harm suffered, the greater the exchange value. To explain how this currency is formed and the role of the media in transforming the victim into a commodity, two components are taken into consideration: demand and supply.

When looking at the process of the commodification of the ideal victim, Green (2011) refers to the demand for security as a key factor. As to what drives this, research has identified a variety of emotions. Initially, the demand for protection was attributed to public fear of crime. Later research identified anger as a trigger (Newburn, 2017). Significantly, whatever the emotion might be, the demand for security depends on assumptions and worries about crime and perceptions concerning one's own vulnerability and potential to become a victim—albeit, this might have nothing to do with a personal experience of victimisation (Green, 2011). Indeed, as explained by Beck (1992), it is the sense of living in a risk society that is instrumental here, where individuals still perceive themselves as being under threat, even as they may never have experienced victimisation. Current national and international threats, financial crises, unknown and inexplicable maladies and the doubtful ability of the government and criminal justice to restore safety, create a sense that we are all in this together. In other words, actual personal harm suffered by a victim is transmuted into a diffuse sense of collective risk. This in turn, as put by Quinney (1972), justifies a legal intervention where the harm has been recognised in the 'public interest'. Hence, the 'ideal victim' has become an abstract legal entity (Best, 1997) emblematic of society's demand for safety. In turn, the socially constructed 'ideal victim'—the one which was officially recognised as 'deserving'—tends to be commodified as the media recognises the social demand for narratives about victimhood, risk, and safety. However, Beck also drew attention to the fallacy of this sense of risk: 'we do not know what it is we don't know – but from this dangers arise, which threaten mankind' (2006, p. 329). And it is this nebulous sense of risk that lends additional power to the media drive to commodify the 'ideal victim', spurred by the constant reminder, that although the danger exists far from us, we might become the next victims.

In this context, the 'selling' of protection is important[22]; indeed, it is the role of the media to provide an immediate, visual and real-time sensual experience which is instrumental to the culturalisation of the victim. Walklate explains that media coverage given to events of a 'risky' nature 'is intended to move us: to encourage us to place ourselves next to the victim, for after all, are they not just like us?' (2012, p. 176). Moreover, thanks to the tools available on the internet, the media's powers lie in its ability to create timeless and space-less platforms; hence, the internet user will be repeatedly exposed to the sensual experience, making it immediate and real-time again and again, irrespective of when it was initially reported or where it happened. In turn, the media not only channels these spaces, but it also expressively sets the terms of and conditions for social conformity; as put by Moore, it instructs 'us on how to morally judge a case and [...] where blame lies' (2014, p. 10). For Furedi (2013), the media helps make sense of moral issues without the constraints of legal and political scrutiny (Djerf-Pierre et al., 2013). The dynamic can be illustrated through readers' comments to an online news article about Savile's crimes. For example, a heavily emotive headline in the *Mail Online*, 'Savile pictured at the Jersey House of Horrors: Paedophile DJ is surrounded by children at care home where 192 suffered abuse' (Allen, 2012), attracted 109 readers' comments. These comments were in turn

---

[22] For example, see discussion on that in Krahmann (2011).

rated by subsequent readers; the number of ratings indicates that the first twenty 'best rated' comments attracted 7345 readers. The highest-rated 'best' comment expressed the following: 'All Savile pictures repulse me, goodness only knows how his victims have felt all these years [...]'; only 22 out of 759 readers rated this comment 'down' (i.e. expressing disapproval). Out of the 109 comments made directly to the article, only 13 were subject to a high level of disagreement, attracting about 4092 subsequent readers; at the top of the score (with 798 readers) as the 'worst' comment was the following: 'Has anything been PROVED??? No...'.

It is difficult to suggest that the contributors to this public debate (who some might see as guardians of social conformity) are engaged in genuine deliberation. Rather, just as trial and punishment have served as a form of entertainment through the ages—what is on display here is a form of armchair outrage. Gewirtz goes as far as arguing that 'the trial can have the organized combat of spectator sports, the emotional tumult of a soap opera, and the heightened suspense of a thriller' (1996, p. 886). Moreover, Presdee defines this more generally as the 'commodification of social life', where social relations 'become both a fetish and a commodity' (2000, p. 26). The real-crime documentary is particularly significant in this context; it can be seen as a commodity which responds to the demand for entertainment on the one hand, while on the other hand, it taps into public consciousness as a commodity with a social purpose (that is, revealing injustice) (Schofield, 2004). Inevitably, the demand for such entertainment is dependent on the media's representation of what it chooses to emphasise as 'real' and 'outrageous'. This will depend on the newsworthiness of the story (Greer, 2007; Moore, 2014). The debate concerning when the first Savile documentary was chosen to be aired well illustrates the changing value attributed to the story. Although the documentary was aired in October 2012, it was meant to be broadcast at Christmas 2011. Instead, given Savile's death in October 2011 the documentary was shelved in favour of two tribute shows. For Greer and McLaughlin (2013), this power to choose what is newsworthy and thus control public interaction with this information, reflects principles of market competition. That is, good news sells, but sensational news sells more. This is where the 'supply' for this demand comes into play.

In supplying entertainment, the media seek to bolster demand, and one way of doing this is to escalate a crime-problem so that it is recast as a scandal. According to Presdee (2000), scandal is mainly fed by 'emotionality'; hence, the more sensational the story is, the higher the rating. Greer and McLaughlin explain that scandalising news increases 'profit through a surge in scandalised consumers' (2013, p. 244). For the scandal to 'succeed' in that, it needs to 'elicit a deep cultural unease' (Jewkes, 2015, p. 56). Indeed, sex-related scandals involving women and/or children have been identified as highly entertaining (Greer, 2007; Jewkes, 2015; Moore, 2014), especially if matched with 'an institutional culture of impunity', and recently, also the 'celebrity' aspect (Greer & McLaughlin, 2013, p. 256). Jewkes (2015) suggests that the representation of the scandal must trigger in the viewer the perception of 'otherness', thus establishing their own 'social conformity' and in turn, acceptance of the narrative presented by the media. In the case of Savile, the media found a fertile ground for triggering the scandal. First, although up until then a national hero, Savile could not counterargue the allegations brought after his death—hence, the public was presented with one predominant narrative. Also, the coincidence of having several other celebrity sex-offence allegations emerging around the same time meant that the construction of a crime-problem and hence a scandal could not have been easier. However, rather than it having a social purpose, scholars have considered that these media revelations are part of a 'feeding frenzy' aiming to guarantee the media's economic survival (Greer & McLaughlin, 2012). This considered, it is difficult to see how this seemingly democratic media-driven public sphere can, as suggested by Norris, truly facilitate the 'development of an informed public opinion as an independent check on the power of the state' (2010, p. 6).

Implications: Reproducing Violence

It might feel unjust criticising the media when it is serving—as in the Savile case—to reveal injustice. In a way, the Savile documentaries might be seen to have empowered victims; indeed, the report published following the Operation Yewtree investigation into the allegations was titled 'Giving Victims a Voice'. Scholars have also considered the notion that the media facilitates a space for a sort of social therapy (Bainbridge, 2020). A headline article in the *Telegraph* suggested this too: 'How the Jimmy Savile scandal helped victims to speak out' (O'Donovan, 2016). The article implicitly praised the media's civic dutifulness in bringing to light the victims' testimonies:

> What was never in doubt was the importance of these victim's stories being heard. Not only by those whose silence conspired – however unintentionally – to hide Savile's crimes for decades. But by all of us, and especially anyone who might still have had any lingering doubts as to the devastating and long-lasting effects of sexual abuse'.

However, we must be mindful of the difference between reporting facts as they are, as opposed to constructing them, or worse—appropriating and commodifying them for gain. It is not clear who has, if at all, assigned to the media the role of 'guardians of social conformity', as mentioned earlier. However, there is no doubt that joining the victim industry, as Best calls it (1997), has been profitable. The real-crime-*victim* documentary has emerged in a cultural context where victimisation has become increasingly salient and marketable. Significantly, the public learns about the latest social anxiety from the media. 'Anxiety' is on-point here, because although the reporting of news is meant to convey 'a knowledge', this is constructed with what Osborn argues is an 'immediate and sensationalized impact [...] with little depth of analysis or contextualisation' (2002, cited in Jewkes, 2015, p. 32). Indeed, the presenter of the BBC's Savile documentary aired in 2016 opens by saying that 'for decades there was a secret at the heart of British life' (2016). This crime-problem was declared from the start to be a national scandal, and, in turn, the victims' personal stories merely fed into the media narrative of public shame and scandal. Thus, personal lives have become the nation's business, constructing and positioning them 'at the heart of the market economy' (Taylor, 1999, cited in Green, 2011, p. 106).

The victims in the Savile documentaries were, very simply, recruited as film Extras (i.e. background actors) where the main actor was Jimmy

Savile. The story presented by the documentaries was one-sided, and the victims were represented one-dimensionally. The possible nuances and complexities that each different victim's experience might have had, was lost. In other words, the documentaries marginalised the complex experience of multi-layered sexual victimisation; some of the victims revealed, by-the-way, that they were subject to repeated victimisation by multiple perpetrators since a young age. Instead, the victims' representation in the documentaries was aimed at producing a portrait of individual, pathological predator and institutional failure—the victims, merely needed to validate this story by confirming that they are 'deserving' victims. For example, the first scene in the BBC 2016 documentary shows one of the female victims and her husband sitting on a sofa; the shot is framed by a darkened living room with a spotlight on the couple. The husband speaks first: 'There wasn't secret, it was shame'. This is followed by what could be interpreted as a puzzled look by his wife. To this reaction, the husband responds: 'Wasn't it? You were ashamed of it' (Lambet, 2016, 00:21). The visual staging of the participants' narrative in these glossy documentaries is fundamental; it helps build up the social scandal. Crucially, the victim mentioned above is *told* that she was ashamed. This assertion of shame—as something that a victim must feel—contributes to the standardising of emotional response, while also setting this narrative as one of 'ideal' victimhood. The documentaries leave little room for compassion for the victims, as their main aim is to create the opposite in relation to Savile—despite the victims' stories providing the narrative basis for the documentaries, the underlying aim is to produce a particular emotional reaction to the perpetrator. For example, the ITV 2012 documentary's presenter opens up by stating that Jimmy Savile was a friend of the rich and famous (although no mention is made of the huge mob of fans he had). The presenter continues by stating that 'tonight *Exposure* investigates allegations that away from the cameras Sir Jimmy Savile was far from a genial eccentric […]' (Gardiner, 2012, 00:32).

To get the scandal going, the Savile's documentaries had to shake public perception; yet, to entice belief and trust in the story, they also needed to reassure Savile's fans that even the victims were not aware that they were tricked by him. Indeed, the documentaries stress that the whole nation was tricked. For example, by introducing himself as a former police officer and a child protection specialist (Gardiner, 2012, 03:19) rather than an investigative journalist for ITV (his current profession), the presenter of the 2012 ITV documentary established not only the reliability of the story told, but also, that the story is told by an expert—someone who really knows, and is able to see through Savile's subterfuge. In an House of Commons debate about child protection, a Member of Parliament suggested that the 2012 ITV documentary was 'game-changing', leading to an 'extraordinary turn of events' and that he (the Member of Parliament) 'pay[s] tribute for what…[the ITV documentary presenter] has set in motion as a result' (HC Deb, 12 September 2013). On closer inspection, what the documentary achieves is a decidedly unnuanced characterisation of victimisation, with the audience continually being given cues as to how to feel and react, cues that stem not from the victims' experience of events, but from an externally derived interpretive frame. An adult tongue-kissing a 14 year old girl in public, for example, is offered up as simply unacceptable, but the use of the word 'shock' by the now-adult victim, when asked about this past event, instructs us on how we are expected to feel rather then what she felt when this happened (Gardiner, 2012, 28:39). Several of the witnesses, in both documentaries, use phrases such as: 'looking back now as an adult I realise he was grooming me […]' (Gardiner, 2012, 28:53). These are then matched by visual reconstructions of the evidence and dramatic music, helping to sensationalise the narrative—not 'as they happened', according to victims' testimony, but rather as they are now interpreted, through twenty-first-century ideas about (amongst other things) grooming.

The high production values of the 2016 BBC documentary with its sophisticated shots, sharp and high-resolution images and arrangements of light and colour, further enhance the level of emotional intimacy—as if we were sitting in witnesses' living room, perhaps holding their hands. In a recent interview with the British broadcaster and presenter Sue Perkins (Brown, 2020), she revealed how the producers of the television programme *The Great British Bake Off* encouraged the contestants to express greater levels of emotional distress by 'pointing cameras in the bakers' faces and making them cry and saying, "Tell us about your dead gran"'—all for the sake of high audience ratings. It is impossible to comment on the filming technique used in the Savile documentaries; nevertheless, the simple format of an interview broadcast in 2012 as opposed to the sophisticated glossy documentary shot in 2016, might suggest that the interviewee was asked to improve her dramatic screen-performance. Indeed, the woman identified as victim in the 2016 BBC documentary explained that she regretted that she came across as 'detached' from her testimony in the previous interview with ITV news in 2012 (Lambet, 2016, 14:49). Indeed, the original footage is of a simple interview—a person talking to another person by way of following a question and answer format—the interviewee does not wear makeup, the image resolution is relatively low, the room is poorly lit, the wall behind the interviewee is decorated with a patterned purple wallpaper while the wall behind the interviewer is fluorescent pink—to a great extent unexciting, unengaging, hence with little emotional impact. The title of the interview does not do much to entice empathy either, using the words 'alleged victim' and 'alleged attack' (ITV News, 2012). In fact, the 2016 BBC documentary confirms that the allegation made was not taken positively by the public (Lambet, 2016, 21:32). However, in the revised and glossy version of the 2016 BBC documentary—aided by the sensationalising effects of contrasting lights, closeup shot, background music and background colour and setting—the same victim's story is framed in such a way as to boost credibility, not least of all because we're shown footage of her crying. In this 'improved' version, the victim says that she is reluctant to tell the story 'as a matter of fact [...] because it is messy' (Lambet, 2016, 15:23). Yet, her story *is* told as a matter of fact (it is given less than 7 minutes in the documentary)— she was just another story to be added to the pool of events for the construction of the scandal. Victims' subjective experience are rendered irrelevant—for Green, this is in keeping with a broader tendency in the media to make victim testimony into a product, 'an objective unit to be bought and sold' (2011, p. 106). In fact, in this instance the media's triumph could not have been greater: the ITV documentary won three Royal Television Society journalism awards in 2013. It also won the 'scoop of the year' and it was named as the 'best home current affairs programme' (O'Carroll, 2013).

It effect, it must not be forgotten that the media reconstruction of reality is aimed at sensationalising events. It has been already clarified that the 'real' crime documentary is, after all, a form of artistic expression—a one-sided narrative, revealing only one version of the events, and presenting this as the authoritative 'truth' of the matter. Peter Spindler's confession—Metropolitan Police Commander and head of the specialist investigation on the Savile case in 2012—illustrates that. He revealed a few years after the investigation took place, that the comment he made in an interview to the BBC that 'at this stage [...] it is quite clear that Savile was a predatory sex offender' (BBC, 9 October 2012; Lambet, 2016, 39:41) was a 'risk' (Lambet, 2016, 39:22). According to him, the police did not have substantial evidence to corroborate this claim; Spindler explained that 'we could not have done what we did with a live suspect; we would have kept very quiet' (Lambet, 2016, 39:04). Further illustrating the point that the documentaries' investigation was one-sided is the concern that other possible witnesses' testimonies might have been ignored. For example, recent research by Smith and Burnett (2018) funded by the Economic and Social Research Council (ESRC) has revealed some new, challenging evidence. The study brings evidence of Anna Raccoon (pseudonym), a former resident of Duncroft; she refutes the claim made by another former resident who said that Savile assaulted her in 1965 when she was 15 years of age. Anna said that she shared a dormitory with her during this period but she never saw Savile at Duncroft at that time. Rather, another former resident interviewed for the study suggests that she was the one who introduced Savile to Duncroft, and this only happened in 1974—this was confirmed by Surrey Police's Operation Outreach (Surrey Police, 2015). Corroborated evidence by other former residents and former school staff suggests that the censorious culture at Duncroft promoted by the headmistress and her deputy during the 1960s and 1970s meant that it was unlikely that anyone would have had unsupervised access to the residents' dormitories (Smith & Burnett, 2018).

Even if we choose to ignore the question of evidence, it still remains that these documentaries took the place of a legal process. The media's tendency to encourage a mob of public opinion, as referred to by Gewirtz (1996), is not a new occurrence. For Foucault (1977), for example, the public attending executions in England during the late seventeenth and eighteenth centuries fulfilled a necessary rite for the verification of the offender and its elimination. The need to create a 'spectacle' (Debord, 1970, cited in Greer & McLaughlin, 2011, p. 27) was as fundamental then as it is now to confirm and evidence the notion that justice has been achieved (Moore et al., 2019). The difference, however, is that the real-crime-*victim* documentary demonstrates the idea that, in the court of public opinion, people are guilty until proven innocent (Greer & McLaughlin, 2011). By having an accused who is deceased means that innocence can hardly be proven; the illusion created by the documentaries that they are reclaiming justice by returning it to the people, further emphasises the frivolous attitude of the media to the pronouncement of Savile's guilt (Smith & Burnett, 2018). Perhaps some might consider that the implications of making allegations are redundant, if the accused is deceased[23]; and yet, although not affecting the dead, this still might have repercussions for the living. Indeed, research by Hoyle et al. (2016) evidences how these historical events have brought about not only an increase in the reporting of sex crime, but also an increased number of false allegations.

However, beyond concerns for legal formalities, victims' speaking out (Serisier, 2018) in the context of the documentaries' representation is far more problematic. The victims are represented, especially in the 2016 BBC documentary, as if the documentary gave them the opportunity to finally speak up: 'it was like releasing the pressure on a slow cooker, it felt good, because now everything is out there' (Victim 1. Lambet, 2016, 01:37); 'I need to share now, and I need to talk now' (Victim 2. Lambet, 2016, 07:18); 'back then, it never occurred to me to say anything – who would believe me?' (Victim 3. Lambet, 2016, 07:25). The witnesses speak to the camera, hence directly to the public, in their living rooms. What the viewers get is the sense that it is now safe to talk about sexual abuse; what perhaps we forget, is that this public exposure is not instrumental to the victims' wellbeing, protection or safeguard. As pointed out by Boyle (2018a), a victim's identity is usually protected

---

[23] However, Scarre (2012) brings several counter arguments to that, looking more generally on what does it say about us, as a society, when we posthumously negatively talk about the dead.

from the media and thus from the public. The openness with which the victims speak in the documentary makes us forget that this is not a reality show; it makes us forget to ask whether those who spoke of a burden to speak out received adequate expert support (Boyle, 2018a). For example, it was discussed previously that the victims escaped the secondary victimisation typical of the trial process. However, Boyle (2018a) suggests that those participating in the documentaries were still subject to it, although this time at the hands of the media. For one thing, and as indicated above, victims' narratives were appropriated by the documentary creators and used for an aim other than telling these victims' stories. Beyond this, there are clear examples of secondary victimisation. The case of Karen Ward is a stark example of this. The first person identified by the BBC documentary's producer as a victim, Ward's story was derived from her private autobiography, originally published and found on the World Wide Web. It only included a small paragraph concerning her encounter in her teenage years with a certain 'JS' (Ward, 2016). Karen Ward (2016) reveals in her post-documentary book that initially, once the journalists got hold of her phone numbers, she had to switch her landline and mobile off 'just to endeavour to maintain a modicum of peace'; she adds that 'the upshot of this was that I could then add trapped, beleaguered and hopeless to my descriptors of how I was doing; being hounded by the media is not at all conducive to recovery' (2016, Chapter 13).

Moreover, accrediting the documentaries with recognising victims of sex crimes as deserving-ideal victims, should be taken with caution. True, the documentaries provoked public and governmental awareness for the need of better protection. In a House of Commons debate, a member of parliament suggested that child protection and child abuse 'have probably never had a high profile, and have never triggered such a response and awareness among the public at large, which is probably the one compensation of the whole sordid Jimmy Savile affair' (HC Deb, 12 September 2013). However, the notion that each victim counts, is an illusion. What the Savile documentaries—and other real-crime victim documentaries beside—demonstrate is that women victims only matter in multiples (Boyle, 2018b, 2018c). Indeed, the case of Savile illustrates that individual sexual violence allegations tend to be overlooked. Several of the victims suffered sexual abuse throughout their childhood, but it was only when multiple allegations emerged against one and same person that their cases gained attention, both in terms of media coverage and a criminal justice response. In this respect, the documentaries have changed very little, despite the idea that they were 'game-changing'. Serisier argues that 'breaking the silence, despite its significant cultural impact, has not ended sexual violence, nor does it seem to have significantly reduce it' (2018, p. 12). In fact, a recent report identified that rape and sexual assault 'victim-survivors continue to face challenges at each stage of the criminal justice process' (Brooks-Hay et al., 2019). The London Victims Commissioner, Clair Waxman, reports similar findings. She presents the experience of a victim of non-recent abuse, as follows:

> [Chris] first reported in 1979 and 1988, but her case was marked as No Further Action on both occasions. Chris reported again in April 2016 and waited 14 months for her case to be sent to CPS. The CPS then requested social media records two years after the crime was reported (May 2018) and Chris finally received a No Further Action letter from the CPS via the Police in November 2018, with no explanation around the decision. (Waxman, 2019, n.p)

Conclusion

The media appears to have taken the role of guardian of social conformity. However, the suggestion that it promotes transparency, democratisation of access to information and serves as a whistleblower, righting injustices, should be considered carefully. It is true that, in the case of Jimmy Savile, the media played a major role in unveiling a troubling reality. It also raised awareness about prevention, apprehension and protection—in turn, this mobilised the public and the criminal justice system. However, we cannot ignore the fact that the mass media today is at the heart of the capitalist marketplace. We must be critical of how the Savile documentaries have represented the victims and used their testimonies for filmmaking purposes—they became the site for a de-facto trial. It is a 'trial' that would have not been possible if the accused was alive: his crime would have been first verified in a court of law. The documentaries gave the impression that their purpose was to show that justice is being done after all—by drawing upon multiple victims' stories, and enlarging each story so as to focus on the Savile experience, the documentaries promoted the idea that the problem is institutional rather than social. Indeed, by deflecting responsibility, the public could see itself as a victim of the system too, rather than part of the problem; hence, the documentaries and ensuing media coverage skillfully guided the public's sensitivities by tapping into our fears and sustaining the demand for real-crime entertainment.

Study Questions

- What characteristics are associated with the 'ideal victim'? Identify some examples of this cultural construction being used in media treatments of violent crime.
- In what sense did the documentaries about Jimmy Savile distort and mis-appropriate victims and survivors' testimonies?
- How do these distorted depictions reflect and sustain myths about sexual violence and victimisation?
- Why is it a problem that 'real crime' documentaries are a product of the entertainment industry? What are the implications of this for the depiction of violence and victimhood?

Bibliography

Allen, H., & Savigny, H. (2012). Selling scandals or ideology? The politics of business crime coverage. *European Journal of Communication, 27*, 278–290.

Aust, R., & Holdsworth, A. (2017). The BBC archive post-Jimmy Savile: irreparable damage or recoverable ground? In J. B. Kay, C. Mahoney, & C. Shaw (Eds.), *The past in visual culture essays on memory, nostalgia and the media* (pp. 170–184). MacFarland & Company.

Bainbridge, C. (2020). Who will fix it for us? Toxic celebrity and the therapeutic dynamics of media culture. *Celebrity Studies, 11*, 75–88.

Beck, U. (1992). *Risk society: Towards a new modernity*. Sage.

Beck, U. (2002). The terrorist threat, world risk society revisited. *Theory, Culture & Society, 19*, 39–55.

Beck, U. (2006). Living in the world risk society, A Hobhouse Memorial Public Lecture given on Wednesday 15 February 2006 at the London School of Economics. *Economy and Society, 35*, 329–345.

Best, J. (1997). Victimisation and the victim industry. *Society, 34*, 9–17.

Boyle, K. (2018a). Television and/as testimony in the Jimmy Savile case. *Critical Studies in Television, 13*, 387–404.

Boyle, K. (2018b). Hiding in plain sight: Gender, sexism and press coverage of the Jimmy Savile case. *Journalism Studies, 19*, 1562–1578.

Boyle, K. (2018c). Television and/as testimony in Jimmy Savile case. *Critical Studies in Television, 13*, 387–404.

Brooks-Hay, O., Burman, M., & Bradley, L. (2019). *Justice Journeys: Informing policy and practice through lived experience of victim-survivors of rape and serious sexual assault* (The Scottish Centre for Crime & Justice Research, No. 4). https://www.sccjr.ac.uk/projects/justice-journeys-informing-policy-and-practice-through-lived-experience/. Accessed 30 May 2020.

Brown, M. (2020, March 17). Bake Off's Mel and Sue quit on day one after tears left a bad taste. *The Guardian online*. https://www.theguardian.com/tv-and-radio/2020/mar/17/bake-offs-mel-sue-quit-day-one-after-tears-left-bad-taste. Accessed 29 May 2020.

Brownmiller, S. (1976). *Against our will: Men, women and rape*. Penguin Books.

Bruzzi, S. (2016). Making a genre: The case of the contemporary true crime documentary. *Law and Humanities, 10*, 249–280.

Christie N. (1986). The ideal victim. In Ezzat A. Fattah (Ed.), *From crime policy to victim policy* (pp. 15–30, 18). Macmillan.

Collie, H., & Irwin, M. (2013). 'The weekend starts here': Young women, pop music television and identity. *Screen, 54*(2), 262–269.

Djerf-Pierre, M., Ekstrom, M., & Johansson, B. (2013). Policy failure or moral scandal? Political accountability, journalism and new public management. *Media, Culture and Society, 35*, 960–976.

Duggan, M. (2018). *Revisiting the 'ideal victim': Developments in critical criminology*. Policy Press.

Du Mont, J., Karen-Lee, M., & Terri, L. M. (2003). The role of "real rape" and "real victim" stereotypes in the police reporting practices of sexually assaulted women. *Violence Against Women, 9*, 466–486.

Fattah, E. A. (1986). Prologue: On some visible and hidden dangers of victim movements. In E. A. Fattah (Ed.), *From crime policy to victim policy* (pp. 1–14). Palgrave Macmillan.

Foucault, M. (1977). *Discipline and punish: The birth of the prison*. Penguin Books.

Fuhs, K. (2014). The legal trial and/in documentary film. *Cultural Studies, 28*, 781–808.

Furedi, F. (2013). *Moral crusades in an age of mistrust: The Jimmy Savile Scandal*. Palgrave Pivot.

Gewirtz, P. (1996). Victims as voyeurs at the criminal trial. *Northwestern University Law Review, 90*, 863–893.

Gray, D., & Watt, P. (2013). *Giving victims and voce: A joint MPS and NSPCC report into allegations of sexual abuse made against Jimmy Savile under Operation Yewtree*. https://www.nspcc.org.uk/globalassets/documents/research-reports/yewtree-report-giving-victims-voice-jimmy-savile.pdf. Accessed 24 May 2020.

Green, S. (2011). Crime, victimisation and vulnerability from. In S. Walklate (Ed.), *Handbook of victims and victimology* (pp. 91–117). Routledge.

Greer, C. (2007). News media, victims and crime. In P. Davies, P. Francis, & C. Greer (Eds.), *Victims, crime and society* (pp. 20–49). Sage.

Greer, C., & McLaughlin, E. (2011). 'Trial by Media': Policing, the 24-7 news mediasphere and the 'politics of outrage'. *Theoretical Criminology, 15*(1), 23–46.

Greer, C., & McLaughlin, E. (2012). A paedophile scandal foretold: Sir Jimmy Savile, child sexual abuse and the BBC. *British Society of Criminology Newsletter, 71*, 7–11.

Greer, C., & McLaughlin, E. (2013). The Sir Jimmy Savile scandal: Child sexual abuse and institutional denial at the BBC. *Crime Media Culture, 9*, 243–263.

Greer, C., & McLaughlin, E. (2015). The return of the repressed: Secrets, lies, denial and historical institutional child sexual abuse scandals. In D. Whyte (Ed.), *How corrupt is Britain?* (pp. 113–123). Pluto.

Harris, J., & Grace, S. (1999). *A question of evidence? Investigating and prosecuting rape in the 1990s*. Home Office.

Hay, D., Linebaugh, P., Rule, J. G., Thompson, E. P., & Winslow, C. (1975). *Albion's fatal tree: Crime and society in eighteenth-century England*. Pantheon Books.

Hay, D., & Snyder, F. (1989). Using the criminal law, 1750–1850: Policing, power and the state. In D. Hay & F. Snyder (Eds.), *Policing and prosecution in Britain 1750–1850* (pp. 3–52). Oxford University Press.

Hoyle, C., Speechley, N.-E., & Burnett, R. (2016). *The impact of being wrongly accused of abuse in occupations of trust: Victims' voices.* University of Oxford, Centre for Criminology. https://www.law.ox.ac.uk/sites/files/oxlaw/the_impact_of_being_wrongly_accused_of_abuse_hoyle_speechley_burnett_final_26_may.pdf. Accessed 27 July 2020.

Jewkes, Y. (2015). *Media and crime.* Sage.

Jordan, J. (2001). Worlds apart? Women, rape and the police reporting process. *British Journal of Criminology, 41*, 679–706.

Kearon, T., & Godfrey, B. S. (2007). Setting the scene: A question of history from. In S. Walklate (Ed.), *Handbook of victims and victimology* (pp. 17–36). Routledge.

Kirchengast, T. (2006). *The victim in criminal Law and justice.* Palgrave Macmillan.

Krahmann, E. (2011). Beck and beyond: Selling security in the world of risk society. *Review of International Studies, 37*, 349–372.

Lampard, K., & Marsden, E. (2015). *Themes and lessons learnt from NHS investigations into matters relating to Jimmy Savile, Independent report for the Secretary of State for Health.* https://www.gov.uk/government/publications/jimmy-savile-nhs-investigations-lessons-learned. Accessed 10 May 2020.

Langbein, J. H. (1983). *Albion's fatal flaws, past and present* (Faculty Scholarship Series). https://digitalcommons.law.yale.edu/fss_papers/545. Accessed 20 May 2020.

Leyshon, C. (2012, October 12). The downfall of a British television icon. *The New Yorker.* https://www.newyorker.com/culture/culture-desk/the-downfall-of-a-british-television-icon. Accessed 07 Oct 2021.

Moore, S. (2009). Cautionary tales: Drug-facilitated sexual assault in the British media. *Crime Media Culture, 5*, 305–320.

Moore, S. (2014). *Crime and the media.* Macmillan.

Moore, S., Clayton, A., & Murphy, H. (2019). Seeing justice done: Courtroom filming and the deceptions of transparency. *Crime Media Culture* (online first), 1–18.

Newburn, T. (2017). *Criminology.* Taylor & Francis.

Norris, P. (2010). *Public sentinel: News media and government reform.* The World Bank.

Orth, U. (2002). Secondary victimisation of crime victims by criminal proceedings. *Social Justice Research, 15*, 313–325.

Presdee, M. (2000). *Cultural criminology and the carnival of crime*. Routledge.

Quinney, R. (1972). Who is the victim? *Criminology, 10*, 314–323.

Rehavam (Gandhi) Ze'evi. (1926–2001). Israeli Knesset Political Biographies. Knesset.gov.il. Accessed 07 Oct 2021.

Scarre, G. (2012). Speaking of the dead. *Mortality, 17*, 36–50.

Schofield, K. (2004). Collisions n culture and crime: Media commodification of child sexual abuse. In J. Ferrell, K. Hayward, W. Morrison, & M. Presdee (Eds.), *Cultural criminology unleashed* (pp. 121–131). Routledge.

Serisier T. (2018). *Speaking out*. Palgrave Macmillan.

Silbey, J. M. (2005). Filmmaking in the precinct house and the genre of documentary film. *Columbia Journal of Law & the Arts, 29*(2), 107–180.

Silbey, J. M. (2010). Evidence verite and the law of film. *Suffolk University, Law School, Legal Studies Research Paper Series, 31*(4), 1257–1922.

Smith, J. (2016, February 25). *Review Report, An independent review into the BBC's culture and practices during the Jimmy Savile and Stuart hall years*. http://downloads.bbci.co.uk/bbctrust/assets/files/pdf/our_work/dame_janet_smith_review/conclusions_summaries.pdf. Accessed 10 May 2020.

Smith, M., & Burnett, R. (2018). The origins of the Jimmy Savile scandal. *International Journal of Sociology and Social Policy, 38*, 26–40.

Strobl, R. (2004). Constructing the victim: Theoretical reflections and empirical examples. *International Review of Victimology, 11*, 295–311.

Surrey Police. (2015). *Operation outreach*. http://mandatenow.org.uk/wp-content/uploads/2015/04/Operation-Outreach-29-4-2015-11186-link.pdf. Accessed 2 June 2020.

Walklate, S. (2012). Who is the victim of crime? Paying homage to the work if Richard Quinney. *Crime and Culture, 8*, 173–184.

Walklate, S. (2017). *Handbook of victims and victimology*. Routledge.

Ward, K. (2016). *Victim Zero: Jimmy Savile tried to ruin my life. I was the first victim to fight back*. John Blake.

Waxman, C. (2019, July, press release). *Stark findings in major review of rape cases*. Mayor of London, London Assembly. https://www.london.gov.uk/press-releases/mayoral/stark-findings-in-major-review-of-rape-cases. Accessed 18 Jan 2021. Report available in Waxman, C. (2019, July). The London Rape Review: A review of cases from 2016. Mayor of London, Office for Police and Crime. https://www.london.gov.uk/sites/default/files/london_rape_review_final_report_31.7.19.pdf. Accessed 18 Jan 2021.

Weis, K., & Borges, S. S. (1973). Victimology and rape: The case of the legitimate victim. *Issues in Criminology, 8*(2), 71–115.

Other

HC Deb. (2013, September 12). Vol. 567, Col. 1200. https://bit.ly/3kGyC7B Accessed 18 Nov 2020.
Prosecution of Offences Act 1985 c.23.
Sexual Offences Act 1956 c.69.

Media (by Author and Chronologically)

Allen, E. (2012, October 16). Savile pictured at the Jersey House of Horrors: Paedophile DJ is surrounded by children at care home where 192 suffered abuse. *Mail Online*. http://www.dailymail.co.uk/news/article-2218517/ Jimmy-Savile-pictured-surrounded-children-Jersey-care-home-192-suffered-abuse.html. Accessed 7 June 2016.
Barber, L. (2020). 10 years of the Sunday review: 22 July 1990—Lynn Barber Interviews Jimmy Savile; "I was nervous when I told him: 'What people say is that you Like little girls...'" (The Independent on Sunday, 1990, October 2). *The Independent*. https://www.independent.co.uk/arts-entertainment/tv/features/lynn-barber-i-was-nervous-when-i-told-jimmy-savile-people-say-you-like-little-girls-8193169.html. Accessed 29 Apr 2020.
Barford, V., & Westcott, K. (2012, October 29). Jimmy Savile: The road to hypervigilance. *BBC News*. http://www.bbc.co.uk/news/magazine-200 93812. Accessed 24 Nov 2020.
BBC News. (2012, October 9). *Jimmy Savile abuse claims: Police pursue 120 lines of inquiry*. https://www.bbc.co.uk/news/uk-19887019. Accessed 24 Nov 2020.
Bull, S. (2011, October 31). A proper British eccentric: Tributes pour in as DJ, TV presenter and charity marathon runner extraordinaire Sir Jimmy Savile dies. *Mail Online*. https://www.dailymail.co.uk/tvshowbiz/article-2055045/Jimmy-Savile-dead-DJ-Jimll-Fix-It-presenter-dies-home-aged-84.html. Accessed 28 Apr 2020.
Casciani, D. (2013, March 12). The missed chance to get Jimmy Savile. *BBC News*. http://www.bbc.co.uk/news/uk-21756150. Accessed 13 Apr 2017.
Easton, M. (2015, February 26). Savile: 'How could this be allowed to happen?' *BBC News*. http://www.bbc.co.uk/news/uk-31628420. Accessed 18 July 2016.
ITV News. (2012, October 2). *Exclusive: Alleged victim tells ITV News of alleged attach by Sir Jimmy Savile*. Interview by Lucy Manning. https://

www.itv.com/news/2012-10-02/alleged-victim-of-sir-jimmy-savile-speaks-out and https://www.youtube.com/watch?v=PuEMI9rCXCk&feature=emb_logo. Accessed 18 Nov 2020.

Llewellyn-Smith, J. (1994, January 10). How Sir Jim has fixed it for himself. *The Times*.

O'Carroll, L. (2013, February 21). ITV scoops three awards for coverage of Jimmy Savile sex abuse scandal. *Theguardian.com*. https://www.theguardian.com/media/2013/feb/21/itv-rts-awards-jimmy-savile. Accessed 23 July 2016.

O'Donovan, G. (2016, April 11). How the Jimmy Savile scandal helped victims to speak out. *The Telegraph*. http://www.telegraph.co.uk/tv/2016/04/11/abused-the-untold-story-jimmy-savile-victims-review/. Accessed 19 July 2016.

Sillito, D. (2016, February 25). Analysis: How did Savile get away with it? *BBC News*. http://www.bbc.co.uk/news/entertainment-arts-35659358. Accessed 18 July 2016.

Sweeting, A. (2011, October 29). Sir Jimmy Savile obituary. *The Guardian*. https://www.theguardian.com/music/2011/oct/29/sir-jimmy-savile. Accessed 28 Apr 2020.

Leaving Neverland: Michael Jackson and Me. Director Dan Reed, production Amos Pictures, release 2019 (aired in the UK by Channel 4). https://www.channel4.com/programmes/leaving-neverland-michael-jackson-and-me/on-demand/63905-002. Accessed 27 July 2020.

Gandhi—The true story behind the Myth. (2016, April 14). Channel 2 Keshet. http://www.mako.co.il/tv-ilana_dayan/2016-2659ae10426f3510/Article-7a7cca401651451006.htm. Accessed 20 Apr 2016.

Abused: The Untold Story. (2016, April 1). BBC, 1 Director Olly Lambet. https://vimeo.com/162907735. Accessed 10 May 2020.

Stoke Mandeville nurse: Jimmy Savile took my innocence. (2015, February 26). *BBC News*. http://www.bbc.co.uk/news/uk-31506266. Accessed 18 July 2016.

Exposed: The Other Side of Jimmy Savile. (2020, October 3). ITV1, Director Lesley Gardiner, Presenter Mark Williams-Thomas. http://www.dailymotion.com/video/xv03is_exposure-the-other-side-of-jimmy-savile-3th-oct-2012-full-documentary-itv_news. Accessed 10 May 2020.

YouTube. (2012). *Jimmy Savile Shame: Girl-Molesting live on 'Top of The Pops'!* https://www.youtube.com/watch?v=puyKtlPcmzU. Accessed 24 May 2020.

When Louis Met...Jimmy. (2000). Director will Yapp, writer and presented Louis Theroux, release 2000 (aired in the UK by BBC2).

Sir Jimmy Savile. (2011, October 29). *The Telegraph*. https://www.telegraph.co.uk/news/obituaries/8857428/Sir-Jimmy-Savile.html. Accessed 28 Apr 2020.

The British Broadcasting Corporation (BBC) (Top of the Pops [TV Series 1964–2019])—IMB. https://www.imdb.com/title/tt0139803/. Accessed 28 Apr 2020.

Top of the Pops [TV Series 1964–2019]—IMDb. (2003–2019). https://www.imdb.com/title/tt0139803/reviews?ref_=tt_urv. Accessed 28 Apr 2020.

3

"Don't Let Netflix Tell You What to Think!": Debates on Getting to Know the Accused/Convicted in *Making a Murderer* and Other Injustice Narratives

George S. Larke-Walsh

Introduction

Making a Murderer (Demos & Ricciardi, 2015, 2018) is a true crime series from Netflix about the 2005 murder of Teresa Halbach in Wisconsin, USA. Detailing the trial and subsequent conviction of Steven Avery and Brendan Dassey, it also encourages audiences to "get to know" both men, in order to validate their appeals, understand their convictions and critique the institutions involved. Both seasons have been hugely successful, but they have also received a great deal of criticism, especially for their emotive and biased narrative tactics. This chapter does not intend to undermine such criticism, but it will offer a slightly different assessment of the tactics. It focuses on how the documentary's distinctive approach to character creation and emotional engagement provides opportunities for the convicted to be acknowledged and explored beyond

G. S. Larke-Walsh (✉)
University of Sunderland, Sunderland, UK
e-mail: Georgelarke-walsh@sunderland.ac.uk

© The Author(s), under exclusive license to Springer Nature
Switzerland AG 2021
M. Mellins and S. Moore (eds.), *Critiquing Violent Crime in the Media*,
https://doi.org/10.1007/978-3-030-83758-7_3

just the crime to which they are connected, and the affect this may have on audiences. Consideration of the development of documentary as entertainment including attendant "storytelling tendencies" as noted by Dirk Eitzen (2018) will help to provide an important context for understanding what I'm here calling "injustice narratives" as a unique form. In contrast to traditional true crime narratives that focus on the successful investigation and capture of a guilty person and, with it, "a good old-fashioned reordering of the chaos wrought by crime" (Murley, 2008, p. 3), injustice narratives, including *Making a Murderer*, extend investigative intrigue to encourage audiences to consider processes of enacting justice and to question notions of fair practice within the institutions involved.

Injustice narratives are true crime documentaries that focus on the accused, or convicted perpetrators of crime. These are not new, nor especially controversial. As Yardley et al. note (2017), investigative journalism has a "moral duty to expose injustices and champion the public's right to know" (p. 468). On a surface level, the prominence and popularity of serialized narratives appears to suit a focus on the accused/convicted for the simple, yet sad, reason that there is always an end point in stories about the victim, whereas stories about the accused are potentially more open-ended and ongoing. Such decisions on the part of the producers inevitably raise questions about motivation and suggest at least the possibility that injustice narratives are exploitative rather than socially responsible. However, ever-increasing revelations of corruption and bad practice, especially in the USA's justice system, have served to provide injustice narratives, in both documentary films and streaming series, with significant social credibility. *The Paradise Lost Trilogy* (Berlinger & Sinofsky, 1996, 2000, 2011), *Murder on a Sunday Morning* (Lestrade, 2001), *The Staircase* (Lestrade, 2004–2018), *The Trials of Darryl Hunt* (Stern & Sundberg, 2006), *The Central Park Five* (Burns & Burns, 2012), *Making a Murderer* (Demos & Ricciardi, 2015, 2018), *Southwest of Salem: The Story of the San Antonio Four* (Esquinazi, 2016), *The Kalief Browder Story* (Furst, 2017), *The Case Against Adnan Syed* (Berg, 2019, adapted from *This American Life's* podcast spin-off, *Serial* (Koenig,

2014) and *The Innocence Files* (Netflix Limited Series, 2020)[1] are just a few examples. What began as isolated stories of bad practice has quickly grown into widespread recognition of a broken justice system. The significance of injustice narratives is established in their desire to challenge the discourses of truth and justice traditionally dominated by legal institutions. They achieve this by championing more populist approaches to fairness and the public's right to know. This chapter turns now to consider some of the criticisms concerning *Making a Murderer*, before proceeding to consider how this particular injustice narrative encourages audiences to "get to know" its protagonists.

Criticisms of Injustice Narratives

Injustice narratives have been criticized for a variety of reasons, and the popularity of *Making a Murderer* has arguably encouraged extra scrutiny. The series even alludes to its own notoriety at the beginning of Season Two in a montage of praise and criticism that includes a stand-off between opposing audience types; "don't let Netflix tell you what to think!" is the final accusation used in this segment. Most criticism alludes to the tendency for true crime to simplify arguments. For instance, the intention in a series such as *Making a Murderer* is to encourage audiences to see the accused/convicted as "good people". It has been suggested that this decontextualizes the crime, feeds into simplistic demands for certainty (Worden, 2020), and reduces the focus to "good" guys versus "bad" guys (Horeck, 2019; La Chance & Kaplan, 2019; Seltzer, 2007). *Making a Murderer* certainly identifies "bad" guys, not least in both the chief prosecutor, Ken Kratz, and Dassey's original defense lawyer, Len Kachinsky, and suggests their unprofessional behavior are defining factors in both convictions. La Chance and Kaplan argue the focus on one case—that of the defendant—"works to distance the viewer from a sense of being implicated in what they witness" (2019, p. 12). They also argue the impact of events is reduced to an entertaining mystery,

---

[1] The nine episodes in this limited series were directed by Roger Ross Williams, Jed Rothstein, Sarah Dowland, Alex Gibney, Liz Garbus and Andy Grieve.

and the fetishization of innocence perpetuates a "procedural rather than substantive vision of justice" (La Chance & Kaplan, 2019, p. 3). Such is the broad cultural salience of this particular injustice narrative that transmedial responses to *Making a Murderer* have taken on an extraordinary range of forms, from serious political inquiry to comedy memes and have influenced a perception of audiences as "armchair jurors". Horeck argues that any sense of social responsibility encouraged in the series is illusory, because it relies on emotional rather than critical responses from its audience. Furthermore, she states audiences may well be misled by injustice narratives into thinking that "watching (or listening to) and 'interpreting' these accused men and sharing our affective responses to them through networked digital media actually accounts for something" (Horeck, 2019, p. 126).

Both Seltzer (2007) and Worden (2020) argue that forensic analysis in true crime is too often presented as an infallible science, capable of providing proofs from the minutest particles of evidence. Futhermore, they suggest the genre is fixated with identifying culprits and assigning guilt in order to provide narrative closure. Even in the injustice narrative, where the identity of the real criminal is in doubt, narratives tend to still assign guilt to at least one individual (such as the prosecutor in *Making a Murderer*, or an alternative accused in *The Paradise Lost* films). Worden argues these practices present certainties that ignore major socio-political realities of modern society, where poverty is so often a contributing factor to crime and a hindrance to meaningful justice. The genre's reliance on concrete evidence and identifying guilt is viewed as an impediment to effective interrogation of the legal system for, as Worden states, it both mis-represents the "structural conditions of exploitation that target the poor" (Chapter 4) as well as over-simplifies the traumatic events that in reality "cannot be resolved or achieve closure" (ibid.). These criticisms and more are at least partially directed at the narrativization of criminal cases and/or the emotional intensity of the content that has the accused/convicted at the center. Such criticisms are valid, especially in the case of *Making a Murderer* whose long form, high intensity structure and singular focus on two convicted killers have, as yet, failed to prove innocence. However, in spite of all its short-comings, *Making a Murderer* is about much more than establishing guilt or innocence and has indeed helped to disseminate interest within the mainstream about much-needed justice reform. Hook et al. (2016) suggest the series is an example of "shifts in reportage and media literacy" (p. 15) that is "oriented toward real-world outcomes" (ibid.) and transmedial responses are evidence of how it "spark[s] investigation" (ibid.). They conclude their analysis with a list of real-world outcomes that can be attributed to such responses associated with the series. These include attention to legal practices as well as critical reflections on the role of media in helping, or hindering defendants. Therefore, while criticisms of injustice narratives can reflect a healthy skepticism toward the social purpose of popular media trends, such judgments must not negate the possibilities such media may also offer for public debate. No matter how distasteful we may consider the popular true crime format, or how much we may prefer more substantive and intellectual discussion of important social issues, reducing complex institutional practices into simple "good" versus "bad" characters provides a gateway to a topic of significant social import. It is also important to note, as cognitive theorists have successfully argued and this chapter will address later, emotion and logic are not disconnected impulses. Therefore, appealing to emotions does not automatically discount the impulse to critically reflect. *Making a Murderer* does indeed exploit generic tropes in its desire to reach the widest possible audience and it deserves criticism for that, but nonetheless it also includes significant strategies that operate beyond sensationalism and encourage audience engagement with a set of intellectual issues that should not be completely dismissed.

Populist Discourses and Gossip in True Crime Narratives

One reason true crime narratives continue to be distrusted is their association with the persistent rise of populist discourses within mainstream documentary. This development has raised concerns around the popularity of certain topics, such as crime, or celebrity and the balance between entertainment and information. Documentaries since the 1980s have continued to grow in popularity and some of this is due to an increased reliance upon narrative and tonal features usually associated with entertainment as a media form. Paul Arthur (1998) identifies a sub-genre in the 1990s he calls "tabloid documentaries". John Corner (2002) similarly suggests reality television has created a new function for documentary as a "diversion", while Keith Beattie suggests some documentaries now fall into the umbrella category of "popular factual-entertainment". All of these terms seek to categorize the shift from documentary as a sober presentation of information to documentary as an entertainment form. In the introduction to a special edition of the journal *InMedia* (2019) which focuses on such developments, David Lipson and Zachary Baqué suggests the shifts as having a profound effect on our assessment of truth-claims. However, in contrast to the earlier scholars, they do not necessarily suggest these effects as negative for they believe documentaries remain largely ethical spaces even when they entertain. Lipsom and Baqué's overview is important here because, while it has been tempting to consider any connection to entertainment as the signal of crisis in documentary filmmaking, it is important to pause and consider why that has to be considered the case. It seems that any focus on entertainment, that may include examples of overt characterization, performance, and delivery of information through anecdote, trivia, or chatty gossip, is subsequently identified as insincere. This is most likely due to a long-held but overly generalized agreement that non-fiction must always be a serious form, or as Nichols calls it, a "discourse of sobriety" (1991, p. 3).

Dirk Eitzen's (2018) response to this debate is significant, because he not only defends the use of populist discourse in the documentary, but he also reminds us that, while we should be cautious of all narratives in what he describes as our "post-truth world", it is not necessary to dismiss every truth claim as irrevocably damaged. He argues that many documentaries make emotional appeals to viewers and that these appeals often "bear a striking and illuminating resemblance to the appeals of gossip" (Eitzen, 2018, p. 102). Contemporary documentaries trade in stories rather than facts and within that he suggests gossip has a significant and maybe even positive social function:

Gossip has a nasty reputation. People tend to think of it as entirely harmful and evil. In fact, it has powerful positive aspects. Psychologically, it makes us feel stronger and more connected. Socially, it binds us to others and fosters reciprocity. Morally, it shapes and strengthens our sense of right and wrong. Politically, it serves the less powerful by creating group solidarity and marshalling group pressure to keep bullies and cheats in line. Much of documentaries' power for good lies in the same positive potentials. (Eitzen, 2018, p. 104)

The political power of gossip in the creation of group solidarity and as a counterpoint to institutional discourse is significant for injustice narratives. It reminds us that dismissing the opinions of ordinary citizens, or the accused/convicted simply on the basis they lack the credentials (such as a law degree), and hence a legitimized voice in the legal system is also assuming the system is somehow beyond reproach from the people it is supposed to serve. Hence, injustice narratives have social value in giving voice to those who would normally be ignored. In this context, explaining legal procedures to a mass audience in ways that resemble gossip or the anecdotal sharing of stories is a positive social process; it encourages audiences to consider and judge both institutional and personal discourses on a similar "human" level.

Kristen Fuhs (2014) has argued for an understanding of trial documentaries as a reflection of the very real processes of storytelling that occur in courtrooms every day. She labels them as "juridical" rather than injustice documentaries and shows how they "use the legal trial as both a platform and a structuring device to contest the evidentiary value of testimony" (Fuhs, 2014, p. 783), or as "meta-trial[s] on the legitimacy of the actual trials" (p. 784) involved. She uses the example of de Lestrade's *Murder on a Sunday Morning* to show how the film offers evidence (including a characterization of the accused, Brenton Butler) to counter "each of the prosecutor's claims" (Fuhs, 2014, p. 787) about him as the accused. She argues that convictions often hinge on the quality of a prosecutor's, or defense's storytelling in the courtroom and so documentaries that wish to challenge accusations or convictions are simply offering a rebuttal to the original presentation of the case. They are simply doing so in an alternative "public" arena. *Murder on a Sunday Morning* is an exploration of a prosecution that was ultimately proved unfounded and so it is quite easy for Fuhs (2014) to justify and celebrate the documentary.[2] *Making a Murderer* utilizes the same tactics, but in a television series, rather than a single film and perhaps most significantly has so far only managed to create widespread interest in the case, but has not produced an alternative resolution.

While the truth of a case is still under debate there will always be arguments about the veracity of any new information offered, or opinions challenged by a documentary. However, Eitzen (2018) cautions against aligning any concerns about documentary storytelling with issues such as those surrounding "fake news", because in his opinion they "do different things and stem from different impulses" (p. 94). However, he does acknowledge that much contemporary political and social discourse is fueled by emotion and this is crucial to an understanding of contemporary documentary. In this context, injustice narratives, at their best, attempt to identify how emotional discourse has been abused by individuals, or is in fact already hidden within the institutional practices that guide actions, all of which impacts access to fair-minded justice. This is especially evident for those involved in high-profile cases and/or for people in minority groups. However, the quandary for many documentary-makers is that in order to show the manipulative effects of emotional discourse they end up re-stating its use by including footage of the original reporting, investigation, and trial of a crime, such as the press conferences and news reporting included in *Making a Murderer*, that result in the series participating in, or at least reflecting, such discourses themselves. While *Making a Murderer's* inclusion of press coverage is relatively limited, other true crime films have explored some of the worst aspects of crime reporting and are thus in danger of operating in similar histrionics in their own argument. For instance, the *Paradise Lost Trilogy* walks a very delicate path in attempting to show the level of hysteria that surrounded the child murders and led to the conviction of the Memphis teenagers. This has led some critics, most notably Seltzer (2007), to argue the trilogy willingly participates, or capitalizes on the sensational nature

---

[2] *Murder on a Sunday Morning* won an Academy award for "Best Documentary Feature" in 2002. It also won a Prix Italia award for "Best Television Documentary" 2002.

of events. However, it could also be argued the films are in fact offering a critique on such media practices and are also attempting to present the influence such emotional discourses have had on the entire case and its aftermath.

In this respect, part of the strategy of injustice narratives is to identify emotion and the associated manipulation of facts as a major factor in causing miscarriages of justice in the first place. Many injustice narratives use storytelling and anecdotal knowledge to explain the processes by which homophobia or political corruption result in a rush to convict a person on limited, or biased evidence. All of these emotive factors can be argued to be symptomatic of a post-truth society. For instance, *Southwest of Salem* argues the four women were convicted of child molestation primarily because of cultural ignorance about, and prejudice against, the identification of the women as lesbians. The film points to exaggerated fears of both homosexuality and Satanism, fueled by unsubstantiated stories and hearsay that nevertheless prevailed in both legal and social services in the early 1990s. The film argues such fears are no more than gossip, but it also suggests they are the most likely cause of the rush to believe the inconsistent accusations from two very young girls against the women. As these fears were eventually proved unfounded, it is entirely relevant for the documentary to argue how the women's convictions were influenced by shared stories and gossip rather than objective evidence. Similarly, the convictions central to the *Paradise Lost* trilogy are also connected to a communities' shared gossip and fears of Satanism, including unfounded assertions that teenage "goth" identities are directly attached to devil worship. Storytelling by corrupt political and law enforcement actors is blamed for the trials and convictions in both *The Staircase* and *Making a Murderer*. For instance, Michael Petersen's defense team (*Staircase*) reference Petersen's contentious Mayoral election campaign as a possible motivation for the prosecution's behavior and eagerness to assign guilt. *Making a Murderer* suggests Avery's pending civil case against the Manitowoc County Sheriff's Office influences officer participation in the creation of a plausible timeline for Avery's involvement in Halbach's death. This is achieved not only through officer testimony, but also includes possible evidence tampering, such as the planting of Halbach's car keys in Avery's house. To this end, the behavior of District Attorney Ken Kratz highlighted in *Making a Murderer* is the most obvious example of a legal system's exploitative emotional strategies against the accused. The highly emotive language employed in Kratz's pre-trial press conferences that includes unsubstantiated assertions of Avery's physical and emotional state during events is meant to create a picture of Halbach's suffering as well as to establish Avery's guilt as self-evident. The inclusion of this press conference in the narrative is one of the many instances when the documentary asserts the hypocrisy of the legal system's claim to objectivity. Given all of the above examples, it is evident that gossip and storytelling have a powerful influence on the enactment of justice in real life court cases. It also suggests how powerful gossip and the sharing of stories are to creating a social understanding of crime and criminality.

Mark Seltzer's (2007) critical account of *Paradise Lost* not only suggests it is sensationalist, but overly simplistic in its attempts at identifying an alternative culprit. Again, such criticism highlights the double-bind that most injustice narratives experience in their attempts to address the causes, effects as well as solutions to wrongful convictions. They often attempt to identify the central cause of individuals' actions in order to show how institutional discrimination is not an abstract entity, but is enacted by real people in real situations, and most importantly affects people's entire lives. For instance, *The Trials of Darryl Hunt*, *Murder on a Sunday Morning*, and *The Kalief Browder Story* all focus on institutionalized racism in the legal system and focus on various actors, such as district attorneys and witnesses who participate in the rush to judge an innocent man based almost solely on his race. Thus, the films identify these actors as alternative culprits in order to show how their behavior affected the legal process as well as individual lives. In the case of *The Trials of Darryl Hunt* the actions of district attorney, Dean Bowman, who continually denies Hunt access to a fair retrial, take precedence in the documentary narrative, more than the revelation and conviction of the real murderer. This is not only because of the filmmaker's desire to focus on the injustices inherent to a biased appeals system, but also to suggest why the victim's family continually refuses to accept Hunt's innocence even after the real murderer was identified by the court.[3] Rather than a weakness, the search for an alternative culprit mirrors the process of legal inquiry as it is enacted in the courtroom. In this respect, it might look like an attempt to find coherence and closure to a criminal event, but on second glance might be doing something more. The acceptance of innocence by the victim, or victim's family is the most rewarding way to offer a coherent emotional closure for an injustice narrative. *Making a Murder* includes it in the acquittal of Steven Avery for an earlier rape conviction through an interview with the victim, it is also evident in *Southwest of Salem: The San Antonio Four* when one of the victims recants her testimony. However, acceptance is rare and rather than a weakness of such narratives is in fact evidence of how such closure is so often unattainable for those involved in criminal cases. Injustice narratives encourage emotional engagement that is often quite contradictory and because of their subject matter they are unable to offer complete, or satisfactory narrative closure. In such cases, identifying an alternative culprit is a way to create balance and to encourage audiences to consider the accused/convicted as more than the crime.

None of the arguments discussed so far suggest injustice narratives should have carte blanche to use emotion or anecdote however they want, or that the relevation of a miscarriage of justice justifies their means. Documentaries should strive for honesty, relevance, and understanding. At best, injustice narratives achieve this by recognizing the conflicting issues involved in solving and punishing a crime. Films such as *The Trials of Darryl Hunt, Murder on a Sunday Morning* and *Southwest of Salem* eloquently address issues of race and gender identity while still criticizing the system. Arguably, *The Staircase, Paradise Lost,* and *Making a Murderer* are less measured and more passionate and demonstrative. However, it is evident that these latter films and series engage their audiences in similar debates about the American justice system

---

[3] This is presented in the film by the inclusion of a statement from Evelyn Jefferson (mother of Deborah Sykes, the murder victim), who maintains her belief in Hunt's guilt, despite the court's decision. Arguably, the film includes this statement, not only to show the continued prejudice against Hunt, but also to show how miscarriages of justice create mistrust and hurt for all involved to the extent that any decision fails to provide complete and satisfactory closure.

and still encourage critical assessments of how different social groups are viewed and treated. To dismiss their social value on the basis that some arguments are over-simplified is to ignore that these films do much to reveal the emotive tactics commonly used by the justice system to ensure convictions.

Making a Murderer suggests claims of objectivity made by justice systems are myths, and themselves a hindrance to justice. Hence, its own use of emotion can be justified as a rebuttal to the abuse of it in legal practices. The behavior of the special prosecutor, Ken Kratz, is its prime target, but in Season Two it also conducts a forensic analysis of coercive techniques in police interviews through repeated analysis of Brendan's video-taped confession as well as provides information on his upbringing and educational level. Similarly, all the evidence against Steven is systematically challenged, especially in Season Two, while extra information is provided on his extended family and other relationships. The intention is to show the systemic flaws in the current justice system and to extend the characterization of both Steven and Brendan beyond their involvement in a crime. Season Two spends significant time creating emotional engagement with Brendan. This has not only an emotional appeal to audiences, but constitutes an argument for him to be recognized within the justice system as a fully rounded human being rather than as simply part of a crime. At one point, Brendan's mother asserts her belief that prosecutors would recognize Brendan's innocence if they would just "get to know him". It is this "getting to know" the accused/convicted that is a revolutionary practice in the context of a supposedly objective legal system. It goes beyond a reliance on the processing of facts and enters the environment of human emotional engagement. In the depiction of the US Court of Appeals process (Season Two, episode six), the defense team's request for Brendan's exoneration hinges on the judges' acceptance that Brendan was manipulated into confessing to a crime he did not commit. To do this, it is suggested the judges have to accept the process of interrogation as emotional coercion and also accept Brendan's susceptibility to such tactics. At one point, two out of the three judges (Judge Williams and Rovner) acknowledge the emotional manipulation of Brendan while the third (Judge Hamilton) continually refuses to accept the idea that emotion could play any part in causing a false confession. While some of Judge Hamilton's comments raise significant questions about ideologies surrounding masculine identity and individual courage, it is primarily a segment designed to emphasize the impact of that judge's opinion on Brendan's access to justice. The documentary is encouraging audiences, not only to get emotionally involved in Brendan's predicament, but to see the judge's decision as a result of emotional biases rather than objective analysis. To this end, the series is justifying its own tactics by presenting the judge as an emotional human being operating from personal bias, rather than an impervious assessor of facts. It is suggesting once again that emotional bias exists in all aspects of pre and post-conviction legal practices and remains a hindrance to fair justice if it is not acknowledged.

Creating Character and Encouraging Emotional Engagement: "Getting to Know" the Accused/Convicted in Injustice Narratives

If identifying emotional bias was all injustice narratives involved themselves in, then they might not receive the amount of criticism they so often do. However, the associated primary function of injustice narratives is to invite audiences to "get to know" the accused/convicted, and they achieve this by centering their narratives on processes of characterization, which is another source of contention in the reception of documentary texts. The creation of characters and emotional engagement are topics primarily associated with fiction film. However, a great deal of academic work has developed, especially from within studies of cognition, to address how such processes also occur in the documentary. For instance, Carl Plantinga (2018) states quite clearly the similarities between fiction and non-fiction when he announces "documentary filmmakers represent people, and in so doing, they *characterize* them" (p. 115). While non-fiction is influenced by significant ethical requirements, such as the implicit contract between filmmaker and audience that asserts documentaries as "accurate or reliable guides to the film's subject" (ibid.), this does not mean the process of representing a person on screen is neutral. Indeed, all documentaries encourage particular allegiances and/or antipathies regarding the people involved. This is important to a study of true crime documentaries, and especially injustice narratives, because the subject matter is focused almost entirely on encouraging audiences to judge the people involved. In traditional true crime, audiences are encouraged to trust in the processes of justice and so representations of police officers and prosecutors will involve opportunities to construct allegiances. In contrast, an injustice narrative wishes to cast suspicion on such processes and so it will find opportunities to create antipathies in its characterization of the law, as seen in *Making a Murderer*'s consistent accusations against the Manitowoc police department. The extent to which the construction of such allegiances and antipathies are implied or explicit are in part found in a documentary's use of more open or formal voices in its narrative structure. The concept of the documentary voice stems from Bill Nichols' (1983) article on documentary styles and point of view, later solidified in his seminal work on documentary modes (1991). Plantinga (1997) expands this to a study of rhetorical strategies in documentary, where he aligns the open voice with the principles of observational documentary and its emphasis on "showing" information with minimal explanation. In contrast, he suggests a more formal voice occurs in expository films, because its interests lie in a more assertive "telling" of information. In his recent study of characterization he argues these impulses have an impact on the construction of characters not least because "the more the filmmaker attempts to mold viewer perceptions of character through editing, music and shot composition, for example, the further toward the formal and away from the open (or observational) voice the film movies" (Plantinga, 2018, p. 130). Again, the importance of this analysis is evident when we consider how much injustice narratives have a specific interest in molding viewer perceptions of character. While they mostly eschew the explicit formalities of voice-over, they are nonetheless examples of conscious efforts to encourage emotional engagement through character construction. It is evident that in creating characters, injustice narratives are "telling" audiences about the subjects of their film, or series.

Documentaries, as already noted by Eitzen (2018) are in the business of storytelling, and as Ib Bondebjerg (2014) argues; they "use all kinds of communicative strategies [that] appeal not only to reason, but also to feelings and the more sensual dimensions of our reality" (p. 14). Injustice narratives are committed to encouraging audiences to emotionally engage with their central characters. They do this primarily to promote their innocence and to direct criticism of the justice system that enacted a false conviction. However, they also do it to encourage audiences to empathize and see the convicted as "ordinary", or possibly as "people like us". Hence, processes such as finding an alternative culprit, or questioning objectivity in the legal system, as detailed earlier, are all ways to provide the context through which the central character (the accused/convicted) can be viewed sympathetically. It is these elements that encourage criticism, but if considered carefully, it also raises the social purpose of injustice narratives beyond the presentation of isolated cases. If audiences find points of connection with the characters involved then the narrative is more likely to also encourage critical reflection on some of the causes for false convictions; in other words, the emotional engagement operates as the initial "buy-in" for audiences. It is impossible to adequately pinpoint the locus of all audience responses, but it is evident that the chances of encouraging critical debate are not completely undermined by the inclusion of emotional engagement. It is as legitimate to state, as do Hook, Barrios-O'Neill, and Dyer that *Making a Murderer* encourages "meaningful engagement [and] critical thinking" (2016, p. 15) as it is to suggest it takes a "melodramatic, lowbrow approach to its subject matter" (La Chance & Kaplan, 2019, p. 6).

Studies of emotional engagement in the documentary are crucial to understanding the power of character creation, but also serve to caution against seeing such creative choices as a hindrance to critical reflection. Scholars utilize cognitive theories to explain how audiences are encouraged to respond to non-fiction film. They are built upon and largely accept the ideas put forward in cognitive linguistics by George Lakoff and Mark Johnson that the mind and body are linked when it comes to the processing of information (1999) and therefore emotional responses are not the opposite of objective reasoning. From the study of emotion in fiction film (Grodal, 2009; Plantinga & Smith, 1999; Smith, 1995) to the more recent work on documentary (Brylla & Kramer, 2018), a recognition that "emotions are not dysfunctions that interfere with our rationality" (Smith, 1999, p. 103) is central to recognizing how crucial emotion is as part of the process by which we make sense of information. Furthermore, while Jans Eder (2006) argues that "audiovisual representations of characters can be conceived of as dense streams of cues that trigger a wide range of mental reactions in viewers, including perceptions, feelings and imaginings" (p. 69), he also reminds us that our perceptions of on-screen characters are based on social cognition learned "in encounters with real people" (ibid.). Thus, the ways in which audiences engage with on-screen characters cannot be differentiated into fiction versus non-fiction, when the processes for both are already so similar to that which takes place in the everyday. When linked to Eitzen's (2018) recognition that contemporary political and social discourse tends to focus on emotions, rather than truths, it is evident just how important an understanding of emotional engagement is to understanding the power documentary narratives have to influence critical thinking.

As already stated, criticism of true crime, and *Making a Murderer* specifically, draws attention to the ways in which it reduces the central conflict to "good" versus "bad" people. Such criticism is valid, but rarely identifies exactly how the series creates this binary and thus does not thoroughly explore its effects. It is evident the construction of characters is the primary source of binaries and therefore will provide a key to understanding audience-members' emotional engagement. Plantinga's (2018) study suggests the common literary distinction between "flat" and "round" is useful in distinguishing levels of characterization in documentary, because while most texts do not have time to offer "fully-rounded" examples, the degree to which a character is explored will affect audience responses. This is not as simple as saying "more screen time" equates to more rounded characters, or even "more sympathy" equals more engagement; it is the level of complexity that is key. He notes how flat characters are "uncomplicated, unchanging and characterized by only one, or two traits" (Plantinga, 2018, p. 122), while round characters are obviously more complex. *Making a Murderer's* use of flat characters is immediately obvious in its presentation of prosecutor Ken Kratz, detective James Lenk and defense lawyer Len Kachinsky. All three are limited to specific behaviors that suggest them as over-confident, untrustworthy characters. From Kratz's infamous pre-trial press conference (Season One, episode six), Lenk's unconvincing testimony in court (Season One, episode seven) and Kachinsky and Michael O'Kelly's egregious bullying behavior toward Brendan (Season One, episode five), the series reduces these characters to oppressive agents of an uncaring system, whose primary goal appears to be to gain convictions by any means they deem necessary. None of these three are provided with significant screen time or character complexity that may contradict, or even complicate this assessment. In Season Two, episode two Kratz's press conference is replayed, in order to remind audiences of his villainous role in the case, while later in episode six, footage of a further press conference is suggested as Kratz's attempt to manipulate media responses to Brendan's appeal for exoneration. Most importantly, in Season Two, episode two, the filmmakers employ their most explicit construction of Kratz as an alternative culprit. Using audio from phone interview with Steven over a montage of images of Kratz at work, Steven accuses the prosecutor of having "too much power" and of failing to provide "justice for Teresa's family". This is a clear case of the documentary "telling" audiences how to view Kratz, one that is in no way implicit, or hidden. In both seasons there is no attempt to hide disdain for this man, or to present him as anything beyond a flat characterization of villainy.

In contrast, the filmmakers create more complex characterizations, and sympathy for both Steven and Brendan and attempt to maintain that sympathy throughout 20 episodes. Presenting them as flat "good" characters in this instance would be unsustainable, but it is also counterproductive to their intentions, so they work to construct more complex fully rounded characterizations. Plantinga (2018) reminds us that such a task is extremely difficult as; "a round characterization provides a sense of a person's personality, of their deepest motivations and beliefs" (p. 123). He goes on to state how physical gestures, interactions with others, other people's opinions of them, as well as changes over time are all necessary elements to present a truly rounded character. Such complexity is a challenge with even the most open and accessible person, but in the case of *Making a Murderer* the filmmakers are denied direct access to either of their central characters beyond intermittent telephone calls. Interestingly, *Making a Murderer* appears more interested in Steven and Brendan and rebutting the presentation of them as criminals, than it is in actually solving the crime involved. It continually asserts them as victims of a broken legal system. Again, this justifies some of the harshest criticisms of the series reflected here in Horeck's (2019) statement that it "operates according to presumptive, predetermined binaries, that [..] elide the female victim" (p. 132). She argues the series is so obsessed with exploring the state's treatment of Steven and Brendan that it fails to provide adequate respect and consideration for the victim. This is not only true of the series, but also many other discussions that surround the case since the series aired. A book by Steven's lawyer, Jeffrey Buting (2017) suggests:

> Whether convinced of Steven Avery's innocence or guilt, most viewers of *Making a Murderer* agree that the investigation, prosecution, and trial of Teresa Halbach's murder were tainted by law enforcement conflict of interest; biased pretrial publicity generated by an unethical prosecutor; and evidence that led to more questions than answers about what happened to Teresa. This is a travesty of justice for her, too. (Buting, 2017, p. 9)

While it's important to note that he ends here with justifying the need for investigation as a tribute to Teresa Halbach, it is still the state's treatment of Steven Avery that remains his central focus. It is evident that, in order to achieve their goals, the defense lawyers, as well as the documentary as a chronicle of such defense, will be intent on providing as much information about Steven and Brendan as possible in order to keep the focus exactly where they want it to be. An injustice narrative is exactly what it seems, a text that focuses on the injustice of an accusation and/or conviction and therefore it invites audiences to get to know the person[s] involved in the prosecution. In so doing it almost inevitably reduces the crime and its victims to a secondary level of consideration.

The challenges of creating complex characterizations and audience emotional engagement with Steven and Brendan are addressed in various ways throughout *Making a Murderer*. The opening credit sequence for both series remains focused on Steven and includes a prominent photograph of him as a child. Similarly, one of the most prevalent images of Brendan from the series is his slumped posture during the long police interrogation. Both of these examples are crucial because they are the primary images upon which their more rounded characterizations are built. In essence, both series wish to constantly remind audiences of these men as sons, or children. Not in a way that reduces their characters to one or two traits, but as a connection to the primary characters to whom the filmmakers have consistent access. Both of the series use the men's parents, Dolores and Allan Avery, and Peter and Barbara Dassey,[4] as physical and emotional surrogates for the men they cannot access. This not only allows for the more complex and contradictory elements of the men's characters to be explored through interviews, but it means that such information is filtered through the sympathetic and, perhaps most importantly, legally innocent, parents. It can be argued that this decision is primarily situational, in that much of the filmmakers' access to Avery and Dassey occurs through the men's phone calls to their family, but it is also extremely useful in creating stand-ins for characters whose physical presence is otherwise confined to court appearances and prison photographs.

Creating characterizations beyond their status as convicted criminals is crucial to rebutting the evidence provided in the courtroom, and interrogation sequences. In other injustice narratives similar techniques are employed, or addressed, depending on access to the primary characters. For instance, in *Southwest of Salem*, all four women are interviewed while in prison. While this emphasizes their status as convicted, the interviews are conducted using close-ups and long takes. This encourages emotional engagement with the women that acts as a precursor to then encouraging audiences to reflect on the reasons for such miscarriage of justice to occur. Similar techniques are used in *The Innocence Files*, where interviews with the convicted are a primary source of information on the consequences of injustice. As noted, Fuhs' (2014) discussion of *Murder on a Sunday Morning* shows how interviews with family members, as well as various

---

[4] Scott Tadych, Brendan's step father appears more often than Peter Dassey, but an interview with Peter in season 1, episode 1 is one of the most significant examples of characterizing Brandon through a blood relative.

photographs, create Brenton Butler as a rounded character, and the same technique is used for Darryl in *The Trials of Darryl Hunt*. These strategies are all designed to lift the characterization of the central subject away from accused/convicted, so they may be recognized as "ordinary" or "like us", and thus encourage meaningful audience engagement with their plights. These techniques would not work with flat characterizations that demand audiences see *only* innocence and morality, but they are techniques that, through attention to more rounded detail, introduce the possibility that innocence and morality is indeed part of their character; a possibility it is argued the prosecution did not allow in the courtroom. Injustice narratives use a variety of techniques and so cannot be confined, or reduced to simple manipulations, but their intention always includes certain tactics that operate as rebuttals of the characterization used in the original conviction.

Making a Murderer's focus on parents as stand-ins for their sons is an evident tactic to encourage emotional engagement with the convicted. It is illustrated in Season One in Dolores' attendance at the trial in the latter episodes, but is used to a far greater degree in Season Two in successive interviews about hopes for an exoneration. The parents are obvious defenders of their sons' innocence, but they also discuss them as family-oriented, loving, and generous men. Thus, while interviews with the parents are used to create a sense of urgency, such as the desperate desire to have Steven freed before his increasingly frail parents pass away, or for Brendan to be freed while he is still young enough to perhaps have his own family, these aspects are in many ways tangential to the primary, but implicit, use of the parents' physical presence to provide characterizations of Steven and Brendan. The most obvious example of this is an interview with Peter Dassey in Season Two, episode one. Not only does Peter say Brendan is "like me", but Peter also has similar speech patterns and physical appearance to that seen in the limited footage of Brendan. He discusses Brendan's placid and caring nature while attendant footage shows his own tidy home and attentive character. Hence, the purpose of this interview is not an exercise in learning about Peter, but is in fact all about Brendan. Through Peter's physical demeanor, audiences are encouraged to see Brendan and this provides a more rounded characterization than can be obtained from the archive footage, or prison photographs available to the filmmakers. The same is true of interviews with and attendant footage of Barbara Dassey whose demeanor is similarly placid. Over the course of the two seasons Brendan's characterization is created using evidence from family and lawyers with whom he has regular interactions, but his physical presence, in gestures and demeanor, is provided by engagement with his close family. Similarly, Allan Avery's work ethic and Dolores stoic, but weary patience are suggested as physical stand-ins for Steven's character, while their declining health suggests similar physical attributes in him as well. In stark contrast to the flat characterization of Ken Kratz as a conceited and powerful man, both Steven and Brendan, with minimal real-time participation from either of them, are consistently connected to humble and physically benign citizens and this operates as a consistent and powerful rebuttal of the prosecution's characterization of them as killers.

Conclusion

Getting to know Steven and Brendan through watching *Making a Murderer* is a heavily constructed process, partly because the filmmakers have limited access to them and partly because they want audiences to see them as the "good guys" in the narrative. Characterization is a natural part of all documentary representations, but it is especially evident in true crime injustice narratives where audiences are encouraged to judge participants and to reconsider the processes of a particular legal case. It is an emotionally charged arena where encouraging emotional engagement with the convicted is a contentious tactic, especially when the accusation or conviction has not been proven false, because it not only suggests a dismissal and disrespect of the victims, their families, and legal system, but it may also provide undeserved attention for the convicted and prejudice the appeals process. However, characterization is also a justified tactic in resisting the idea that the convicted can be understood simply in terms of the crimes to which they are attached and is essential in creating emotional engagement with a criminal case sometimes long after it has been accepted as solved. While objective evidence is still accepted as the pinnacle of fair justice, appeals to emotion are an effective first step to encourage interest in a closed case and point to the reasons why reevaluating, or critically reflecting upon legal processes is a human issue and not just an institutional one. While *Making a Murderer* employs many tactics more readily associated with "telling", rather than "showing" information this does not mean audiences are unable to critically reflect on the processes it reveals. Until faith in the US legal system is restored, the extent to which audiences find the tactics used in *Making a Murderer* as exploitative, or justified will depend on a huge variety of factors. These may include exposure and attitudes to other true crime texts, or other documentary forms, learned opinions about the criminal justice system and those who are accused/convicted of crimes, pre-conceived ideas of gender, race, and class in American culture as well as many other sociopolitical factors. This is not to suggest *Making a Murderer* has no ethical role to play in its characterizations, but it is also important to note that criticisms of its worth are often attached to wider ideological assumptions about the roles of documentary, entertainment, and justice reform. To suggest that audience responses to *Making a Murderer* are always naïve, or based on uncaring, selfish principles of voyeurism and fingerpointing is to miss the potential that even popular mainstream media has to disseminate meaningful information about important social issues. As a film scholar it is hard not to cringe at its narrative manipulations and theatrical re-enactments of pop-forensic science, but to argue that in watching *Making a Murderer* Netflix is "telling you what to think" is to give it more credit, and audiences much less credit, than either deserve. Regardless of its simplistic tactics, it encourages audiences to think about events in their immediate world. For every audience member who takes true crime on face value as purely entertainment, or dismisses it as exploitation, there are many others who will question what they see and in response to what they have been "told" are encouraged to know more.

Study Questions

- What are "injustice narratives" and what criticisms have been raised about this narrative form?
- What techniques does *Making a Murderer* deploy to encourage us to "get to know" Steven Avery and Brendan Dassey?
- Larke-Walsh sees "true crime" documentaries' attempts to get us to emotionally engage with their protagonists in a positive light. What is her argument, and do you agree?

Bibliography

Arthur, P. (1998). Media spectacle and the tabloid documentary. *Film Comment, 34*(1), 74–80.

Bondebjerg, I. (2014). Documentary and cognitive theory: Narrative, emotion and memory. *Media and Communication, 2*(1), 13–22.

Brylla, C., & Kramer, M. (Eds.). (2018). *Cognitive theory and documentary film.* Palgrave MacMillan.

Buting, J. F. (2017). *Illusion of justice: Inside making a murderer and America's broken system.* Harper-Collins Publishers.

Corner, J. (2002). Performing the real: Documentary diversions. *Television and New Media, 3*(3), 255–269.

Eder, J. (2006). Ways of being close to characters. *Film Studies, 8,* 68–80.

Eitzen, D. (2018). The duties of documentary in a post-truth society. In C. Brylla & M. Kramer (Eds.), *Cognitive theory and documentary film.* Palgrave Macmillan.

Fuhs, K. (2014). The legal trial and/in documentary film. *Cultural Studies, 28*(5–6), 781–808. https://doi.org/10.1080/09502386.2014.886484

Grodal, T. (2009). *Embodied visions: Evolution.* Oxford University Press.

Hook, A., Barrios-O'Neill, D., & Mairs Dyer, J. (2016). A transmedia topology of *Making a Murderer. Journal of European Television History and Culture, 5*(10). https://doi.org/10.181146/2213-0969.2016.jethc117

Horeck, T. (2019). *Justice on demand: True crime in the digital streaming era.* Wayne State University Press.

La Chance, D., & Kaplan, P. (2019). Criminal justice in the middlebrow imagination: The punitive dimensions of *Making a Murderer*. *Crime, Media, Culture*. https://doi.org/10.1177/1749659019835249

Lakoff, G., & Johnson, M. (1999). *Philosophy in the flesh: The embodied mind at its challenge to Western thought*. Basic Books.

Lipson, D., & Baqué, Z. (2019). Rethinking the convergence of documentary and entertainment. *InMedia, 7*(2).

Murley, J. (2008). *The rise of true crime: Twentieth century murder and American popular culture*. Praeger.

Nichols, B. (1991). *Representing reality: Issues and concepts in documentary*. Indiana University Press.

Nichols, Bill. (1983). The Voice of Documentary. *Film Quarterly, 36*(3), 17–30. https://doi.org/10.2307/3697347.

Plantinga, Carl. (1997). *Rhetoric and representation in non-fiction film*. New York. Cambridge University Press.

Plantinga, C. (2018). Characterization and character engagement in the documentary. In C. Brylla & M. Kramer (Eds.), *Cognitive theory and documentary film*. Palgrave Macmillan.

Plantinga, C., & Smith, G. M. (1999). *Passionate views: Film, cognition and emotion*. John Hopkins University Press.

Seltzer, M. (2007). *True crime: Observations on violence and modernity*. Abingdon, UK: Routledge.

Smith, M. (1995). *Engaging characters: Fiction, emotion, and the cinema*. Clarendon Press.

Smith, G. M. (1999). "Local emotions, global moods, and film structure." In C. Plantinga & G. M. Smith, (Eds.), *Passionate views: Film, cognition and emotion* (pp.103–126). Baltimore: John Hopkins University Press.

Worden, D. (2020). *Neoliberal non-fictions: The documentary aesthetic form from Joan Didion to Jay-Z*. University of Virginia Press.

Yardley, E., Wilson, D., & Kennedy, M. (2017). "To me its [sic] reallife": Secondary victims of homicide in newer media. *Victims and Offenders, 12*(3): 467–496. https://doi.org/10.1080/15564886.2015.1105896

4

From 'Forensic Narratives' to 'Narratives of Forensics': Telling Stories About the Murder of Gay Gibson

Alexa Neale

Introduction

Recent documentaries and podcasts suggest the emergence of a new true crime genre, characterised by public participation and focus on wrongful convictions or miscarriages of justice (Bruzzi, 2016; Stratton, 2019). Content displays 'a forensic, almost fetishistic, fixation with evidence', scientific techniques applied to past cases to reach conclusive truths, catch killers or correct judicial wrongs reached by inferior evidentiary standards of the past (Bruzzi, 2016, p. 251). For example, recent true crime depictions of the murder of Eileen (known as 'Gay') Gibson aboard a British ship off the coast of South Africa in 1947 have seen an author and programme-maker arguing that the absolute truth of 'what actually happened' lies in DNA on a 70-year-old hairbrush with problematic provenance, supported by uncontextualised partial police files

A. Neale (✉)
University of Sussex, Brighton, UK
e-mail: a.neale@sussex.ac.uk

© The Author(s), under exclusive license to Springer Nature Switzerland AG 2021
M. Mellins and S. Moore (eds.), *Critiquing Violent Crime in the Media*,
https://doi.org/10.1007/978-3-030-83758-7_4

(Brown, 2018; Latto & Doherty, 2018). Using the Gibson murder as a case study, this chapter tracks murder narratives from archived case file documents through true crime media up to 2020, highlighting the ways in which failure to historicise murder narratives can create rather than correct injustices.

Introducing the Gay Gibson Case

When James Camb was found guilty of the murder of Gay Gibson, death by judicial hanging was the mandatory sentence in England and Wales and so it was pronounced upon him by the judge. However, not all death sentences recorded were carried out. Between 1942 and 1955, for example, white male defendants like Camb had a 41% chance of reprieve (Seal & Neale, 2020b, p. 886). Juries, judges, UK Director of Public Prosecutions, the Court of Criminal Appeal, Prison Commission and Home Office frequently tempered capital sentences by recommending mercy, recording some degree of sympathy, mitigating circumstance deserving of clemency or even doubt in their legal pronouncements, private correspondence or secret memoranda. Even in the worst cases, where discretionary powers to commute the death sentence to a term of imprisonment could not be justified, prosecution narratives were often neutralised in some way by contemporaries in the criminal justice system or in subsequent institutional memory. This was not so in the Camb case, however. Archives of crime and justice demonstrate an unusual level of longitudinal and unilateral commitment to the police and prosecution narrative: that James Camb was a serial sexual predator and his fatal attack on Gay Gibson was the middle of seven known and recorded assaults on girls and young women. His *modus operandi* involved using his position as hospitality staff to select, pursue and isolate female guests, invading their bedrooms and assaulting them without consent. Gibson's murder was a consequence of Camb's asphyxiation paraphilia. Contemporaries did not use this phrase, but survivors of attacks before and after Gibson described how Camb used his hands or body to apply pressure to restrict or stop their breathing. Police believed that an attack just prior to that on Gibson had taught Camb that suffocating his victims left visible marks on their faces. According to this narrative, it was to destroy evidence of his crime that Camb disposed of Gibson's body by pushing her through the porthole of her cabin at sea.[1] Despite rigid adherence to this narrative of Gibson's murder by Camb in the official historical and judicial record, it is a counter-narrative that has become the dominant popular memory of Gibson's death, traceable through true crime media over three quarters of a century: Camb's defence counsel alleged that Gibson died suddenly from a health condition during consensual sex. That narrative was the only way to save his life within the law considering the evidence; a specifically *forensic* narrative.

Life-saving forensic narratives were not necessarily the whole truth as seen by those who told them. As Lizzie Seal and I have argued elsewhere, once a particular mercy narrative emerged and proved successful 'it remained as a possible story to tell' due in no small part to the high stakes involved (Seal & Neale, 2020b, p. 887). The term 'forensic narratives' is used here to encompass mercy narratives, defence narratives and other stories contingent upon legal definitions, courtroom conditions and/or potential punishments—drawing on the meaning of the word 'forensic' as 'suitable or analogous to pleadings in court' (OED, 2020). Forensic narratives take complex events and nuanced characters and shape them to fit offence frameworks defined by legal statute, precedent and possible punishment according to a forced adversarial binary: crown/prosecution vs defendant/defence, victim vs criminal, murder vs an alternative somewhere between slightly lesser culpability and total non-involvement, death by hanging vs life in prison. When the axe falls on one of the two sides, common sense dictates that the opposing case is discredited; but even recently newspapers and members of parliament have been criticised for promoting the notion that a 'not guilty' verdict ratifies the defence narrative (The Secret Barrister, 2020). In actuality, juries declare a verdict of 'not guilty' or favour a less serious conviction for a variety of reasons including a scintilla of doubt, failure of prosecution evidence to meet the required standard of proof, or the mandatory punishment associated with the charge deemed too harsh. For example,

---

[1] The official record concerning this case consists of police officer accounts, court documents, official correspondence, and Home Office papers at The National Archives (TNA) including: ASSI 26/59/1; MEPO 3/2860; PCOM 9/643. See also Kemble (1948).

juries were less likely to find defendants guilty when death was the mandatory sentence and likely outcome of a conviction (see Seal, 2014). On the other hand, given that the burden of proof lies with the prosecution, a guilty verdict does, at least partially, indicate the jury's acceptance of the prosecution narrative and rejection of the defence. This context is important because forensic narratives which defended against a murder charge did not have to meet the same rules and standards of evidence because the burden of proof did not lie with them. Forensic narratives deployed in defence are not required to be proven to the same degree as prosecuting forensic narratives. Rather they are told in order to explain away prosecution evidence, to cast doubt and suggest alternative circumstances which could mitigate the crime, suggest an alternative charge was more appropriate (such as manslaughter) or simply anticipate a verdict of guilty of murder but arouse sympathy which would see a jury and judge recommend mercy.

As attempts to save a life at any cost, mercy narratives and defence narratives during the period preceding the abolition of capital punishment in England and Wales (1965) frequently called upon damaging stereotypes about, amongst other things, sex, gender and race. Inspiring sympathy for the defendant often required damning indictments of the victim's character, who, if they were deceased, would be unable to offer a challenge in the courtroom or speak out when the press inevitably focused on such details of a case. (A phenomenon also observed recently in relation to the 'rough sex defence'—itself an example of a forensic narrative—by campaign group, We Can't Consent to This—see Bows & Herring, 2020). Given sexual double standards in the past and present, and the high prevalence of male on female domestic and/or sexual killings in which women are regarded as culpable in their own murders (Bows & Herring, 2020), reviving a defence narrative after the jury has found in favour of the prosecution and rejected the alternative has the effect of resurrecting stories given little or no credit by contemporaries and prioritizing evidence which did not meet an equivalent standard of proof. Further, out of the context of the courtroom, exhibits of evidence preserved in archives or discussed in newspaper reporting are seen without the rigorous adversarial interrogation, questioning and examination of expert witnesses and first-hand observers that helped the jury understand, contextualise and weigh them. Exhibits the jury rejected after rigorous courtroom debate, and the elements of the forensic narratives they illustrated, are archived alongside those judged most compelling and persuasive. Taking forensic narratives out of their forensic (legal) context, therefore, risks misrepresenting many forensic moments, past and present (Neale, 2020a). True crime media about the Gibson case, for example, actively muted the voices of survivors within months of mainstream public attention to #MeToo, a movement which encouraged survivors of sexual assault to speak up and the rest of the world to listen (Phipps, 2019).

In this chapter I use archive case files to identify the origins of the forensic narratives in the case, the contexts and circumstances under which they were constructed and deployed. I prioritise the voices of young women, recently muted by true crime media on the case, to tell the prosecution narrative which was ultimately endorsed by Camb's conviction. I then chronologically track true crime depictions of the murder of Gay Gibson from contemporary forensic narratives to recent narratives of forensics, identifying trends in true crime media that have contributed to the transformation of the story over time, including true crime retrospectives and sensationalised serialisations in tabloid newspapers, whose apparent opening up of a tiny space for debate has been over-emphasised by later true crime publications. In the decades following the trial, true crime media including books written by male legal and scientific 'experts' emphasised their own superior scientific and legal knowledge of a non-existent female body. I show how their claims to empirical fact, combined with Camb's serialised criminal biography, began to modify the public memory of the case despite his return to prison for similar violent sexual offences against girls. I go on to show how true crime authors from 1991 to 2020 have promoted outrageous interpretations of the case, doing serious injustice to the experiences of survivors and the memory of an innocent dead woman. In the final part of this chapter I suggest ways in which these damaging narratives can be fruitfully critiqued using the same technologies and approaches to injustice offered by present true crime media (Stratton, 2019). Exploring how forensic narratives have been transformed into narratives of forensics by the interests and characteristics of true crime widens their application to injustice(s), I argue, recognizing that true crime can be untruthful and unjust in its treatment of historical cases. First, I will describe how this chapter defines 'true crime'.

Analysing the Truth in True Crime

Law defines crime. As Lizzie Seal and I have highlighted separately and together, narratives associated with real-life murders are contingent on legal framing and courtroom contexts in the first instance, including mercy narratives in the form of petitions, and visual narratives through crime scene photographs (Neale, 2020a). Stories about crime in and out of the courtroom are telling of the historical, cultural, and political moments in which they are told, reflecting common social tropes. True crime is also deserving of scholarly attention because these public narratives represent a popular criminology, with capital crime identified as a particularly pervasive and persistent theme in British popular culture, communicated via a variety of media forms for centuries (Biressi, 2001; Seal, 2014). Besides following contemporary cases, the repeated telling and retelling of past events is an enduring feature of true crime stories, as is the pre-eminence of murder and morality tales about the accused in which the path to crime, sometimes for victim as much as defendant, can be traced biographically and offer a salutary lesson to consumers. There is also a historical precedent for novel-length non-fiction which complicates the 'truth' of true crime by expanding creatively on real-life murders (Biressi, 2001). For the purpose of this chapter, 'true crime' is defined broadly as entertaining and/or informational media, from contemporary press to retrospective podcast via TV and streaming documentary, which references real-life individuals and the familiar circumstances of a particular (alleged) unlawful event.

Viewing modern techniques as uniquely able to uncover miscarriages of justice and solve cold cases inaccurately assumes a smooth upward trajectory of forensic history climaxing at a point of scientific and empirical superiority, objectivity and certainty (Adam, 2020). Such a view also overlooks instances where there was contemporary public debate questioning police investigation techniques or judicial decisions and their crime narratives in the past (Wood, 2020). The Gibson case reveals, too, that true crime narratives, despite seeming to offer up an unvarnished 'truth', are a product of various biases and assumptions. For example, true crime stories which promote Camb's lesser culpability in accordance with the defence forensic narrative include gendered double standards of sexuality, male experts as the most authoritative voices on women's bodies, and latterly the notion that the infallible and final 'truth' lies dormant and encoded in (non-existent) genetic material. In reaching for legitimacy they prioritise certain perspectives and voices, silencing others and alienating potential audiences. Exploring how forensic narratives have been transformed into narratives of forensics by the interests and characteristics of true crime recognises that case outcomes that can be resolved are not the only injustices deserving of attention, and that exploring past cases and associated media demands 'sensitivity to the particular contexts and the diversity of audiences when it comes to the telling of [crime] stories' (Wood, 2020, p. 177).

Forensic Narratives in the Gay Gibson Case

'Forensic narratives' refer to stories originating in the courtroom or in accordance with legal frameworks which draw on prominent social and cultural tropes and recent legal precedent to construct a story of crime with a particular legal outcome, verdict or punishment. For example, judges and juries in 1940s England and Wales were sympathetic to returning soldiers who killed their wives if they constructed a narrative which evoked short- and long-term factors compatible with contemporary social concerns for gendered roles and family reconstruction, the concept of provocation and increasing involvement of psychiatric understandings of behaviour in legal practice and punishment policy. These sympathies often neutralised crimes initially defined as 'murder' leading to lesser convictions or complete acquittal, despite no doubt that the accused was the killer (Neale, 2020a, Ch. 5). Sexual double-standards are common to many twentieth-century forensic narratives, women's sexuality is a common feature of arguments for manslaughter when death was the mandatory penalty for murder. Outside the courtroom, sex sells, but the possibility of capital punishment is added to public interest and circulation of forensic narratives in true crime media (Seal, 2014).

In the period of the Gay Gibson case, true crime stories tended to encourage escapist fantasies amongst their audiences, no doubt as a means of offering a cultural alternative to the austerity and rationing that characterised everyday life in post-war Britain. That cultural backdrop is well-illustrated by the British film, *It Always Rains on Sunday*, released 25 November 1947. Rose Sandigate wakes up on a typical Sunday morning to the relentless demands of postwar domestic drudgery in a drab, damp and bomb-damaged environment. One of her few joys is a cup of tea in bed with her husband while he reads the Sunday papers and she asks him 'any murders?' (Hamer, dir., 1947; Nead, 2017). Sunday murder stories were as traditional and as British as roast beef according to George Orwell in 1946. Favourite narratives included middle-class characters, sex, celebrity, familiar settings or everyday situations and an extraordinary coincidence or occurrence (Orwell, 1965). The murder of Gay Gibson ticked almost every box.

The Sunday Pictorial's front page on 26 October 1947 read: 'THE GIRL IN CABIN 126 … pretty, red-headed Eileen (Gay) Gibson, 21, London actress' who had disappeared from passenger ship *The Durban Castle* 'on the homeward voyage from South Africa' (*Sunday Pictorial*, 1947, pp. 1, 8, 9). Crew had reportedly searched vessel and waters with no sightings and the Captain was certain the young woman must be dead, her body lost at sea. The story offered escapism, mystery, glamour, foreign travel—restricted under wartime regulations still in operation and by general austerity—and celebrity. Gay Gibson was not a household name, but boxer-turned-actor Eric Boon was. Pictured together as co-stars in centre pages, he described hearing his friend speak of a job offer in London, hopeful for her future acting career (*Sunday Pictorial*, 1947, p. 9). That Gibson envisioned a positive future enhanced the melodrama but also inoculated against a common narrative explanation for disappearance at sea: suicide. Attempted suicide was a criminal offence until 1961 and rarely named in 1940s newspapers, which referred to self-destruction only euphemistically. As Adrian Bingham (2009) has highlighted, newspapers were also reluctant to name extramarital pregnancy and crimes like abortion and rape. This reticence is reflected in archives of criminal justice and policing; perceived causes of suicidal intentions including romantic disappointment were raised and refuted in the Gibson case, often without naming the crime.[2] Journalistic practices, story selection and motivations for constructing press crime narratives can be frustratingly opaque but it was certainly in the interests of selling papers to amp up the intrigue while maintaining press reporting powers by adherence to legal guidelines (Wood, 2016). Framing Gibson's initial disappearance as a 'mystery' and following the investigation and courtroom action to reveal the case piecemeal served the dual functions of serialisation to keep readers buying newspapers and adhering to rules that restricted crime reporting before a trial was concluded. Politicians were concerned that the press may influence the course of justice and frequently sought to censor them if they stepped beyond the bounds of propriety. For example, shortly before Gibson's disappearance, contempt of court charges were brought against a newspaper that referred to John George Haigh as a murderer before he had been convicted.[3] Newspaper true crime reports must therefore be seen in light of various codes: moral, legal, written and implied, with the promise of story-longevity adding an additional spur to reporting.

The first statements recorded and archived regarding Gibson's disappearance indicate that her alleged killer, like Haigh, had received the notion that there could be no murder conviction without a body and he adjusted his narrative of events to fit evidence as it emerged.[4] When Gibson was missing from her cabin on the morning of 18 October 1947 and crew were questioned, deck steward James Camb denied having ever been in her room but told a colleague she had confided in him that she was pregnant, unmarried and depressed. He hoped to infer a narrative of suicide (Casswell, 1961, p. 296; Dunboyne, 1953, p. 17). When confronted with competing evidence—including that Gibson had pushed her bedside call buttons to summon the night watchman, who

---

[2] TNA: ASSI 26/59/1; MEPO 3/2860; see also Clark (1949).

[3] TNA: HO 45/25849: Home Office Registered Papers: Crime: Financing by Newspapers of the Defence of Criminals: Attempts by Prisoners Held on Capital Charges to Publish Their Stories (1933–1955).

[4] TNA: MEPO 3/2860: Police reports and witness statements; Kemble (1948).

had opened the door and seen Camb's face—he changed his story: she invited him, they made love, she clutched him tightly and there was sadness in her eyes when he said goodbye, evoking a romantic melodrama in which the lovelorn actress was the tragic star. Each passenger and crew member who had spoken with the young woman could not countenance suicide; she was hopeful for the future, she had plans, she did not seem depressed. Crew working on deck had not seen her, she could not have gone overboard from there unobserved. Threads from Gay's missing dressing gown were found caught on her open cabin porthole, suggesting her exit. As the last person to see her alive and caught in a lie about it, Camb was under close observation. Conspicuously wearing his heavy jacket in stifling equatorial heat rather than the lighter uniform that exposed his arms made colleagues suspicious. He was examined by the ship's surgeon who found recent parallel wounds on his wrist and shoulder consistent with fingernails. Camb said he had been scratching heat rash. Police were notified and officers met the *Durban Castle* before it docked at Southampton to examine Gibson's cabin and interview Camb. If the woman had died from something other than his violence, now was the time to say so, police told him. Camb seemed to realise the possibility of a counter-narrative to murder for the first time and thought very carefully before he offered a new statement. This time he said Gibson died suddenly during consensual sex and he pushed the body out of the porthole in a panic.[5] It was critical to his survival that James Camb's narrative of Gay Gibson's disappearance did not fit legal definitions of the offence of capital murder, rather it had to render him either completely inculpable (as his suicide story suggested) or guilty of a lesser charge with a lighter sentence (such as manslaughter). If he was found guilty of murder, death was the mandatory sentence, though on average 40 per cent of men whose death sentence was reviewed by the Home Office in the twentieth century were reprieved through the secretive and discretionary process of mercy (Seal, 2014). A sentence would be commuted to imprisonment only if a sympathetic mercy narrative could be constructed by a prisoner's legal representatives (Seal & Neale, 2020b). The only alternative was to apply to appeal post-conviction,

---

[5] TNA: ASSI 26/59/1; MEPO 3/2860; Kemble (1948); Clark (1949).

which usually relied upon a courtroom technicality such as the judge failing to accurately describe the legal definitions which applied to the prosecution and defence narratives.[6] These considerations are crucial to comprehending how forensic narratives became a true crime story: they were constructed to explain a death as unlawful, to define it as murder or manslaughter, to lessen culpability or criminal intent, and to appeal for merciful treatment. Crime narratives required a legal frame, a forensic context, from which to hang (Althoff et al., 2020).

What Camb, like Haigh, did not realise was that a body was not required to convict for murder (especially at sea); Home Office files and police narratives describe it as uncommon but not unknown (Kemble, 1948). Twenty-first-century popular culture views circumstantial evidence as a poor substitute for that which is directly observed, physical or scientifically testable, but in the twentieth-century courtroom opening and closing speeches, prosecuting counsel frequently referred to material exhibits (objects), documents, crime scene photographs and witness testimony as fragments of a puzzle requiring only common sense by the jury to reach a guilty verdict (Neale, 2020a). Defence counsel would attack by any means the authenticity or believability of a prosecution witness or their evidence, including medical experts, to cast reasonable doubt on the prosecution's case. But the most effective defences offered a counter-narrative that explained the same evidence given by the prosecution—equally as believable but with less deadly consequences for their client. Camb had already confessed to pushing Gibson's body out of the porthole by the time counsel consulted with him and so his life depended on: (1) Her having died, but not by his hand, before he put her in the water; (2) A reasonable explanation for disposing of her body—for which he offered fear of suspicion and discovery of his affair (Camb would lose his wife, child and career). Thus, the defence began to construct the only forensic narrative that would save Camb's life. Rape had to be excluded because where the intention to rape, and not to kill, could be proved, and the victim died as a result of force or injury, murder was charged and death sentences rarely reprieved.[7]

---

[6] See for example TNA: DPP 2/1728: CAMB, J: Murder appeal (1948); Clark (1949).
[7] TNA: HO 384/158: Capital Cases vol. 1, pp. 430–50.

Here, defence counsel would have some difficulty because as the police investigation advanced, a new narrative emerged: Gay Gibson was the fourth young woman James Camb had assaulted in as many weeks. He had twice invaded passengers' bedrooms and partially asphyxiated two minors. To be clear; I do not claim these attacks '*prove*' conclusively that Camb murdered Gibson, just as the verdict against him is not infallible. Rather, they persuaded police and prosecution that the evidence was sufficiently strong, even without a body, for a jury to reach a positive conviction for murder. It was an open and shut case.[8]

Stella Durham, aged 19, was travelling First Class on the *Durban Castle* with her Aunt and six-year-old cousin when it left Southampton on 11 September 1947. Within a day 'Jimmy' Camb had asked for her name and cabin number. She gave him neither. 'He was apt to be forward but I never took any notice of his attentions he paid to me' she said. He kept trying to talk to her, offering pretexts such as 'he wanted to tell me something' but she ignored him. Feeling seasick on the second day at sea, Stella went to lie down in her cabin at 2.30 p.m.[9] Passengers were advised not to lock their doors in case of emergencies and anyway the geography of the accommodation areas and assignment of cabins by gender and family groups ensured no passing strangers; the only crew allowed were the Cabin Steward or Stewardess on duty, or a night watchman after hours. Deck Stewards like James Camb had no business being in the main hallways, let alone the alleys branching off which led to clusters of passenger cabins. He was certainly not allowed to go into their rooms.[10] But when Stella suddenly woke from her nap Camb was kneeling next to her bed. She sat up, but he pushed her down on her back by her shoulder. She struggled to get away 'but did not succeed as Jimmy got on top of me with his whole body covering mine. In view of the weight of this man on top of me, I was unable to shout'. Pressing down on her chest, Stella could not breathe while Camb pinned her down, touching her breasts and trying to kiss and undress her. She 'eventually succeeded in pushing him away' and finally able to draw breath and speak 'I told

---

[8] TNA: MEPO 3/2860: Metropolitan Police Report, 11 November 1947, p. 3, plus affidavits.
[9] TNA: MEPO 3/2860: Affidavit of Stella Durham, taken by Detective Sergeant J.M. Visser, South Africa Police, Johannesburg, 5 November 1947.
[10] TNA: ASSI 26/59/1: Deposition of Eileen Field, 24 November 1947; see also Clark (1949).

him that my Aunt was next door'. 'This had the desired effect and Jimmy got up, but for a second time he forced me down on the bed again. This time I knocked on the wall ...' Camb abruptly left the cabin and Stella 'immediately ran on deck to go and tell my Aunt ... but I did not find her and never told her what had actually happened, because I found it to be embarrassing ...'. Stella sought out a crew member, telling him only that Camb had been in her cabin. She was too embarrassed to share details or involve the Captain. Instead Camb was warned to keep away from accommodation areas and crew would be keeping an eye on him for the rest of the voyage to Durban. 'After this Jimmy never approached or attacked me again, and I kept out of his way', noted Stella.[11]

On the same journey out of Southampton, Laura Temple, aged 19, worked as a nanny travelling with her employer and two children. Camb's responsibilities included stowing equipment, deck chairs and games in a small room or large cupboard where he also occasionally took breaks and made tea. This was where he asked Laura to meet him less than a week after he had attacked Stella in her cabin. They sat on deck chairs and drank cocktails Camb fetched for them, chatting 'quite pleasantly' until another steward tried to enter and Camb shooed him away and locked the door. Laura 'realised that I should not be there' and tried to leave but Camb said he would not let her go until she kissed him. She refused.

> The next thing I remembered I was in a kneeling position on the floor with my back against the seat of the chair and the back of my neck on the deck chair. Camb was kneeling by me. He had his one hand on my throat, strangling me, and his other hand he had round the back of my neck. He was pressing my head down on the deck chair...There was blood from my mouth on the collar of his white jacket. His face was dripping in perspiration .... (Affidavit of Laura Temple, 1947)

Laura cried and Camb tried to quiet her. 'He said that he hoped for my sake as well as his that I would not say anything ... He said he could not understand what came over him. He said he was sorry'. Camb let

---

11 TNA: MEPO 3/2860: Affidavit of Stella Durham.

Laura out and in her haste or dizziness she fell downstairs but did not meet any other passengers on her way to the cabin she shared with one of the children who was asleep. 'I looked in the mirror, my eyes were bloodshot. My face was purple'.[12] Laura saw those petechiae—capillaries burst from the pressure of asphyxiation—every time she looked in the mirror for the following month before they finally cleared. She hid them with sunglasses and told her employer they were caused by the fall because she feared losing her job if it were known she had willingly met with Camb at night.[13]

Laura disembarked at Durban where the ship took on new passengers before departing for Port Elizabeth, Cape Town (where Gay Gibson would board) and eventually Southampton. Sixteen-year-old Anna Jarvis and her family were travelling between Durban and Cape Town on holiday, departing 3 October 1947. When the ship called at Port Elizabeth on the 5th, the deck steward suggested Anna accompany him ashore but she refused. The next night she danced with some of the officers but Camb asked them to stop so the band could retire at 11 p.m. Anna returned to her cabin, packed her trunk ready to disembark the next day, turned off her light and went to sleep. She woke to find Camb standing over her. Confused and sleepy, she asked him what time it was. He said it was just after midnight.

> He then told me that he was sorry that he had to stop the dance as the officers were not allowed to dance with the passengers. I told him that he was not allowed to be in my cabin either, but he just laughed and sat down on my bed. (Affidavit of Anna Jarvis, 1947)

Camb put his arm around Anna and tried to kiss her. She asked him to go and tried to push him away 'but he still held on to me'. It is unclear whether Anna was responding to questions or offering spontaneous prose when she deposed that she had not screamed for help because she 'wasn't scared' of Camb, or did not want him to think she was. To avoid his repeated attempts to kiss her, she turned her back and buried her face

12 TNA: MEPO 3/2860: Affidavit of Laura Temple, witnessed by Detective Constable van Niekerk, Commissioner of Oaths, Cape Town, 5 November 1947.
13 TNA: MEPO 3/2860: Affidavit of Laura Temple.

in the pillow. He remained sitting on her bed for 20 minutes until he abruptly 'got up, switched off the light, closed my cabin door and left'.[14] The next morning Anna told an officer that Camb had been in her cabin, but their conversation was interrupted by her little brother and Camb himself coming into the room. She left the ship at Cape Town a few hours later.[15]

While it was docked at Cape Town, *The Durban Castle* welcomed new passengers including 21-year-old actress Gay Gibson. She was a frequent traveller, having emigrated with her family from their native Merseyside for her father's career on at least two occasions. She had also travelled alone and with colleagues for acting jobs touring Britain, Europe and recently South Africa. After her last theatrical role there ended and she was dissatisfied with radio work, Gay decided to follow-up on some contacts and possible roles in London. She spent a few days with her mother, now settled in South Africa with her father, before sailing for Southampton on the *Durban Castle*.[16] It was on this journey that she met James Camb and her death.

In early November South African press reported James Camb had been arrested on suspicion of murder and his legal representatives had travelled there seeking information in support of his defence. They suggested that information about Gibson's behaviour and alleged romances during her stay in South Africa, already receiving damning comment in British and colonial press, could save Camb's life. Anna, Laura and Stella each separately recognised that their experiences added other context and went to police but, as Stella put it 'I wish to request that, if possible, my evidence, if required, be taken on commission and not for me to appear in Court'.[17] Each of the young women was under the age of legal majority and their statements reflect that they were not considered adults like other witnesses. They would have relied on permission from parents or employers to make the long round trip to England for the trial, where there was no hope of remaining anonymous or staying out of the press.

---

[14] TNA: MEPO 3/2860: Affidavit of Anna Jarvis, sworn before J. Pienaar, Commissioner of Oaths, Durban, 5 November 1947.

[15] TNA: MEPO 3/2860: Affidavit of Anna Jarvis.

[16] TNA: ASSI 26/59/1; MEPO 3/2860.

[17] TNA: MEPO 3/2860: Affidavit of Stella Durham.

In contrast, actors who had known Gibson in South Africa stood only to benefit from publicity and free travel if they responded to the same headlines. Tales of Gibson's alleged romances transformed the tellers into heroes because her sexuality reduced Camb's culpability and likelihood of going to the gallows (Clark, 1949, pp. 11–12, 27). This reflects the contemporary trope of women with a sexual past as less 'rape-able'—a notion with a long history, the legacies of which are still felt in the present despite legislative attempts at reform (Smith, 2018, p. 98). As Olivia Smith has argued, this narrative of women with a sexual history as less able to withhold their consent, and the tropes about women as emotional or childlike that bolstered it, were partly perpetuated by the specific contexts of law and courtroom. Performed adversarialism, techniques of questioning and the different practices of prosecution vs defence with regard to the presentation and interrogation of evidence and the burden of proof, or lack thereof: all such factors shape forensic narratives about dead women being culpable in their own murders (Smith, 2018, pp. 127, 128).

The omission of the female witnesses' affidavits from later narratives of the Gibson case (see below) demonstrates the ways in which gendered sexual double standards operated in favour of male murderers from the very earliest stages of investigation to true crime retellings decades later. Stories about Gibson's alleged romances were deemed highly relevant to her murder, mitigating Camb's crime in press and courtroom, whereas the three affidavits about Camb's history of assaults were deemed inadmissible by the magistrate as they pertained to his character (Clark, 1949, pp. 11, 12, 27). This impacted the archival record because only exhibits of evidence passed through this filter were sent to higher courts of Assize or Old Bailey and archived with court depositions. Yet it is these highly selective files or the discarded documents and copies kept as career souvenirs by police officers involved in the case that are most often consulted by researchers for the purposes of modern true crime television, treated as complete dossiers of all evidence collected in the case and therefore a suitable resource for reinvestigating murder at vast temporal distance.[18] In addition, newspapers could say what they liked about the dead but risked contempt of court charges if they referred to a defendant's character negatively before the conclusion of the trial.[19] This factor further skews twenty-first-century true crime depictions of historical cases because digitised newspapers are the most readily available contemporary source.[20] Though no character restriction applied after Camb was found guilty of murder and sentenced to death, the conclusion of the case could not be eked out over as many newspaper editions as had the investigation and trial. Newspapers now commented upon the assault affidavits, using them to endorse Camb's conviction—with headlines such as '3 girls said Camb assaulted them'—but did so on a single occasion compared to repeated reporting on Gibson's alleged past. At the same time, they stuck rigidly to contemporary sexual double standards; Camb was married and had a woman in every port but Gibson was 'an easy victim'; 'twenty one, neurotic, hysterical and fond of male company' (*Daily Mirror*, 1948, pp. 1, 8)—despite this being a central factor in the now-rejected narrative of the defence. As the next section will show, it is the narrative of Gay Gibson as sickly, sexually available and overly emotional that has been absorbed into the true crime memory of the case, not the chronology of sexual assaults that ratified the jury's verdict of Gibson's murder as the final act in a series of increasingly deadly, violent sex attacks by Camb.

When Camb was sentenced to death his defence counsel reused the narrative of consensual sex and natural death in applications to appeal and petitions for mercy (Clark, 1949, pp. 252–255). As Lizzie Seal and I have shown elsewhere, mercy narratives were not necessarily reflective of genuine opinions, they were a story that could be told strategically to save a life (Seal & Neale, 2020b). With deepening ambivalence about the death penalty in the 1940s, mercy petitions from the public to the Home Secretary may have been motivated by general objection to the death penalty rather than doubt about Camb's guilt specifically. However

---

[18] See for example Benson (prod.) 2018. For some of these problems see Seal and Neale (2020a).

[19] TNA: HO 45/25849.

[20] Available via databases such as Findmypast and The British Library, *The British Newspaper Archive*, www.britishnewspaperarchive.co.uk (2020).

as Seal (2014) has shown, petitions were more likely to cite specifics of a case derived from defence narratives—communicated through press in the case of public petitions—rather than give their general objections. 'A Would-be Helper' wrote to Scotland Yard suggesting a forensic narrative of Gibson's death that reduced Camb's culpability; could he have accidentally killed her in his efforts to escape on having been discovered stealing from her room? The postscript suggests the author was motivated by concern about capital punishment more than sympathy for Camb: 'we public often read that the smallest mite has hung [sic] a man'.[21] The possibility of alternative narratives or doubt about degrees of culpability often influenced the Home Secretary to recommend mercy, keeping the precise reasons secret but recording them in the index which constituted a working reference and institutional memory of capital cases.[22] It is telling that the forensic narrative of Camb's case recorded there defines the case as a killing in the furtherance of rape, and that Camb escaped the gallows *only* because a bill was being debated in parliament which would see the suspension of capital punishment.[23] But the question remains; if the defence narrative was repeatedly rejected by police, jury, judges, Home Secretary and press, why has it dominated true crime media on the Camb case, reappearing down the decades as a narrative of forensics that can be scientifically 'proven' to exonerate the memory of a convicted murderer and sex offender? The next section shows how true crime stories circulated by the media have favoured narratives of forensics over forensic narratives.

---

[21] TNA: MEPO 3/2860: Anonymous and undated letter to Scotland Yard from 'A Would-be Helper'. This is not to say that those who wished to see Camb reprieved blithely accepted misogynistic press framing of Gibson, see for example Readers' Letters, *Sunday Pictorial* (1948, p. 5) only that they had few arenas to express it.

[22] An ongoing research project (2019–2022) funded by the Leverhulme Trust is exploring Home Office precedent books including those cited in this chapter. Alexa Neale, 'Black Books: The Institutional Memory of Hanging and Mercy at the Home Office' ECF-2018-448.

[23] Camb benefitted from a blanket reprieve policy applied in secret (so as not to allow the public to believe that they could get away with murder) while the bill made positive progress through parliament, only to be defeated in the House of Lords at the end of the year. TNA: PCOM 9/643: 'Suspension of Capital Punishment, inc. Camb'; HO 384/158.

Narratives of Forensics in the Gay Gibson Case

On 11 September 1949 (18 months after Camb's conviction), the *Sunday Pictorial* invited readers to 'Consider your verdict!' in a 'new crime series' about 'notorious *murderers*' of which Camb was the first. 'Would you have hanged them?' the paper asked (*Sunday* Pictorial, 1949, pp. 1, 6–7). Other publications began to appear at this time which drew on the traditions of revisiting historic cases for true crime entertainment promoting public debate (for example, Lustgarten, 1949; see Seal, 2014 for more). These examples show that there is nothing new in the fascination with potential miscarriages of justice associated with present true crime like *Making a Murderer* and *Serial* (Stratton, 2019). But they do demonstrate the role of media format in shaping content. 'Consider your verdict' rehashed courtroom narratives as a device for selling newspapers rather than reflecting a genuine scepticism about the justice of the trial outcomes. It did not provide a platform upon which readers could share opinions, it merely suggested they might have them. The following decades saw the development of the true crime genre as it expanded into new media and, as the examples from the Camb case show, each one helped to promote narratives of forensics and more particularly the defence narrative that Gay Gibson died of natural causes. The result, as this section shows, is the promotion of a retrospective narrative of forensics and the silencing of victims of sexual assault.

While 'Consider your verdict' was repeating the same newspaper's earlier treatment of the Camb case, publications emerged which attempted to distinguish themselves from sensational newspaper reporting. Junior counsel Geoffrey Clark's *Trial of James Camb* book for the Notable British Trials Series was published in 1949, followed by various legal actors' case histories in the following decades, including Sir Travers Humphreys' *Book of Trials* in 1953, many of which had been previously serialised in newspapers. Notable and Great Trials series' introductions and career retrospectives by judges and barristers promoted narratives of forensics by highlighting their own skills and influence in the courtroom. Describing how they overcame contentious evidence or deployed effective legal argument, advocated for their client or the victim and expertly questioned witnesses including medical experts, they attempted to adopt a tone that was more legal education and less entertainment. This distinction has been perpetuated as more recent true crime authors have selected these publications as somehow neutral accounts of, for example, reactions from the courtroom during a trial and the behaviour of witnesses and defendants (which are not described in official shorthand transcripts) (Brown, 2018, pp. 225–228). However, these texts were arguably consumed by audiences with the same interests as those who read sensational true crime and stuck rigidly to the prosecution/defence outcome narrative with which each author had been involved, while ultimately acknowledging the general fairness of the judicial system (D'Cruze, 2006; Stewart, 2017). For example, Joshua Casswell, who defended Camb, found a way to consolidate the jury's verdict against his narrative, rendering him the 'loser' in the case, with his commitment to that narrative: Camb was a bad man, but not a murderer (Casswell, 1961, p. 305). An almost identical copy of Clark's *Trial of James Camb* was published in 1950 for a US audience as a paperback pulp novel with the title *The Girl in the Stateroom*. Its brightly illustrated cover portrays Gay Gibson as seductress, reclining on a bed with stocking-tops revealed, engaging in the same sexualised sensationalism that promoted Camb's defence narrative. However, the cover is not reflective of the contents. The authors view Camb's conviction as just and the survivor affidavits as endorsing his guilt, revealing how true crime in the 1950s did not necessarily have to wholly reject one narrative in order to appeal to its audience's tastes for sex and crime (Boswell & Thompson, 1951).

Another true crime tradition revived and accelerated after the Second World War was the serialised criminal biography sub-genre, of which *The Sunday Pictorial* and *News of the World* newspapers established themselves as the leading titles. An example exposing the legal contingency of narratives perpetuated by true crime media is Brian Donald Hume. Involved in 'shady racketeering' associated with the rationing black market during the wartime and postwar years, Hume was accused of the murder of Stanley Setty in 1950 but claimed he had only disposed of the body on behalf of three gangsters who did the murdering. This defence narrative was accepted and he was acquitted of Setty's murder but imprisoned as an accessory after the fact. *The Sunday Pictorial* covered his story as part of the same wave of true crime serials that had started with Camb's 'Consider your verdict!' in late 1949 (*Sunday* Pictorial, 1950, p. 1). Signalling changing tastes toward narratives of forensics, in 1958, the same paper paid Hume £2000 for his serialised confession to Setty's murder (once acquitted he could not be tried for the same crime a second time) complete with staged photographs showing how he prepared the dismembered body and disposed of it from a plane (Butler, 1976, p. 98). The timing coincided with another moment of legal change as the Homicide Act was introduced which restricted the death penalty to certain types of murder, reviving interest in crime narratives and public comment on the operation of justice (Seal, 2014, pp. 23–26).

James Camb was paid £2500 for his serialised post-release story in the late 1950s. Dragged out over weeks but giving no new revelations, the paper drew readers in with the sensational front-page headline: 'You did not kill Gay Gibson'. The news story described a meeting between recently released Camb and one of the three medical witnesses at the trial, Professor J.M. Webster. The latter was reported as telling Camb 'I have a scientific conviction that your story was the true one'. The issue promised Camb's own words over the following weeks (*Sunday Pictorial*, 1959a, p. 1), as indicated in the line: 'My name is James Camb, and I now wish to make a free and open admission concerning the events leading to the death of Gay Gibson ...'. Promising 'the whole truth', the serial delivered only a repetition, in sensationalised language, of Camb's defence narrative that Gibson died in his arms following consensual sex and his only mistake was to try to cover his tracks (*Sunday Pictorial*, 1959b, p. 1). 'It was a tragic, terrifying end to what I had intended to be a night of casual love-making', he boasted, placing Gibson as the latest in a long line of conquests which included a South American millionaire and other unaccompanied young women travelling first class. Of the sexual assaults he claimed:

> There had been complaints about me before. On the outward voyage to Capetown there had been an incident when a young girl invited me down to her cabin and exasperated me by her teenage behaviour. I put her over my knee and gave her a good spanking. (*Sunday Pictorial*, 1959c, p. 8)

Gibson continued to be morally culpable in her own murder rather than the innocent victim of a sudden medical episode according to Camb's narrative. At a moment he described as the natural conclusion to love-making, he said her whole body tensed, she gripped his arm and then completely relaxed in a sort of swoon. Alluding to orgasm as the point at which Gibson's heart stopped beating underscored her consent and his innocence.[24]

On 21 May 1971 the *Daily Mirror* (weekday daily to the *Sunday Pictorial/Mirror*) featured a short article:

'GAY GIBSON KILLER ACCUSED BY THREE GIRLS: A man convicted of murder twenty-four years ago yesterday admitted making indecent advances to little girls. James Clarke - formerly known as James Camb ... 54, admitted three charges of 'lewd and indecent practices' ... The prosecution said that he followed the ten-year-old girl into her bedroom, pushed her on to her back and tried to kiss her ... ' later the same night he returned to the room and attempted to assault the two eleven-year-olds sleeping there. (*Daily* Mirror, 1971, p. 21)

The Times reported on his sentencing at the Scottish High Court, where his licence was withdrawn and he returned to prison 'for an indefinite period of what is inaccurately referred to as life imprisonment'. He served a further seven years (*The Times*, 1971, p. 1).

Again, I do not claim these offences were something like 'proof' of Camb's murder of Gibson. Rather, I am interested in their role in the popular memory of the case, including recent true crime media. Survivors' affidavits were considered by contemporaries to increase the veracity of the prosecution narrative that Camb had raped and murdered Gibson (see above) and equally, Camb's 1971 convictions were recorded by the Home Office beside their index entry regarding his murder conviction and the micro-narrative of the case.[25] Why then, if the 1971

---

[24] The series concluded on 25 October 1959 declaring 'NOW, THE VERDICT IS YOURS' though again, it does not seem to have invited readers to share their views (*Sunday Pictorial*, 1959d, p. 23).

[25] See archival resources: TNA: HO 384/158: Capital Cases vol. 1, 431.

crimes worked so strongly against it, did Camb's defence narrative survive the following decades in true crime?

To understand this better, we need to turn to think some more about how narratives of forensics work to privilege forensic science such as DNA and other expert technologies as superior forms of evidence in stories about crime. Cultural Criminology recognises the influence of forensic investigation depicted in various crime media, true and fictional, US and UK, on public perceptions of the speed, infallibility and superiority of scientific methods in crime detection and prosecution (Cavender & Jurik, 2016; Turkel, 2009). These perceptions have, in many instances, been supported by the career memoirs and professional autobiographies of experts in law, policing and criminalistics who contributed to true crime by describing their own advanced skills and techniques—elevating the science as well as themselves (Adam, 2015). In the Gibson case, the absence of a corpse allowed Camb to construct his own narrative of her death and many medical men declared themselves experts on Gibson's imaginary body. Denis Herbstein's, 1991 book, for example, is preoccupied with the defence narrative and prioritises the memories of medical witnesses and similar true crime over the three 1947 affidavits and the 1971 sexual offences against children. In fact he identifies a further sexual offence in 1967 which I have been unable to find in any other sources, an eighth victim: an eight-year-old girl who complained to her mother when Camb showed her a picture of a naked woman and then—characteristically selecting quotes which minimise sexual assault—"he allowed his hand to wander a bit on the little girl and she told her mother who complained to the police ...".[26] Herbstein (1991) does not cite sources for this information nor accompanying quotes but says that Camb was charged with indecent assault and pleaded guilty, but the magistrate extended his probation rather than recalling him to prison. Herbstein (1991) is repeatedly sympathetic to Camb more than his eight victims, even suggesting that one of the incidents of which he was convicted for sexually assaulting a child might have been caused by lack of sex because he was living apart from his wife (Herbstein, 1991, pp. 240–244, 248, 249, 251, 252).

---

[26] Herbstein, p. 240.

In 2018 Mirror Books published *Death of an Actress* by Antony M. Brown, the second book in his series 'Cold Case Jury True Crime Collection'. Reinventing Gay Gibson's murder as a 'Cold Case' suggests a crime unsolved and unpunished, erasing the trial, conviction, sentence and punishment that brought her murderer to justice and saw him serve 18 1/2 years in prison (including the revocation of his license for sexual offences against children in 1971). Brown (2018) takes jurifying the public to an extreme, arguing that a modern audience—informed by his book—is capable of reaching a more accurate and meaningful conclusion than the 1947 jury. As described above, archives of crime preserve only a fraction of selected evidence and online repositories favour the type of true crime media that comes with bias baked in. But Brown's book prioritises past true crime books and newspapers as source material over 'The National Archive [sic]', as well as elevating the testimony of 'expert' witnesses on the medical issues beyond the weight it was given in its original forensic context (Brown, 2018, pp. 225–228). As 'the first researcher to inspect … the complete police record'—more accurately a fragmentary private collection—he states inaccurately that three verdicts were possible in the Camb case: misadventure, murder or manslaughter and offers the latter as 'The Verdict: My Judgement' (Brown, 2018, pp. 122, 123, 220). Yet he spends most of the book favouring the defence narrative and endorsing tropes of Gay Gibson as sickly, over-sexed and a willing partner to Camb in his creative reconstructions stitched together with offensive and outdated sexist tropes. For example, he contends that Gibson's ownership of a contraceptive device (which she kept buried in her suitcase), is proof positive of her sexual activity and by implication her undiscerning availability for sex with anyone, including the man who killed her (Brown, 2018, p. 129). Brown's treatment of the affidavits of the young women whose assaults preceded Gay's murder is indifferent at best. Of fourteen documents or collections of documents he reinvents as 'Exhibits' (a misleading appellation since most were not exhibits of evidence at the trial), the one that contains their affidavits is the only one of which Brown demands 'corroboration' (Brown, 2018, pp. 131–133, 202–206). The affidavits do not feature amongst the six pieces of evidence Brown regards as key to the case, preferring instead to devote an entire chapter and significant research to a secondhand statement regarding Gibson's missing pyjamas (see below) (Brown, 2018, pp. 134–144, 150–154). Lizzie Seal (2012) has encouraged scholars to tune into rather than censor feelings of allegiance, outrage and ambivalence when researching women and crime, a reflexive approach which deepens sensitivity to derogatory depictions and ethical engagement. Antony Brown's treatment of James Camb's victims; Stella Durham, Laura Temple, Anna Jarvis, Gay Gibson and four unnamed little girls, left me feeling angry and sick.

As part of Brown's demolition of the case against Camb he invites readers to give their verdict on it and his other 'cold cases' (which are not) on his website. The way Brown frames the options is both problematic and revealing:

> Select your verdict from one of the choices below. Which is the most likely in your view?
> *Misadventure*: Gay Gibson died suddenly while having consensual sex with James Camb
> *Murder*: Gay Gibson was strangled by James Camb when his advances were rebuffed
> *Manslaughter*: Gay Gibson died suddenly during a sexual assault by James Camb.
> (Brown, 2020)

As explored above, jurifying the public after-the-fact has a long history, even in this case. The problem is that Brown's framing of the options brings in tropes that are offensive *and* inaccurate. Manslaughter was not offered as a potential narrative in the Camb case, it had no legal justification. Further, to say that if it was murder it was because 'his advances were rebuffed' implies some space for discretional sympathy given the context of murders of women by men in the mid-twentieth century. In cases where men killed women who resisted sex where there was reason to expect their sexual availability, the Home Office could be sympathetic and was more likely (horrifyingly) to reprieve.[27] This was not how contemporaries saw the Camb case. The conclusion to Brown's poll on his website endorses his own pet theory: 'As of 09:45 on 5 August 2020,

---

[27] Capital Cases vol. 1.

the verdict of the Cold Case Jury is: MANSLAUGHTER Gay Gibson died suddenly during a sexual assault by James Camb'.[28]

In 2018, the same year his *Death of an Actress* was published, Brown collaborated on a TV documentary broadcast as factual programming on BBC News Channel. Presenter Richard Latto introduced the Gibson case as '*The Porthole Murder*', describing it as 'still debated today' and argued that his research into Gibson's possible health conditions bring 'the truth of what *actually* happened in cabin 126' within touching distance, 'rewriting history'. Latto explains: '[a]fter *a lot* of research I managed to track down … Gloria J Dimick, Forensic DNA Analyst.' Interviewing her via Skype, Latto explains that the police trophy archive of uncertain provenance contains a hairbrush which he is certain belonged to Gay Gibson.[29] The hairs adhering to it are definitely from Gibson's head, he asserts. Dimick suppresses a smile as she explains how the hair cannot be tested in the way Latto proposes and that, *if* any hair follicles contained sufficient material for a DNA sample to be taken it would be mitochondrial DNA and not a full sequence that could be obtained. She summarises: 'Unfortunately [the DNA in the hair] would not have information relating to a disease state in your victim' (Latto, 2018). Latto ignores the problematic nature of the object and prefers a failure of the science:

> It's very frustrating. This [holds up the brush] *actually belonged* to Gay Gibson … it seems technology isn't practical enough to tell us what information might actually lie in the strands and follicles on the brush. But maybe one day it can give us a true picture of Gay Gibson's health. The future could really be the key to the past. (Latto, 2018)

Latto assumes the superiority of modern empirical values as uniquely able to deliver justice. Further, his dissatisfaction with the expertise of a female scientist reflects his prioritisation of male voices more generally, including

---

[28] Brown, *Cold Case Jury Case 2: Jury Verdict*. http://coldcasejury.com/case02/juryverdict1.asp 'Jury Size: 313 / Manslaughter: 50% / Murder: 33% / Misadventure: 17%' (2020) [last accessed 13 August 2020].

[29] See archival resources: TNA: ASSI 26/59/1: Camb: List of Exhibits #20: hairbrush retained by prosecution.

a discarded statement offered to police by a man who met a stranger in a pub. The stranger, the man said, told him that his dentist owned Gay Gibson's mysterious missing pyjamas. The prosecution had contended that the pyjamas were unaccounted for because Gibson went through the porthole wearing them, whereas Camb claimed that she met him in her dressing gown (under which she was naked) and his defence counsel cited this as proof of sexual consent. Police gave no credence to the man's story about Gibson's pyjamas coming into the possession of an acquaintance twice-removed. However, Latto asserts it 'could have completely changed the verdict of the jury.' He argues that '[The man's statement] clearly supports James Camb's insistence that she was not wearing any pyjamas. It could've been enough to convince them that Camb was an honest man and believe his whole story.' Latto dismisses the survivor affidavits entirely, consigning Camb's later convictions for sexual assaults of children to a footnote at the end of the programme:

> In 1959 Camb was released from prison and in his only interview continued to protest his innocence. He was later arrested again for other sexual offences, but the only accusation he ever faced of being violent was at the trial of 1948. The events surrounding this detailed case are still debated today but maybe one day we'll know the undisputable [sic] truth behind the porthole mystery. (Latto, 2018)

Later in 2018 an episode of BBC regional programming's H2O 'podcast' covered the case. It consisted of Latto's documentary edited to audio with added archive sound (BBC Radio Solent, 2018). 'Podcast' is a contentious appellation here, retrospectively applied to radio shows and audio recordings to appeal to the latest media trend. More recently, it is true crime podcasts that have helped define the medium. *Serial* is perhaps the most popular podcast of all time and an example of the hosted investigation style of true crime podcast, featuring pre-recorded audio and commentary by the host, following them as their research unfolds on a single case over weeks. *My Favorite Murder* is of a more conversational style, each week features a different case explored and dissected by a pair of hosts who share their uncensored views on critical aspects of a past case and associated media. Both styles allow listeners—most commonly young women motivated by escapism and entertainment—to get to know a little of the personality and motivations of the hosts (Boling & Hull, 2018; Kilgariff & Hardstark, 2016; Koenig, 2014). In other instances, podcasts involve little more than the reading out a common version of a case narrative, usually from Wikipedia or recent true crime. For examples, *Futility Closet* (Ross, 2019) and *The Unseen Podcast* (Episode 22, 2019), though highly listenable, do little more than read a summary of the case in their respective episodes dedicated to it, relying by their own admission on Latto and Brown, which are problematic to say the least, as we have seen. In contrast, *Fresh Hell Podcast* is reflective of more of the critical opportunities the format offers. Including contextualising web searches based on their own interests, hosts Annie and Johanna freely express their conviction that Gibson's sexual history is irrelevant to her murder in their episode dedicated to it.

> *Annie*: …the defence said that that it was important to determine if she had been – quote – overly friendly with men making her rape likely. No huge surprise here given the time but also fuck that guy and his judgemental patriarchal bullshit. This is partly why I really wanted to cover this case because I was shocked reading it how victim-blamey the whole thing is.
> *Johanna*: But seriously, how can that still shock you?
> *Annie*: I know. It shouldn't. But some of this stuff is relatively new… it's not like these books were written forty years ago. (*Fresh Hell Podcast* Episode 65, 2020)

Fresh Hell Podcast is arguably more accurately reflective of post-#MeToo true crime which pays attention to sexual assault survivor voices.[30] The podcast format offers unique potential for discussion and critique, responding quickly to true crime media (Buozis, 2017). In the hands of women like Annie and Johanna, the true crime podcast is a 'potential site of doubled resistance' (Greer, 2017, p. 153). By offering critical and

---

[30] See, for other examples: Liz Garbus, Elizabeth Wolff, Myles Kane, Josh Koury (dirs), *I'll Be Gone in the Dark* [TV miniseries] HBO USA/Netflix first broadcast 28 June 2020; Nigel Bellis, Astral Finnie (writers, directors) *Surviving R. Kelly* [two part TV miniseries], Lifetime USA/Netflix, first broadcast 3 January 2019 and 2 January 2020; Lisa Bryant (dir.), *Jeffrey Epstein: Filthy Rich* [TV miniseries] Netflix, 27 May 2020.

contextual information, particularly the forensic—legal—context from which such narratives emerged, more nuanced conversations can be had that still satisfy the traditions of true crime as escapism and entertainment. I suggest a diversity of voices have new insights to offer about forensic narratives from crimes past *and* about true crime narratives of forensics—stories that have much to tell without 'proof' by laboratory science.

Conclusion

Accepting and regurgitating, without analysis or critique, the surface meaning of narratives about crime and justice risks misunderstanding historical social norms and their relationships with policing and justice. The contexts within which a forensic narrative emerged bring into focus the specific conditions and contingencies of the legal system that demanded the use of such tropes (Seal & Neale, 2020b). Repeating them as widely accepted fact, on the other hand, overlooks the agency of contemporary audiences and their ability to interact with the law. It also underestimates the ultimate discretionary power of the Home Office to mitigate sentences or overrule jury and judge recommendations by granting or withholding mercy in capital cases, and contributes to the culture of secrecy with which they closely guarded their reasons for mercy decisions.

Contemporary true crime's preoccupation with the potential for scientific certainty or forensic objectivity demands to be unsettled and contested. Certainly, we should continue to explore injustices wherever we see them, past or present. However, we must also acknowledge the empirical values that formed the basis of the evidence, and narratives, we interrogate. As I have described elsewhere, exhibits of evidence used in twentieth-century courtrooms were created according to empirical codes that differ from those operating in the present. Objects, traces, models and photographs were deployed to endorse narratives told by witnesses whereas narratives of forensics elevate such exhibits to the status of indisputable artefacts (Neale, 2020a, 2020b). Viewing the past through the lens of true crime media presents potential pitfalls but also opens opportunities. The podcast format, in particular, extends public participation in crime, creates communities of feeling and concern for miscarriages of justice and the more subtle injustices created by inequalities woven into legal systems in the past, including discretion, sexism, sexual double standards, over-policing of some communities and institutional racism.

By way of conclusion, I argue that the outrage-inducing injustice in the case of Gay Gibson's murder is not James Camb's conviction. It is the wrongful treatment of Gibson after-the-fact. Even a novel inspired by the case, which invents an entirely fictional killer, still promotes the idea that the real-life Gay Gibson was hysterical, sickly, over-sexed and culpable in her own violent murder (Heath, 2009). In real-life, the flimsy narrative of Camb's lesser culpability deployed to save his life spoke to sexist contemporary tropes but was rejected by the jury, judge and Home Office who remembered the case as a brutal rape and murder deserving of the harshest punishment. The idea of a 'debate' in the case was created by press to sell newspapers and male 'experts' attempted to further their careers and expertise by pushing the notion of Camb's innocence, interrogating Gibson's body (despite none ever having examined it) in their own true crime publications and interviews. That this narrative of forensics has been resurrected and given unequal attention by a true crime television programme and book in the twenty-first century ignores our own contemporary context of #MeToo and other prominent sexual abuse scandals. It retrospectively re-silences Camb's victims, glossing over the guilty verdict, death sentence and withdrawal of parole that legitimised their experiences. Finally, by situating the murder as a mystery they can solve, speaking to the present taste for miscarriages of justice in true crime, and by insisting that, were the science advanced enough, it would endorse their theory of Camb's innocence through revealing Gibson's health problems, written in her DNA despite the destruction of her body, these true crime advocates bias their 'cold case jury' to their own verdict. Worse, they help to normalise gendered violence, sexual assault and victim culpability in the past *and* present.

Study Questions

- How has the Gay Gibson case been subject to cultural revision over the years? Think, here, about how the figures of Gibson and Camb have been reimagined in these depictions.
- How and why has this case been subject to revision? Think, here, about the role of what Neale calls 'forensic narratives' and 'narratives of forensics'.
- Are there general lessons to learn here about the construction of the 'cold case'?
- What does the media retelling of the Gay Gibson case tell us about attitudes to gender and justice in the present?

References

Archive Sources

The National Archives (Kew, UK)
ASSI 26/59/1: Assizes Depositions, Murder: Camb, James (1947)
DPP 2/1728: Director of Public Prosecutions Case Papers: CAMB, J: Murder appeal (1948)
HO 384/158: Home Office Noters Section Precedent Books: Capital Cases, 1901–65 Vol. 1
HO 45/25849: Home Office Registered Papers: Crime: Financing by Newspapers of the Defence of Criminals: Attempts by Prisoners Held on Capital Charges to Publish Their Stories (1933–55)
MEPO 3/2860: Metropolitan Police, Commissioner Correspondence and Papers: Murder of Eileen (Gay) Gibson by James Camb (1947–8)
PCOM 9/643: Prison Commission and Home Office: Suspension of Capital Punishment for Murder during Time the Criminal Justice Bill Was Going through Parliament, inc. Case of James Camb (1948)

Bibliography

Adam, A. (2015). *A history of forensic science: British beginnings in the twentieth century*. Routledge.

Adam, A. (Ed.). (2020). *Crime and the construction of forensic objectivity from 1850*. Palgrave Macmillan.

Akrivos, D., & Antoniou, A. K. (Eds.). (2019). *Crime, deviance and popular culture*. Palgrave.

Althoff, M., Dollinger, B., & Schmidt, H. (Eds.). (2020). *Conflicting narratives of crime and punishment*. Palgrave/Springer.

Annie and Johanna (surnames not given). (2020, June 10) *Fresh Hell Podcast Episode 65: Murder—GayGibson*. https://freshhellpodcast.com/2020/06/10/episode-65-murder-gay-gibson/

BBC Radio Solent. (2018, December 28). *H20 podcast: The porthole mystery*. https://www.bbc.co.uk/programmes/p06w9n5w

Bellis, N., & Finnie, A. (Writers, Directors) (2020). *Surviving R. Kelly* [two part TV miniseries], Lifetime USA/Netflix, first broadcast 3 January 2019 and 2 January 2020.

Benson, M. (Producer). (2018). *Murder, mystery and my family* [TV series]. Chalkboard Television for BBC.

Bingham, A. (2009). *Family newspapers? Sex, private life, and the British popular press 1918–1978*. Oxford University Press.

Biressi, A. (2001). *Crime, fear, and the law in true crime stories*. Palgrave.

Boling, K. S., & Hull, K. (2018). Undisclosed information—Serial is my favorite murder: Examining motivations in the true crime podcast audience. *Journal of Radio & Audio Media, 25*(1), 92–108.

Boswell, C., & Thompson, L. (1951). *The girl in the stateroom*. Fawcett Books.

Bows, H., & Herring, J. (2020). Getting away with murder? A review of the 'rough sex defence.' *The Journal of Criminal Law, 84*(6), 525–538.

Brown, A. M. (2018). *Death of an actress: A cold case jury true crime*. Mirror Books.

Brown, A. M. (2020). *Cold case jury true crime collection*. https://www.coldcasejury.com Last accessed 13 August 2020.

Bruzzi, S. (2016). Making a genre: The case of the contemporary true crime documentary. *Law and Humanities, 10*(2), 249–280.

Bryant, L. (Director). (2020). *Jeffrey Epstein: Filthy rich* [TV miniseries]. Netflix, 27 May 2020.

Buozis, M. (2017). Giving voice to the accused: Serial and the critical potential of true crime. *Communication and Critical/cultural Studies, 14*(3), 254–270.

Burney, I., & Hamlin, C. (Eds.). (2019). *Global forensic cultures: Making fact and justice in the modern era.* Johns Hopkins University Press.

Butler, I. (Eds.). (1976) *The trials of Brian Donald Hume.* Celebrated Trials Series. Newton Abbot: David & Charles.

Byers, M., & Johnson, V. L. (Eds.). (2009). *The CSI effect: television, crime and governance.* Lexington Books.

Casswell, J. D. (1961). *A lance for liberty.* George G. Harrap and Co., Ltd.

Cavender, G., & Jurik, N. (2016). Crime, criminology and the crime genre. In P. Knepper & A. Johansen (Eds.), *The Oxford handbook of the history of crime and criminal justice* (pp. 320–337). Oxford University Press.

Clark, G. (Ed.). (1949). *Trial of James Camb (The Port-Hole murder)* Notable British Trials Vol. 71. William Hodge & Co.

D'Cruze, S. (2006). 'The damned place was haunted': The gothic, middlebrow culture and inter-war 'notable trials.' *Literature and History, 15*(1), 37–58.

Daily Mirror. (1971, May 21). p. 21.

Daily Mirror. (1948, March 23) pp. 1, 8.

Dunboyne. (Eds.). (1953). *The trial of John George Haigh: (The Acid Bath Murder),* Notable British Trials Vol. 78. William Hodge & Co.

Findmypast and The British Library, *The British Newspaper Archive.* www.britishnewspaperarchive.co.uk

Garbus, L., Wolff, E. Kane, M., & Koury, J. (Director). (2020, June 28). *I'll be gone in the dark* [TV miniseries]. HBO USA/Netflix.

Greer, A. (2017). Murder, she spoke: The female voice's ethics of evocation and spatialisation in the true crime podcast. *Sound Studies, 3*(2), 152–164.

Hamer, R. (Director) (1947). *It always rains on sunday* [film]. Ealing Studios, UK.

Heath, R. (2009). *The Finest Type of English Womanhood.* Hutchinson.

Herbstein, D. (1991). *The porthole murder case.* Hodder & Stoughton.

Humphreys, T. (1953). *A book of trials.* Heinemann.

Johansen, A., & Knepper, P. (Eds.). (2016). *The Oxford handbook of the history of crime and criminal justice.* Oxford University Press.

Kemble, C. S., & H.S. . (1948). The murder without a body. *The Police Journal, 21*(4), 261–270.

Kilgariff, K., & Hardstark, G. (2016). *My favorite murder* [podcast]. https://myfavoritemurder.com/. First broadcast 13 January 2016.

Koenig, S. and This American Life. (2014). *Serial season 1* [podcast]. https://serialpodcast.org/season-one. First broadcast 3 October 2014.

Latto, R. (Writer, Producer), & Doherty, P. (Director) (2018). *The porthole mystery* [TV documentary], BBC News Channel. First broadcast 23 March 2018.

Latto, R. (Writer and Presenter) for BBC Radio Solent. (2018). *H20 podcast: The porthole mystery* (28 December 2018). https://www.bbc.co.uk/progra mmes/p06w9n5w

Lustgarten, E. (1949). *Verdict in dispute*. Allen Wingate.

Creutzfeldt, N., Mason, M., & McConnachie, K. (Eds.). (2019). *(2019) Routledge handbook of socio-legal theory and methods*. Routledge.

Nead, L. (2017). *The tiger in the smoke: Art and culture in post-war Britain*. Yale University Press.

Neale, A. (2020a). *Photographing crime scenes in twentieth-century London: Microhistories of domestic murder*. Bloomsbury Academic.

Neale, A. (2020b). Murder in miniature: Reconstructing the crime scene in the English courtroom. In A. Adam (Eds.), *Crime and the construction of forensic objectivity from 1850* (pp. 43–67). Palgrave Macmillan.

Orwell, G. (1965.) *Decline of the English murder and other essays* [originally published 1946]. Penguin

Oxford English Dictionary Online. (2020) "forensic, adj. and n." *OED Online*, Oxford University Press. www.oed.com/view/Entry/73107. Accessed 13 August 2020.

Phipps, A. (2019). The fight against sexual violence. *Soundings, 71*(71), 62–74.

Ross, G. (2019, June 24). *Futility closet podcast episode 254: The porthole murder*. https://www.futilitycloset.com/2019/06/24/podcast-episode-254-the-porthole-murder/

Seal, L. (2012). Emotion and allegiance in researching four mid- 20th-century cases of women accused of murder. *Qualitative Research, 12*(6), 686–701.

Seal, L. (2014). *Capital punishment in twentieth-century britain: Audience, justice, memory*. Routledge.

Seal, L., & Neale, A. (2019). Encountering the archive: Researching race, racialisation and the death penalty in England and Wales, 1900–1965. In N. Creutzfeldt, M. Mason, & K. McConnachie (Eds.), *Routledge handbook of socio-legal theory and methods* (pp. 289–300). Routledge.

Seal, L., & Neale, A. (2020a). 'In his passionate way': Emotion, race and gender in cases of partner-murder in England and Wales, 1900–39. *British Journal of Criminology, 60*(4), 811–829.

Seal, L., & Neale, A. (2020b). Racializing mercy: Capital punishment and race in twentieth-century England and Wales. *Law & History Review, 38*(4), 883–910.

Secret Barrister. (2020) *Fake law: The truth about justice in an age of lies.* Picador Palgrave Macmillan.

Smith, O. (2018) *Rape trials in England and Wales: Observing justice and rethinking rape myths.* Palgrave.

Stewart, V. (2017). *Crime writing in interwar Britain, fact and fiction.* Cambridge University Press.

Stratton, G. (2019). Wrongful conviction, pop culture, and achieving justice in the digital age. In D. Akrivos & A. K. Antoniou (Eds.), *Crime, deviance and popular culture* (pp. 177–201). Palgrave.

Sunday Pictorial. (1947, October 26). pp. 1, 8–9.

Sunday Pictorial. (1949, September 11). pp. 1, 6–7.

Sunday Pictorial. (1950, January 29). p. 1.

Sunday Pictorial. (1959a, September 13). p. 1.

Sunday Pictorial. (1959b, September20). p. 1.

Sunday Pictorial. (1959c, October 4). p. 8.

Sunday Pictorial. (1959d, October 25). p. 23.

Sutton-Vane, A. (2020). Murder cases, trunks and the entanglement of ethics: The preservation and display of crime records and scenes of crime material. In A. Adam (Ed.), *Crime and the construction of forensic objectivity from 1850* (pp. 279–301). Palgrave Macmillan.

The Times (1971, May 29). p. 1.

Turkel, W. J. (2009). The crime scene, the evidential fetish, and the usable past. In M. Byers & V. M. Johnson (Eds.), *The CSI effect: television, crime and governance* (pp. 133–146). Lexington Books.

Unseen Podcast. (2019, April 28). *Unseen podcast Episode 22: The porthole murder.* Via Spotify https://open.spotify.com/episode/2yddzS7XryjtfSFwlL xesF

Wood, J. C. (2016). Crime news and the press. In P. Knepper & A. Johansen (Eds.), *The Oxford handbook of the history of crime and criminal justice* (pp. 301–319). Oxford University Press.

Wood, J. C. (2020). Sympathies and scandals: (Counter-)narratives of criminality and policing in inter-war Britain. In M. Althoff, B. Dollinger, & H. Schmidt (Eds.), *Conflicting narratives of crime and punishment* (pp. 161–180). Palgrave/Springer.

5

In Consideration of Serial Violence: The Perils of Repetition and Routine in 'true crime' Documentaries

Sarah Moore

Introduction

Seriality rules when it comes to the media treatment of crime in the early twenty-first century. Spend a few moments thinking about your favourite media depictions of crime, and the chances are that you've brought to mind a television crime show, podcast series, or documentary mini-series. And what these serial media formats tell us about crime is that it tends to be cyclical, a problem of repeated patterns and relationships, reproduced with sickeningly violent effects. Think again of your favourite media treatment of crime, and consider how often the focus is multiple acts of violent crime, perpetrated by that most emblematic criminal of the modern era, the serial killer.

This chapter suggests that the 'true crime' genre offers a particularly interesting and revealing demonstration of seriality, such that it requires

S. Moore (✉)
University of Bath, Bath, UK
e-mail: sm2315@bath.ac.uk

© The Author(s), under exclusive license to Springer Nature Switzerland AG 2021
M. Mellins and S. Moore (eds.), *Critiquing Violent Crime in the Media*,
https://doi.org/10.1007/978-3-030-83758-7_5

us to re-think what's going on when we re-enact an event, over and over. It is anchored in a discussion of two 'true crime' documentaries: the television mini-series *The Staircase* (De Lestrade, 2004–2018) and Season One of the podcast *Serial* (Koenig, 2014). This discussion explores two key ideas about repetition in media depictions of violence. First, that cultural seriality, and the repetition that is a fundamental feature of this format, involves an evacuation of meaning, a replaying and rehashing that serves no other function than to titillate and feed an appetite for repeat-consumption. Secondly, that repetition can be a haunting of sorts, bringing the past into painful and troubling coexistence with the present, and signalling a need to come to terms with lost-futures.

This is to think about repetition as a cultural and behavioural pattern that arises under particular socio-psychological conditions where the need to remember becomes especially acute, and is especially likely to be thwarted. 'True crime' documentaries translate these into concrete problems. What happens when we re-run and re-run a violent event, using various props to stand in for the person-lost? Do we end up going round in circles when we re-enact an event? Why are we so apt to miss what's been in front of us all along and forget things that seemed important at the time? Who should we trust more when reconstructing events: those who claim to remember perfectly, or those who claim to have forgotten entirely? In raising these troubling, often unresolvable, questions, the 'true crime' documentaries discussed in this chapter offer a way of thinking about the perils of repetition and routine—even as they embody, too, the problems that come from transforming violence into serial entertainment. They tell us, amongst other things, that repetition for its own sake—without any consideration of what exactly is being remembered and what it means to see anew—can be a frustratingly fruitless endeavour. This chapter turns now to consider in more detail the role and meaning of serialisation in media treatments of violent crime, before discussing in detail two 'true crime' documentaries and what they might tell us about repetition and routine.

Over and Over and Over Again: Serialised Crime in Theoretical Perspective

In the late twentieth, early twenty-first century there has been what seems like a resurgence of interest in serial crime stories, most notably, perhaps, in the form of television series and podcasts. In fact, serialisation has long been a key feature of the media treatment of crime, and popular culture more broadly. The nineteenth-century detective novel, then, and still now, amongst the most popular of genres, was originally issued periodically, its individual chapters serving as new instalments. The penny dreadful, aptly named, for it provided sensational, cheap fictionalised accounts of the lives of infamous criminals, was amongst the most widely-read formats of the early-mid nineteenth century and it too took an episodic form.[1] As Pittard (2015) points out, serialisation shaped both the content and meaning of the crime stories that became such a key feature of Victorian popular culture and beyond. Certainly, the serial format of crime stories is inextricably linked to a set of narrative devices that, in the twenty-first century, we have become wholly familiar with as seemingly essential elements of the crime story. Chief amongst these is repetition. Series are long-form stories, told in segments, and this means that they need to sustain our interest and provide us with the means to follow what's happening, all the trickier when their plots are labyrinthine and their social worlds expansive—think *Game of Thrones*—and when there is a gap in time between episodes being released. To keep us on track, series provide us with regular reminders of what happened last and tantalising glimpses of what's 'up next'. This replaying of key events itself takes on a familiar pattern, with episodes often moving from revelation, to twist, to cliffhanger (and repeat).

These narrative devices encourage certain emotional responses—for fans, it's a familiar repertoire of feeling—chiefly shock and enervation, and also, when the subject-matter is violent crime, a likely sense of horror. The vast body of criminological literature concerning the relationship between media coverage of crime and public attitudes towards

---

[1] See Pittard (2015), for a useful overview of these serialised crime story formats in the nineteenth century.

crime largely focuses on the content of that coverage (for a review, see Moore, 2014a). This chapter is more interested in how the formal features of crime stories, in particular repetition, shape their meaning and possible effect. Their serial structure is part of this, but so too is their reliance on re-enactment and reinvestigation, as well as their interest, thematically, in repetitious behaviours and double-identities.

The following section explores these uses of repetition through a focussed discussion of two 'true crime' documentary series. Before that I want to discuss and draw together two strands of contemporary thinking that help make sense of the cultural tendency to replay violent events: writing on repetition as a particular product of late modern society and criminological work on hauntology. I don't mean to suggest that these two theoretical strands of writing constitute different approaches to the same phenomena. Writing about seriality as a cultural product tends to be interested in repetition as a structural feature, and sees seriality as pathological in terms of its origin and effects, that is, as evidence of deeper, darker psycho-social drives to repeat and replay. Hauntology is more interested in the tone of crime stories, and sees the coexistence of the past and the present in stories and spaces—which often, but by no means always, involves repetition—as a potentially radical response that refuses to rid the present of discomforting traces of the past. My aim in this chapter is not to reconcile, nor to suggest the primacy or greater purchase of either strand of writing, but rather to take from both—and then, hopefully, in the section that follows, develop—suggestive ideas about the role of repeating, remembering, and re-seeing in 'true crime' documentaries.

We'll turn first to the idea that serial crime stories are a product of a set of cultural-economic conditions that promote serial production and consumption, creating a culture stuck 'on repeat'. Take, by way of example, stories about serial killing. Dyer (2015) details the huge growth of media interest in serial killing in the last century, and points out that whilst this has become a pervasive cultural concern, its incidence in the media is at 'extravagant variation to its incidence in reality' (Dyer, 2015, p. 5). He notes—as others in this collection do—that the serial killer is a modern invention, a term that only really gained purchase during the 1980s and came to legitimise a new field of pseudo-scientific study. 'Serial killer', Dyer points out, supplanted other empirical-sounding formulations ('psychopath') as well as more morally-laden terms ('monster') (Dyer, 2015, pp. 18–20). In short, as with these earlier designations, the 'serial killer' is fundamentally a social construction, and it's one that belongs firmly to the modern social world.

For one thing, in the act of killing again—in a horrifying pattern of repetition and escalation—each murder becomes 'an episode in a serial', ready-made for the sort of cultural consumption that has become dominant under conditions of late capitalism (Dyer, 1997, p. 14). More generally, Dyer wants to alert us to the central role of repetition—and not just cultural repetition—in contemporary social life:

> Both labour — the production line, the modern office, the internet — and the majority culture — the press, cinema, television, internet — are characterised and organised by repetition, so much so that repetition may be taken to be a fundamental experience of what it is to be human in contemporary society. (Dyer, 2015, p. 10)

He means, as he goes on to explain, mechanical, unthinking repetition for its own sake—of work-tasks and cultural consumption—rather than the sort of 'natural' repetition that might shape the life and work of agrarian communities. The modern consumerist impulse is a key part of this, and, as various social theorists have pointed out, it's distinguished by a seemingly insatiable appetite for—simply—more stuff. Seriality, cultural repetition more broadly, is a cultural format that feeds that appetite by leaving us expecting and wanting more, whether that's the next episode, the next season, or the new version of our favourite story-format. To return to Dyer (2015): serial stories of serial killers fit a world built around serial consumption. Or, to be truer to his thesis: a world built around serial consumption is especially likely to produce a phantom such as the serial killer and make this the basis for serialised stories.

The implication here is that we can think of repetition—seriality, too—as an urge, one that can become an inexhaustible and sometimes pathological desire, that springs from particular social conditions associated with late modernity, not least of all unfettered consumption. The social theorist Georg Simmel (2004—originally 1900) made a similar point in his writing about the modern money economy and how it shapes human relationships and behaviour. His book *Philosophy of Money* ranges across vivid examples, from sex work to loan sharks. In one part of the book he considers two apparently contradictory character-types: the miser and the spendthrift. The spendthrift is addicted to spending money, and so never keeps it for that long. Misers, in contrast, can't let go of the stuff; they horde money and come to cherish it. What unites these two character-types, Simmel (2004) argues, is a valorisation of money in and of itself, of (simply) having it, on the part of the miser, and (simply) spending it, on the part of the spendthrift. Both have lost a sense of any value beyond this experience of having-and-spending, both are stuck in an endless, unsatisfying loop with no ultimate end-point. The miser will never stop collecting money (can you ever have too much of the stuff?), and the spendthrift will never stop spending it (can you ever tire of shopping?) Simmel's (2004) broader point is that the advent of the modern money system as a means of exchange introduced to human behaviour and relationships a profound problem of meaning, and in particular a distorted sense of what's valuable and why. This manifests itself as, first, the tendency to replay and repeat, and secondly, a tendency for those repetitions—whether a cultural treatment or behavioural—to feel loop-like, serving nothing beyond.

As Dyer (2015) also notes, the modern construction of the serial killer is precisely this character: he (and it is most usually a 'he') is somehow stuck in a behavioural pattern governed (seemingly) by pure want, creating rituals, symbols, and patterns not for any higher purpose, but simply to mark out the act of killing itself. As consumers of serial killer stories, we are also, most of us, unable to resist the urge to replay and repeat (and, to follow through the implication of the discussion above, this can mean getting stuck in a binge-watching loop where we're watching for the sake of it). There is more going on here than a cultural impulse to replay, again and again. The desire to re-watch, re-listen, or re-read reflects, too, an uncomfortable desire to trace back to an event that is elemental and abhorrent, yet so fundamentally beyond our reach. In most serial killer stories, what we encounter first is the trace of a crime: a perceptual outline of both killer and event (served up to us as a profile and crime scene). The original act—sickeningly present in our thoughts—remains, usually, always-in-the-past, never truly recoverable, but always very much the main point of interest.

Ernst Bloch (1980—originally 1960) saw the detective novel in similar terms. Here he is describing the peculiar structure of this genre (and, we might add, any crime-story that has detection as a central element):

> Before the first word of the first chapter something happened, but no one knows what, apparently not even the narrator. A dim focal point exists, as yet unrecognised, whither and thither the entire truckload of ensuing events is mobilized – a crime, usually murder, precedes the beginning. In all other narrative forms both deeds and misdeeds develop before the omnipresent reader. Here, on the contrary, the reader is absent when the misdeed occurs, a misdeed that, though conveniently home-delivered, shuns the light of day and lingers in the background of the story. (Bloch, 1980, p. 37)

For Bloch (1980), this makes fictional accounts of detection similar to the task of psychoanalysis, in as much as the latter, too, involves tracing back and replaying past events again and again in a bid to make sense of them. These attempts to work-back and replay are, Bloch argues, thwarted where they seek to return to an original, primal event of elemental violence. Thwarted, because enactment is, in both detective stories and psychoanalysis, inevitably a *re*-enactment and the misdeed, as Bloch puts it, 'shuns the light of day'. In making this point, I don't want to suggest—as those critical of psychoanalysis sometimes have— a problem of veracity with recovered memories of past trauma. Rather, I want to focus on what all this tells us about the motivation for producing and consuming serial crime stories. Is it the case, as Bloch (1980) suggests, that we consume such stories over-and-over—and that crime stories themselves have such a repetitious structure—because of a deep-seated desire to glimpse and make sense of a deeply disruptive, but fundamentally elusive violent event? And how do we then form an understanding of that violent event, once we've realised the limits of empirical reconstruction?

The ambivalent desire to return to and make sense of the past is a concern, too, for criminologists interested in hauntology. This is an idea that has gained purchase across the humanities over the last fifteen years, and originates in the work of the philosopher Jacques Derrida. In his *Spectres of Marx* (2006, originally 1993), widely seen as the text that introduced hauntology, Derrida suggested that marxism—at that point, largely seen as a failed project—would 'haunt' western European societies as a much vaunted future that didn't quite come to pass. His point is that cherished ideologies that come to be deeply embedded in the cultural consciousness don't simply evaporate at the point at which they come to seem obsolete—they leave a residual trace in the culture. Some ideas, perhaps full ideological systems, *haunt* us, they—again—seem to return and repeat, as if they never quite fully went away.

For cultural criminologists, a similar point holds about violence and crime: we might be encouraged to see these as discrete, fleeting events, but their impact (both emotional and material) are in many respects lasting. Our daily lives are full of uncanny reminders of these events, so much so that we might come to experience a decidedly disjointed sense of time: what's in the past appears stubbornly to resist being laid to rest, and instead pops up to impose itself, uncannily, in the here-and-now. Flowers left by a roadside, old police ticker-tape left on-site, broken glass outside city-centre pubs, tatty 'missing' posters on lamp posts, adversarial graffiti marking out territory and inflaming disputes—our daily lives are full of such emblems of moments-past that are also part of the here-and-now.

This isn't a simple matter of being 'stuck in the past'. It's easy to imagine that repetition is all backwards-looking, but in the discussion above—when we considered the connection between psychoanalysis and fictional feats of detection—we thought about the possibility that repeatedly tracing back reflects a desire to move forwards by resolving the past. We discussed, too, how attempts to complete, resolve, and move on might be thwarted when repetition becomes a habit, an urge even—think, again, of the serial killer, the miser, the spendthrift.

Hauntologists would add that what stops us moving on is a sense that an imagined future is no longer possible. This is another reason why serial killer stories are so popular: our deep sense of unease comes not just from thinking about a terrible event-in-the-past, but also a lost future. News stories play upon this: they pique our interest in 'what happened' as well as the life-cut-short. For hauntologists, this sense of a lost future is pervasive. Fisher, in sketching out the uses of hauntology in film studies, notes that '[w]hat haunts the digital cul-de-sac of the twenty-first century is not so much the past as all the lost futures that the twentieth century taught us to anticipate' (Fisher, 2012, p. 16). We're back, again, to that Derridean idea that the failure of the twentieth-century marxist project would be experienced as a collective haunting.

Hauntologists suggest that the contemporary culture is more generally shaped by an unsettling temporal dislocation, a tendency to loop back to troubled, unresolved past events, and to experience recurring dreams of futures-lost. Time, as hauntologists have it, 'is out of joint'. The phrase comes from Shakespeare's *Hamlet*, from an early episode in the play that Derrida uses to explain the experience—key to hauntology—of linear time being disrupted. The phrase is uttered by Hamlet, Prince of Denmark, after a troubling visitation from the ghost of his recently deceased father. Hamlet learns from this apparition that the new king—his father's brother, so at once now Hamlet's step-father, uncle, and king—murdered Hamlet's father to take the crown. Those who have seen or read the play will know that the ghostly visitation causes Hamlet to unravel, and much of the drama that ensues involves him endlessly circling round a set of disturbing questions. Can he trust a ghost? Does even countenancing the ghost's story put him on the wrong side of morality? In spending so much time worrying about the veracity of the ghost's account, is he putting off doing the right thing and usurping the new king? And how much does his mother, who has hastily re-married her brother-in-law, know about what's going on? Fiddler, in setting out the importance of this scene in Hamlet for hauntologists, notes that the spectre of Hamlet's father 'destablizes the distinction between past and present and, as a result, opens up the future' (Fiddler, 2019, p. 468). The ghost—a remnant of the past—is stuck in the present, refusing to let things move on, and at the same time a newly-settled future, both in terms of the royal succession and Hamlet's own destiny (as future king), is thrown into disarray.

There's something else in this episode that I think is worth noting, and that is Hamlet's profound sense that he needs to bring about a radical change in perspective as a result of this new knowledge—that all must be recast. In his first soliloquy after the ghost's visitation he vows to 'wipe away all trivial fond records' from his memory to live only by the ghost's 'commandment' to get revenge, because now Hamlet sees, for the very first time, a fundamental truth: '[t]hat one may smile, and smile, and be a villain'. In fact, he is anything but urgent in his actions. For the remainder of the play we watch Hamlet replay the original event again and again—even staging a play that re-enacts his uncle's crime—as he troubles over the fact that he didn't see what was there all along and needs to effect a radical re-versioning of the past. This crisis over seeing and not seeing, mis-remembering and re-remembering—manifesting as a compulsion to repeat—is, I want to suggest, of central concern for twenty-first century 'true crime' documentaries. The next section provides an introduction to the 'true crime' format and takes a close look at two 'true crime' documentaries. The final, concluding discussion returns to think about what seriality, re-enactment, and the rehearsing of 'the facts' in 'true crime' documentaries might tell us about the promise and problems of repetition.

Ever-Recurring Moments and Deceptive Doubles in 'True Crime' Documentaries

Much has been written over the last decade about the popularity of the 'true crime' documentary (most notably Bruzzi, 2016; Selzer, 2007). This format assembles and assesses evidence—re-examining existing accounts and rooting out new ones—in such a way as to suggest a new way of looking at a case. Revelation and exposé are, then, key features of the 'true crime' documentary format, as is an investigatory tone and structure, customarily directed towards revealing miscarriages of justice, as Walsh points out in an earlier chapter. Linnemann (2015) reminds us that an interest in real-life crime is by no means specific to the twenty-first century. Indeed, towards the start of this chapter, I mentioned several formats that we might think of as 'true crime' that were popular in the nineteenth century. At the same time, there's been an evident proliferation of 'true crime' accounts in the opening decades of the twenty-first century, reflecting the increased public availability of data and film footage (not least of all, courtroom filming), an interest in portrayals of 'real life' crime, and a particular cultural mood of cynicism in relation to criminal justice processes and outcomes (see Moore, 2014b for a fuller discussion). Within this broader interest in 'real' and 'true' crime, one particular format—the 'true crime' documentary—has become especially popular, and Bruzzi (2016) convincingly argues that we should see this as an emergent genre, with shared and familiar conventions. Amongst other things, she points out, there is an evident 'relaxation of the boundaries between 'fact' and 'fiction'' in 'true crime' documentaries; they both offer up 'the facts' and dramatise events. For Bruzzi (2016, p. 257), this reflects 'an acceptance [amongst documentary filmmakers] that reality...is not fixed, finite or stable'.

Criminologists and media studies researchers tend to approach this differently, arguing that 'true crime' documentaries claim to reveal 'what really happened', but actually prioritise a particular view of events. Investigative neutrality, here, is conceived of as a rhetorical device that urges particular attitudes to criminal justice and crime. LaChance and Kaplan (2020), for example, argue that the phenomenally popular 'true crime' documentary television series *Making a Murderer* (Ricciardi & Demos, 2015–2018) works to entrench punitive attitudes by focussing squarely on the question of defendant guilt (rather than the thornier question of how we treat those convicted of crime).

This chapter largely leaves aside these questions about veracity and rhetoric—important though they are—and is instead specifically interested in the role and meaning of repetition and seriality in 'true crime' documentary. In doing so, I want to move the discussion away from questions about reality and truth, and instead towards questions about time, memory and the urge to replay events. This section focuses on two popular 'true crime' series: the television mini-series *The Staircase* (described by Bruzzi as the 'touchstone or foundational text' in the 'true crime' documentary genre—Bruzzi, 2016, p. 250) and Season One of the podcast series *Serial*, still, some eight years after its original release, amongst the most downloaded podcasts. Both were originally transmitted in the early twenty-first century and both are based in the USA (although *The Staircase* was directed and produced—initially, at least—by a French team, funded by Canal+). In common with 'true crime' documentaries more generally, both series revolve around a central male protagonist accused of a horrific violent crime, in each case, the murder of a woman. The narrative arc, in both series, is shaped by the male protagonist's claim to be innocent—persecuted, even; a victim.

The Staircase, originally broadcast in 2004, follows the case of Michael Peterson, accused of the murder of his wife, Kathleen Peterson, who in 2001 was found dead at the bottom of the staircase in the family home. The series starts with events six weeks after Kathleen's death, with Michael Peterson grappling with having been charged with her murder. The first eight episodes (which made up the original series that was released in 2004) chart Peterson's preparation for trial, the trial itself, and eventual conviction. This part of the story is anchored in a set of episode-by-episode revelations: that Peterson was intimately connected to a prior, eerily similar case in Germany some years beforehand; that Peterson is bi-sexual and was romantically involved with men whilst married to Kathleen; that local law enforcement agencies have a grudge against Peterson; the late discovery of the alleged murder weapon, the blow-poke.[2] This structure of serial revelation—most episodes begin with a big reveal and end with a cliffhanger—might suggest a steady pace of story-development. It's also a predictable pattern, and by episode eight, once we've learned the outcome of the trial and been urged to feel its illogic, that structure may well strike us as deeply unproductive. No amount of serial revelation has saved Peterson from being convicted, and once we get there, it seems strangely and discomfortingly inevitable.

As the series extends past its original eight episodes—into the final five episodes that were added in 2013 and 2018—we move into the post-conviction and appeal stage and the narrative arc that was provided by the trial falls away. We're left with a story of a man in stasis. Repetition is key here, too. In these episodes, as we follow Paterson in prison, pursuing an appeal, and then under house arrest, there is a continual sense that we're watching events on repeat. The appeal affords this sense of repetition—it's a re-serialisation of the original trial—and so too do the plodding routines of prison life and then house arrest.

In other respects, too, repetition is a central theme in *The Staircase*. The prosecution wants to suggest a pattern to Paterson's behaviour, and

---

[2] A grate-side tool for stoking fires.

so we're offered up prior episodes where he lost his temper, was insensitive to Kathleen, and—most strikingly—was connected to an identikit death some years before. It offers up the tantalising idea that Peterson might be a repeat-killer who has replicated a murder and then re-staged its cover-up.

The two key settings for the original series—the Peterson home and the courtroom—are, too, places of familiar routine (though, as hinted at above and discussed further below, whether these are productive or harmful routines remains an open question throughout). We return, again and again, to one particular part of the Peterson home: the eponymous staircase, the scene of Kathleen's death. It's a confined space located in the recesses of the Peterson household, tucked-away and narrow. So much of the activity that goes on within the Peterson home, so much, too, of what we see and are asked to think about, is oriented around that staircase and the past that haunts it. Our first glimpse of it comes roughly six minutes into the first episode, in a series of scenes that set out Peterson's account of what happened the night Kathleen died. As we listen to his 911 call—his voice wild and panicked—we're shown low-grade camera footage, shot on a hand-held camera, of the Peterson home. It lingers and zooms in on a blood-smeared doorway, then it travels around the space, capturing Christmas decorations at the foot of a grand entrance staircase (it's not *the* staircase, then). We bob seamlessly through a space cordoned-off with police ticker tape, as Peterson's 911 call becomes ever more desperate.

We cut away, briefly, to the here-and-now, to Peterson's son describing how he came upon the scene, and then, within 30 seconds, we cut back to the on-site, just-in-the-aftermath hand-held camera footage. We've jumped to an inner recess of the home, and now we're travelling down a dark hallway, with Peterson's 911 call again serving as voice-over. He's crying now, and has become totally detached from the conversation with the operator (*is the phone off the hook?*) We notice, as we make our way along the hall, a dark mass at the end, and as we get closer, we make out a body, sprawled out on the floor at the foot of a stairwell, blood everywhere, as Peterson's voice-over becomes a low, continuous sob.

There's so much to say here—about, for example, the documentary's early support for Peterson's version of events, by pairing his 911 call with grainy camera footage that 'discovers' Kathleen, so that the latter seems to serve as empirical evidence for the former—but I want to focus on how this set of scenes collapse the past and the present. We cut, immediately after, to a talking-head account from Peterson in the documentary's here-and-now, and he tells us: 'I vividly remember finding Kathleen'. This moment, this scene, is forever superimposed on all others in this documentary, so much so that we too will continually bring to mind (and be asked to bring to mind) this moment of terrible loss. It is an imprint of a horrible, never really knowable, immediate past: did Kathleen suffer a terrible fall before ending up in this state, or was she, as the prosecution claim, murdered?

We return to the scene of her death, in most cases, several times each episode, starting with the title sequence, where we slowly swoop down a stylish, computer-enhanced version of the staircase, its steps and walls becoming digital screens showing footage from the documentary. We return to different versions of this space as we follow Peterson around the house, in the courtroom when looking at photographs of Kathleen's dead body, alongside the expert witnesses and jurors as they visit the home. And beyond these direct viewings of the staircase, we're frequently asked to bring this space to mind.

Take, by way of example, a set of scenes in the defence attorney's office where we watch the defense's blood splatter expert perform an extraordinary demonstration of how to read blood splatter patterns. He daubs strands of hair into a pot of red ink and then flicks it in broad strokes at a white board in an attempt to recreate the blood splatters in the stairwell ("*that* much hair did all that?", one of the defence lawyers asks, appreciatively). It's a re-enactment, of sorts, of Kathleen's last moments and it culminates in the blood splatter expert taking a mouthful of ketchup, tipping his head back, and coughing up the sauce onto the white board to recreate the effect of, presumably, one last, labourful cough. It's done with jocularity, and he invites others to have a go (they do, and with unimpressive results). It's partly an evidence-building exercise, partly a team-building exercise. Both sit uncomfortably against the fact that we're also listening to a horrifyingly antiseptic replaying of a woman's brutal death. There's a parallel, equally discomforting, set of scenes at the end of

Episode One, where the defence team re-enacts Kathleen's death to determine if Peterson could have heard her screams (*did she scream?*) from where he claims to have been at the time, outside, pool-side. They set up a tape player, balanced on one of the lower stairs—covered in Kathleen's now-dry blood—and play a recording of a woman shouting for help, her voice moving to different pitches, presumably in an attempt at greater scientific validity. We cut between this stand-in for Kathleen and Peterson, surrounded by his defence team and dogs, pool-side, silent and craning to listen. Whether it's Peterson not-quite-hearing the mocked-up sound of Kathleen dying-at-a-distance, or the blood splatter expert's re-creation of the material 'facts', we replay, again and again, the story of Kathleen's death in the stairwell, told in different ways, by different people.

Bruzzi astutely points out that the layers of re-enactment in *The Staircase* are what make it compulsive viewing, adding that 'this simultaneous existence as a re-enactment of events that have concluded and an enactment of those same events as if they have not yet happened' produces 'a temporal duality responsible for the series' disquieting uncanniness throughout' (Bruzzi, 2016, p. 254). The re-enactments of Kathleen's death, as described above, are a striking example of this. Kathleen, we know is dead, but here we watch and listen to 'her' dying again, the evidentiary nature of the set-up serving to reinforce the idea that this is actually how it happened. Except, of course, it's not her that we're watching or hearing; this is categorically not 'what happened', this is the documentary's here-and-now.

We're back to that idea of time being out of joint, and in the examples above that temporal dislocation comes from the very particular aims and demands of re-enactment done for the purpose of legal case-building. It creates a version of the past that leaves out so much that matters—most noticeably, Kathleen herself—and nonetheless claims to prove 'what happened'. Meanwhile, the past in a more fundamental way remains unresolved. No wonder, like the ghost in Hamlet, it just keeps coming back in unreconstructed form (that haunting image of Kathleen's body, those blood splatters). Bruzzi (2016) draws a connection, as I did above, between re-enactment and psychoanalysis, and specifically the Freudian idea that repetition 'is a displacement activity, a substitute for remembering; a symptom, therefore, of *not remembering*' (Bruzzi, 2016, p. 253—original italics). It's commensurate with the idea—discussed above—that repetition and seriality contribute to an evacuation of meaning and value, a failure to complete and close and reconcile and realise. *The Staircase* acknowledges that this is horrifying, even as it does little to bring Kathleen back into the frame in such a way that might allow us—and the Peterson family—to reconnect with the events of the past and move beyond them. What we have, instead, is *Peterson's* observation that what's missing, both from the trial and the ensuing media coverage, is any understanding of Kathleen as a person.

The same holds for our understanding of Michael Peterson. We're offered multiple perspectives on him, round and round, back in time, but never back all the way to the moments that we really want to see. Never—we realise after the ninth episode—forwards, to who he might become after or despite this set of events. We watch him in the courtroom, moved to tears as he—us and the jurors, too —listen to his 911 call after discovering Kathleen at the bottom of the stairs. (*Or was it after killing her?*) It's a device that is commonly used in 'true crime' documentaries: the in-the-moment, not-for-*this*-moment recording of a voice, its tone and pitch maybe betraying what really happened. The convention, in 'true crime' television documentaries, is for the camera to remain fixed on the listening face of the accused as they—we—hear a version of them speaking from a different time and place. Doubling is an especially uncanny effect of the repetition that forms a key feature of the 'true crime' documentary genre. Here, we may well ask ourselves whether *this* Peterson sat in the courtroom is the *same* Peterson that we're listening to, caught in a moment of terrible shock? Can we discern a telling gap, between this original moment and the version we're being asked to believe now, one that suggests that what we're seeing now is a performance? Worse still, are we hearing what happened, or is this, too, put-on? In other words, are we watching someone listening to a recording of themselves staging an event? The repetitions proliferate like images in a hall of mirrors. It's a metaphor that alerts us to a key effect of repetition in 'true crime' documentaries, and that is to suggest that the material traces of a case do not give up the truth, they're just the imprint or the echo of a terrible thing that happened. Sometimes, this works to sensationalise events, to tantalise audience members by taking them so *near* to what happened, yet never quite all the way. In other instances, it works to alert us to the possibility that focussing on the imprints or echoes of a violent episode can mean we get further away from the event itself. Perhaps reclaiming such events and the people lost to them involves moving them out of an empirical frame of reference, and insisting on other ways of looking at them.

In *The Staircase* there is a suggestion that continually retracing our steps doesn't in itself yield much, and certainly doesn't necessarily awaken new ways of seeing. The discovery of the blow-poke, the alleged murder weapon, is a case in point. A gift from Kathleen's sister, the suspiciously missing blow-poke is an essential part of the prosecution's case. In the courtroom, for the benefit of the jury, the prosecution team re-enacts the fatal strikes with—another double—a duplicate version of the real thing. The Peterson family circle back to the missing blow-poke in their conversations at home: they've looked everywhere, turned the house upside down—as have the police—and their repeated attempts to locate it have been fruitless. Until, one day, out of the blue, it's re-discovered in the garage, covered in cobwebs, but by no means hidden. It's been there all along. Everybody looked for it and most likely *at* it, but nobody noticed it.

It's no coincidence that the blow-poke is found in the Peterson home, amongst the familiar paraphernalia of domestic life, and more specifically in amongst the heap of much-used, rarely noticed stuff in their garage (and it could, of course, have been a spare room, a shed, a bedside cabinet, a porch, a hallway drawer). Most of us have had a version of this very same experience: we're *sure* we put our house-keys in the tray, we've looked everywhere for them, they're not anywhere else (except they are—they're on the table in the kitchen, where we've checked several times over). We're susceptible to mental habits of seeing that allow us to imagine things where we expect them to be, miss things in plain sight, and stop us from accurately inventorising spaces that we know very well indeed. In instances such as this, replaying an event—retracing our steps—doesn't help; in fact, the force of repetition is such that it can make us even more blinkered, even less likely to see clearly, even more inured to the day-to-day placement of people and things.

A parallel problem confronts the podcast-maker Sarah Koenig and her audience, in the first season of *Serial*. The 12-part series unpacks a historic case for which the central male protagonist, Adnan Syed, has already been convicted. Syed, at the point that *Serial* was first made available, had spent fourteen years in prison for the murder of his ex-girlfriend, Hae Min Lee. Hae, a popular, bright 17-year old, disappeared after school on January 13th, 1999. Her body was found nearly a month later, half-buried in Baltimore's Leakin Park. We learn in the course of the series that the case was mired by unreliable witnesses and contestable evidence, but chief amongst the problems with this case—and central to the prosecution's case—is that Syed simply can't remember what he was doing on the afternoon that Hae disappeared.

Koenig makes much of this in the opening episode, and she pursues it as an abstract empirical question: is it possible for us to lead busy, organised lives and for these everyday events simply not to register with us—and those we're with—in any lasting way? She asks her audience: can *you* remember what you were doing on any given day a month ago? Even with the benefit of newer technology—more sophisticated mobile phones, for example—remembering these events as distinct and discrete is surprisingly hard. That's at least partly because of the routine and repetition in our everyday lives. I can remember what I did on my last birthday, or on Christmas Day; the rest is distinctly unmemorable, even as, at the time, they might have seemed like notably good or bad days.

A similar point might be made about our memory of familiar spaces, and this too is a particular problem in Season One of *Serial*. A key piece of testimony revolves around the idea that Adnan made a phone call from a pay-phone in the car park of the local electronic store, Best Buy. No one, it transpires, can recall this pay-phone—its placement in this space, whether it actually existed. Koenig digs out the original plans for the space, but there's doubt about the accuracy of even this, an official record of decision-making. All of this amounts to an extraordinary ellipsis in collective memory, one that indirectly lends credibility to Syed's seemingly strange inability to call to mind the events on the day that Hae went missing.

In *Serial*, Syed's lack of memory is set against the equally uncanny ability of Jay, the state's key witness, who claims that Syed enlisted his help to bury Hae's dead body, to recall in great detail. Jay changes his testimony multiple times, but still holds firm to the idea that he can remember what happened. *Serial* at times presents the case as a straightforward matter of who we believe: Syed or Jay. With that comes another, broader question. Which account has greater purchase: one where someone claims to be able to remember entirely, or one where someone claims not to be able to recall at all? In the opening decades of the twenty-first century, where the empirical bases of 'the truth' seem less certain, the claim to be able to recall with total accuracy and without prejudice might seem at best questionable, at worst part of the problem.

The tendency for amnesia and mis-seeing might strike us all the more likely when it comes to acts of violence in intimate relationships and domestic settings. Both *The Staircase* and Season One of *Serial* suggest that this is at least a possibility; that extraordinary acts of violence occur against a backdrop of everyday life that is unmemorable in its normality. Criminologists remind us that such acts can be—most usually *are*—an extension of normal, everyday relationships, and that's what makes them so very difficult to recognise, both by onlookers, apt to assume that there's 'nothing to see here' and those subject to violence. In this respect, Season One of *Serial* and *The Staircase* suggest an obverse relationship between normality and routine to that suggested in fictional treatments of serial killers. For the latter, abnormal desires become the basis for a pathological routine and repetition. An alternative, also sickening idea holds in the 'true crime' documentaries discussed here: 'normal' routine and repetition might give rise to (and then hide) abnormal desires. Even as we might believe Syed and Peterson innocent of the crimes of which they are accused, this is the possibility that we're asked to countenance.

As in *The Staircase*, *Serial* answers to this problem by undertaking a huge investigatory project in a bid to recover the past. Where Adnan can't—or perhaps won't—remember, Koenig takes over the task of piecing together the timeline of 'what happened', reviewing witness accounts and evidence from telephone companies. A very particular type of seriality holds here: we return, episode after episode, to different versions of 'what happened', from the media-friendly, condensed version, complete with cliffhanger (in Episode One), to the longer-view of Syed and Hae's relationship (in Episode Two), to the prosecution's version of events (Episode Six), to a close-up look at Jay's testimony and perspective (Episode Eight), to the swirling rumour-mill about the case (Episode Eleven). The overall lesson is: the truth might be 'out there', but it's also available in multiple forms. One consequence of this rehearsing of different versions of 'what happened' and the telescoping in and out, from specific moments to the broader view of the case, is that multiple versions of Syed emerge. He is at once (except, he *can't be both*) the 'good son' and prone to lying to his parents (about, amongst other things, his relationship with Hae). We get troubling glimpses of a darker version of Syed, one that writes notes to classmates about wanting to kill Hae for having dumped him. This is set against the Syed that we hear in the here-and-now of the podcast, in telephone conversations with Koenig, him in prison, her voice made crisper from being in a professional radio studio. The effect is to make Syed's contributions to these conversations seem all the more relaxed—*his* voice is the unedited one (however erroneous an impression this might be). Koenig ponders, at points, whether his off-guard comments might reveal a double-identity and with it, a gap between 'reality' and performance. This is the prevailing problem for Koenig, and one that she never resolves: who is the *real* Adnan Syed?

As with *The Staircase*, then, in Season One of *Serial* the back-and-forth replaying of events, conversations, and experiences creates a flurry of doubles. Here, unlike in *The Staircase*, this gives rise to a fundamental unknowability about Syed's innocence, and with it (perhaps because of it) a deeply felt need to find out for sure. This is most clearly expressed in Episode Five, centred on Koenig's re-enactment of events according to the prosecution's timeline. We accompany her on the car ride, trying to make the journey from Hae and Syed's school to Best Buy in 21 min or less (in line with the prosecution's model of 'what happened'). Koenig is multi-tasking all the way—keeping an eye on the clock, pondering about whether any of this would have been possible, conscious of the need to commentate what is an otherwise uninteresting drive through suburbia. It's a re-enactment that might put us in mind of the blood splatter expert's re-enactment of Kathleen Peterson's last moments. In both cases, we're offered a replaying of 'what happened' that is both tantalising in bringing us closer to the original event and jarring in its not-really-realness. And in both cases there's an evident displacement of attention away from Hae and Kathleen, and towards the empirical coordinates that fasten their deaths in time and space. *Serial* ultimately fails to reframe events in such a way as to allow Hae to take centre-stage. What it does tell us, though, is that empirical investigation is insufficient in answering the questions that really matter about this case. Koenig's conclusion, after all this work of tracing and re-playing events, is that there's very little that we know with any degree of certainty when it comes to Hae's murder. What makes this conclusion all the more extraordinary is the revelation in Episode One that someone actually might know where Adnan was on the afternoon that Hae disappeared; a schoolmate who gets in contact with Adnan after he's arrested to say that she saw him in the school library, but his defence team didn't pick it up and follow-up the testimony. Koenig tracks her down, and she's certain of what she saw, and when. It's a 'gotcha' revelation, akin to the discovery of the blow-poke in *The Staircase*—there all along, available to anyone who tried to look for it, but strangely unnoticed for so long. And as with the discovery of the blow-poke in *The Staircase*, Syed's alibi has no impact on the outcome of his trial. Nor does it sway Koenig towards believing that he's innocent. It's worth noting here how strikingly at odds this is with the standard narrative trajectory of crime stories, where a revelation or discovery almost always serves to resolve events, either by proving that someone is after all innocent or that someone is incontrovertibly guilty. Not so here, in the 'true crime' documentaries that have formed the focus for our discussion. The effect is to suggest that, no matter how hard we work to determine 'what happened' by replaying events, knowledge empirically derived is not enough to determine 'the truth', or rather, the revealing of empirical facts is not enough to prompt us to see and think differently. That, as Hamlet found, takes a more profound effort to reorder our understanding of human behaviour.

Concluding Discussion

Repetition as a means of recovering 'what happened' is an especially fraught experience when what's being replayed is a violent event. The 'true crime' documentaries discussed in this chapter might put us in mind of Bloch's (1980) observation that detective stories are peculiar in structure and focus, betraying a deep fascination with an original, violent moment that can never be recovered as it really was. There is an urgency to this task of charting backwards—we want to know and see 'what happened'—but that desire is met with a fundamental problem: the impossibility of laying witness to that terrible event. Bruzzi (2016, p. 253) reminds us that repetition, both as a cultural mode and individual behaviour, can become a 'displacement activity', a way of '*not remembering*'. In other words, the re-enactment of violent events is liable to become a process of endless rehearsal, one that belies the impossibility of retrieving 'what happened' and stops us from thinking about what we might need to remember in order to resolve things and move on.

There is something universal about this set of relationships between violence, repetition, and (not) moving on, but it's worth thinking, too, about the more particular features of 'true crime' stories and their depiction of violence. For one thing, and as noted above, these almost always involve violence against women. This should give us pause to think again about what it means to repeat and not (really) remember. In both *The Staircase* and Season One of *Serial*, the fundamental loss at the heart—but also, decidedly *not at the heart*—of the story is a woman's violent death, that of Kathleen Peterson and Hae Min Lee respectively. Despite both documentaries acknowledging that the investigatory work obscures Kathleen and Hae, their focus remains squarely on the question of whether the men accused of their murders are innocent. The repetition of key events is directed towards answering this (unanswerable) question. There is a compulsiveness to this—both to the serial repetitions of 'what happened' and in the act of consuming them—and this might put us in mind of our earlier discussion about the contemporary cultural tendency for unthinking, unending repetition. As Dyer (2015) points out, there is a particular problem here when it comes to depictions of male violence against women. It means, for one thing, that we get hooked into a cycle of repeating the event, as an event, rather than moving beyond, towards an explanation. The corollary of this is that the female victim is liable—likely, even—to become incidental to these serial retellings; relatively unimportant as a 'someone', but crucial in material terms, as a 'something'. This is why they are so readily substituted with props and facsimiles. *The Staircase* and *Serial* contribute to these problems, even as they acknowledge them.

In other respects, repetition in these series has a more nuanced, and potentially more radical meaning. As discussed above, in both of these 'true crime' documentaries, the familiar pattern of repetition—re-enactment of the events, as well as a reliance on a recurring structure of revelation-and-cliffhanger, and a thematic interest in repetition—is combined with open recognition that repeating doesn't lead to resolution. After the tightly organised, repetitive structure of the original eight episodes of *The Staircase*, we get a set of episodes—after Peterson is found guilty of murder—that rely, still on the repetition of the appeal process and a life of incarceration, but in such a way as to emphasise the inertia of the criminal justice system and the stasis of a family stuck perpetually in a moment of time. In Season One of *Serial*, too, we're made acutely aware that Syed is 15 years (and counting) into a life sentence for Hae's murder. Here too, repetition of 'what happened' is so evidently a fruitless, endless endeavour.

Both documentaries tell another story besides about repetition: that it potentially hides more than it reveals. As discussed above, these series suggest that everyday relationships and routines can make us blinkered. They cause us to miss what's in plain sight (the long-missing blow-poke in *The Staircase*, propped up against a wall in the family's garage), and they make us unreliable witnesses to the events and relationships that play out under our very noses (Syed's lost memory concerning the day Hae disappeared). Familiarity gives rise to amnesia and omission. And both *Serial* and *The Staircase* reflect a deep fear that it might also breed contempt. At the heart of both lies the horrifying possibility—more a lingering fear than a worked-through thesis—that intimacy can give rise to violence and that Peterson and Syed are not who they say they are *Serial*, in particular, keeps this possibility open throughout, but both series dramatise the question of whether Peterson and Syed have double-identities. I have suggested, above, that the tendency for a series of doubles to emerge in 'true crime' documentaries is related, too, to the reliance on repetition: it means that a host of different versions of the central male protagonist emerge from the serial re-running of evidence and witness testimony. This structural tendency is intimately connected to the series' interest in the question of whether the central protagonist is who they claim to be, and in particular whether the here-and-now version of this person (eminently likeable and available to us) is consonant with the earlier version of them we glimpse through recordings of 911 calls, friends' testimony, ad hoc notes, and private messages. That both Peterson and Syed are at once, on the one hand, the 'good father and husband' and the 'good son and boyfriend', and at the same time *not only* these things, is crucial to the overall effect here, as is Koenig's refusal to decide on Syed's guilt. It's an indeterminacy that hauntologists would applaud as potentially radical and critical, because it alerts us to the possibility that a wholesale change in seeing is needed to reconcile the deep discomfort and contradictions that arise when we let the past butt up against the present.

This is a problem that confronts us all, as we grapple with the serial challenges to hegemonic thinking in the early twenty-first century—amongst them, the media revelations about the sexual violence of the once-loved television presented Jimmy Savile, the #MeToo campaign, and the Black Lives Matter movement. These mark collective, cultural problems of remembering, reliving, and re-seeing, but they're felt, too, at an individual level much as Hamlet experiences the fracturing of past-present-future. Did people see, but not register the bad things that were going on around them? How should we re-enact and make amends for those past events? What's the balance to be struck between returning 'to the scene of the crime' and moving forwards? This chapter has suggested that these are also the central concerns for twenty-first century 'true crime' documentaries, and they provide us with an insight into both the promise and challenges of re-engaging with and replaying past events. For one thing, they teach us about the deeply entrenched barriers to recognising what's been in plain sight all along, in particular our tendency to look-past and not notice. They hint, too, at the problems that arise when we imagine that finding out 'the truth' is a purely empirical project of locating new evidence, retracing our steps, and fastening the coordinates of a violent event in time and space. In the early twenty-first century, there is a collective sense that this isn't enough, that objective confirmation (or rebuttal) of 'the facts' doesn't in itself close the matter and treat deep injustices.

Study Questions

- How does serialisation as a media format shape the meaning and consumption of crime stories? Think, here, about how we engage/interact with these stories, their emotional impact, and the common narrative devices used in serialised stories.
- What do hauntologists mean when they refer to time being 'out of joint'? Can you think of examples of this temporal dislocation at work in crime stories, and how does that affect the tone and effect of those stories?
- How is repetition used in 'true crime' documentaries, and why is this such a key feature of these crime stories?
- What do the 'true crime' documentaries discussed in this chapter tell us about the perils of social routine?

References

Bloch, E. (1980). A philosophical view of the detective novel. *Discourse, 2*(Summer), 32–52.

Bruzzi, S. (2016). Making a genre: the case of the contemporary true crime documentary. *Law and Humanities, 10*, 249–280.

De Lestrade, X. (Dir.) (2004). *The Staircase.* Anal+ (Episodes 1–10); Netflix (Episodes 11–13).

Derrida, J. (2006). *Specters of marxism: The state of the debt, the work of mourning and the new international.* London: Routledge.

Dyer, R. (1997). Kill and kill again. *Sight and Sound, 7*(9), 14–17.

Dyer, R. (2015). *Lethal repetition: Serial killing in European Cinema.* London: British Film Institute.

Fiddler, M. (2019). Ghosts of other stories: A synthesis of hauntology, crime and space. *Crime Media Culture, 15*(3), 463–477.

Fisher, M. (2012). What is hauntology? *Film Quarterly, 66*(1), 16–24.

Koenig, S. (2014). 'Serial' (Podcast) Season One. WBEZ.

LaChance, D., & Kaplan, P. (2020). Criminal justice in the middlebrow imagination: The punitive dimensions of Making a Murderer. *Crime Media Culture, 16*(1), 81–96.

Linnemann, T. (2015). Capote's ghosts: Violence, media and the spectre of suspicion. *The British Journal of Criminology, 55*(3), 514–533.

Moore, S. (2014a). *Crime and the media.* Palgrave Macmillan.

Moore, S. (2014b). Real-life crime and cop-work in Cops. In S. Moore (Ed.), *Crime and the Media* (pp. 275–288). Palgrave Macmillan.

Pittard, C. (2015). The Victorian context: Serialization, circulation, genres. In C. Berberich (Ed.) *The Bloomsbury introduction to popular fiction,* (pp. 11–29). Bloomsbury.

Ricciardi, L., & Demos, M. (2015). *Making a Murderer.* USA: Netlix.

Selzer, M. (2007). *True crime: Observations on violence and modernity.* Routledge.

Simmel, G. (2004). *Philosophy of Money* (3rd ed.). Routledge.

Part II

Representations of Victims—Survivors

6

'Stay Sexy and Don't Get Murdered': Depictions of Female Victimhood in Post-Me Too True Crime

Megan Hoffman and Simon Hobbs

Introduction

The true crime genre has a rich tradition spanning multiple media, including books, films, television and, most recently, podcasts. In maintaining its relevance, the genre has adapted to account for a series of social and cultural changes that shape the way it is produced and consumed. Historically, men have dominated true crime as its producers and subjects. From "classic" examples such as Truman Capote's *In Cold Blood* (1965) and Norman Mailer's *The Executioner's Song* (1979) to documentaries such as *The Thin Blue Line* (Morris, 1988) and more

M. Hoffman (✉)
Independent Scholar, Southsea, UK
e-mail: megan.hoffman@port.ac.uk

S. Hobbs
University of Portsmouth, Hampshire, UK
e-mail: simon.hobbs2@port.ac.uk

© The Author(s), under exclusive license to Springer Nature Switzerland AG 2021
M. Mellins and S. Moore (eds.), *Critiquing Violent Crime in the Media*,
https://doi.org/10.1007/978-3-030-83758-7_6

recent approaches in the form of podcasts like *Last Podcast on the Left* (Kissel et al., 2011–present), men have controlled narratives which primarily focus on male perpetrators. However, there is evidence that true crime is a genre that is primarily consumed by women, and that this is not a recent trend. In 1984, a readership survey for three major true crime magazines found that over 85 percent of its respondents were women (Cameron & Frazer, 1987, p. 50). Similarly, in 2010, Amanda Vicary and R. Chris Fraley concluded that more women than men read true crime books (p. 83), and in 2018, Kelli Boling and Kevin Hull conducted a study which found that women compose 73 percent of the true crime podcast audience (p. 103). Boling and Hull, furthermore, suggest that true crime podcasts specifically have "cultivated a very participatory online audience" that is "predominantly female, active, involved and interested in the material covered" (p. 106). The true crime genre's changing landscape is characterised by opportunities for increased audience engagement and, perhaps not surprisingly, growing reflection on the genre's potential for social and political activism. These developments have also coincided with a shift in the ways that female victimhood is framed in these stories, which often exhibit either a deliberate rejection or a conscious reframing of the genre's conventions. As Tanya Horeck notes, "the current cultural moment may be ripe for a feminist rearticulation of the genre" (2019, p. 176). In this chapter, we examine the potential of this feminist rearticulation by examining recent attempts by women across different media to produce true crime narratives that centre female voices and perspectives. We argue that the ways in which these stories are told in podcasts like *My Favorite Murder with Karen Kilgariff and Georgia Hardstark* (2016–present), books such as Hallie Rubenhold's *The Five: The Untold Lives of the Women Killed by Jack the Ripper* (2019) and documentaries including BBC Four's *The Yorkshire Ripper Files: A Very British Crime Story* (Williams, 2019a) and Amazon's *Ted Bundy: Falling for a Killer* (Wood, 2020a) expose and critique the misogyny embedded within previous narratives and, consequently, within wider legal, social and cultural institutions.

Notably, the steady rise in both popularity and production of true crime narratives by and about women has coincided with activism instigated by the Me Too movement against sexualised violence, and crucial to this chapter will be a reading of these texts in the light of post-Me Too discourses. The Me Too movement was started by social justice activist Tarana Burke in 2006 in order to support young Black women and girls who had experienced sexual violence, and Burke first used the phrase "Me Too" as a means for survivors of sexual violence to express solidarity. The movement remained largely within the context of Burke's work until October 2017, when American actress Alyssa Milano used the phrase on Twitter in reaction to highly publicised sexual abuse allegations against Hollywood producer Harvey Weinstein, asking her followers to "write 'me too' as a reply to this tweet" if they had been "sexually harassed or assaulted," and suggesting that this "might give people a sense of the magnitude of the problem" (Milano, 2017). Milano's tweet went viral, and within twenty-four hours the hashtag #MeToo had been shared or reacted to millions of times on Twitter and Facebook (Lawton, 2017). The hashtag provided a platform for victims of sexual violence to discuss their experiences openly, expose perpetrators and bring heightened attention to the importance of recognizing sexual violence as a systemic problem rather than as isolated incidents experienced by individuals. The sharing of stories through engagement with the #MeToo hashtag not only works to "expose the structural nature of men's violence" (Boyle, 2019, p. 12), but it also provides a catalyst for personal healing as "victims of sexual violence or harassment feel empowered when others acknowledge it [...] and receive significant benefits to recovery when positive responses from others are received after disclosing" (Hosterman et al., 2018, p. 85). The effect of the Me Too movement has been to provide a prominent platform for a type of activism that reframes female victimhood by centreing women's voices and experiences and calling attention to pervasive, systemic misogyny in the wider culture.

It is this reframing that has enabled a key shift evident in recent true crime narratives from a focus on the recounting of a male killer's sensationalised—and even glamorised—exploits to an examination of how female victimhood is represented, not only in true crime but also, implicitly, in a wider cultural context. Jean Murley observes that as in traditional crime fiction, true crime narratives rely upon certain genre conventions: a murder, the search for a killer, an exploration of the killer's motives and personality and resolution in the form of the killer's punishment (2019, p. 204). In many true crime narratives, a significant aspect of this formula is a focus on the exceptionalism of the (usually male) killer and the sensational details of the crimes, constructing the killer as the "hero" of the story (Cameron & Frazer, 1987, p. 36) and "disconnect[ing] these individuals from the social fabric in order to present them as aberrations and freaks" (Schmid, 2005, p. 176). The effect of this type of narrative focus not only creates fascination about the killer as a pathological individual, but also downplays the presence of victims, who appear in the form of destroyed bodies or (if their lives are discussed at all) as one-dimensional archetypes whose risky or foolhardy behaviour played a role in their own demise.

We observe a recent trend in true crime narratives that, while still offering the pleasures of narrative conventions to their consumers, attempt to complicate those conventions by engaging with post-Me Too culture. They do so by reworking well-known true crime stories to focus on victims through interviews with families and friends and emphasising the details of victims' lives over the circumstances of their deaths; creating space for female survivors of crimes to recount their experiences in their own words; using women's voices to narrate and provide commentary (often critiquing the ways those stories have been told in the past) and placing the crimes within the context of a continuum of systemic violence against women influenced by various sociocultural factors rather than constructing the killer as an aberration. There is no doubt that there are positive aspects to the reframing we have observed in recent true crime narratives; however, we also wish to explore the ways in which these forms still raise ethical concerns that are intrinsic to true crime as a genre and that progress and reaffirm problematic discourses that have often seen female victims overlooked or exploited. Overall, we seek to place female-led true crime within the very specific social context of Me Too and assess how a more aware society understands a genre that has often exploited the destruction, degradation and rape of female bodies.

"Nobody Knows Who the Women Were": Displacing the Killer as Protagonist

In the case of particularly infamous true crime stories—especially those involving serial killers—reframing the story to reflect a more victim-centred narrative can be a powerful strategy. Many conventional serial killer narratives focus on the killer's abnormal psychological state, providing representations of his chequered background and murderous exploits that are designed to horrify, titillate and even, at times, elicit admiration from the reader, viewer or listener. Cameron and Frazer point out that this has the effect of constructing the killer as the story's "hero": "one meaning of hero in contemporary usage is 'chief male character in a book or play' and this is exactly the role of the murderer in popular discourse, whether his exploits are celebrated or reviled (or both at once)" (1987, p. 36). The dominance of the serial killer in particular within the true crime genre has been examined at length by scholars including David Schmid, who argues in *Natural Born Celebrities: Serial Killers in American Culture* (2005) that certain individuals have become so embedded within popular culture that they enjoy a kind of celebrity status themselves. Consequently, any discourses that surround these killers and their crimes will further contribute to the killer's mythology and their victims' marginalisation. Focusing on the killer as an exceptional individual also has the effect of shutting down nuanced discussions of the wider sociocultural implications of violence, and how serial murder can be read within these. Two examples of recent true crime outputs that deliberately depart from these well-established genre conventions are Amazon's five-part documentary *Ted Bundy: Falling for a Killer* (referred to hereafter as *Falling for a Killer*) and Rubenhold's book *The Five: The Untold Lives of the Women Killed by Jack the Ripper* (referred to hereafter as *The Five*). Both use a victim-centred framework to present alternative retellings of serial killer cases that have been covered extensively within the true crime genre, and both carefully set the crimes within larger contexts of misogyny and violence against women. In doing so, these narratives provoke reflection upon the true crime genre itself, and how victims have been exploited within it.

Directed by Trish Wood, *Falling for a Killer* examines the effects of infamous serial killer Ted Bundy's crimes on victims, victims' families and those who were close to Bundy himself. The title alludes specifically to the participation of Elizabeth Kendall, Bundy's former girlfriend, who says during her first moments on camera that "The story has been told many times by men. I want to tell the story because I think there are lessons to be learned. Now is the time to talk about this [...] my story from beginning to end" (Wood, 2020b). The documentary quickly frames itself as a retelling of this famous true crime story by women—Kendall's assertion that she wants to talk about her experiences because the story has been "told many times by men" is reinforced by Laura Healy, the sister of Bundy victim Lynda Ann Healy, who notes the way the "Bundy story has been recycled over and over and over again. It makes for great entertainment. He's a fascinating evil character" (Wood, 2020b). The text instantly positions itself in opposition to the traditional retellings of Bundy's crimes, which are described by author Ginger Strand in the same montage to be "a discounting of the stories of the women, in favour of the central hero being the most important character [...] And that is a failure to look deeper and think harder about violence against women in our culture" (Wood, 2020b). In doing so, the documentary offers a retelling of the Bundy case that advocates for a higher edifying (and even pedagogical) purpose than other Bundy narratives—the viewer is told that "there are lessons to be learned" and is invited to "look deeper and think harder". It is suggested that the documentary has larger value than serving as "great entertainment" for true crime fans, and its educational tone is strengthened by *Falling for a Killer*'s efforts to position its narrative within wider contemporary discourses by emphasising links between misogyny in the 1970s to the present day. Care is taken throughout the documentary to build social and political context: many of the episodes incorporate footage from the 1970s accompanied by background information on events such as the "Battle of the Sexes" between Billie Jean King and Bobby Riggs, popular culture outputs associated with feminist sensibilities such as *The Mary Tyler Moore Show* (Brooks & Burns, 1970–1977), and protests supporting the women's liberation movement. Interviews with women who lived in the Seattle area during the time of Bundy's crimes also contribute to creating an image of the 1970s as a time when women's roles in society were being furiously debated. One such interviewee, Py Batemen, the founder of the Feminist Karate Union at the University of Washington, explains "Men who were growing up in the time when women were subservient and came of age when women were moving past that—I believe it triggered some very strong feelings in them, and in some of them it was rage" (Wood, 2020b). The documentary frames Bundy as the embodiment of this rage, and his well-groomed aesthetic and Republican political connections place him in direct opposition to the progressive values of the hippie counterculture and the women's liberation movement and align him with the more "traditional" attitudes to gender roles that were being contested at the time. In this way, the narrative's focus is not solely on Bundy's evil, but on how his violent acts function within wider systems.

It is the ways in which *Falling for a Killer* treats its female subjects that sets this documentary apart from previous retellings of Bundy's crimes. Significantly, its narrative is not constructed as an examination of Bundy's background, but as Elizabeth Kendall's story. Kendall relates how she was a divorced, single mother who met Bundy when she relocated to Seattle after deciding to move away from her conservative family, seeking an "adventure" (Wood, 2020b). Bundy is introduced into the documentary as Kendall's boyfriend only after she has spoken about her own background. Rather than constructing Kendall as the peripheral love interest of a more "famous" man, the documentary focuses on Bundy's place in Kendall's life, which has the effect of casting Kendall, not Bundy, as the story's protagonist. A similar strategy is used throughout the documentary in its treatment of women interviewees—the women being interviewed are invited to talk about their own lives and backgrounds, or those of their murdered loved ones, before the discussion turns to Bundy. This holds true not only for the interviewees who knew Bundy or were his victims, but also for those who were clearly chosen for the documentary because they were *women* who were involved with the case. Although men are also interviewed, they do not provide the most prominent perspectives, and, unlike the women interviewees, their personal stories are never explored (except in the case of Bundy's brother, Richard Bundy, who is treated sympathetically as a victim). For example, the first law enforcement perspectives in the documentary are provided by two women police officers, Cheryl Martin and Kathleen McChesney, and they are both given the opportunity to talk about their experiences of misogyny rising through the ranks in the police before even touching upon their contributions to the Bundy investigation. These women's personal stories, and those of other women involved in the case either directly or tangentially including lawyers, news reporters and academics, provide a narrative of women facing discrimination in male-dominated professions that serves to place Bundy's acts within a larger context of systemic misogyny. Ultimately, *Falling for a Killer* suggests the existence of a cultural reckoning point for the devaluing of women's stories, and interviews with female family members and friends of Bundy's victims, female law enforcement officers, female cultural commentators and Elizabeth and Molly Kendall, shape the documentary's women-centred narrative. Wood explains that this was a deliberate choice: "I think everybody knows [Bundy's] name. Nobody knows who the women were. [...] And I think that any future endeavors like this should focus more on the people who survived and who can talk about the culture in which it happened" (Geller, 2020). Wood's statement places the documentary as part of a post-Me Too discourse, implying a turning point after which there is a moral imperative for future narratives to adopt a more culturally critical perspective.

Rubenhold is similarly aggressive in her reframing of a well-established true crime narrative, writing early in *The Five* that "It is for [the five victims of serial killer Jack the Ripper] that I write this book. I do so in the hope that we may now hear their stories clearly and give back to them that which was so brutally taken away with their lives: their dignity" (2019, p. 16). *The Five* places its advocacy for victims within broader feminist discourses by beginning with an epigraph by Audre Lorde: "I write for those women who do not speak, for those who do not have a voice because they were so terrified, because we are taught to respect fear more than ourselves. We've been taught that silence would save us, but it won't" (Rubenhold, 2019, p. vii). By introducing the narrative with a quotation from a feminist writer well-known for criticising systems of oppression, the text immediately encourages the reader to understand the following recounting of the lives of five nineteenth-century murder victims as part of an ongoing conversation about systemic violence against women and the empowering potential of giving voice to women's experiences. Noting the manner in which stories about Jack the Ripper's crimes have supported a true crime "industry" built upon the killer's mystique at victims' expense, Rubenhold further positions her book as a new approach to a tired and potentially damaging narrative:

> In order to keep [Jack the Ripper] alive, we have had to forget his victims. We have become complicit in their diminishment. When we repeat the accepted Ripper legend […] without questioning the origins of the story and its sources, without considering the reliability of the evidence or the assumptions that contributed to forming it, we not only assist in perpetuating the injustices committed against Polly, Annie, Elizabeth, Kate and Mary Jane but we also condone the basest forms of violence. (2019, p. 348)

The book discusses the murders themselves only in the vaguest and briefest terms at the end of its compelling depictions of the victims' lives, which were often plagued by personal tragedies resulting from the hardships of being working class women in a deeply misogynistic and classist society. *The Five* directly encourages the reader to re-examine their presuppositions about victims' culpability gleaned from consuming previous Jack the Ripper narratives and from their own beliefs about gender , class and sex work. Both *The Five* and *Falling for a Killer* therefore imply that the true crime consumer has a moral obligation to carefully consider the type and quality of narrative they consume, and, more importantly, that this consumption can itself become a form of activism. In displacing the killer as the "hero" of the narrative in order to focus on victims and their stories, the true crime genre moves beyond its status as "entertainment" and achieves a more noble objective of contributing to wider discussions about systemic misogyny. In privileging the victims' suffering over the killer's actions, these newer true crime narratives also add valuable insight to the longevity of the type of misogynistic behaviour to which the Me Too movement responds. Thus, these victim-centred texts exist simultaneously as the result of recent social change and as further evidence of the need for sustained activism.

"He's Said What He's Going to Say by Murdering a Bunch of Women": The Importance of the Female Voice

In positioning women as interviewers, interviewees, narrators and writers, these texts allow the female voice to reappropriate power from the male voices that so often control these stories (whether these are members of the justice system, journalists or, most worryingly, the killer himself). Here, it is not so much about what is being said—although that is of course important—but the fact that these newer retellings provide women's perspectives on the wider social, cultural and political contexts that surround these crimes. This strategy has been deployed most effectively in aural mediums such as podcasts, wherein the disembodied female voice negates the true crime genre's previous reliance on showing or reconstructing the degraded, violated and assaulted bodies of female victims (Greer, 2017, p. 153). The female voice—with its ability to amass an increased feeling of connection, solidarity and sympathy from its largely like-minded audience—is central to the success of true crime comedy podcast *My Favorite Murder with Karen Kilgariff and Georgia Hardstark* (referred to hereafter as *My Favorite Murder*). In offering an unapologetic reframing of true crime which explicitly attacks patriarchy, the pair have become a unique voice within the genre, and, in an important move towards women gaining more power within the true crime industry to retell and reframe, have created their own podcast network, Exactly Right. This allows Georgia Hardstark and Karen Kilgariff to tell the stories however they like, control interactions with their devoted fanbase (lovingly dubbed "Murderinos") and ultimately enjoy levels of flexibility perhaps unavailable to women in more established forms of the media.

The show's simple format, which involves each host taking a turn to tell her co-host about a murder she has been researching, affords Kilgariff and Hardstark the space to weave together sections of humour and feminist discourse with narratives of care and affection. In becoming overwhelmed by the stories being told, Hardstark and Kilgariff strengthen the show's connection to the female victims (Greer, 2017, p. 162) and explicitly align themselves with the suffering of the victim and their loved ones. They use their voices to interrupt each other with whimpers, cries of despair, angry retorts and disappointment at the state of the situation being recounted. For example, in episode 23, "Making a Twenty-Thirderer" (Hardstark & Kilgariff, 2016), Kilgariff tells the story of the attempted murder of Sarah Brady, who while nine months pregnant killed her attacker and potential "fetus-napper" Katie Smith. As Kilgariff recounts the moment Brady fought off Smith's attacks, Hardstark—almost uncontrollably—continues to utter the words "no" or "god," before admitting "I don't think I can deal with this one" (2016). Consequently, Kilgariff and Hardstark—in their role as listeners—act as in-text surrogates for the consumer by offering the "correct" response to these stories. This is equally true in moments of anger. When discussing Netflix's 2019 Ted Bundy documentary *Conversations with a Killer: The Ted Bundy Tapes* (Berlinger)—a text whose release saw Bundy become a sex icon on social media[1] and drew attention to the problematic discourses that still surround true crime content that focuses on the killer rather than the victims—Hardstark offers her frank and unapologetic opinion:

> I watched two episodes and I was like 'why am I so angry and not enjoying this?'. And I am usually interested in Ted Bundy shit, and I realise it's because I have to hear his fucking voice and that's the point of the show [...] And I fucking hate him so much [...] He's a fucking megalomaniac, he's a fucking known liar, and it's not diabolical, he's a little pussy who was intimidated by women and wanted to be famous [...] Like why are we listening to him and his side of the story? (2019b)

In admonishing Netflix's approach, *My Favorite Murder* sends out a rallying cry for the importance of victim-centred true crime content.

---

[1] Following viewers' enraptured responses on social media to Bundy's physical appearance and intellect, Netflix tweeted "I've seen a lot of talk about Bundy's alleged hotness and would like to gently remind everyone that there are literally THOUSANDS of hot men on the service—almost all of whom are not convicted serial murderers" (Netflix, 2019). Even as the documentary itself drew criticism for its focus on Bundy's voice, the platform's reprimand to overly flippant viewers acknowledges the existence of a tension within the true crime genre between the need to provide entertainment and a growing sense of ethical responsibility.

The rawness of Hardstark's impassioned delivery borders on activism, wherein she uses her platform and voice to draw attention to the shortcomings that continue to obscure and negate the significance of the victims' stories. When taken as a whole, *My Favorite Murder* illustrates the potential for female voices to fill long-standing deficiencies in the current media landscape. This ability to counteract traditional true crime models is furthered during the hosts' frequent discussions of their own mental health, which shows them to be, as Horeck notes, "just like us—interested in the prurient details of murder cases, which are now readily available online [. . .] but also ethically minded and appropriately outraged at gross social injustices as we click from source to source to source" (2019, p. 2). This combination—which positions Kilgariff and Hardstark as a caring yet (importantly) hostile voice in the true crime genre—assures the audience that they are equipped to handle the troubling and difficult stories that lay at the core of their show.

The BBC's *The Yorkshire Ripper Files: A Very British Crime Story* (referred to hereafter as *The Yorkshire Ripper Files*)— although it is a documentary and therefore does not benefit from the same level of freedom enjoyed by podcasts—uses the disembodied voice to similar effect. A useful companion piece to *Falling for a Killer*, Liza Williams's documentary about the mishandling of the Yorkshire Ripper manhunt gives voice to a group of previously silenced survivors. Akin to Wood's American counterpart, the series positions serial killer Peter Sutcliffe as a product of his social surroundings, which, in this case, is a northern Britain reacting to growing women's rights activism in the 1970s. However, while the documentary uncovers the roles institutional sexism (particularly the dehumanisation of sex workers), racism and classism played in allowing Sutcliffe to evade police for so long—and are thus central to the more general directives of post-Me Too true crime—it is the role Williams holds as narrator that is worthy of further consideration here. Like Kilgariff and Hardstark, Williams's tone is natural, comforting, stern and authoritative without being alienating or patronising. Laced with a regionality that is too often absent in serious factual programming, Williams states:

My name is Liza Williams. I'm a filmmaker who grew up in the North and heard stories about the Yorkshire Ripper. Now I want to go back 40 years to look at this case with fresh eyes to find out what went so wrong and how the attitudes of 1970s Yorkshire shaped the investigation. (2019b)

In positioning herself within the region where the crimes took place—both in terms of *what* is said and *how* it is said—and stating her personal interest in the case, Williams uses her voice to instantly frame the narrative as hers. She continues in this personal vein by addressing the audience with open-ended questions ("I want to ask: how did 1970s Britain enable its deadliest killer?", 2019b); admitting when she does not have all of the information ("despite the police assumption that Wilma [McCann, Sutcliffe's first victim] was a prostitute, I can't find any clear evidence that she was—maybe the fact that she was a poor single mother, living and socializing within a red light district, was enough", 2019b), and offering her own opinion on the case ("It feels to me that the name 'Ripper' gave the new killer a persona, and one that reinforced the police's theory that he was on a mission to kill prostitutes", 2019b). This mixture of regionality, personal investment, honesty and opinion enables Williams to achieve the type of connection to the audience enjoyed by the hosts of *My Favorite Murder*, even within the more formal framework of a documentary produced by an established institution like the BBC. This is telling of the broader positive movements in the true crime genre, as traditional media outlets—not just newer content providers like streaming services and podcasters—are entrusting women with a platform to reshape these narratives.

Cash-Tag MeToo: Merchandise, Marketing and the Monetisation of Women's Rights Activism and True Crime Content

Nevertheless, efforts to connect with an audience can also raise issues that are intrinsically problematic to the true crime genre, particularly when those efforts are geared towards marketing and possible financial gain for the narrative's producers. When producers use social media to promote their work, wider discourses such as the Me Too movement can be invoked with the use of hashtags. Rubenhold used the hashtag in a Facebook post promoting her book *The Five*: "Proofs of *The Five* have arrived! Publication on 28 February (UK) and early April (US). If you are interested in receiving a copy and are a reviewer, bookseller or work in events or media, let me know! #thefivewomen #metoo #jacktheripper" (Rubenhold, 2018). Rubenhold's post places her work as part of the discourses surrounding Me Too, suggesting a victim-centric approach; however, it also attempts to draw the attention of "reviewers, booksellers, and those who work in events or media" by using this hashtag as well as the hashtag #jacktheripper. The use of this additional hashtag provides context for her work, but it also inevitably evokes the particularly well-known—and often sensationalised—narratives of those murders by using the killer's famous nickname in order to increase interest and promote sales. Although in her work Rubenhold criticises the celebrification of serial killers at their victims' expense, the sales and publicity of that work depend upon readers' knowledge of and interest in previous narratives of the crimes, which have overwhelmingly employed the true crime tropes of the glorification of the killer as an evil genius and the extensive forensic examinations of the victims' mutilated bodies. Though Rubenhold has also invoked #MeToo on social media and in interviews in ways that more directly draw attention to her work's focus, the use of the hashtag for promotional purposes raises an ethical concern that is central to true crime as a genre: does profiting from stories of murder and violence, even if those stories are framed as part of a victim-centric discourse, "[exploit] the lives and experiences of those who have already been exploited too much" (Biressi, 2001, p. 16)?

Another text that can be accused of mobilising the #MeToo hashtag as a recognisable brand across its social media pages is *Killing Theodore* (Calderon, n.d), a yet to be released Bundy docuseries whose marketing has focused on its victim-centred approach. On the docuseries' Twitter, Instagram and Facebook pages, promotional teaser posts are interspersed with—and even interwoven within—posts condemning violence against women as well as those that support crime victims more generally. Most tellingly, *Killing Theodore* directly interacts with social media affiliated with the official Me Too movement. In one such example, *Killing Theodore* reposted an Instagram post from the Me Too movement reading "We are a movement that will always center the needs of survivors" (@metoomvmt, 2019). @killingtheodore responded "We tend to believe that the individuals in our series found a healing factor when they told their stories. Updates on the series coming soon! #metoo #timesup #Theodore #Theodoredocumentary #theodoreadocuseries #believewomen #believesurvivors #rememberthe- victims" (@killingtheodore, 2019). Like Rubenhold, director Celine Beth Calderon recognises Me Too not only as an important part of contemporary women's rights activism, but also a channel through which a producer can achieve increased exposure and attention. Nonetheless, the makers of the documentary did refuse the urge to monetise the prop- erty further, with Calderon claiming that the rise in murderabilia coupled with Bundy's "iconic" status forced them to reconsider the production of T-shirts and other assorted merchandise (Iwasaki, 2020). Even though the sales of these items would have funded the production of the docu- mentary and thus would have ultimately helped to create a platform from which victims could tell their stories, the refusal to profit from Bundy's image draws into focus the myriad of ethical questions surrounding the monetising of true crime content. This need to carefully consider who profits from whose image is particularly important not only within the post-Me Too climate but also with the growing visibility and influence of the Black Lives Matter movement, which has cast the obligation to be socially aware as a key concern for any media producer or consumer. Interestingly, even as *My Favorite Murder* actively targets a young, female audience who would define themselves as sensitive to and aware of these important social movements, the podcast produces a wealth of official merchandise for listeners to consume. Although this is not murderabilia in the sense that Calderon warned, as it promotes the show rather than the murderers, it still utilises true crime, and therefore the stories of murder, rape, incest, cannibalism and paedophilia that act as corner- stones of the genre, as an income stream. The store section of the show's official website offers their Murderinos approximately fifty-three products (at the time of writing—although there have been far more previously), including t-shirts, cups, welcome mats, pins, key rings and puzzles. The sheer variety of goods available rivals that of many mainstream blockbusters or a long-running TV series and shows the manner in which *My Favorite Murder* can be accused of positioning itself as a fandom–a place wherein listeners invest both cultural and economic capital—rather than a platform of change, as we saw in the works of Wood, Williams and Rubenhold.

Most of the products are simple variations on a set formula; a famous saying from the show is placed on a selection of different goods. The sayings themselves have included those celebrating the characteristics and speaking style of the hosts ("Here's the Thing," "Fucking Hooray," and "Spell It Like You Say It"), empowering statements that challenge patriarchal dominance ("Toxic Masculinity Ruins the Party Again" and "Goddammit, Patriarchy, Go To Your Room!"), rude slogans that aid the construction of the listeners' countercultural identities ("Absofuckingtively" and "Ga' Fuck Yourself"), and direct references to true crime ("You're In A Cult, Call Your Dad," "Lock Your Fucking Door," "Starts Bad, Gets Worse," "Stay Out of the Forest," and "Stay Sexy, Don't Get Murdered"). It is, of course, the latter group that raises the most ethical concerns, as they often—even if unintentionally—make light of stories involving the murders or attempted murders of women. For example, "Stay Out of the Forest" originated during a discussion of Marina Vircheva, who survived being thrown down a well by Russian serial killer Alexander Pichushkin. The full quote—"just get a job, buy your own shit, stay out of the forest" (2016) problematically props up the idea that certain kinds of lifestyles or behaviours lead to victimhood. Instead of the progressive reframing seen in *Falling for a Killer* and *The Yorkshire Ripper Files*—where the social–cultural system is investigated in order to explore where these killers came from and why they were allowed to operate for so long—Hardstark and Kilgariff suggest that being economically reliant on men places women in a position of vulnerability and ultimately implies culpability for their own murders. In doing so, *My Favorite Murder* fails to hold the killer completely accountable for his actions and instead engages in problematic discourses around victim blaming. Soon after urging listeners to "stay out of the forest," Kilgariff directly encourages the commercialisation of this problematic content and progresses stereotypes about female victimhood the pair ostensibly set out to challenge by saying "any time we list something in threes, we want you to put it on a poster!" (2016). Although this episode of the podcast pre-dates the popularisation of Me Too movement—and thus took place in an era of less heightened awareness and sensitivity—the merchandise it spawned is produced and consumed within a post-Me Too climate while being attached to a show that clearly identifies itself with the type of content produced as a result of ongoing activism by women. "Starts Bad, Gets Worse"—which was coined during a live show in Baltimore in 2019 and has previously featured on items within the webstore—raises further questions about the show's ability to truly move away from the worrying dialogues that have typified true crime. In addressing potential "outsiders" in the audience who may not be prepared for the comedy aspects of the show, Kilgariff states:

> There are people here who need a bit of an explanation [...] We need you to know that this is, [sic] although, comedy is involved we don't think the worst thing that can happen to a human being is funny, it's not what we joke about [...] That's just how conversationally we process this incredibly terrible news that you will be getting from us, just the worst. Starts bad, gets worse. That's our guarantee to you. (2019a)

This staunch defence of their approach is met with laughter and cheers from the audience, and it clearly adds to the unapologetic tone that defines the show. Yet it is followed by the story of fourteen-year-old Carolyn Wasilewski, who, although being the victim of an unsolved murder that made national headlines in 1954, becomes incidental during the live show. Instead, the hosts spend a significant amount of the time allotted to discussing her murder talking about Baltimore filmmaker John Waters, whose film *Crybaby* (1990) was inspired by her death. More problematically, Kilgariff mocks Wasilewski's appearance, stating "sorry, she's fourteen, what the fuck [...] She's the principal of my grammar school" (2019a). Although minutes before Kilgariff assured the live crowd that "we don't think the worst thing that can happen to a human being is funny," it is the victim—rather than the system, the police or the killer—that becomes the punchline of a joke. The audience is encouraged to laugh at the murdered girl rather than sympathise with her family, condemn the killer or mourn her death. In making a flippant line that precedes a troubling and badly handled story a marketable slogan, the hosts of *My Favorite Murder* show a willingness to exploit the stories in their care for monetary gain. In memorialising these sayings on merchandise, the victim's legacy is no longer under the control of the deceased or her family and friends. Nor is she held as someone to be grieved, an incident to be learnt from, or a casualty of systemic sexism. Instead, the victim becomes a comedic prop; a commercial vessel through which Hardstark and Kilgariff can make related merchandise that fans can consume. Herein, any implied moral obligation to victims is jettisoned in favour of brand building and commerciality.

Still Sexy Even Though He Murdered

As victim-centred true crime grows in prominence and popularity, the tropes that defined previous retellings become increasingly challenged and outmoded. However, regardless of the producers' intentions, some outputs still rely on the damaging traits that dominated true crime prior to the post-Me Too recalibration that is evident in some of the genre's newer productions. The recycling of problematic approaches is seemingly more common when the focus is placed on well-known serial killers as each new output unavoidably feeds the killer's individual brand and swells their mythical status. As has been discussed, victim-centred narratives have worked to mitigate these issues by shifting the focus away from the killer. Despite the problematic aspects outlined earlier, *My Favorite Murder* has often been presented as a significant and much celebrated voice in post-Me Too true crime coverage, wherein its commitment to reacting, fighting, sharing, caring, crying, laughing and talking counteracts male dominance and misogynistic frameworks. Yet when the show tackles the cases of the more prominent figures—such as in the episode "Live at the Neptune" (2017), which focuses on Bundy's crimes—its reliance on traditional true crime storytelling techniques sees the victims discarded and overlooked in favour of a fetishisation of the celebrity killer. Following Hardstark's recounting of the murder of Punk singer Mia Zapata (notably, this is a carefully curated victim-centred story that has all the positive hallmarks of post-Me Too true crime content), she jokingly—but with a sad and remorseful tone—says "take it away Karen! Man I really set you up for failure didn't I?" (2017). Rather than acknowledging the story's emotional impact, Kilgariff confidently states:

Kilgariff: 'Nope [audience laughter]. You wanna know why?'
Hardstark: 'Why?'
Kilgariff: 'Because I'm doing Ted Bundy' [Hardstark and audience erupt in cheers, ohhs, ahhs and applause]. (2017)

Although the crowd's response is not controlled by Kilgariff, her showboating and decision to include a dramatic pause before announcing Bundy's name suggests his brand identity is used to raise the stakes, best Hardstark's story, and impress the live crowd. Once the extended cheers die down, Kilgariff sing-songs Montell Jordan's "This Is How We Do It" (Jordan, 1995) in an act that feeds off the energy of a crowd excited to hear about the crimes of one of the most infamous serial killers in history. Capped off with Bundy being called a "Hometown Super Monster", this opening passage sets the tone for the rest of the show in that it directs attention towards Bundy as a local celebrity, rather than to his victims and the effects of his crimes.

Throughout this show, Kilgariff panders to the live audience, mentioning names of places such as bars and college campuses so as to receive knowing cheers and applause. Although the hosts chastise the audience at times for this reaction, the script is written in such a way that it encourages the crowd to feel connected to *Bundy's* story and actions rather than reflecting on the women he killed. Even in moments when the victims' stories do come into focus, a sense of hurriedness on Kilgariff's part further diminishes their significance:

Kilgariff: 'And when I say murderous rampage, I'm talking about five pages of eleven-point font rampage shit. So, let's blaze through this'.
Hardstark: 'Get comfy everyone'. (2017)

The idea that the crimes—and therefore the life stories of certain victims—need to be "blazed through" directly contradicts the pedagogical value, care and time given to the female agents (be those survivors, family members, friends or those in the justice system) in the likes of *The Yorkshire Ripper Files* and, more tellingly, *Falling for a Killer*, and positions Bundy's prolificness as a hindrance to effective storytelling rather than a tragedy to be examined. In the documentaries—and, for that matter, in many episodes of *My Favorite Murder* that are not recorded in front of a live audience where there is pressure to pander to that audience's regional pride and excitement to hear retellings of well-known local cases by their favourite podcasters—producers provide women with a platform on which they can tell their stories, shifting focus away from the male killer and onto the aftermath left by their actions, and, by extension, the systems that allowed them to operate. *My Favorite Murder*'s approach to the Bundy case does not allow for the same level of consideration, effectively reducing the victims to a list of names whose staggering number is to be marvelled at. In conflating the victims into a tale of one man's evil rather than the loss of thirty women's lives, *My Favorite Murder* positions Bundy as the lead, the star, the returning hero, and problematically furthers the stereotype of the celebrity killer, playing to the audience's fascination with Bundy as an individual and knowingly adding to his status in the space where his impact was most tellingly felt.

However, the podcast—due to its roots as a DIY medium and the continuing lack of professional gatekeepers (Spinelli & Dann, 2019, pp. 7–8)—lends itself to a more spontaneous style of discussion. While this allows for hosts and producers to offer marginal views uncontested, the lack of regulation can lead to an inconsistent and widely variable final product. Horeck, in her discussion of the freedoms enjoyed by true crime podcasts , suggests that the hosts of *My Favorite Murder* "openly privilege their affective responses over rigorous research" (Horeck, 2019, p. 28), which, she claims, has the tendency to annoy some listeners. As we show in our analysis, *My Favorite Murder* can at times be accused of releasing outputs that are not diligent enough to effectively reframe these stories. However, slipping back into potentially damaging narratives can occur in even the most sensitive and carefully constructed texts. While we have largely celebrated the approach of *Falling for a Killer*, episode four of the documentary, "Take Care of Yourself, Young Man" (Wood, 2020d), sees certain genre conventions return unchecked. For example, journalist Steve Winn frames Bundy as a migratory animal who moved to Tallahassee in search of prey, adding to the prevailing image of Bundy as a monstrous entity by evoking images of him as an inhuman lone wolf driven solely by his murderous desires (Wood, 2020d). This is emphasised later in the episode when former Pensacola Police Chief Norman Chapman talks about noticing Bundy's eyes during their first meeting, and the impending sense of doom that seemed to emanate from him. This, Chapman claims, would always be the feeling he got when he was around somebody who murdered someone (Wood, 2020d). Perhaps unsurprisingly, this attempt to "other" Bundy occurs right before the introduction of Kimberly Leach's murder. Most likely due to her age— Leach was twelve years old when she was murdered by Bundy—she is not treated like the other victims. Rather than a description of her life and personality, the documentary instead relies on interviews with people expressing their shock and horror at the fact that she was a child when she was killed. This treatment of Leach removes the discourses so important to creating a fully formed, fully human victim, and with no details of her life preceding her contact with Bundy, Leach is defined by her death at his hands. This allows Bundy to take centre stage, wherein he is given the classic serial killer treatment—he is dehumanised as an animal, a monster, an aberration. Gone too is the cultural context so painstakingly built throughout the rest of the documentary that has suggested that Bundy's violence is part of a larger system of violence against women. The "battle of the sexes" that was set up so clearly in earlier episodes is abandoned in favour of a discussion of Bundy's various performances (in the prison and the courtroom) and the familiar story of Bundy as a charismatic, evil showman who does not "fit the type."

Conclusion: "I Didn't Want to be Marked as a Victim. Ever"

The final part of this chapter shows the inherent problems within the true crime genre and the difficulty in creating content that is able to critically discuss infamous killers without adding to their appeal. As we have demonstrated, even narratives that are sensitively constructed around the victim's story of suffering can lean heavily on tropes that centre on the killer and cast him as a mythologised, monstrous figure. However, the true crime narratives we discuss often deny genre conventions in other important ways. In recent years the examination of victims' bodies in minute forensic detail has become a common motif, and even, for those true crime consumers who enjoy the illusion of participation in the case's solution, part of the genre's overall appeal. As Abigail Biressi argues, these innovations in and popular depictions of forensic science have caused a dehumanizing shift in focus to the victim as an object of forensic investigation rather than a fully realised person. The refusal of the producers considered within this chapter to dwell upon graphic details of victims' post-mortem bodies or how they were killed could be read as a reaction to this trend and as an attempt not only to return humanity to the victims, but also to refuse the victim's—always feminised and, as Biressi maintains, sexualised—objectification (2001, p. 160). In each of the narratives we discuss, the convention of lingering upon every forensic detail of the victims' ravaged bodies is deliberately avoided—for example, the hosts of *My Favorite Murder* often shy away from describing exceptionally violent murders out of professed respect for victims, while *The Five* almost completely removes detailed accounts of some of the most famous crime scenes in history, bar a poignant list of personal effects found on each victim's body. When graphic descriptions of injuries and mutilation to the victims' bodies are otherwise avoided, the impact created can be all the more effective when the power to relate these details is given to the women affected by violence. A key example of this appears in *Falling for a Killer*, when Karen Sparks—a Bundy survivor—recounts her own injuries in her first on-camera interview (Wood, 2020b). Sparks's honest and frank description of her ordeal is even more compelling because Bundy's violence towards his other victims is not examined as directly. In refusing to fill the documentary with discussions and images of mutilated bodies, Wood provides Sparks with an opportunity so often denied victims of abuse—the opportunity to speak about their experiences on their own terms. Sparks's ability to tell her own story means that her body is not objectified or fetishised as a site of forensic examination; rather, her body becomes a vessel through which she can continue to challenge Bundy's actions and exemplify the victim-centred nature of the documentary and the Me Too movement at large. This is typified by her powerfully defiant final line: "Even though I was victimised I wasn't a victim [...] I just wanted to do normal things, be a normal person. I didn't want to be marked as a victim. Ever" (Wood, 2020c). And it is ultimately this possibility for victims to reclaim their stories, bodies and memories in ways not readily available or commercially acceptable pre-Me Too that has defined new directions in post-Me Too true crime content. Although the stories themselves sometimes perpetuate the genre's problematic aspects, their circulation in the mainstream media and increasing popularity offer a platform for more women to create, narrate and engage with a type of true crime that takes into account their voices and their stories.

Study Questions

- What are the pros and cons of engaging with a true crime audience through means such as social media, the sale of merchandise, live podcast episodes, etc.?
- What are the potential dangers of representing the serial killer figure as an aberration or monster?
- How does the podcast format move the true crime genre away from a reliance upon gratuitous depictions of violence?
- Is victim-centred true crime capable of providing the healing and support associated with the Me Too movement, or are such narratives still limited by problematic genre conventions that exploit and/or ignore abused and murdered women?

Bibliography

Biressi, A. (2001). *Crime, fear and the law in true crime stories*. Palgrave Macmillan.
Boling, K. S. (2019). True crime podcasting—Journalism justice or entertainment. *Radio Journal: International Studies in Broadcast & Audio Media, 17*, 161–178.

Boling, K. S., & Hull, K. (2018). Undisclosed information—Serial is my favorite murder: Examining motivations in the true crime podcast audience. *Journal of Radio & Audio Media, 25*, 92–108.

Boyle, K. (2019). *#Metoo, Weinstein and feminism*. Palgrave Macmillan.

Cameron, D., & Frazer, E. (1987). *The lust to kill: A feminist investigation of sexual murder*. Polity.

Capote, T. (1965). *In cold blood*. Random House.

Conversations with a Killer: The Ted Bundy Tapes. Television Programme. (2019). Directed by Joe Berlinger. USA: RadicalMedia, Elastic, Gigantic Studios and Outpost Digital.

Crybaby. Film. (1990). Directed by John Waters. USA: Universal Pictures and Imagine Entertainment.

Geller, L. (2020). '*Falling for a Killer*'. Director Trish Wood wants you to stop trying to psychoanalyze Ted Bundy. *Women's Health*. https://www.womens healthmag.com/life/a30700481/ted-bundy-falling-for-a-killer-director-eli zabeth-kendall/. Accessed 4th May 2020.

Greer, A. (2017). Murder, she spoke: The female voice's ethics of evocation and spatialisation in the true crime podcast. *Sound Studies, 3*, 152–164.

Hardstark, G., & Kilgariff, K. (2016). *My favorite murder with Karen Kilgariff and Georgia Hardstark*, 2016–present [Podcast episode 23 "Making a Twenty-Thirderer"]. Retrieved August 4, 2020, from https://castbox.fm/ episode/23-Making-A-Twenty-Thirderer-id2532140-id215932466?countr y=gb.

Hardstark, G., & Kilgariff, K. (2016–present). *My favorite murder with Karen Kilgariff and Georgia Hardstark* [Podcast audio]. Retrieved August 4, 2020, from https://castbox.fm/channel/2532140?country=gb.

Hardstark, G., & Kilgariff, K. (2017). *My favorite murder with Karen Kilgariff and Georgia Hardstark*, 2016–present [Podcast episode 61 "Live at the Neptune"]. Retrieved August 4, 2020, from https://castbox.fm/episode/61-Live-at-The-Neptune-id2532140-id215932527?country=gb.

Hardstark, G., & Kilgariff, K. (2019a). *My favorite murder with Karen Kilgariff and Georgia Hardstark*, 2016–present [Podcast episode 159 "Live at the Lyric Baltimore"]. Retrieved August 4, 2020, from https://castbox.fm/episode/ 159-Live-at-the-Lyric-in-Baltimore-id2532140-id215932726?country=gb.

Hardstark, G., & Kilgariff, K. (2019b). *My favorite murder with Karen Kilgariff and Georgia Hardstark*, 2016–present [Podcast episode 158 "Burn Day"]. Retrieved August 4, 2020, from https://castbox.fm/episode/158-Burn-Day-id2532140-id215932724?country=gb.

Horeck, T. (2019). *Justice on demand: True crime in the digital streaming era.* Wayne State University Press.

Hosterman, A. R., Johnson, N. R., Stouffer, R., & Herring, S. (2018). Twitter, social support messages, and the #MeToo movement. *The Journal of Social Media in Society, 7,* 69–91.

Iwasaki, S. (2020). New title 'Killing Theodore' breathes new life in Ted Bundy documentary. *Park Record.* https://www.parkrecord.com/entertainment/new-title-killing-theodore-breathes-new-life-in-ted-bundy-documentary/. Accessed 7th August 2020.

Jordan, M. (1995). *This is how we do it.* Oji Pierce and Slick Rick. Def Jam.

Kendall, E. (2020). *The phantom prince: My life with Ted Bundy* (updated and expanded ed.). Abrams.

Killing Theodore (@killingtheodore). (2019, September 22). We tend to believe that the individuals in our series found a healing factor when they told their stories. Updates on the series coming soon! #metoo #timesup #Theodore #Theodoredocumentary #theodoreadocuseries #believewomen #believesurvivors #rememberthevictims. *Instagram Post.* https://www.instagram.com/p/B2uJkBGhNJB/.

Killing Theodore. Television programme. TBC. Created Celene Beth Calderon and Timothy John Psarras. USA: Red Spur Films.

Kissel, B., Parks, M., & Zebrowski, H. (2011–present). *Last podcast on the left* [Podcast audio]. Retrieved August 4, 2020, from https://open.spotify.com/show/3yZg2MCkf31pPXiG4nznrg?si=S4AtuVIuQ9mNhtGJ6HXGiQ.

Lawton, G. (2017). #MeToo is here to stay: We must challenge all men about sexual harassment. *The Guardian.* https://www.theguardian.com/lifeandstyle/2017/oct/28/metoo-hashtag-sexual-harassment-violence-challenge-campaign-women-men. Accessed 12th March 2020.

Mailer, N. (1979). *The executioner's song.* Little, Brown & Co.

Me Too Movement (@metoomvmt). (2019, September 20). We are a movement that will always center the needs of survivors. *Instagram Post.* https://www.instagram.com/p/B2pWSUcCDDf/.

Milano, A. (@Alyssa_Milano). (2017, October 15). If you've been sexually harassed or assaulted write 'me too' as a reply to this tweet. *Twitter.* https://twitter.com/alyssa_milano/status/919659438700670976?lang=en.

Murley, J. (2019). Aftermath: The true crime memoir comes of age. In D. Akrivos & A. Antoniou (Eds.), *Crime, deviance and popular culture: International and multidisciplinary perspectives* (pp. 203–229). Palgrave Macmillan.

Netflix. (@netflix). (2019, January 19, 6:18 p.m.). I've seen a lot of talk about Bundy's alleged hotness and would like to gently remind everyone that there are literally THOUSANDS of hot men on the service—Almost all of whom are not convicted serial murderers. *Twitter*. https://twitter.com/netflix/sta tus/1089950741064601600.

Rubenhold, H. (2018, October 23). Proofs of the five have arrived! Publication on 28 Feb (UK) and early April (US). If you are interested in receiving a copy and are a reviewer, bookseller or work in events or media, let me know! #thefivewomen #metoo #jacktheripper. *Facebook*. https://www.fac ebook.com/HallieRubenholdBooks/photos/proofs-of-the-five-have-arrived-publication-on-28-feb-uk-and-early-april-us-if-y/1907474186003271/.

Rubenhold, H. (2019). *The five: The untold lives of the women killed by Jack the Ripper*. Transworld Publishers.

Schmid, D. (2005). *Natural born celebrities: Serial killers in American culture*. University of Chicago Press.

Spinelli, M., & Dann, L. (2019). *Podcasting: The audio media revolution*. Bloomsbury.

Ted Bundy: Falling for a killer. Television Programme. (2020a). Directed by Trish Wood. USA: Amazon Studios and Saloon Media.

Ted Bundy: Falling for a killer. Television Episode "Boy Meets Girl". (2020b). Directed by Trish Wood. USA: Amazon Studios and Saloon Media.

Ted Bundy: Falling for a killer. Television Episode "Collateral Damage". (2020c). Directed by Trish Wood. USA: Amazon Studios and Saloon Media.

Ted Bundy: Falling for a killer. Television Episode "Take Care of Yourself, Young Man". (2020d). Directed by Trish Wood. USA: Amazon Studios and Saloon Media.

The Mary Tyler Moore show. Television programme. (1970–1977). Created by James L. Brooks and Allan Burns. USA: MTM Enterprises.

The thin blue line. Film. (1988). Directed by Errol Morris. USA: American Playhouse, Channel 4 Television Corporation and Third Floor Productions.

The Yorkshire ripper files: A very British crime story. Television Programme. (2019a). Directed by Liza Williams. UK: Wall to Wall Media and BBC.

The Yorkshire ripper files: A very British crime story. Television Episode "Chapeltown". (2019b). Directed by Liza Williams. UK: Wall to Wall Media and BBC.

Vicary, A., & Fraley, C. R. (2010). Captured by true crime: Why are women drawn to tales of rape, murder, and serial killers? *Social Psychological and Personality—Science, 1*, 81–86.

7

Stalking, the Media and Raising Public Awareness

Maria Mellins

Introduction

This research feeds into a wider context of mounting concern about violence against women and girls. Karen Ingala Smith is identifying and cataloguing the murder of women, by men, in her *Counting Dead Women* blog, and together with Clarissa O'Callaghan has founded the Femicide Census,[1] which reveals a woman in the UK is more likely to be killed by a partner or former partner than any other man, and

---

[1] Definitions of femicide vary. The narrowest definition refers to women killed by their current or former partner, a slightly wider definition extends to women killed by male family members, but as Karen Ingala Smith notes, the Femicide Census looks at a wider definition—women who are killed by men (Femicide Census Webinar for the release of the report, UK Femicides 2009–2018. *If I'm not in on Friday I might be dead*).

M. Mellins (✉)
St Mary's University, Twickenham, UK
e-mail: maria.mellins@stmarys.ac.uk

© The Author(s), under exclusive license to Springer Nature
Switzerland AG 2021
M. Mellins and S. Moore (eds.), *Critiquing Violent Crime in the Media*,
https://doi.org/10.1007/978-3-030-83758-7_7

the number of women known to have been killed by men over the last ten years from 2009 to 2018, reached 1425 (Long et al., 2020). The *We Can't Consent to This* campaign has successfully challenged the use of the 'rough sex' defence in abuse and homicide trials. The murder of Sarah Everard has led to increased media coverage of public concern for women's safety on UK streets, exemplified by the 'Reclaim these Streets' website and the vigil on Clapham Common that saw controversial arrests of women for breaching Covid-19 restrictions. Meanwhile, the Covid-19 lockdowns have prompted media discussion of domestic abuse and femicide. This is a global issue, with Mexico's nationwide protests against femicide following the brutal murder of Ingrid Escamilla and Fátima Cecilia Aldrighett, France's 'NousToutes' (All of Us) protest against rising femicide rates, the 'Not One Less' protest in Argentina, as well as the mass scream against domestic violence and gender inequality in Switzerland, as 'men's violence against women is a leading cause of the premature death for women globally,' (Femicide Census, 2020).

This chapter focuses on one particular type of crime that poses a significant threat in the UK and beyond—stalking. In the UK, one in five women, and one in ten men will be stalked in their lifetime and there were an estimated 1,472,000 victims of stalking in England and Wales in 2018/19 (ONS, 2019, see also Bracewell et al., 2020). Whilst in recent years, stalking has received significant attention from the criminal justice system, support services, charities, researchers and trainers, who aim to educate others on the catastrophic impact of stalking, it is still a crime that is not identified, is under-reported and misunderstood. Sheridan's (2005) research tells us that 75 percent of people suffer 100 incidents of stalking before reporting to the police. The term 'stalking' is often minimised; phrases like, 'I stalked them on social media,' are common in modern life. 'Romantic' narratives of stalking are plentiful in popular culture and most recently stalking has been used as a humorous gesture on Valentine's day cards (for instance, cards are available that depict the character of Joe from the Netflix series *You*—who is shown to stalk, kidnap and murder—accompanying the image of Joe is a strapline 'Stalker is a strong word, I prefer Valentine' and 'From your stalker').

Stalking is also often associated with celebrity. As Lowney and Best (1995) assert, stalking became much more visible in media of the late

1980s when it was framed as a news story of obsessed fans who engage in 'star-stalking.' Such links to celebrity can lead people to believe that stars are the main target, or that it is a crime that is very rare and largely involves strangers lurking behind bushes. However, stalking is a crime that can affect anyone. As Mullen et al.'s (2009) research outlines, motivations for stalking vary greatly and can be broadly organised into five types. Some stalkers are motivated by a fantasised or 'delusional' love for someone that they do not currently have a relationship with, in the belief, or hope that they will achieve one (*Intimacy Seeker* in Mullen et al., 2009). Others are motivated by a desire to get a date with someone or a short-term sexual relationship, but lack the necessary social training, as a result they may pursue someone in a crude, 'inept or unreasonably persistent manner' (the *Incompetent Suitor*). In some instances, stalking is motivated by a sense of 'injustice and/or humiliation,' which is a driver for perpetrators' attempt to achieve retribution and regain a sense of control (the *Resentful* stalker). In some cases, stalking is motivated by a 'sadistic sexuality' that is for sexual gratification or preparatory to an assault (the *Predatory* stalker). However, the most common motivation for stalking behaviour, which makes up around half of all stalking cases, and usually the most violent, high-risk cases, are perpetrated by ex-partners and those who have previously had some form of intimate relationship with the person they are stalking (the *Rejected* stalker). Whilst overall, stalkers can be any gender, nearly 90 percent of perpetrators in the rejected stalker category are men, who predominantly stalk women (Mullen et al., 2009, p. 70).

The impacts of stalking cannot be underestimated. Those who are subjected to stalking are often told to ignore the unwanted attention, or even, to feel flattered by it. However, in reality, during my ISAC training (Independent Stalking Advocacy Caseworker) and my work supporting victims-survivors, I have observed that stalking takes a great deal from people; it has been described as 'emotional rape' and 'psychological terrorism' (Suzy Lamplugh Trust, 2020). Stalking is a complex, insidious crime, where the absence of violence does not necessarily reduce risk to those who are targeted. It can cause extreme alarm and distress and force people to significantly change aspects of their life. These impacts can isolate people from their support networks and social life. Those experiencing stalking may delete social media sites, avoid certain routes to work, not use their garden or even become housebound. It can cause significant emotional and psychological harm and result in mental health conditions such as depression, anxiety and post-traumatic stress, as well as impacting physical health in the form of sleep deprivation, weight fluctuations and dizziness, amongst other symptoms. Stalking has financial implications. People may be forced to invest in expensive security equipment; they may lose their jobs. If a stalker is a previous or current partner, a person may be prevented from accessing their finances, they may be subject to violence and coercive controlling behaviours and this can have devastating effects on children within the relationship and can also lead to people being revictimised through the courts. In high risk, extreme cases, stalking can result in murder and suicide.

Whilst stalking affects all age groups, and it is a misconception that domestic violence and stalking do not impact on older age groups, young people are at a high-risk of being stalked.[2] During their 'Unfollow Me' campaign, *Vice* in collaboration with Paladin National Stalking Advocacy Service and the Alice Ruggles Trust carried out a survey of 12,000 young people aged 13–24, which found that 35 percent of this group had personally been subjected to stalking, whilst 56 percent knew someone who had been a victim (*Vice*, 2018). Fissel et al. also found that 'Stalking victimization prevalence rates for college student samples appear to be much larger when compared to those from the nationally representative adult samples' (2020, p. 21). However, as this chapter will outline through a consideration of Alice Ruggles, recognition and identification of stalking and coercive control is not widespread amongst those of college and university age groups. This is reflected more widely in NUS (National Union of Students) research, 'Hidden Marks: A study of women students of harassment, stalking, violence and sexual assault' (2010). The NUS commissioned the research within universities as they perceived that students were at a higher risk of experiencing stalking

---

[2] Further research into age and stalking cases is crucial to ascertain the specific risks posed to people at certain times of their lives. This is particularly concerned with young people, but there needs to be further understanding of how stalking affects people at other life stages including the lifelong effects on the children of ex-partner stalking cases, as well as people from older age groups and vulnerable categories.

and sexual violence, but that there was 'little awareness of this amongst students.'

> This report is a wake-up call. We must act now to break the silence: violence against women students is widespread, serious, and is hampering women's ability to learn. This report is just the start of the work that the NUS Women's Campaign will be undertaking to tackle violence against women students. But we can't end the violence alone. Institutions, students' unions and students have a pressing responsibility to take immediate action to tackle the problem.
> (Olivia Bailey, NUS National Women's Officer, 2010)

Over a decade later, the recent Statement of Expectations released by the Office for Students continues to call for the implementation of more 'effective systems, policies and processes to prevent and respond to incidents of harassment and sexual misconduct,' (OfS, 2021) demonstrating the urgent need to address safety and young people. Given the myths and misunderstandings of stalking and the prevalence of this crime amongst all age groups, but particularly the younger generation, it is the central aim of this chapter to outline the need for increased societal awareness of stalking and more specifically the requirement for education to tackle this public health issue. This education should come in many forms, including formal education in schools, colleges and universities, but also placing an emphasis on the role of the media to shed light on this important topic, so that they might help the public to recognise stalking behaviour and guide them to much-needed support. This chapter draws on case study analysis of Alice Ruggles, in order to underline key features of stalking behaviour that need to be more easily identified by bystanders, as we never know when our advice may be needed. Whilst factors of the criminal investigation and legislation of stalking will be considered, the focus here is on how Alice's case can be used to raise *public* awareness of stalking, especially amongst young people, so that fixated and obsessive behaviour can be identified. The author would encourage further reading of Alice's *Domestic Homicide Review* (2018) for details of the police response to Alice's case, and how it highlighted an urgency for criminal justice adjustments and reform.

Before addressing Alice's case, it is important to reflect on how this research has been carried out and the methodology employed. The research for this chapter has developed out of my own experience as an Independent Stalking Advocacy Caseworker (ISAC) and a Trustee for the Alice Ruggles Trust. Alongside this practice-based experience, this chapter is also based upon a media analysis of key written and audio-visual documents, such as ITV documentary *An Hour to Catch a Killer*, Channel 5 documentary *Murdered by My Stalker*, *Real Crime Profile* podcast episode 'My Daughter Alice,' and the *Vice Broadly* campaign 'Unfollow Me,' as well as document analysis of Alice's *Domestic Homicide Review*[3] (DHR, 2018), government reviews and legislation. It is important to point out that this chapter focuses on *one* particular stalker typology, the ex-partner or rejected stalker, whose motivation comes from a need for 'reconciliation or revenge for rejection' (Mullen et al., 2009). This chapter's focus on ex-partner stalkers who have been in an intimate relationship with the victim-survivor, is due to the relative commonality of this type of stalker and the high risk that they pose, but ex-partner stalkers have also been selected because this type of stalker is not necessarily what the public, and to some extent, the police, perceive stalkers to be like, when compared to stalking cases that involve strangers (see Weller et al. research on public perceptions of stalking, 2013). It is now crucial to begin this chapter with a rounded understanding of Alice Ruggles; readers are encouraged to read Box 7.1 'Alice's Story,' that shares details of Alice's life.

---

[3] Domestic Homicide Reviews are a multi-agency review that were introduced in England and Wales in 2011, they are a statutory requirement in order to review the circumstances of deaths for the purpose of homicide prevention. With a report of over 100-pages, 32 key findings, and 20 recommendations Alice's *Domestic Homicide Review* presents valuable learnings concerning managing risk and homicide prevention.

Box 7.1: Alice's Story (With Thanks, Alice Ruggles Trust Website)

Alice's family and friends will always remember her for her happy and outgoing personality. She had the ability to cheer anyone up when they were down; she was incredibly quick-witted, a brilliant listener, and genuinely empathetic. She quickly made friends wherever she went.

Alice was the third of the four Ruggles children, and grew up with her sister and brothers in the quiet Leicestershire village of Tur Langton. The family was a close-knit one and Alice always managed to make her presence known, whether by her jokes, her mischievous pranks, or later by the endless banter on the family WhatsApp group. She was a natural entertainer, who could be found not only singing in school concerts but also leading the karaoke at friends' parties when she was as young as nine.

For her senior years at school Alice chose to attend Leicester High School for Girls where her mother Sue worked. Making friends was second nature to her and she was popular and successful there, playing a lead role in the school pantomime, performing comic pieces in house events, singing in the chamber choir, and narrowly missing becoming the victrix ludorum on sports day when she fell flat on her face at the start of her final race (something she thought was hilarious). She also helped younger pupils with their Duke of Edinburgh's Award, helped to organise the school ball ... the list is endless.

The Ruggles family Christmas was a three-day affair: no-one ever missed one, even after the children had moved away from home and everyone was scattered around the country. At Alice's insistence, the serious eating would always kick off with an enormous Chinese meal on her birthday, Christmas Eve.

Having discovered fencing at a PGL camp at age eleven, the sport soon became an important part of Alice's life. Her chosen weapon was the epee, and she represented her home county of Leicestershire and the East-Midlands region on many occasions; she also enjoyed success on the national fencing circuit. By the time she was eighteen, Alice was selecting potential universities based on the strengths of their fencing clubs, and she duly chose Northumbria, where she became club captain. The proudest of her achievements was winning the Women's Epee at the Leeds Open in 2012.

Alice stayed in Newcastle after graduation, having come to love the city. After a while she secured a job at media giant Sky's Newcastle hub, where she was quickly promoted to become site coordinator and PA to the head of sales. One of her colleagues wrote of her: "You know I'm not a man of many words, unless it was badgering you to get my laptop ordered, so I just wanted to list my best memories of you. Genuinely, the most horrific Manchunian accent I have ever heard. EVER. Absolutely awful. And hilarious in equal measure. You taught me the difference between foil, epee and sabre. I still won't watch it at the Olympics. You are more sarcastic than me. Your sense of humour was second to none. So witty and sharp as a tack. Last, but definitely not least, you had the most infectious personality and brightened the office on a daily basis. I can genuinely say any day I spoke to you was a happier one for it. You never failed to make me laugh, and I'm a miserable sod. You could even do it via an e-mail..." and the e-mail attached reads "Laptop wait time is directly proportional to how nice you are to me. Therefore yours is due for delivery in 2074. Thanks, Alice"

Alice Ruggles

Alice Ruggles was kind, clever and beautiful. She had an infectious personality and an incredible sense of humour: she saw the fun side of everything. She loved life, loved her friends and loved her job. She had so much to live for. Tragically, Alice was murdered in Gateshead on 12 October 2016, aged just 24. (Alice Ruggles Trust, 2020)

Summary of Key Events

Alice was originally from Leicestershire, but moved to Newcastle for university and remained living there after she graduated. Alice knew Trimaan Dhillon for just one year. They were introduced online by a mutual friend whilst Dhillon served as a soldier in Afghanistan; he returned to the UK in January 2016 where they met in-person for the first time. Dhillon then flew back to Afghanistan for a further two months. Their face-to-face relationship, which lasted for less than eighteen weeks, started well, but Dhillon increasingly sought to control Alice. She fell out with friends, lost weight and became withdrawn and isolated. In August 2016, Alice received a message from a woman who Dhillon had contacted on social media. This, and discovering Dhillon had told

Fig. 7.1 Image of Alice Ruggles (Courtesy of the Alice Ruggles Trust)

her other lies, spurred Alice to end their relationship. Dhillon then went on to stalk Alice, and despite Alice reporting him to the police and being served a Police Information Notice (PIN), Dhillon continued to bombard Alice with messages, phone calls and letters. He tracked Alice both digitally and physically. On the 12 October, a colleague gave Alice a lift home from work. At this time, Dhillon parked his car down the road from Alice's flat. As he waited in his car, he sent texts to another woman arranging to meet up with her. Fourteen minutes after Alice arrived home, Dhillon broke into her ground floor flat, and brutally

Fig. 7.2 Image of Alice Ruggles (Courtesy of the Alice Ruggles Trust)

murdered her. A short time later, Alice's flatmate returned to the property, but could not gain entry through the front door. Feeling something was terribly wrong, she climbed through the window at the rear of the property and found Alice in the bathroom. She called the emergency services; as she did so, she screamed Dhillon's name. Dhillon was arrested shortly afterwards and was found guilty of Alice's murder. He is now serving a life sentence with a minimum tariff of twenty-two-years for the murder of Alice. Alice's parents, Sue and Clive, her sister Emma, and brothers Nick and Patrick, set up the Alice Ruggles Trust with the mission to help prevent what happened to Alice happening to others.

Alice's case was well-known and attracted widespread media attention. The case became high profile for a number of reasons, not least because it embodied a number of news values that are prominent in the construction and selection of news stories. Jewkes explains that editors and journalists sift and select news stories based on their 'news values' and ability to garner public interest (2015, p. 49). Alice's young age, beauty, warm personality, loving family and friends, good job, in contrast to the shock and devastation enacted by Dhillon, is in line with the news value of 'violence and conflict' that was extremely pronounced in this case. Wider news values such as 'risk' and 'individualisation' were also present in the initial reporting of this case. Another reason for the case's widespread coverage is the visual 'imagery' (Jewkes, 2015, p. 49) available to news outlets. The media had unprecedented access to Alice's case. Documentary filmmakers were already filming *An Hour to Catch a Killer* in Forth Banks Police Station, Newcastle Upon Tyne, when Alice's murder took place. When the 999 call was made by Alice's flatmate, the crew began filming Detective Chief Inspector Lisa Theaker and her team from Northumbria Police force. They followed their movements and for the first time, detectives wore high-definition bodycams, providing unique insights into the investigation, including footage of police and forensic officers as they entered Alice's flat, and later as they arrested, questioned and charged Dhillon with her murder.

Whilst Alice's case included news values that were initially responsible for the story being selected and represented widely within the news cycle, the presence of other important elements has maintained its longevity and relevance as a key case study, used in stalking training and conferences to raise awareness of stalking. This chapter now turns to consider the first of these important features—the prevalence of coercive control within stalking and the need to understand links with domestic abuse and dating violence.

Coercive Control

Coercive control was made an offence under Section 76 of the *Serious Crime Act 2015*. Whilst not all ex-partner stalking cases involved coercive control and intimate partner violence during the actual relationship, these are often key features in this type of stalking case. After relationship separation, the offender, now devoid of their partner to enact these behaviours on, may turn to stalking.[4] In this way, they replace

---

[4] However, this isn't to suggest that for many, these behaviours do not also occur within the relationship, for instance tracking practices may occur at any time, not just after separation, and coercive control certainly continues after a relationship ends.

the time they would have spent with their partner on stalking activities: planning, surveying, tracking, so they exchange one form of control for another. This can be more time intensive than a full-time job. Both coercive control and stalking are pattern based, as opposed to incident based, offences (Scott et al., 2020) and are often undetected by family, friends, law enforcement and even the person who is being subjected to these behaviours. The independent behaviours may not appear threatening in isolation, but when examined as part of a pattern carry a very high risk and are tantamount to what Evan Stark (2007) has called a hostage situation. In his seminal work, *Coercive Control. How Men Dominate Women in Personal Life,* Stark states that whilst coercive control may be interweaved with physical assault which, in the worst cases, can lead to fatality, 'the primary harm abusive men inflict is political, not physical, and reflects the deprivation of rights and resources that are critical to personhood and citizenship' (2007, p. 5). Stark underlines that control is the aim of the offender, and is achieved over time through microregulation of everyday routine roles, such as withholding access to money, food, transport and communication (2007, p. 5).

In her book *See What You Made Me Do: Power Control and Domestic Abuse* (2020) Jess Hill highlights links between the pattern of coercive and controlling behaviour in domestic abuse and Prisoners of War camps in 1950s. Both situations include a perpetrator that lives alongside their captive for a significant amount of time, who gradually isolates them from others and becomes the most important person in their life. It is this gradual take-over that causes the captive person to experience a shift in attitudes and beliefs. Hill states that Albert Biderman (1957) studied the use of coercive control techniques employed in North Korean POW camps where American soldiers had given false confessions. After interviewing POWs on their return, Biderman found that contrary to press claims that Chinese communists in charge of the camps had developed a new weapon of 'brainwashing' and possessed mind controlling abilities that could implant soldiers' brains with new memories; what had actually occurred was the age-old technique of coercive control—instilling dependency, debility and dread (Hill, 2020, p. 15). In this way, the captors gain control of their captive so they become compliant, dependent and begin to share their world view.[5] But as psychiatrist and trauma specialist Judith Herman explains, control is not gained immediately, instead victims-survivors are 'taken prisoner gradually, by courtship' (Herman, 2001, p. 82). Jane Monckton Smith (2019, 2021) asserts in her *Homicide Timeline*, in the early instances of the relationship there is a period of courtship during which perpetrators draw their partner in, seeking 'early and firm commitment.' Jealousy may also be demonstrated during this phase, but positioned as a normal aspect of love (2019, p. 14). This equates to an expedited sense of love and devotion, a 'grand passion' (Fisher 2004 in Monckton Smith, 2019, p. 13) or what Laura Richards terms, when discussing the relationship between Alice and Dhillon, 'love bombing' (Real Crime Profile, 2018).

Initially, Alice and Dhillon's relationship echoed this early phase and was not immediately characterised by abuse. This is not to say that these psychological aspects were not present at this early stage. Alice's brother notes, that initially when Dhillon first met Alice there weren't clear signs, but 'he was trying very hard' (*Vice Broadly* 'Unfollow Me'). He gave Alice gifts and paid her lots of compliments. Dhillon demonstrated intensity, and a need for early commitment from Alice from the outset. Dhillon met Alice after he saw some photographs of her on holiday in Sri Lanka on a mutual friend's social media site. Dhillon messaged the friend, telling her that 'your friend is one of the most naturally beautiful girls I've ever seen and could she help him contact Alice' (DHR, 2018, p. 30). Their online relationship developed, and before long he urged Alice to make their relationship more official and to call him her boyfriend. This intensity also impacted on the amount of contact Dhillon wanted to have with Alice. For the first three months of their relationship, their communication was entirely through phone calls, messages and sending gift parcels. Alice didn't actually meet Dhillon until he returned from his posting in Afghanistan in January 2016. In spite of being separated physically, work friends commented on the amount of contact Alice had with Dhillon. Whilst they appeared to be getting on well at this stage, friends noticed that Alice often spent lunchbreaks calling or texting him

---

[5] Biderman's chart consists of eight techniques – isolation, monopolisation of perception, induced debility or exhaustion, cultivation of anxiety and despair, alternation of punishment or reward, demonstration of omnipotence, degradation, and the enforcement of trivial demands.

and Alice texted her sister saying: 'he speaks [to me] every day [...] and he gets really upset if we can't speak, it's so nice' (DHR, 2018, p. 30).

As the relationship progressed, Dhillon's behaviour became increasingly domineering. The pattern of controlling behaviour was subtle and typically clandestine, Stark refers to these behaviours as 'technologies' including isolation, intimidation and control (2007, p. 228). Over the course of their relationship Dhillon began to isolate Alice from friends and family. She fell out with her housemates and moved to a ground floor flat in Gateshead with her friend and work colleague. Alice's friend articulated Dhillon's isolation of Alice during the documentary *Murdered by My Stalker* (2018). She stated that:

> He wanted to spend all of his time, and her time, in the flat. He wouldn't go out drinking or socialising because he wouldn't want her to be in the pub late, dressed up and having people look at her, and perhaps find her attractive.

Dhillon sought a constant presence in all aspects of Alice's life, to the point where he would arrive uninvited at events, despite the significant geographical distance between them (of approximately 130 miles). Dhillon would confront Alice about items on her social media newsfeed, about where she had been and who she was socialising with. For instance, Alice's *Domestic Homicide Review* contains details of when Alice stayed with her parents for the Christmas period, which also included Alice's birthday on Christmas Eve. Alice still had not met Dhillon face-to-face at this stage. On Alice's birthday, Dhillon was annoyed with Alice for being involved in an event that he didn't want her to attend. In response, he sent her a message about another woman, which upset Alice (DHR, 2018, p. 31). Later in their relationship, when Dhillon returned to the UK, Alice attended a work meeting in Edinburgh, which included a night's stay in a hotel. Alice went out for a meal and drinks with work friends, and colleagues noticed that she was distracted by messages on her phone and 'looked anxious and worried.' One of Alice's colleagues actually took her phone and suggested she contact him in the morning instead, but later that night, Dhillon appeared at the work event and an argument ensued. When they came down for breakfast, colleagues recalled that Alice looked upset, as if 'they'd been arguing all night' (DHR, 2018, p. 32).

The *Vice Broadly* video that was produced as part of the 'Unfollow Me' campaign includes interviews with Alice's parents and brother, which further expand on the extent of controlling behaviour. During the five-minute short film, her father Clive describes how Alice lost friends, her self-confidence diminished, and she was physically losing weight. Her mother Sue underlines how 'he used all sorts of things to persuade her, she didn't have enough money, she shouldn't go out.' By employing controlling behaviour, Dhillon undermined Alice's confidence. This slowly dissolved her self-worth and morphed her perspective on how she viewed herself and others. From the information available in Alice's *Domestic Homicide Review*, it is evident that by carrying out small actions that feed into a wider pattern of micromanagement of everyday routines, from selecting clothes, to comments about her appearance, Dhillon attempted to control Alice and this was carried out with such subtlety, Alice herself was not even fully aware of her control deficit within the relationship.

As time passed, the situation became even worse for Alice. As the Alice Ruggles Trust documents, 'the cumulative effect of Dhillon's behaviour on Alice was very marked indeed. In a few months, from the happy, outgoing, vibrant person she had been, she had become miserable and lonely. Her work was adversely affected' (Alice Ruggles Trust Website, 2020). One particular event that took place a few weeks later, revealed Dhillon to be, in Alice's words, 'possessive, mind-controlling and manipulative.' It was a moment that Alice, herself, felt that he had 'gone too far' (DHR, 2018, p. 36). Alice recounted the circumstances to her flatmate, describing how she had been in the shower, when Dhillon wanted to get in to use the bathroom. He banged relentlessly on the door and once he gained entry, he demanded that she must stand in the kitchen, sopping wet, until he had finished in the bathroom. Alice also discovered that Dhillon had been in contact with other women (the full extent of his unfaithful behaviour emerged later). Having lost trust in Dhillon, Alice ended the relationship. Unfortunately, in keeping with the rejected stalker type, Dhillon would not let Alice leave. The more concrete the separation, the more Dhillon lost control over Alice. He therefore began to adopt other measures to maintain his sense of power and dominance; a campaign of stalking and veiled threats. A text message that he wrote to Alice demonstrates his sense of ownership: 'I'm not used to losing something that belongs to me' (DHR, 2018, p. 40).

Stalking Methods and Risk

Whilst there is no recognised legal definition of stalking,[6] the College of Policing have released a useful mnemonic to outline stalking behaviour. If the behaviour is Fixated, Obsessed, Unwanted and Repeated (FOUR) it should be identified as stalking. Whilst this does function as a useful tool for focusing on behaviours, it is important to keep in mind that the mnemonic does not underline the aspects of fear and distress that are caused by stalking. Paladin National Stalking Advocacy Service defines stalking as, '[a] pattern of unwanted, fixated and obsessive behaviour which is intrusive and causes fear of violence or serious alarm or distress' (Paladin Website, 2020). The methods of stalking are extremely varied and this is reflected in the 'behaviours' outlined in the stalking legislation, the *Protections of Freedoms Act 2012*, which was an amendment to the *Protection from Harassment Act 1997*. For instance, one act of stalking outlined in the legislation concerns 'contacting, or attempting to contact, a person by any means' (Protections of Freedoms Act, 2012). This can be by constant insertion into someone's life, by turning up at work, home, family or friends' homes, or a place of study. It might be writing on a person's social media, incessantly messaging or calling them. Or it might be more manipulative, subtle gestures of driving past their house at the same time every day, leaving notes and gifts. The legislation includes, 'following a person,' or surveillance, this can be 'spying' or 'loitering' in their space, tracking their car. It can be using apps to survey their whereabouts online, downloading data and monitoring phones. There are methods that are designed to appear innocuous to everyone

---

[6] Whilst a definition may be useful to raise awareness, there are benefits to this lack of definition, as if imposed, perpetrators may engage in behaviours at the fringes of the legislative definition and this may quickly result in a narrow, outdated understanding of stalking, which does not fully reflect the spectrum of behaviours.

apart from the person that is being stalked. These can be mental mind games and gas lighting behaviours, which don't appear to be threatening until viewed as a pattern of behaviour. For instance, 'interfering with any property in the possession of a person' (Protections of Freedoms Act, 2012) is often reported in stalking cases, and can involve acts like moving around garden furniture, or removing/inserting items within their home. Actions can be chilling, designed to cause terror and trauma. Justene Reece was stalked by her ex-partner Nicholas Allen, in Staffordshire. Justene tragically took her life in February 2017 as a result of Allen's stalking. Nicholas Allen relentlessly stalked Justene and other people within her life[7]; he threatened her son, committed violent acts, made fake claims about sexual offences of a family member and posted offensive pictures of her mother's grave on social media. Allen was brought to trial on a charge of 'unlawful killing' and was sentenced to ten years for manslaughter. On sentencing the judge stated that Justene took her life 'as a direct result of your sustained and determined criminal actions – actions which you clearly knew were having a profound effect upon her' (Chambers in Tapley & Jackson, 2019, p. 94).

Justene's ex-partner had a history of abusive behaviour dating back to 1998. A report carried out by The Independent Office for Police Conduct found that there were 34 occasions where police received reports of incidents, either reported directly by Justene, or by her friends and family, 16 of these were not cross-referenced and the police investigation failed to see the wider pattern of abuse. Detective Chief Constable Nick Baker of Staffordshire Police acknowledged that 'we did not understand the impact that Nicolas Allen was having on Justene, we did not listen to her as a victim' (Channel 4 News, 2019). The report found that further training was needed for Staffordshire police 'to improve the linking of incidents and crimes' (ICPO website). Given Allen's abusive relationship history (which was on record after Justene had applied for a Domestic Violence Disclosure Scheme) it is crucial for police and wider services to have a joined-up approach that cross references evidence so that serial offenders do not continue to go unnoticed. Missing these

---

[7] Sheridan's research from 2005 found that on average 21 people in the victims life will be impacted.

signposts and deeming violence as 'one-off incidents' can result in fatalities. Clare's Law, named after Clare Woods who was murdered in 2009 by her ex-partner who had a history of violence against women is an important development that recognises the risks of a previously abusive relationship history. Under Clare's Law, partners, close friends or relatives can apply for a Domestic Violence Disclosures Scheme (DVDS), which can reveal information about their partners previous offences and convictions. Whilst this is a step in the right direction, campaigners have called for a more centralised, statutory tracking system for serial offenders.

The *Real Crime Profile* podcast is very effective in using its platform to raise awareness of issues related to stalking, domestic abuse and homicide. The episode, 'Profiling Serial and Serious Domestic Violence Perpetrators and Stalkers,' (2020) documents the campaign for the Domestic Abuse Bill, and particularly the New Clause for 'serial and serious domestic violence perpetrators and stalkers' to be tracked in order to prevent further abuse. During the episode, Laura Richards presents case studies of women who have been murdered by their ex-partner who have a history of abuse. Laura discusses the case of Hollie Gazzard, who was stalked and murdered by Asher Maslin who had been involved in 24 previous violent offences. Kerri McAuley was stalked and murdered by Joe Storey who had convictions for abuse dating back to when he was 14, including two restraining orders. Theodore Johnson murdered Yvonne Johnson in 1981 in her Wolverhampton home, he was sentenced for manslaughter for the 'provocated' murder. He then went on to murder Yvonne Bennett in 1993, and Angela Best in 2016. This episode joins others from the *Real Crime Profile* podcast to raise awareness of these crimes. The discussion provides important insights into the victim's perspective, and also educates the public on the need for change within the criminal justice system. At the time of writing this chapter, the Domestic Abuse Bill has received Royal Assent, but the serial abusers and stalkers amendment (amendment 42) was defeated. Whilst this amendment has not been included in the new legislation, Laura Richard in her podcast *Crime Analyst (2021)*, highlights important changes that will take place as a result of the campaign. These include a comprehensive perpetrators strategy, new Multi-Agency Public Protection System (MAPPS database), new statutory guidance on expanding Category 3, domestic abuse and stalking services to be included at Multi-Agency Public Protection Arrangements (MAPPA) and £25 million invested in government funds.

Returning to Jane Monckton Smith's (2019, 2021) research on the eight stages of the *Homicide Timeline* is useful as this also highlights the need to understand an offender's relationship history. During stage one, 'pre-relationship,' Monckton Smith outlines that a previous relationship history is a risk indicator for intimate partner homicide. 'It was found that a history of controlling patterns, domestic abuse, or stalking was present in every case where a pre-relationship history was recorded' (Monckton Smith, 2019, p. 1274). The history of the pattern of behaviour varied from serial convictions to informal reports and allegations from former partners. Therefore, prominent research within this field is signalling the need to view risk as a pattern of behaviour, and an important part of this pattern is tracking the abuser as he enters new relationships to identify the trajectory of risk. This fundamental need to adopt a broader perspective of stalking, to see the pattern of behaviour, is also echoed in training sessions delivered by Paladin National Stalking Advocacy Service, particularly when using risk assessments such as the DASH Risk Checklist.[8] Alongside previous relationship history, there are a number of risk factors that need to be closely assessed; these indicators include previous use of weapons, suicidal ideation, a sense of entitlement, excessive jealousy, previous incidence of strangulation, sexual abuse, abuse of children, mental health, alcohol and drug abuse, amongst others. However, when considering risk within stalking cases, Paladin underline that it is vital to keep in mind that the DASH, or comparable risk assessments, should not be viewed as tick box exercises. Risk is dynamic. As new behaviours occur, risk levels will shift, which is why it is crucial to repeat risk assessments. Police officers, advocates and wider services must examine the pattern, or what Alice's *Domestic Homicide Review* refer to as 'the clusters of behaviour' involved. Alice's *Domestic Homicide Review* highlights key risk behaviour clusters in stalking cases,

---

[8] DASH Risk Checklist stands for Domestic Abuse, Stalking and Honour-Based Violence Risk Identification, Assessment and Management Model (DASH Risk Model, 2009).

which include (i) a history of stalking behaviour, (ii) the presence of stalking, control or abuse, (iii) separation and (iv) escalation.

History of Stalking

Alice's Domestic Homicide Review contains details about a previous offence, which took place in 2014, when Dhillon appeared before Kent Magistrates Court and was given a restraining order relating to his behaviour towards his ex-partner. Dhillon's ex-girlfriend had arranged to meet her new partner in a busy high-street. On her way to the meeting, Dhillon appeared, and began to behave in an aggressive manner, blocking her path. As the argument ensued, her new partner arrived. The argument escalated and Dhillon's body language became increasingly hostile towards the couple. When his ex-girlfriend asked if he was going to hit her, he moved towards her, spat in her face, and ran off.

The importance of underlining the history of stalking is identified by Clive Ruggles during his discussion with Laura Richards on *Real Crime Profile*. Clive points out that further knowledge of Dhillon's history of behaviour would have impacted on the police investigation, and would also have changed Alice's perspective on what was happening to her. In the conversation, Laura Richard's asserts that 'police should have searched their indices to see the history of the perpetrator.' Clive then articulates the need for a more robust approach that tracks perpetrators backgrounds; 'we have to have joined up databases [...] if it is part of a stalking campaign, you don't concentrate on the one offence, you have to concentrate on the bigger picture,' (Clive Ruggles Real Crime Profile, 2018).

Stalking, Control or Abuse

This chapter has already highlighted the controlling behaviours that Alice was subjected to. Alice consequently ended the relationship in August, 2016. At first, Alice tried to keep the break-up as amicable as possible, but after a number of attempts to try and get her to come back to him, Alice began to ignore Dhillon's messages. Dhillon then approached other people within Alice's life. For instance, he sent messages to her mother, and other friends, asking them to convince Alice to go back to him. Dhillon invested a great deal of time and effort into planning, tracking and victimising Alice, revealing his fixation and obsession. He turned up at Alice's home (despite the significant distance), constantly texted her and left voicemails. He delivered unwanted gifts and he also sent her photographs.

Dhillon used technology-enabled stalking which had extensive impacts on Alice's life and drove her further into isolation. He gained access to Alice's social media, and Alice suspected that he could read her messages and was tracking her phone, which made communicating with family and friends incredibly difficult. On the 15 August, Alice found that she had been locked out of her Facebook account. Dhillon later admitted that he had accessed the account to stop Alice from using Tinder, to prevent her from meeting a new partner. In early September, Alice went on a short break to Germany to visit her sister, who had been posted there as part of her job in the army. Whilst she was there, Alice started a new relationship. Immediately, Dhillon contacted her new partner and began to mislead him about Alice's character; he even suggested (erroneously) that Alice was cheating on him.

Dhillon also told Alice that he possessed private images of her that she would not want other people to see. Although Alice did not know what these images were, Alice was frightened that Dhillon would post these images on social media, resulting in her severe torment and fear of humiliation. This technology-enabled victimisation caused Alice significant distress. The psychological and social impact of digital stalking needs to be foregrounded in ex-partner stalking cases. One of the key findings in Alice's *Domestic Homicide Review* outlines, 'Digital stalking is often a significant factor in abusive relationships and needs to be robustly reflected within future risk assessments' (DHR, 2018, p. 88). The importance of considering the harms of stalking across both digital and physical contexts, and not seeing them as two separate forms of stalking, is also underlined by the Suzy Lamplugh Trust in their 'Unmasking Stalking. A Changing Landscape Report' (2021) that documents a 49% increase in online behaviours for those whose experience of stalking started before lockdown. Similarly, this is also highlighted by Fissel et al.'s research (2020) who propose that 'stalking by the use of electronic technology should be included as one of the tactics or behaviours used to operationalise stalking' (2020, p. 31).

Separation

Separation is considered to be the single biggest risk indicator for homicide (Brennan, 2016 in DHR, 2018 p. 67). As Weller et al. (2013) point out, a number of researchers have underlined the risk involved with rejected stalkers and the increased likelihood that ex-partners may result in violence after separation. But they also point out, drawing on Sheridan and Roberts (2011) that if the prior relationship has included physical or psychological abuse, and contained excessively controlling behaviour; this carries an even higher risk, and is a key predictor of physical assault. Separation in Alice's case, functioned as a trigger point. A sense of 'finality' over a relationship ending is a very dangerous point in a stalking case, in fact the first two months after separation are thought to be the most dangerous (DeKeseredy et al., 2017, p. 38). Finality can also relate to wider elements of separation, such as suicidal ideation and the prospect of losing one's job or home, which can produce 'nothing to lose' or 'last chance' thinking (Monckton Smith, 2019). Alongside relationship separation, these wider factors of finality were also present in this case. Senior officers at Glencorse Barracks were being made aware of aspects of Dhillon's behaviour. They had carried out a welfare check in response to information they had received that Dhillon had made threats to take his own life, and he was also breaching orders. During September, Dhillon was temporarily deployed to barracks in Aberdeenshire, but had returned to Edinburgh without permission. When his Platoon Commander questioned him on this, Dhillon 'immediately broke down in tears and appeared genuinely distressed about a separation with his girlfriend' (DHR, 2018, p. 42). The situation escalated on the 30 September, when Dhillon's behaviour resulted in official involvement from the police, army and local victim services.

Escalation

Escalation points can include varied factors, which are nuanced for each case. These can include meeting a new partner, moving away, death of a friend or family member, pregnancy or birth, and, if not managed correctly, police involvement. Whilst reporting stalking to the police as early as possible is crucial in stalking cases, police involvement can have significant negative impacts on the outcome, as Alice's case demonstrates. Just before ten o'clock on the evening of 30th September, after driving the two-and-a-half-hour journey to Alice's house, Dhillon knocked on Alice's front door. Alice came to the door and looked out the spy-hole, at which time Dhillon concealed himself. Suspecting it was Dhillon, Alice then called his phone to establish his location. Dhillon told Alice he was in Edinburgh. Dhillon knocked on Alice's front door for a second time. Alice once again looked out, but could not see anyone. Some more time passed, Dhillon then climbed over a six-foot-high fence and knocked on Alice's bedroom window, where she lay in bed. When Alice opened the curtains, Dhillon was outside her bedroom window. He had placed chocolates and flowers on her windowsill, and was now backing away with his hands raised skyward. Dhillon then got into his car and drove back to Edinburgh. During this time, he left Alice messages. In one message Dhillon told Alice that he had been outside her flat since five o'clock that afternoon, almost five hours earlier. Dhillon then left Alice the following voicemail:

> You said, guys like me end up killing people. That's why I just left them there and walked straight out. To prove a point that killing you is something that I've never, ever, ever thought about, and I will never ever even think about that. If you want to go to the police, go to the police, but think about what we're talking about, I've literally done nothing, I've never hurt you, never done any physical hurt to you [...] no, I don't wanna kill you, I'm not intending to kill you. That's all I wanted to say, that I didn't want to kill you, that's why I gave you chocolates and flowers and walked out straight away.

The events of that evening, and the continuous repetition of the phrase, 'I'm not going to kill you,' made Alice feel very frightened and prompted her to call the police's non-emergency number 101. The police phone call Alice made appears on all of the television documentaries of this case, as it was one of the major escalation points, and was a moment that should have been dealt with very differently. Alice had called the police prior to this event, but experienced an initial barrier of a long waiting time, during which time she abandoned the call. When she called the police on this occasion, Alice's tone was calm and polite, akin to her general disposition, but she did state that she felt scared. The call handler presented Alice with two options and asked her what course of action she would like the police to take. The conversation ended with the decision that Dhillon would be served a Police Information Notice (PIN). The PIN[9] was then served by the senior officers in the army.

However, one week later, Dhillon breached the PIN and contacted Alice once again. Alice phoned the police expecting that this would result in automatic arrest; however, the officer on the phone 'was less sympathetic, and no action was taken,' (DHR, 2018, p. 4). During Alice's initial conversation with the police, she was given a false expectation of what she could expect if the PIN was breached, as PIN's do not constitute formal legal action. This was both devastating to Alice who lost faith in the police's ability to protect her, and revealed to Dhillon that there would not be consequences for contacting Alice. This incessant contact and complete disregard for Alice and authority in the form of the police and the army demonstrates how relentless and high-risk Dhillon's behaviour had become. On the 12 October, just five days after Alice's phone call to report the breach of the PIN, Dhillon parked his car down the road from Alice's flat. Alice was dropped home by her work colleague at around 5.15 p.m. Fourteen minutes later, Dhillon moved his car closer to Alice's flat, he broke into her home, and brutally murdered her.

The police handling of this case has been well documented.[10] There are a number of issues, oversights and opportunities for safety planning factors that should have been introduced. In summary, some key points include the need for increased training of first response officers so

---

[9] These have been removed from police protocol.
[10] Alice's Homicide Review provides a very thorough report of the police including 20 recommendations.

that they can identify the crime of stalking. The police officer mentions harassment on the phone, but Alice's call was not crimed as stalking, despite the fact that specific stalking legislation has been in place since 2012. 'If the incident had been correctly identified as stalking, in line with Northumbria Policy, the option of a PIN would have been inappropriate, and the case would have been investigated and resulted in the perpetrator being arrested' (DHR, 2018, p. 63). There has been a lot of discussion of the 'victim-led' emphasis on this case, but Alice should not have been put in the situation where she was urged to decide whether Dhillon should be arrested or not. Alice did not have the necessary training to make such a crucial decision. Dhillon had committed a crime, so should have been arrested, but by placing the emphasis on Alice to decide, and this made Alice responsible for the outcome (like Dhillon losing his job), a situation which was likely to make Dhillon feel angry with her and further raise the threat-level. Alice's *Domestic Homicide Review* also states that further training is needed for professionals to develop professional curiosity and effective use of the DASH Risk Indicator Checklist as it did not capture 'all associated risks and issues' (2018, p. 97). In her statement, Alice confirms that she was 'scared' and 'terrified' and that she was 'being stalked and wants it to stop.' Veiled threats had been made to her life; she had recently separated from Dhillon who had a prior offence against another woman. Dhillon's occupation and military training is also an important part of this picture that was not fully considered by all agencies involved. Dhillon's role within the armed forces may have allowed him to gain knowledge of surveillance methods, and handling weapons, which could impact his ability to target Alice, and to plan her murder. He had recently applied (but was unsuccessful) to the Special Forces which demonstrates his interest in reconnaissance and surveillance work. The documentary *Murdered by My Stalker* demonstrates that images taken from Dhillon's phone revealed he had carried out his own reconnaissance of Alice's flat; the documentary includes a photograph Dhillon had taken of an exterior window (he later gained entry through a window into Alice's flat[11]). Whilst the

---

[11] Although on the evening of Alice's murder, Dhillon actually gained entry through a different window into the living room (not the window in the photograph) it has been speculated that the living room window may have been open when he arrived at the property.

army Independent Management Review (IMR) confirms that he did not receive specialist training to warrant these concerns, this was overlooked as a potential risk factor (DHR, 2018, p. 80).

Conclusion. Raising Public Awareness of Stalking

Over the five years since Alice's death, progress has been made. The following year HMICFRS and HM Crown Prosecution Service Inspectorate (HMCPSI) carried out an inspection into how police and the Crown Prosecution Service (CPS) responded to harassment and stalking, which was published in a report entitled 'Living in Fear,' as well as a research report on victim experience. As a result of these findings and further developments in the sector, important change has occurred. This includes the delivery of stalking training to first response areas of the police force, including the College of Policing. There has been an introduction of Stalking Protection Orders in 2019, which if breached, carry a greater likelihood of an offender being remanded in custody. These orders also impose positive restrictions that can be helpful to safeguard those who are being stalked, as well as providing therapies and intervention work with the offenders (although early indications suggest that these SPOs need to be used much more widely). Stalking sentences have been extended to acknowledge the seriousness and high risk of this crime, and specialist stalking units have also been set up. For instance, the Stalking Threat Assessment Unit (STAC) within the Metropolitan Police Service in partnership with Barnet, Enfield and Haringey Mental Health NHS Trust, and the Suzy Lamplugh Trust; the Integrated Anti-Stalking Unit in Cheshire, and the SPOC (Single Point of Contact) system has been further developed. In terms of services, there has been an increase in roles such as Independent Stalking Advocacy Caseworker (ISACs) and the plans for Specialist Stalking Psychological Advocates.

However, as this chapter has found, there is still work to be done. Much of this work is at an institutional level, which includes further training of frontline police and call handling staff as to how to identify and deal with stalking; ensuring investigators look into the history of offenders and consider the wider patterns of behaviour, such as coercive control, abuse, separation and escalation; and the developments of the methods to track stalkers and serial perpetrators. There also needs to be a continued emphasis on considering why people adopt such behaviour. In order to find solutions to stalking, we need to continue to get to the core of the issue concerning what makes someone vulnerable to carrying out stalking behaviours. Important perpetrator focused initiatives are already occurring in the sector, which seek to understand, interrupt and provide therapies, but these initiatives need to be resourced and wholeheartedly supported.

Whilst there is certainly a responsibility to tackle stalking at an institutional and systemic level within the criminal justice system, stalking is also a social problem, and improving societal identification of stalking is vital to affect fundamental, long-term change. Under Finding 20 of Alice's *Domestic Homicide Review*, the authors outline the need for the general public to have a more detailed understanding of stalking behaviour and particularly the risk attached to incidents that may appear innocent, noting that the '[p]ublic are generally unaware of stalking behaviours and associated risks.' The small acts of leaving gifts, or relentless communications may appear innocuous, they may even make people feel as though they are overacting, being dramatic, or wasting police time, but it is precisely 'within this context that greater public awareness of the risk posed by stalking needs to take place to empower both victims and bystanders.' (DHR, 2018, p. 79). Everyone has a role to play in understanding and identifying this crime, so we can support family, friends and colleagues. Increased circulation of stalking definitions such as the FOUR anacronym (*Fixated, Obsessive, Unwanted, Repeated*) and the stalking legislation itself, may be a useful way to outline behaviours. But in order to really make an impact and create a public shift in understanding of stalking, work must be undertaken in educating the public, and especially young people about the risks of stalking.

Collaboration between media content providers and those who have been personally affected by stalking or work in the field, provide rich opportunities for public education. As Lowney and Best (1995) argue in their article, the media has shaped public understanding of stalking in the past, and as the following example demonstrates, these outlets have the potential to raise public awareness of stalking in a meaningful way in the future. We can note these possibilities during the 'My Daughter Alice' episode of *Real Crime Profile*. During the episode, Clive Ruggles points out that the initial barriers for people being subjected to stalking lie with identifying what is happening to you, and then with the next steps to take:

> We have to raise awareness. Even when the advocates are there, people have to realise that they need them [...] We can create a public change of attitude where stalking is one of the serious issues. (Clive Ruggles)

The discussion continues to underline the need for further signposting to the services that are available to ensure that those who recognise they need help and advice can find these valuable resources. *Real Crime Profile* co-presenter Lisa Zambetti, then points out:

> The number one topic that our listeners write to us about are concerns over those people in their lives that are being stalked or coercively controlled. We get this every single week, sometime every day, it is a huge issue out there, and sometimes the victims don't see themselves as victims. (Lisa Zambetti, Real Crime Profile, 2018)

In this way *Real Crime Profile* functions as an educator, awareness raiser and also a valued service that directs its listeners to help and support. *Real Crime Profile*, along with other documentaries on Alice's case and particularly the *Unfollow Me* campaign produced by media business *Vice* and Paladin National Stalking Advocacy Service, can be used to deliver information to the public and explain these crimes. As this chapter has demonstrated, Alice's case possesses various news values that have resulted in its extensive coverage. The media campaigns and documentaries that depict the tragic circumstances that led to Alice's death have made a lasting impact on viewers; it is a news story that engages public attention. Therefore, further comprehensive coverage of Alice's case and other stalking cases is key to enhance public identification of stalking. Whilst it is true that the media can contribute to unhelpful narrow representations of stalking that can minimise this crime, as Helen Benedict (2005) points out in her analysis of media language of rape, the media also has the potential to lead the way in molding public understanding of sexual violence. 'The media reflects public opinion, to be sure, but it also shapes it, for it is through the media that the public receives all its news and most of its information.' (2005, 127).

Alongside the media, the education system is also an important way to inform younger members of the public about stalking and coercive control, as Murphy also highlights in her chapter within this book on Modern Slavery and Human Trafficking. The Alice Ruggles Trust have already collaborated with the PSHE Association to introduce relationship safety resources in schools and have recently developed a suite of Ofqual regulated SAfEE qualifications to help raise awareness with those working in education environments (Stalking Awareness for Education Environments). Teaching young people about stalking and coercive control will provide staff and students in schools, colleges and universities with the tools to firstly promote healthy relationships so that these behaviours may be identified, and secondly, to signpost where to go for advice if you are experiencing stalking, including the National Stalking Helpline, Paladin National Stalking Advocacy Service, and specialist local services. To be successful, education must address both the potential victims-survivors of stalking, and also, importantly, the potential perpetrators of this crime, as reducing stalking cases will not be possible without early intervention work with potential offenders. Since the publication of the NUS 'Hidden Marks' study in 2010, some positive changes in thinking have begun to occur in the Higher Education sector. University regulators, the Office for Students (OfS), have put forward a set of proposals designed to tackle harassment and sexual misconduct within universities[12] (2020/21). As this chapter has outlined, their Statement of Expectations, outlines a requirement for 'visible commitment from senior leaders and the governing bodies' to prevent forms of harassment and sexual misconduct. But there is a long road ahead

---

[12] Their plans draw on findings from previous reports such as Universities UK's 'Changing the Culture' report, (October 2016) and 'The Equality and Human Rights Commission's Review' (October 2019).

to ensure that young people who are subjected to crimes of stalking and sexual violence are identified, managed and supported at university level. Further research and initiatives that specifically consider stalking and young people are needed. As the Alice Ruggles Trust underline on their website, 'We want to know that the next generation, that Alice should have been part of, will recognise stalking for the vile crime that it is — not as a bit of a joke' (Alice Ruggles Trust Website, 2020).

Study Questions

- What are some of the stalking behaviours outlined in this chapter?
- What are the impacts of stalking on peoples' lives? Primarily consider the victim-survivor here, but also think about their family and friends. What about the person who is stalking?
- Why might young people be subjected to stalking more than other age groups? If your friend told you they were being stalked what advice would you give them?
- What are the different motivations behind stalking? Can you think of ways that we might intervene to prevent escalation?
- How can we improve public awareness of stalking?

Bibliography

Benedict, H. (2005). The language of rape. In E. Buchwald, P. Fletcher, P. R. Fletcher, & M. Roth. (Eds.), *Transforming a rape culture*. Milkweed Editions.

Biderman, A. (1957, September). Communist attempts to elicit false confessions from Air Force prisoners of war. *Bulletin of the New York Academy of Medicine, 33*(9), 616–625.

Bracewell, K., Hargreaves, P., & Stanley, N. (2020). The consequences of the COVID-19 lockdown on stalking victimisation. *Journal of Family Violence.* https://doi.org/10.1007/s10896-020-00201-0

Christie, N. (1986). The ideal victim. In E. A. Fattah (Ed.), *From crime policy to victim policy*. Palgrave Macmillan.

DeKeseredy, W. S., Dragiewicz, M., & Schwartz, M. D. (2017). *Abusive endings*. University of California Press.

Douglass, S. (Independent Chair), Reed, D., & Adam, L. (2018). Domestic homicide review into the death of Alice Ruggles. Gateshead Council. *Gateshead.Gov.Uk.* https://www.gateshead.gov.uk/article/11258/Domestic-homicide-review-into-death-of-Alice-Ruggles. Accessed 26 April 2020.

Fissel, E. R., Reyns, B. W., & Fisher, B. S. (2020). Stalking and cyberstalking victimization research: Taking stock of key conceptual, definitional, prevalence, and theoretical issues. In H. Chan & L. Sheridan (Eds.), *Psycho-criminological approaches to stalking behavior*. Wiley.

Henley, S., Underwood, A., & Farnham, F. (2020). National stalking clinic: A UK response to assessing and managing stalking behavior. In H. Chan & L. Sheridan (Eds.), *Psycho-criminological approaches to stalking behavior*. Wiley.

Herman, J. L. (2001). *Trauma and recovery*. Pandora.

Hill, J. (2020). *See what you made me do*. C Hurst and Co.

Humphreys, C. J, & J Towl, G. J. (2020). *Addressing student sexual violence in higher education*. Emerald Publishing.

Ingala-Smith, K., & O'Callaghan, C. (2020). Femicide census—Profiles of women killed by men. *Femicidescensus.Org.* https://femicidescensus.org/. Accessed 3 December 2020.

Jewkes, Y. (2015). *Crime in the media* (3rd ed.). University of Bath.

Long, J., Harvey, H., Wertans, E., Allen, R., Harper, K. Elliot, K. Brennan, D., Ingala Smith, K., & O'Callaghan, C. (2020). *UK Femicides 2009—2018, If I'm not in on Friday I might be dead*. https://femicidescensus.org/. Accessed 3 December 2020.

Long, J., & Harvey, H. (2018). *Femicide census*. Women killed by men in UK 2018 annual report. https://femicidescensus.org/wp-content/uploads/2020/02/Femicide-Census-Report-on-2018-Femicides-.pdf. Accessed 12 September 2020.

Lowney, K., & Best, J. (1995). Stalking strangers and lovers: Changing media typifications of a new crime problem. In J. Best (Ed.), *Images of issues: Typifying contemporary social issues*. Routledge.

MacKenzie, R., McEwan, T. E., Pathe, M., James, D. V., Ogloff, J. R., & Mullen, P. E. (2009). *Stalking risk profile: Guidelines for the assessment and management of stalkers*. Monash University.

Monckton-Smith, J. (2012). *Murder, gender and the media*. Palgrave Macmillan.

Monckton Smith, J. (2019). Intimate partner Femicide: Using Foucauldian analysis to track an eight stage progression to Homicide. *Violence against Women, 26* (11), 1267–1285. https://doi.org/10.1177/1077801219863876

Monckton Smith, J. (2021). *In control: Dangerous relationships and how they end in murder*. Bloomsbury.

Mullen, P. E., Pathé, M., & Purcell, R. (2009). *Stalkers and their victims*. Cambridge University Press.

Phipps, A. (2010). *Hidden marks: A study of women students' experiences of harassment, stalking, violence and sexual assault*. National Union of Students. Accessed 6 May 2020.

Scott, A., Rajakaruna, N., & Handscomb, N. A., & Waterworth, G. A. H. (2020). Public familiarity and understanding of stalking/harassment legislation. In H. Chan & L. Sheridan (Eds.), *Psycho-criminological approaches to stalking behavior*. Wiley.

Sheridan, L. (2005). *Network for surviving stalking 2005 survey report key findings*.

Stark, E. (2007). *Coercive control: How men entrap women in personal life*. Oxford: Oxford University Press.

Tapley, J., & Jackson, Z. (2019). Protections and prevention: Identifying, managing and monitoring priority perpetrators of domestic abuse. In A. Pycroft & D. Gough (Eds.), *Multi-agency working in criminal justice: Theory, policy and practice*. Policy Press.

Tutchell, E., & Edmonds, J. (2020). *Unsafe spaces: Ending sexual abuse in universities*. Emerald.

Weller, M., Hope, L., & Sheridan, L. (2013). Police and public perceptions of stalking: The role of prior victim-offender relationship. *Journal of Interpersonal Violence, 28*, 320–339.

Websites and Other Resources

Alice Ruggles Trust. (2020). http://alicerugglestrust.org. Accessed 3 January 2020.

Broadly. (2019). https://www.vice.com/en_us/broadly. Accessed 12 April. 2020.

Channel 4 News. (2019). https://www.channel4.com/news/police-failed-to-link-stalking-reports-before-womans-death. Accessed 4 March 2021.

DASH Risk Model. (2009). www.dashriskchecklist.co.uk. Accessed 16 February 2020.

Domestic Abuse Bill 2019–21—UK Parliament. (2020). *Services.Parliament.UK*. https://services.parliament.uk/bills/2019-21/domesticabuse.html. Accessed 1 June 2020.

HMIC & HMCPSI. (2017). *Living in fear–the police and CPS response to harassment and stalking: A joint inspection by HMIC and HMCPSI. HMIC 2017*. Available from: https://www.justiceinspectorates.gov.uk/hmicfrs/publications/living-in-fear-thepolice-and-cps-response-to-harassment-and-stalking/. Accessed 1 June 2020.

Office for National Statistics. (2019). *Stalking: Findings from the crime survey for England and Wales*. https://www.ons.gov.uk/peoplepopulationandcommunity/crimeandjustice/datasets/stalkingfindingsfromthecrimesurveyforenglandandwales. Accessed 30 August 2020.

Office for Students. (2021). *Prevent and address harrassment and sexual misconduct*. https://www.officeforstudents.org.uk/advice-and-guidance/student-wellbeing-and-protection/prevent-and-addressharassment-and-sexual-misconduct/statement-of-expectations/. Accessed 21 April 2021.

Paladin National Stalking Advocacy Service. (2020). Accessed 3 January 2020.

Protections of Freedoms Act. (2012). https://www.cps.gov.uk/legal-guidance/stalking-and-harassment. Accessed 9 January 2020.

Real Crime Profile. (2018). https://wondery.com/shows/real-crime-profile/ Accessed 12 April. 2020.

Suzy Lamplugh Trust. (2020). https://www.suzylamplugh.org/. Accessed 3 January 2020.

The Femicide Census. (2020). https://www.femicidecensus.org/wp-content/uploads/2020/11/Femicide-Census-10-yearreport.pdf. Accessed 3 Januaury 2021.

Vice. (2018). https://unfollowme.vice.com/. Accessed 7 January 2021.

8

Human Trafficking and Coercive Control: Representations in Media and Challenges in Legislation

Carole Murphy

Introduction

This chapter intends to bring together and discuss coercive control in two very different contexts: domestic abuse/intimate partner violence (DV/IPV) and modern slavery/human trafficking (MSHT). Disparate as these contexts appear, they have one major factor in common— that is, both are perpetrated out of sight of the public domain. And yet, legislation recognising coercive control in both circumstances was only recently implemented (2015). Section 76 of the *Serious Crime Act (England and Wales)* criminalised coercive control within domestic abuse/intimate partner violence. The *Modern Slavery Act* was introduced to tackle the growing problem of human trafficking and modern-day slavery in the UK. Within this policy, coercion is recognised as one of the tools used in the recruitment and control of victims. However, the

C. Murphy (✉)
St. Mary's University, Twickenham, UK
e-mail: Carole.murphy@stmarys.ac.uk

© The Author(s), under exclusive license to Springer Nature
Switzerland AG 2021
M. Mellins and S. Moore (eds.), *Critiquing Violent Crime in the Media*,
https://doi.org/10.1007/978-3-030-83758-7_8

introduction of legislation does not necessarily guarantee a solution to a criminal act. The social world is complex and the interaction of a variety of factors within the criminal justice system, its interplay within the public domain and intersection with media reports and representations can lead to misunderstandings and misinformation.

Therefore, this chapter first sets out a discussion of the two pieces of legislation referred to above, including an overview of how coercive control and its myriad of features are described in government documents. As will be seen, the list is long and complex and may include elements not readily perceived as coercive control. Indeed, for many members of the public, some of the behaviours described may be all too familiar, 'everyday' experiences. The discussion that follows though attempts to unpick some of these bland descriptions and provide examples from literature of how coercion is used as a tool of control in circumstances of DV/IPV and MSHT. Drawing from a large body of research including the work of Baldwin et al, 2014; Stark, 2007; Hopper & Hidalgo, 2006 and Biderman, 1957; the similarities from these diverse contexts are explicated and analysed. However, understanding these experiences ex post facto (or after the fact) does nothing to prevent the exploitation and abuse, nor to assist the victims at an earlier stage. It is important then to know about coercive control and this knowledge must come in accessible formats. In this regard, the media play a crucial role in disseminating information about 'hidden' issues and have indeed represented coercive control in DV/IPV, and to a lesser extent, as we shall see in cases of MSHT. To uncover and analyse media reporting and representations in film and other forms of popular culture, and its impact on understanding or otherwise, a three-pronged approach was taken by the author. First, studies undertaken on public understanding of coercive control in both domains were critically analysed to provide a realistic context of the issues for the reader. Second, a key word search of news media reports in Lexis Nexis enabled analysis of how news media report on the topic; and finally, recent representations in soaps and dramas were analysed for accuracy. Whilst media representations are very much a feature of how we, the public, understand complex issues, this chapter then turns to an analysis of how coercive control is understood and utilised in the criminal justice system (CJS), especially for female victims who, according to the UK government, tend to be overwhelmingly over-represented in DV/IPV cases. Women's experience of the CJS reflects their wider experiences of a lack of agency in which they feel disempowered (Walklate & Fitz-Gibbon, 2019). For victims of DV/IPV and MSHT, this is highly problematic as it tends to mirror their experiences whilst being controlled. Applying the concept of coercive control in the criminal justice system therefore may be harmful to victims. The chapter concludes with a deliberation about the importance of improving knowledge of coercive control within both professional and public spheres in order to lead to better protection of victims and improve the potential for prevention through earlier identification.

Coercive Control Legislation and Intimate Partner Violence

Coercive control was introduced as a concept for greater understanding of the dynamics that occur in cases of domestic abuse/intimate partner violence (DV/IPV). The phrase, adopted by Evan Stark (2007) from colleagues during his many years' experience working in the field of domestic violence, was instrumental in shifting understanding of control and coercion within intimate partner violence. However, despite a growing awareness of coercive control as a factor in cases of DV/IPV, and the introduction of legislation in other countries (e.g. Sweden 1998; France 2010), coercive control was not formally enshrined in UK law until 2015 under Section 76 of the *Serious Crime Act (England and Wales)*. Within the legislation, controlling and coercive behaviour is identified as 'not a single incident' but 'a purposeful pattern of behaviour which takes place over time in order for one individual to exert power, control or coercion over another'. The 'range of acts' perpetrated are 'designed to make a person subordinate and/or dependent by isolating them from sources of support, exploiting their resources and capacities for personal gain, depriving them of the means needed for independence, resistance and escape and regulating their everyday behaviour' (Home Office, 2015, p. 3.) Coercive behaviour is also a range or 'pattern of acts' that include 'assault, threats, humiliation and intimidation or other abuse that is used to harm, punish, or frighten their victim.' (Home Office, 2015, p. 3). The types of behaviour used to control and coerce are many and varied,[1] and can include such behaviours as ownership and entitlement, isolation from family and friends, rape and threats to kill. The similarities between IPV cases and cases of modern slavery and human trafficking (MSHT) are evident and will be discussed further below in relation to coercive control. Additionally, it is important to note the inclusion of coercion and control in legislation surrounding MSHT. Before going on to assess these similarities, this discussion will first outline how coercion and control are conceptualised within modern slavery and human trafficking legal frameworks. As the legislation demonstrates, unlike historical forms of slavery in which slaves were often physically restrained, recent methods involve more subtle forms of coercion and control which inflict enormous psychological damage on victims and therefore are important to consider in cases of MSHT.

Modern Slavery and Human Trafficking Legislation

The Palermo Protocol, the 'Protocol to Prevent, Suppress and Punish Trafficking in Persons *Especially Women and Children*,' was ratified in 2000 to supplement the United Nations Convention against Organised Crime (author's emphasis). The Palermo Protocol was an important piece

---

[1] Such behaviours might include: •; isolating a person from their friends and family; •; depriving them of their basic needs; •; monitoring their time; •; monitoring a person via online communication tools or using spyware; •; taking control over aspects of their everyday life, such as where they can go, who they can see, what to wear and when they can sleep; •; depriving them of access to support services, such as specialist support or medical services; •; repeatedly putting them down such as telling them they are worthless; •; enforcing rules and activity which humiliate, degrade or dehumanise the victim; •; forcing the victim to take part in criminal activity such as shoplifting, neglect or abuse of children to encourage self-blame and prevent disclosure to authorities; •; financial abuse including control of finances, such as only allowing a person a punitive allowance; •; threats to hurt or kill; •; threats to a child; •; threats to reveal or publish private information (e.g. threatening to 'out' someone). •; assault; •; criminal damage (such as destruction of household goods); •; rape; •; preventing a person from having access to transport or from working. This is not an exhaustive list.

of international legislation aiming to address human trafficking. Legislation in other jurisdictions including the *Modern Slavery Act UK 2015* (MSA) and the *Trafficking Victims Protection Act 2000, US* (TVPA) draws upon this definition and recognises coercion and control as factors in cases of human trafficking. The Protocol (2000) states:

'Trafficking in persons' shall mean the recruitment, transportation, transfer, harbouring or receipt of persons, by means of the threat or use of force or other forms of *coercion*, of abduction, of fraud, of deception, of the abuse of power or of a position of vulnerability or of the giving or receiving of payments or benefits to achieve the consent of a person having *control* over another person, for the purpose of exploitation. Exploitation shall include, at a minimum, the exploitation of the prostitution of others or other forms of sexual exploitation, forced labour or services, slavery or practices similar to slavery, servitude or the removal of organs. (author's emphasis)

Prior to the introduction of these key pieces of legislation nationally and internationally, slavery has most commonly been depicted using images of transatlantic slavery in which physical restraints such as chains, shackles and masks were used alongside extreme physical violent acts such as whippings, beatings, confinement and debasement. Consequently, it is easier to understand 'slavery created with chains', especially when considering the possibility, or not, of escape (Hopper & Hidalgo, 2006, p. 188). It is far more difficult to understand why people stay without physical constraints. Even so, legislation recognises that although coercion by traffickers can be non-violent, it nonetheless can create 'an environment of fear' through a variety of means which may include threats of violence towards the victim and/or their family and loved ones (Hopper & Hidalgo, 2006, p. 188). Victims of abuse in many different contexts are also submitted to extreme forms of psychological control. For instance, there are many commonalities between coercive control in DV/ IPV and human trafficking cases and these are discussed in the following section in greater detail.

Psychological Coercion, Domestic Violence and Human Trafficking

A number of comparisons have been made between DV and victims specifically of sex trafficking. The gendered nature of human trafficking and the vulnerability of women and girls to trafficking is highlighted in the Palermo Protocol as emphasised above. Gender inequality is evident in statistics on human trafficking. The International Labour Organisation (ILO) report that 71% of victims are women and girls, although due to the hidden nature of the crime, it is very difficult to gather reliable estimates. Nevertheless, the ILO are one of the most 'trusted sources for understanding the global situation' (Stop the Traffick, 2020) and these statistics indicate the vulnerability of women and girls to exploitation within the context of wider gender inequalities internationally. Within these gendered dynamics, it is unsurprising that control and coercion are also used as tools by human traffickers and modern-day slavers in controlling women. It must be noted that these methods can also be used on men, but this chapter focuses on the particular vulnerabilities of women.

Likewise, the gendered nature of coercive control is acknowledged within DV/IPV contexts. Even though there is a recognition that intimate partner violence can be perpetrated by women, the use of controlling or coercive behaviour by men is far more common; it 'targets gender identity' and is perpetrated through systems of male domination (Stark, 2007, p. 1509). UK legislation also recognises the gendered nature of this offence, supported by statistics on offences from the year prior to introduction of Section 76 (2014) showing that '92.4% of offenders were male and 84% of victims were female'. The report states that '[c]ontrolling or coercive behaviour is primarily a form of violence against women and girls and is underpinned by wider societal gender inequality' (Home Office, 2015, p. 7).

Further, due to the dearth of research on psychological coercion in cases of human trafficking and modern slavery, Hopper and Hidalgo (2006, p. 188) drew on studies about experiences of 'prisoners of war, torture victims, cult members, and *victims of domestic violence*' to gain greater insight into how 'psychological manipulation is used in various conditions of control' (authors emphasis). The list of methods of psychological coercion used on prisoners of war and torture survivors incudes: detention, often in cramped or overcrowded spaces; isolation/solitary confinement and/or lack of privacy and sensory deprivation. Physiological needs are also denied including access to food, water, sleep, toilet and bathing facilities, and medical care. Deprivation of social contacts, 'humiliation and verbal abuse'; 'threats of violence'; 'exposure to ambiguous or contradictory messages'; violation of taboos or religious beliefs; being forced to betray or harm others and being forced to witness atrocities performed on others' are also identified (adapted by Hopper & Hidalgo, 2006, p. 189[2]). In cases of domestic violence, psychological tactics are also used to maintain control, to create conditions of *psychological captivity* (Walker, 1984). The use of the phrase psychological captivity here denotes the non-physical restraints enforced on victims. Common forms of psychological control used in domestic violence situations include creating an environment of fear in which self-blame and guilt on the part of the victim is common. Alternating between kindness and threats is also usual and used by the abuser to create a sense of uncertainty, producing dependency and learned helplessness (Boulette & Anderson, 1986). In DV/IPV, it is rare that physical barriers (such as being tied up or kept captive) are used (Herman, 1992), confirming the reality of *psychological captivity* (Walker, 1984).

Roe-Sepowitz et al. (2014) address other similarities and differences between DV and MSHT, and report that there is evidence that domestic violence and sex trafficking can co-occur (Bruggeman & Keyes, 2009). They cite the Polaris Project's (2010) claim that domestic abuse can be a push factor for being vulnerable to sex trafficking, as victims have few financial or social supports. Additionally, the relationship dynamics mirror to some extent that of the domestic violence situations. Women reported that they experienced 'unpredictable violence combined with a sense of love and admiration' resulting in feelings of disorientation and unreality (Williamson & Cluse-Tolar, 2002, cited in Roe-Sepowitz et al., 2014, p. 3). Characteristics that are similar to both circumstances

---

[2] Physicians for Human Rights, Interrogations, Torture and Ill Treatment: Legal Requirements and Health Consequences 9–10 (2004), *available at* http://phrusa.org/research/pdf/iraq_medical_consequences.pdf.

include: *Secrecy; Violence; Dominance and Power; Rules; Psychological Abuse and Instability; Relationship-Based Grooming; Traumatic Events; Financial Control; Barriers to Disclosing their Victimisation; Consequences of Victimisation; and Challenges of Escaping/Leaving* (Roe-Sepowitz et al., 2014, pp. 7–10).

In Roe-Sepowitz et al.'s (2014) discussion of these different characteristics, coercive control is merely mentioned as an aspect of *Dominance and Power*, and as such, suggests that coercion is *only* an element of *Dominance and Power*, when in fact, it underpins all other characteristics listed above. For example, in order to maintain *Secrecy*, the victims have reasons to hide the reality of their situations either through fear of further violence, or fear of responses such as disbelief from law enforcement or other statutory services. This can then be taken as evidence of the power of the coercion, underpinned by the fear of violence. Similarly, *Violence* can include withholding of food, erratic moods and sudden changes to living circumstances (Roe-Sepowitz et al., 2014). These themes emerge throughout the discussion and it is evident that there is much congruence with those conditions identified as elements of control in various situations of abuse. Though this paper is useful in determining the similarities between DV and sex trafficking, it is less useful in drawing conclusions about how these similarities feature aspects of coercive control.

A more constructive approach is taken by Baldwin et al. (2014) utilising Biderman's Framework of Coercion (1957) to understand the experiences of women trafficked into the US for domestic work and work in the sex industry. Biderman's framework was developed whilst examining techniques used to elicit false confessions from US service personnel during the Korean War. The framework was unknown outside of US military until 2008, when it was reported as the basis for interrogation of suspects in Guantanamo Bay (Baldwin et al., 2014). Biderman outlined 'eight methods of coercion used to establish compliance: *Isolation; Monopolization of Perception; Induced Debility or Exhaustion; Threats; Occasional Indulgences; Demonstration of Omnipotence; Degradation; and Enforcing Trivial Demands*' (cited in Baldwin et al., 2014, p. 1).

In applying the framework in her study, Baldwin et al. interviewed twelve women who had been trafficked, mainly for domestic servitude.

Findings revealed that traffickers had utilised similar techniques as those identified by Biderman, resulting in high levels of risk for 'acute and chronic mental and physical health problems' (2014, p. 2). The women were isolated, even from other staff in domestic situations, and were banned from talking to anyone other than the employer. They were not allowed contact with family, had their actions monitored constantly and were not allowed out without an escort. Exhaustion was common, brought about through a combination of overwork, long hours and increased duties, such as having to work at parties until the early hours every weekend. Sleeping on the floor, being forced to drink alcohol and the denial of medical attention also contributed to feelings of debility. Threats were commonplace. Identification documents were held by the slavers and 'threats of arrest or deportation' become very real in these circumstances (2014, p. 5). Threats were also made against family members, and threats of violence and death were normal.

In many cases, perpetrators would claim associations with powerful people including law enforcement, immigration officials and in several cases, deities. For example, Juju, also 'interchangeably referred to as "witchcraft," "voodoo," "spirits," "muti," "black magic," "demons," "satanism," and "curses,"' (Van der Watt & Kruger, 2017, p. 78) is a well-known technique of control and coercion in Nigeria. It is a widespread form of traditional/religious practice used to control women in cases of trafficking through forced oath taking and threats of punishment from deities (Dunkerley, 2018; Ikeora, 2016; Van der Watt & Kruger, 2017). The Juju ceremony is an important aspect of gaining control. The victim is brought before the Juju priest and required to undress, thus increasing the sense of vulnerability. Naked, the body is easily accessed in order to insert cuts which are rubbed with a mixture of soot and the victim's human tissue so that the spirit can enter the body and the victim 'can never escape from it' (Van der Watt & Kruger, 2020, p. 12). Slavers use victims fear of the spirit to instil further terror and to limit their attempts to escape. The power of Juju should not be underestimated and has become so popular in Benin City (Nigeria) that 'it has developed into an alternative to the official justice system of the state' (ibid., 2019, p. 12).

Such techniques create or increase a sense of paranoia in victims in which they doubt their 'own sense of reality and sanity' and this confirms their lack of control over their lives (Baldwin et al., 2014, p. 8). Degradation in the form of physical acts such as slapping or hair pulling, purposely creating a mess to be cleaned up by the slave and other unreasonable trivial demands are common. In addition, expectations of achieving perfection in tasks—difficult to accomplish when suffering sleep deprivation and physical and psychical pain—all contribute to the overall experience of lack of control and feelings of worthlessness. Their sense of identity has been impacted; in some cases, they have been given a different name by the trafficker (Hopper & Hidalgo, 2006) or had a mark of ownership tattooed on their body (Fang et al., 2018; Goldberg et al., 2017).

As noted earlier in cases of DV, alternating between kindness and threats creates a feeling of disorientation and uncertainty (Roe-Sepowitz, 2014). Likewise, in Biderman's framework, occasional indulgences are used to garner obedience on the part of the victim. For example, one women's 'indulgence' was Tylenol painkillers for her headache (Baldwin et al., 2014, p. 6), demonstrating how small acts of 'kindness' can be used as control mechanisms. Just like survivors of DV/IPV, the psychological impact of physical neglect and abuse, psychological coercion and lack of control that is experienced by women in trafficking cases has been well documented. Taken as a series of small actions that can be normalised in the life of the victim of trafficking, it can be extremely difficult for the survivor to realise the extent of the impact on their mental and physical health, and in some cases to even recognise the abnormality of their situations. However, the wounds incurred through the experience of coercive control should not be underestimated. Trafficked people are psychologically abused, intimidated, emotionally manipulated and marginalised (in Gajic-Veljanoski & Stewart, 2007, p. 343). They are usually physically isolated and are sometimes relocated and may be dependent on drugs. Abuse begins often in transit and includes physical, emotional and sexual abuse in the form of deprivation of food and drink, repeated rape and physical assaults (Hossain et al., 2010). Numerous studies demonstrate post-traumatic stress disorder, suicidal thoughts or suicide attempts, depression and drug and alcohol abuse (Iglesias- Rios et al., 2018; Abas et al., 2013; Altun et al., 2017; Oram et al., 2015; Cwikel et al., 2004; Raymond et al., 2001; Hossain et al., 2010).

Guidance for supporting survivors in recovery and rehabilitation recognise these extremes of experiences. For example, Zimmerman and Borland's instructions for health providers (2009) draw a contrast between the more severe and physical methods used by traffickers such as 'extreme physical abuse or torture-like violence, such as beating, burning, rape and confinement' (2009, pp. 8–9) to coercive measures, such as 'less obvious—but nonetheless coercive and menacing—tactics' (2009, p. 9). More recently, the Helen Bamber Foundation and the Organization for Security and Co-operation in Europe (OSCE) crucially raised awareness of the linkages between human trafficking, torture and other forms of ill-treatment (Witkin, 2013) and provided in-depth guidelines for assessing survivors, understanding 'complex trauma' (2013, p. 84) and the importance of sustaining victims from referral to recovery. It is important though to recognise that in some cases, despite the abuse and neglect, the relationship between the victim and the perpetrator can develop into what Raghavan and Doychak (2015) have termed 'trauma coerced-attachment'.

Trauma-Coerced Attachment

Because of the intense nature of the relationship and the victims attunement to the moods and vagaries of the trafficker, over time a 'traumatic bonding' can occur. Also known as 'Stockholm Syndrome', victims 'tend to magnify small acts of kindness of their captors and may be sympathetic to them' (Hopper & Hidalgo, 2006, p. 199). However, recognising the role of coercive control, Ragavhan and Doychak propose that 'trauma bonding be reconceptualised as trauma-coerced attachment to adequately reflect the abusive dynamics at play' (2015, p. 583). The sex trafficking relationship involves 'complex dichotomies'; victims can be 'romantic and coerced with enforcers and competitive and violent with peers' (Ragavhan & Doychak, 2015, p. 583). Numerous studies are cited to support the argument that 'pathways to these bonds includes a complex interaction' of exploiting the 'power imbalances within the relationship' through dynamics of abusive control and switching between reward and punishment (Ragavhan & Doychak, 2015, p. 583).

Consequently, the attachment should be understood as a 'traumatic response to a terrifying chronic stressor rather than as a dysfunctional attachment that reflects masochism, weakness, or social vulnerability in the victim' (Raghavan & Doychak, 2015, p. 583). Although the concept of trauma-coerced bonding is not new and underpins complex PTSD, within a trafficking context the nature of prolonged traumatic interpersonal trauma has been underexplored. Raghavan and Doychak (2015) argue that the concept of coercive control is useful for examining these experiences of trafficked women and their relationships with their perpetrators and sheds light on the invisible nature of the abuse and control which may be little understood outside of support services. For victims in recovery, as well as accessing trauma informed support to address their physical and psychological needs, furthering understanding of the impact of trauma-coerced attachments on victims' pathology is critical for comprehensive and empathetic responses. In the public domain, comprehending psychological coercion is crucial to identifying situations of abuse and reporting suspected cases to authorities. However, there are many barriers to achieving this position.

Public Understanding of Psychological Coercion in Human Trafficking: A Case Study

As noted, historical depictions of slaves controlled by whips, beatings, chains and other physical restraints as forms of control are more visible and easier to understand. As part of a broader study about modern slavery in the West Midlands, a highly populated area of the UK, Dando et al. (2016) explored public understandings of trafficking and psychological coercion within an environment of increasing reports in news media and online sources. Both the *Modern Slavery* Act and Clause 76 of the *UK Serious Crime Act* had been introduced in 2015, ensuring the timeliness and value of this study.

Utilising surveys with a mix of fixed and open response options, the researchers asked members of the public questions about human trafficking and psychological coercion. The invisible nature of psychological control is challenging in the public domain generally. Unless the public can spot signs of psychological coercion, they can offer little support to law enforcement and other statutory agencies in identifying victims. Drawing on Biderman's framework (1957) to analyse responses regarding knowledge of psychological coercion, Dando et al. (2016) reported that overall 51% of respondents were familiar with the term and 49% were not. Sources of information for the positive responses included news media, social media, online sources and radio.

However, when assessing the *actual* understanding of psychological coercion, the most commonly recognised forms of control were more obvious practices that have been reported in media for some time, for example, 'verbal pressure to commit crime, verbal pressure to behave against free will and verbal intimidation resulting in reduced cognitive functioning and decision-making abilities' (Dando et al., 2016, p. 9). Less familiar types including 'undermining self-confidence; social control; being nice' were understood by fewer than 55% of respondents. Perhaps unsurprisingly then, the results of the study displayed that a majority of respondents (more than 65%) believed that psychological coercion equated with physical imprisonment. Dando et al. (2016) argue that this gap in knowledge originates from government and Non-Governmental Organisation (NGO) messaging on the topic of modern slavery in the UK in which psychological coercion is not addressed in any detail, limiting understanding about its role in 'breaking down victims survival responses' in the process of gaining control (Dando et al., 2016, p. 9). Arguably, the media also play a role in disseminating this messaging from government and NGOs and an examination of some examples of media reporting sheds further light on the lack of knowledge and understanding of psychological elements of control, both in DV and MSHT.

Media and Coercive Control

In media contexts, evidence demonstrates that all forms of media can tend towards sensationalising stories, particularly those that concern sex and murder (Moore, 2014). Moreover, 'moral panics', particularly around women's sexual activities and relationships draw on tropes of virgins or vamps and often result in victim blaming (Benedict, 1993), including cases of DV/IPV. Prior to recent examples (described below), the term coercive control was rarely used in media representations and reports, contributing to a lack of clarity about what it actually entails. Rachel Horman, a practicing lawyer on domestic violence cases argues that accurate reporting in media is important in raising awareness of this issue. Once awareness is gained about the subtleties of coercion, it is impossible to 'un-see' (Horman, 2019). Its commonplaceness becomes apparent and it can be read between the lines of media reports and representations. Raising awareness of coercive control is therefore crucial to gaining a clearer understanding of how to identify and support victims. In recent years, media depictions of some of the subtleties of coercive control have become more commonplace. For example, in 2019, Channel 4 screened *I am...Nicola*, a story of a woman stuck in a coercive relationship. The programme focuses on the very subtle aspects of control in relationships as opposed to more extreme and obvious signs apparent in physical violence. In a review of *I am...Nicola*, Guardian journalist Lucy Mangan reports that *I am...Nicola* captures 'the emotional manipulation, the erosion of a supposedly loved one's mental freedoms, the gentle battering of a psyche into submission' (Mangan, 2019, n.p.). This quote from Mangan encapsulates the disintegration of identity and autonomy experienced by victims of coercive control, and touches on themes discussed earlier in the chapter about victims' paranoia in which they doubt their 'own sense of reality and sanity' (Baldwin et al., 2014, p. 8). A recent storyline in the popular UK soap, *Coronation Street* (2020) characterised coercive control in the relationship between Yasmeen and Geoff, the culmination of which was applauded by viewers as a true representation of their experiences and was reported broadly in news media. In an article about the storyline, a BBC news headline stated 'Coercive control is all of our business' (Faulkner, 2020).

Equally, it is important to improve messaging on modern slavery. Kenway (2020) discussed media reporting in 'Messaging Modern Slavery' (Focus on Labour Exploitation (FLEX) YouTube, 2020). Critical of media framing on the topic of modern slavery (see also Birks & Gardner, 2019) she identified some key barriers to understanding the complexities of modern slavery and raised three areas of concern that need to be addressed to move beyond stereotypes and clichés. First, modern slavery is often represented as similar to historical slavery. Second, it is represented as an illness and third and probably most familiar, as a crime. Kenway (2020) argues that this erroneous framing is problematic on a number of levels. Constructing similarities with historical slavery sends a message that slavery is an aberration, whereas it is an ongoing, long-term and endemic problem in society. It operates on a continuum of exploitation and is part of broader societal and economic structures. These ideas are not new (see for example O'Connell-Davis, 2015) but are less likely to be discussed in the public sphere as they represent enormous structural challenges to tackling broader exploitation.

Likewise, characterising slavery as an illness suggests that it can be treated and cured. Finally, framing the issue as a crime ensures that it joins a pantheon of other acts that are constructed around the notion of us and them, of 'baddies' and good people. Kenway uses the metaphor of a drop of ink in clear water to demonstrate the way that modern day slavery is fabricated as 'contamination of the social fabric rather than part of the social fabric' (2020, YouTube). Within this framing, the notion of the 'perfect victim', or what Nils Christie (1986) calls the ideal victim, is perpetuated and makes space for the 'heroes'—which Kenway (2020) identifies as businesses and politicians in particular—to intervene and enact a rescue operation. In support of this argument, Kenway identifies four frames regularly used within media reporting:

1. Criminal—concerning criminal justice approaches to tackling modern slavery and utilising the 'shock and awe' approach
2. Consumerist—the idea that consumer action and ethical shopping can reduce exploitation

3. Factual/incidental—reporting on facts alone without context, for example, X number of people were found in conditions of modern slavery in X part of the country
4. Systemic—the least common form of reporting, which provides information about the wider social and economic drivers of exploitation.

In these frames, modern forms of slavery are seen as an anomaly outside of normal society and take no heed of continuums of exploitation, nor focus on the structural issues that underpin its modern expansion. Reporting on systemic factors has the potential to change the narrative from that of an anomaly to a more truthful version in which modern slavery is understood as a common feature of the modern world and not as an aberration.

Moreover, and confirming some of the themes discussed above, Gregoriou et al. (2018) address how victims and perpetrators are characterised within news media, true crime and fiction. The authors identify that the impetus to turn human trafficking into 'newsworthy stories' tends to report 'trends and practices that generate stereotypes, clichés and formulaic human trafficking narratives' (Gregoriou 2018, p. v). For example, images tend to show women tied up with rope or chained to beds. Dando et al., (2016, p. 9) note that 'media-grabbing pictures/images of physical restraint' are used in reports, including victims in handcuffs or prison cells. The focus on physical restraints communicates erroneous messages about the nature of control in trafficking cases. A study by Birks and Gardner (2019) on reporting in local newspapers in the UK, utilises a content analysis of 148 articles supplemented by three focus groups. It found that whilst reporting had increased over time, much of it focused on sexual exploitation of women and children. Based on sensationalised stories about the lavish lifestyle of the perpetrators in contrast to the extreme conditions in which slaves were kept, the stories did little to improve understanding of victims' personal narratives and their recovery journeys. In one example, the Connors family controlled up to 100 victims over a period of years on their farm in Bedfordshire. The reporting on this case tended to draw attention to the 'palatial residences' of the family in contrast to the 'squalid conditions' of the slaves (BBC, 2013, 2020). Moreover, reports used 'simplified victim framing, with victims frequently characterised as passive and vulnerable women, who have been deceived rather than more complex stories that explore individual agency and choice' (Birks & Gardner, 2019).

The film *Taken* (2008) is a prime example of this type of victim framing using specific tropes, stereotypes and clichés: the white female virgin as the ideal victim who is kidnapped from a hotel; the white male who comes to the rescue (in this case the victim's father); the victim's friend who was not a virgin and thus was not important to the story other than to show what happens to 'bad girls', (linking in with Nils Christie's [1986] concept of the ideal victim); the stereotypes of the traffickers as Albanian criminal gangs, and of the purchaser of the victim, a Middle Eastern Sheikh. This film could be regarded as an extreme example of stereotypes and clichés; however, there is little evidence of more nuanced reporting in news media more broadly. These representations lead to misunderstanding about trafficking and are misleading about how people are recruited into trafficking situations. They rarely address the acts of coercion and control perpetrated by the traffickers. These critiques of media stories on modern slavery are mirrored, to some extent, in reports on DV/IPV. Following the introduction of the *Modern Slavery Act* and Clause 76 of the *Serious Crime Act* in 2015, media reporting increased on both issues. In the context of DV/IPV, controlling or coercive behaviours in an intimate or family relationship were specifically recognised and discussed in media (Dando et al., 2016). However, coercive control is rarely reported in media discussions about modern slavery/human trafficking. To support this assertion, a review of news media was conducted as outlined below.

News Media Analysis

A search utilising Lexis Library News (08/2020) was undertaken to examine how coercive control was reported in news media in the UK, with no date restrictions. However, given that the legislation introducing the concept of coercive control was quite new (2015), it is unsurprising that there were no reports prior to 2014 (one in 2014 mentioned the upcoming legislation). Using the search terms 'coercive control' AND 'human trafficking' OR 'modern slavery' returned 24 articles. Of those, although human trafficking and/or modern slavery *and* coercive control were mentioned in 18, two of these were repeats of the same incident reported in different newspapers. This story concerned a change in the law on age of workers in 'sexual entertainment' shows in Cheltenham, relaying that recruits would see materials about modern slavery and coercive control in their changing rooms. One article reported on the outgoing director of Public Prosecutions Alison Sanders and her contribution to improving understanding of coercive control. Three articles reported on Theresa May's role in introducing coercive control and modern slavery into the political arena, and one reported on other women who had championed 'women's issues', including coercive control and human trafficking.

The most recent article was about the impact of Covid-19 on the World's longest running soap opera *The Archers*, (Radio 4) and also referenced its recently introduced storyline on modern slavery and coercive control. Other stories were about police knowledge and behaviour. The first of these recounted that, following an inspection, Suffolk Police were found to lack knowledge on coercive control but were more knowledgeable on modern slavery. The other report refers to a story about the ineffectiveness of police in protecting victims of domestic violence and modern slavery. Likewise, the remainder of the reports did not mention coercive control as an element of human trafficking and modern slavery. Even when mentioned, none of the reports define or explain what the term means. Thus, it is unsurprising that understanding amongst the general public is deficient, (also noted in Birks & Gardner, 2019) but more concerning that police may also not understand its impact. Although this news report only provides evidence of one police force, other studies have identified gaps in police knowledge of modern slavery (Murphy, 2018; HMICFRS, 2017). Gaps have also been identified in the implementation of legislation as discussed below.

Coercive Control Legislation

McClenaghan and Boutaud (2017) address the gap between coercive control legislation and its implementation. Evidence confirms very low numbers of cases reported using the new legislation. Police stated that 'charges are "hard to achieve" and "challenging to prove" (McClenaghan & Boutaud, 2017). Walklate and Fitz-Gibbon (2019) also question whether criminalising coercive control benefits or disadvantages victims in DV/IPV cases. Additionally, although clearly defined in the legislation, Hamberger et al. (2017) found that the concept was operationalised and defined in more than 22 different ways, leading to a plethora of different emphases. Lack of agreement on concepts within the criminal justice system has implications for outcomes and in the case of coercive control, may be damaging to the victim. In addition to the slipperiness of the concept, Walklate and Fitz-Gibbon (2019) also argue that 'coercive control creep' is problematic. Coercive control creep in this case means that the term is used frequently and in an uncontested manner, which is unacceptable within criminal justice settings. Walklate and Fitz-Gibbon (2019) argue that use of coercive control in legal cases has the potential to do more harm than good, especially with regard to the experiences of women in the criminal justice system that can mirror the lack of control in their relationships. From the first point of contact with a frontline officer, through to presenting evidence in court, there are many hurdles to face that may also be impacted by ethnicity, class and cultural background in addition to gender.

In this regard, 'the creation of a new offence (coercive control) does not deal with any of the well-documented concerns women have about engaging with the criminal justice process' (Walklate & Fitz-Gibbon, 2019, p. 102) and may lead to what Douglas (2018) calls 'legal systems abuse' in which perpetrators use the system to perpetrate further abuse on their partners. Likewise, victims of MSHT, because of their perception of the power relationship with the trafficker, may perceive people in positions of authority, such as social workers and law enforcement, as similar to traffickers (Preble, 2019). Further, lack of conceptual clarity surrounding coercive control makes it difficult to measure and without accurate measurements about violence towards women, it will be difficult to persuade the government to take action (see Walby & Towers, 2018). Within the CJS, Walby and Towers argue, the term 'domestic violence crime is preferable to that of coercive control when seeking to explain variations in domestic violence' (2018, p. 7).

Although coercion is recognised as a method of recruitment and control in the Palermo Protocol and the MSA, in modern slavery cases in the UK, coercive control is not used as a defence. In a recent case, R-v-Ahmed, the first case of a husband being jailed for domestic servitude, the victim, his wife, was subjected to abuse ranging from violence to having her movements controlled. She was not allowed to socialise or leave the home alone (Walker, 2016). However, the legislation used in this case to prosecute the offender was in relation to 'the victim unable to change their circumstances' (for slavery, servitude and forced labour, Barlow, 2020) as opposed to coercive control. Although there was clear evidence of coercive control, the modern slavery legislation was used in this instance. Thus, whilst coercive control as a feature of modern slavery and human trafficking cases has been recognised for some time (see for example Hopper & Hidalgo, 2006), learning from its inclusion in DV/IPV cases could usefully inform its potential negative impacts prior to its use in cases concerning modern slavery. Modern slavery and human trafficking cases are notoriously difficult to prosecute. Victims/survivors are often key witnesses within a bureaucratic system that can mirror their lack of control and agency within the trafficking situation. Many victims have high levels of distrust towards people in authority, especially the police. Numerous factors contribute to this distrust, including corruption and abuse in their country of origin, having been forced to commit criminal acts, and/or being lied to by traffickers about how they will be treated by law enforcement. Even when agreeing to provide testimony against their traffickers, the onus is often on the victim to prove their enslavement, a difficult task when there is no evidence of physical restraint. Additionally, victims themselves may not know they are victims of a crime and will almost certainly be unaware that they have been subjected to coercive control. Without expert support and guidance for both victims and law enforcement to improve understanding of coercive control and its impacts, victims may not get the justice they deserve.

Conclusion

This chapter introduced the concept of coercive control as it is used in intimate partner violence/domestic abuse cases. How it is understood more broadly, and how it is represented in a variety of media highlighted the lack of factual information communicated through these sources. Likewise, slavery as it is depicted in everyday circumstances and framed by the media is also misleading, resulting in a lack of understanding of control through the mechanics of psychological coercion. Biderman's (1957) framework was presented to aid understanding of the complexity of coercive control, and its use in various scenarios of abuse from torture to intimate partner violence. Similarly, trauma coerced bonding (Raghavan & Doychak, 2015) emphasises the complexities of the perpetrator/victim relationship and the role of power in perpetuating a dependent and damaging bond.

Knowledge and understanding about coercive control can be poorly understood—unsurprising considering the multiplicity of definitions that exist. Moreover, attitudes of police towards victims of IPV and modern slavery have been found to be wanting. As Horley states 'A "canteen culture" of negative attitudes towards women still exists in forces where domestic violence is not taken seriously—"it's just a domestic" is still a refrain heard today.' (cited in Travis, 2016). Likewise, the misrepresentation of human trafficking and modern slavery has long been recognised. News media images of victims controlled through physical constraints are common, and victims in screen media are often constructed in stereotyped and idealised forms. Although highly pertinent as an element of control used within modern slavery/human trafficking situations, there is a dearth of literature on the topic of coercive control. A review of sources on Lexis Library confirmed that the terms are rarely used concurrently and when they are, are not used in relation to each other. Coercive control is not clearly defined in media representations and as Dando et al. (2016) discovered, public understanding is unclear about the signs and symptoms of coercive control, most often viewing it as verbal commands. Clearly, much work is needed in the public domain to increase understanding of coercion as a method of control within DV/IPV and the trafficking/modern slavery relationship.

Representations in popular culture including *I am...Nicola, Coronation Street* and *The Archers,* could be regarded as a step in the right direction towards improving knowledge and understanding amongst members of the public in two domains: first, about the everyday nature and existence of this phenomenon, and second about the continuum of violence experienced within intimate partner relationships and modern day slavery, from extreme physical brutality to more subtle but no less damaging forms of coercive control.

The case of R-v-Ahmed confirms the overlap between modern slavery and domestic abuse and highlights that legislation on coercive control was unnecessary to obtain a conviction in this case. Indeed, Walklate and Fitz-Gibbon (2019) present a convincing argument against relying on coercive control in cases of IPV because of the slipperiness of the concept. Moreover, Hamberger et al.'s (2017), review of the literature shows that almost equal numbers of men and women report IPV and the discrepancy in awareness of this may be related to how the concept of control is understood. Without adequate measurement, appropriate action will be limited and the well-recognised negative experiences of women in the criminal justice process will not be ameliorated. Walklate and Fitz-Gibbon (2019) argue that there may be more effective methods to deal with coercive control in IPV cases, outside of the CJS. In a similar way that learning from cases of torture, prisoners of war, cults and domestic abuse (Hopper & Hidalgo) was used to inform understanding of psychological coercion in human trafficking, taking learning from IPV cases and the experiences of women in the CJS may be a more fruitful way forward to address coercive control in MSHT cases and support victims more effectively.

As discussed in this chapter, although coercive control was introduced in legislation for IPV/DV cases in 2014, its features remain hidden in a cloud of confusion for many members of the public. Professionals who encounter victims are often unaware of how to identify this phenomenon, its impact on victims and the type of support victims need to overcome the long-lasting psychological effects. Engaging in criminal justice processes can be disempowering for women in these cases and can contribute to further damage. In modern slavery and human trafficking cases, coercion is recognised as a feature of control by the perpetrator over the victim. Yet this recognition does nothing to allay the fears of victims, or counteract the psychological damage incurred due to their imprisonment-without-chains. Training for professionals who encounter individuals who have been subjected to coercive control needs to ensure that relevant knowledge and expertise leads to a targeted and prompt response to prevent further psychological damage. In the CJS, the impact on women should take priority and a range of alternative interactions considered.

Greater awareness amongst the general population could be gained through informed media campaigns, documentaries, films and other popular cultural artefacts to considerable effect with the potential to identify victims sooner, alleviating further damage. As Mellins (2022) discussion of stalking and coercive control (chapter 7) also highlights that education within schools, further and higher education could also improve knowledge of the methods of coercive control so that young people can take action against the perpetrators. First, to ensure that those who have personal experience of being coerced or controlled know where to report this, which may include a combination of family and/or experts (teachers, safeguarding officers, youth workers, police, counsellors, social workers). Second, young people should be provided with opportunities to discuss the particular challenges they face in the context of twenty-first century social media, sites in which potential perpetrators prey. By understanding coercive control, they can begin to identify the danger signs for themselves and others and report their fears to supportive adults. Finally, they can also be agents of change through developing campaigns in schools/local communities to raise awareness of coercive control in IPV/DV and MSHT contexts.

Study Questions

- What role does online and screen media play in communicating about coercive control?
- How are modern slavery and human trafficking represented in media?

- What are some of the behaviours associated with coercive control outlined in this chapter? Are they different in DV/IPV and modern slavery and human trafficking cases? In what ways?
- What are the impacts of coercive control on victims' lives? Are they different in DV/IPV and modern slavery and human trafficking cases? In what ways?
- What are the barriers or benefits to including coercive control in criminal cases?
- How can public awareness of coercive control be improved? Outline some key methods of awareness raising for DV/IPV and MSHT.

Bibliography

Abas, M., Ostrovschi, N. V., Prince, M., Gorceag, V. I., Trigub, C., & Oram, S. (2013). Risk factors for mental disorders in women survivors of human trafficking: A historical cohort study. *BMC Psychiatry, 13*(1), 1–11.

Altun, S., Abas, M., Zimmerman, C., Howard, L. M., & Oram, S. (2017). Mental health and human trafficking: Responding to survivors' needs. *Bjpsych International, 14*(1), 21–23.

Biderman, A. (1957). Communist attempts to elicit false confessions from air force prisoners of war. *Bulletin of the New York Academy of Medicine, 33,* 616–625.

Birks, J. & Gardner, A. (2019). Introducing the slave next door. *Anti-Trafficking Review, 13,* 66–81. https://doi.org/10.14197/atr.201219135

Baldwin, S., Fehrenbacher, A., & Eisenman, D. (2014, November 4). Psychological coercion in human trafficking: An application of Biderman's framework. *Qualitative Health Research.* Published Online. https://doi.org/10.1177/1049732314557087

Benedict, H. (1993). *Vamp or virgin: How the press covers sex crime.* Oxford University Press.

Boulette, T., & Anderson, S. (1986). Mind control and the battering of women. *Cultic Studies Journal, 3*(25). Available at http://Csj.Org/Studyindex/Studywomen/Study%20_Womenbatter.htm

Bruggeman, J., & Keyes, E. (2009). *Meeting the legal needs of human trafficking victims: An introduction for domestic violence attorneys and advocates.* Chicago, IL: American Bar Association.

Christie, N. (1986). *The ideal victim. In from crime policy to victim policy* (pp. 17–30). London: Palgrave Macmillan.

Cwikel, J., Chudakov, B., Paikin, M., Agmon, K., & Belmaker, R. H. (2004). Trafficked female sex workers awaiting deportation: Comparison with brothel workers. *Archives of Women's Mental Health, 7*(4), 243–249.

Dando, C., Walsh, D., & Brierley, R. (2016). Perceptions of psychological coercion and human trafficking in The West Midlands of England: Beginning to know the unknown. *PLoS ONE, 11*(5), E0153263. https://doi.org/10.1371/Journal.Pone.0153263

Douglas, H. (2018). Legal systems abuse and coercive control. *Criminology & Criminal Justice, 18*(1), 84–99. https://doi.org/10.1177/174889 5817728380

Dunkerley, A. W. (2018). Exploring the use of juju in Nigerian human trafficking networks: Considerations for criminal investigators. *Police Practice and Research, 19*(1), 83–100.

Fang, S., Coverdale, J., Nguyen, P., & Gordon, M. (2018). Tattoo recognition in screening for victims of human trafficking. *The Journal of Nervous and Mental Disease, 206*(10), 824–827.

Gajic-Veljanoski, O., & Stewart, D. E. (2007). Women trafficked into prostitution: Determinants, human rights and health needs. *Transcultural psychiatry, 44*(3), 338–358.

Goldberg, A., Moore, J., Houck, C., Kaplan, D., & Barron, C. (2017). Domestic minor sex trafficking patients: A retrospective analysis of medical presentation. *Journal of Pediatric and Adolescent Gynecology, 30*(1), 109–115.

Gregoriou, C. (2018). *Representations of transnational human trafficking: Present-day news media, true crime, and fiction* (p. 153). Springer Nature.

Hamberger, L., Larsen, S., & Lehrner, A. (2017). Coercive control in intimate partner violence. *Aggression and Violent Behavior, 37*, 1–11.

Herman, J. (1992). *Trauma and recovery.* Basic Books. Available at https://whatnow727.files.wordpress.com/2018/04/herman_trauma-and-recovery.pdf

Hopper, E, & Hidalgo, J. (2006). Invisible chains: Psychological coercion of human trafficking victims. *Intercultural Human Rights Law Review, 1*,185.

Hossain, M., Zimmerman, C., Abas, M., Light, M., & Watts, C. (2010). The relationship of trauma to mental disorders among trafficked and sexually exploited girls and women. *American Journal of Public Health, 100*(12), 2442–2449.

Iglesias-Rios, L., Harlow, S., Burgard, S., Kiss., S., & Zimmerman, C. (2018). Mental health, violence and psychological coercion among female and male trafficking survivors in the greater mekong sub-region: A cross-sectional study. *BMC Psychology.*

Ikeora, M. (2016). The role of African traditional religion and "Juju" in human trafficking: Implications for anti-trafficking. *Journal of International Women's Studies, 17*(1), 1–18.

McClenaghan, M., & Boutaud, C. (2017, November 24). Questions raised over patchy take-up of Domestic Violence Laws. *The Bureau of Investigative Journalism.* Available at https://www.thebureauinvestigates.com/stories/2017-11-24/coercive-control-concerns. Accessed 20 August.

McMahon, M., & McGorrerry, P. (2016). Criminalising controlling and coercive behaviour: The next step in the prosecution of family violence? *Alternative Law Journal, 41*(2).

Mellins, M. (2022). Stalking, the media and public awareness. In M. Mellins & S. Moore (Eds.), *Critiquing violent crime in the media.* Palgrave Macmillan.

Moore, S. E. (2014). *Crime and the media.* Macmillan International Higher Education.

O' Connell-Davis, J. (2015). *Modern slavery: The margins of freedom.* Palgrave Macmillan.

Oram, S., Khondoker, M., Abas, M., Broadbent, M., & Howard, L. M. (2015). Characteristics of trafficked adults and children with severe mental illness: A historical cohort study. *The Lancet Psychiatry, 2*(12), 1084–1091.

Physicians for Human Rights, Interrogations, Torture and Ill Treatment: Legal Requirements and Health Consequences 9–10. (2004). Available at http://Phrusa.Org/Research/Pdf/Iraq_Medical_Consequences.pdf [Hereinafter Physicians for Human Rights]. Accessed August 2020.

Preble, K. M. (2019). Under their "control": Perceptions of traffickers' power and coercion among international female trafficking survivors during exploitation. *Victims & Offenders, 14*(2), 199–221.

Raghavan, C., & Doychak, K. (2015). Trauma-coerced bonding and victims of sex trafficking: Where do we go from here? *International Journal of Emergency Mental Health And Human Resilience*, 17(2), 583–587. ISSN 1522-4821.

Raymond, J. G., Hughes, D. M., & Gomez, C. J. (2001). Sex trafficking of women in the United States. *International Sex Trafficking of Women & Children: Understanding the Global Epidemic*, 3–14.

Roe-Sepowitz, D., Hickle, K., Dahlstedt, J., & Gallagher, J. (2014). Victim or whore: The similarities and differences between victim's experiences of domestic violence and sex trafficking. *Journal Of Human Behavior in the Social Environment, 24*(8), 883–898. https://doi.org/10.1080/10911359.2013.840552.

Stark, E. (2007). *Coercive control: How men entrap women in personal life.* Oxford University Press.

Travis, A. (2016, May 17). Police treatment of domestic abuse victims to be investigated; Theresa May says too many victims being let down by 'shameful attitudes' of some officers and orders major inquiry. *The Guardian,* Tuesday 7:27 pm. Accessed August 2020 on Lexis Library News.

Van der Watt, M., & Kruger, B. (2017). Exploring 'Juju' and human trafficking: Towards a demystified perspective and response. *South African Review of Sociology, 48*(2), 70–86.

van der Watt, M., & Kruger, B. (2020). Breaking bondages: Control methods, "Juju," and human trafficking. *The Palgrave International Handbook of Human Trafficking,* 935–951.

Walby, S., & Towers, J. (2018). Untangling the concept of coercive control: Theorizing domestic violent crime. *Criminology & Criminal Justice, 18*(1), 7–28. https://doi.org/10.1177/1748895817743541

Walker, L. E. (1984). *The battered woman syndrome.* Harper & Row.

Walklate, S. & Fitz-Gibbon, K. (2019). The criminalisation of coercive control: The power of law? *International Journal for Crime, Justice and Social Democracy, 8*(4), 94–108. https://doi.org/10.5204/ijcjsd.v8i4.1205

Zimmerman, C., & Borland, R. (2009). *Caring for trafficked persons: Guidance for health providers.* International Organisation for Migration.

Websites and Other Resources

Barlow, C. (2020). *Private communication* (prepared court report for R-v-Ahmed case).

BBC. (2020). *Coronation Street.*

BBC news online. (2013). Connors servitude case: More than 100 people may have been held. Available at https://www.bbc.co.uk/news/uk-england-beds-bucks-herts-22446454. Accessed August 2020.

Breen, J. (2015, December 4). Domestic abuse 'champions' in workplaces will help victims. *The Northern Echo* (Newsquest Regional Press).

Channel 4. (2019). *I am...Nicola.*

Chipperfield, D. (2017, March 4). 'Sex slaves' Home is shut by court in police trafficking inquiry. Order prevents others going to house at centre of probe. *Gloucestershire Echo*.

Dando, C. (2020, January 25). Controlling marriages are more common than you'd think; 'Deadwater Fell' is dark, but reflects reality, says the show's consultant psychologist, Coral Dando. *The Daily Telegraph* (London) Coral Dando.

East Anglian Daily Times. (2020, January 7). Police pledge after data inspection finds crime reports go unrecorded. *East Anglian Daily Times*.

Faulkner, D. (2020). *Coercive control is 'all of our business'*. Available at https://www.bbc.co.uk/news/uk-52502409

Garavelli, D. (2016, July 9). Dani Garavelli: Remember the last false dawn of feminism, *Scotsman*.

Gill, M. (2019, July 15). Theresa May's positive legacy? She's a feminist champion; She did good work on domestic violence and FGM, and has been tireless in helping other women to advance. *The Guardian* (London).

Gloucestershire Echo. (2017, May 5). Coercion and rape probe is to go on. *Gloucestershire Echo*.

Gloucestershire Echo. (2020). Age limit for 'sexual entertainment' shows to be increased to 25. *Gloucestershire Echo*.

Her Majesties Inspectorate of Constabulary and Fire and Rescue Services (HMICFRS). 2017. *Stolen freedom: The policing response to modern slavery and human trafficking*.

Home Office. (2015). *Controlling or coercive behaviour statutory guidance*. https://Assets.Publishing.Service.Gov.Uk/Government/Uploads/System/Uploads/Attachment_Data/File/482528/Controlling_Or_Coercive_Behaviour_-_Statutory_Guidance.pdf. Accessed August 2020.

Horman, R. (2019). *A practical guide to coercive control for legal practitioners and victims*. Law Brief Publishing http://www.Lawbriefpublishing.Com/2019/11/Free-Chapter-From-A-Practical-Guide-To-Coercive-Control-For-Legal-Practitioners-And-Victims-By-Rachel-Horman/. Accessed August 2020.

Inge, S. (2016, November 25). An incident of violence in NI homes every 19 minutes sparks call for greater action; 28,000 domestic abuse cases recorded in last year is most since 2004. *Belfast Telegraph*.

Iqbal, N. (2018, October 27). Alison Saunders: 'You wouldn't be human if accusations didn't affect you'. Outgoing director of public prosecutions faced vitriolic criticism despite steering the CPS through turbulent times. *The Observer* (London).

Kenway, E. (2020). *Focus on labour exploitation (Flex) messaging modern slavery: Expert panel and discussion.* Available at https://www.Youtube.Com/Watch? V=Uxmg8cjxxwa&Feature=Youtu.Be

Kerridge, J. (2020, January). Snubbed by critics, adored by readers, MC Beaton was a worthy successor to Agatha Christie. *telegraph.co.uk.*

Lexis Library News (in order of publication, newest to oldest. *indicates refers to coercive control only).

Mangan, L. (2019). I am Nicola review: Rare, stunning TV about an awful phenomenon. *The Guardian.* Available at https://www.theguardian.com/tv-and-radio/2019/jul/23/i-am-nicola-review-inside-toxic-trap-coercive-relati onship. Accessed January 2021.

McGleenon, B. (2020, April 15). Inside China's quest to become an AI superpower. The Belt and Road Initiative has brought an unprecedented influx of Chinese investment to the sleepy fishing town of Sihanoukville in Cambodia. But, as Brian McGleenon discovers, with great capital comes even greater control. *The Independent* (United Kingdom).

McPherson, L., Raimes, V., Mega, M., & Craig McDonald (2014, June 1). Fighting for justice behind closed doors. Prosecutor on why new laws are needed to protect women enduring years of torment leader of legal team wants to put brutes in the dock for years of abuse. *Daily Record and Sunday Mail.*

Mc Lennan, P. (2020). *Coronation street coercive control storyline hits home for emotional viewers.* https://www.radiotimes.com/news/soaps/coronation-street/2020-07-23/coronation-street-control-hits-home/

Modern Slavery Act. (2015). Available at https://www.legislation.gov.uk/ukpga/2015/30/contents/enacted

Murphy, C. (2018). *A game of chance? Long-term Support for survivors of modern slavery.* St. Mary's University. https://www.stmarys.ac.uk/research/centres/modern-slavery/docs/2018-jun-a-game-of-chance.pdf

Neate, P. (2015, December 29). *Women's aid welcomes coercive control law* (Press Release). https://www.Womensaid.Org.Uk/Womens-Aid-Welcomes-Coercive-Control-Law/. Accessed August 2020.

Norris, P. (2017, March 9). Woman arrested during probe into human trafficking. Four alleged female modern slavery victims identified. *Gloucestershire Echo.*

Oppenheim, M. (2020, May 16). 'It's a toxic environment': Honour-based abuse reports surge in lockdown. *The Independent.*

Petter, O. (2018, December 28). The independent's women of 2018: From Christine Blasey Ford to Michelle Obama: The female activists, politicians and actors who campaigned, rallied and fought for equality this year. *The Independent* (United Kingdom).

Phillips, J. (2019, July 19). Swings and roundabouts as May fails to deliver on her best intentions; What, if anything, has Theresa May done for women during her years as Prime Minister? Labour MP. *The Western Mail*.

Pook, L., & Graham, K. (2018, July 1). The secret slavery next door. From the woman who paints your nails to the one cleaning your neighbour's house, we investigate the terrifying world of trafficking that's hidden in plain sight. *The Sun* (England).

Purves, L. (2020, May 26). Barn weddings are off: It's ambridge in the time of corona. *The Daily Mail and Mail on Sunday* (London).

'Sex slaves' Home is shut by court in police trafficking inquiry, The Citizen Gloucester, 04 March 2017.

Stop The Traffick. (2020). *Scale of the issue.* https://www.Stopthetraffik.Org/About-Human-Trafficking/The-Scale-Of-Human-Trafficking/. Accessed August 2020.

Tegeltija, S. (2016, August 1). Wales 'leading the way' in fight against slavery. PM in £33m fund to fight 'the evil trade'. *The Western Mail*.

Travis, A. (2016, May 17). Police treatment of domestic abuse victims to be investigated. Theresa May says too many victims being let down by 'shameful attitudes' of some officers and orders major inquiry. *The Guardian* (London).

UNHCR. (2000). *Palermo protocol, protocol to prevent, supress and punish trafficking in persons especially women and children supplementing the United Nations convention against transnational organised crime.* https://www.Ohchr.Org/En/Professionalinterest/Pages/Protocoltraffickinginpersons.Aspx

Walker, P. (2016, April 1). Briton who made wife live like slave is first to be jailed for domestic servitude. *The Guardian*. Available at https://www.theguardian.com/uk-news/2016/apr/01/man-made-wife-live-like-slave-domestic-servitude-faces-jail?CMP=Share_iOSApp_Other

Western Daily Press. (2020, August 6). New changes for sexual entertainment policy after review. *Western Daily Press*.

Wheeler, C., & Hellen, N. (2019, January 20). New bill to ease court agony for victims of domestic abuse. *The Sunday Times* (London).

Witkin, R. (2013). *OSCE office of the special representative and co-ordinator for combating trafficking in human beings trafficking in human beings amounting to torture and other forms of ill-treatment.* Available at https://www.osce.org/files/f/documents/d/b/103085.pdf. Accessed August 2020.

Part III

Consuming Homicide Narratives

9

That Photograph: Serial Killer as Modern Celebrity

Ian Cummins, Marian Foley, and Martin King

Introduction

In October 1965, the police in Hyde, Greater Manchester received a phone call from David Smith reporting that he had witnessed a murder. Following the phone call, the police went to a house on a housing estate in Hattersley. The house was occupied by Ian Brady, Myra Hindley and her grandmother. The police found the body of Edward Evans. They arrested Brady and four days later Hindley (Cummins et al., 2019). Since that date, the Moors Murders case has never disappeared from popular and media culture. Brady and Hindley became icons of evil, a reference point against which future crimes were measured. The term serial

---

I. Cummins (✉)
School of Health and Society, Salford University, Salford, UK
e-mail: i.d.cummins@salford.ac.uk

M. Foley · M. King
Manchester Metropolitan University, Manchester, UK

© The Author(s), under exclusive license to Springer Nature
Switzerland AG 2021
M. Mellins and S. Moore (eds.), *Critiquing Violent Crime in the Media*,
https://doi.org/10.1007/978-3-030-83758-7_9

killer was not in use at the time of their arrest. However, they were soon inducted into that category by the media. In analysing the wider cultural impact of the coverage of crimes, it is important to emphasise that we are in no way diminishing or underplaying the brutality, violence and degradation involved. We are arguing that one of the results of the salacious media coverage of the case is to do that. It is not that the media coverage sets out to do this. It is rather the cumulative impact of the obsessive mining of the details of the case and Brady and Hindley's relationship to produce a '*definitive account*'.

The Moors Murders case has become an archetype of mediatised murder. This archetype reflects the symbiotic relationship between the media and crime. As previously noted, the '*true crime*' genre is able to keep its market share and reproduce itself by a combination of new stories or new angles on old ones. The Moors Murders has been a feature of British cultural life for nearly sixty years (Lee, 2010). Following the death of Brady in 2017, this may be on the wane. Part of the reason for its position in the news media is the nature of the crimes that Brady and Hindley committed. Alongside this, the case has always been in '*the shadow of the rope*'—the death penalty was abolished whilst Brady and Hindley were on remand. If they had been arrested earlier then they would have almost certainly been executed. The involvement of a woman in such crimes is also a factor in the fascination in the case. Finally, there has been a series of astonishing news stories linked to the case—Hindley's attempted prison escape, the confessions to the murders of Pauline Reade and Keith Bennett and the taking of Brady and Hindley to the Moors— that mean that it has never been that far from the centre of the news cycle.

Features of the Moors case and its aftermath, such as the payment of witnesses for their stories, the focus on exploring the lives of the perpetrators to construct a psychological profile and the exploitation of the victims' families suffering have all become aspects of the modern serial killing industry (Cummins et al., 2019). These events occurred when TV representations of murder and violent crime did not dominate the schedules in the way that they do now. The photographs of Brady and Hindley taken at Hyde police station in 1965 have been produced countless times since. These images have come to play a key role in the representation of Brady and Hindley as icons of evil. They are also key factors in the development of the cult of the serial killer as celebrity. The creation and management of the image and public profile is a key element of modern celebrity culture. These images become texts, on to which the viewer transposes their own readings. Myra Hindley came to be seen as the most evil woman in Britain. In a sense, Brady and Hindley acted as some sort of yardstick, a point of reference for other crimes and acts of evil (Clark, 2011). The photograph links Hindley to other '*evil*' blondes such as Irma Grese, the concentration camp guard who was executed for her role in the Holocaust. This chapter will use an analysis of the famous photographs taken of Brady and Hindley at the time of their arrest as a basis for the exploration of the modern celebrity status of the serial killer. It will then explore the pivotal role of *that photograph* in the construction of Hindley as '*a monster*' (Birch, 1994; Clark, 2011).

The Moors Murders

Following the arrest of Ian Brady, the police recovered two suit-cases belonging to Brady at Manchester Central Station. The suitcases contained photographs and the tape of the torture of Lesley Ann Downey. Lesley Ann Downey had been missing since Boxing Day 1964. Brady and Hindley had abducted her from a fair in Manchester. Her body and that of John Kilbride were recovered from the Moors above Manchester. John Kilbride had been reported missing in November 1963. He had disappeared after helping stall holders clear up at Ashton Market. Brady and Hindley's trial began on 19 April, 1966 at Chester Assizes (Hansford Johnson, 1967). This was the first high profile murder case since the passing of *T*he Murder (Abolition of Death Penalty) Act 1965 which suspended the death penalty for five years. On 6 May 1966, Brady was found guilty of the murders of John Kilbride, Lesley Ann Downey and Edward Evans. Hindley was convicted of two murders and being an accessory in the murder of John Kilbride. During the trial, the tape that Brady and Hindley had made of their abuse and torture of Lesley Ann Downey was played in open Court. Justice Fenton Atkinson described this as a '*truly horrible case*' and Brady as '*wicked beyond belief*'

(Winter, 2002, p. 351). He felt that if Hindley was removed from Brady's influence then there was the possibility that she could be rehabilitated. They were sentenced to life imprisonment. In the 1980s, Brady and Hindley confessed to the murder of Pauline Reade and Keith Bennett who been reported missing in Manchester in 1963 and 1964.

Bricolage

In carrying out the research for this chapter, we use bricolage as a research method. Bricolage as an approach is supported by Levi-Strauss's (1972) ideas on the cultural sphere. It allows for the exploration of complexity and ambiguity via a range of texts and sources. These sources can be historical texts, films, novels and so on. Lincoln (2001) sees the bricoleur as akin to an anthropologist. Wibberley (2012, p. 6) argues 'bricolage brings together in some form, different sources of data'. The result is a form of reflexive commentary (Wibberley, 2012) in which the subject guides or creates the methodology rather than there being 'correct' methodologies that are universally applicable, creating a new hybrid method for each new project.

The continued fascination with the Moors Murders, which we should acknowledge our work contributes to, means that there is a huge range of texts that can be examined. In addition to the famous photographs, this research also explores novels, TV dramas, 'true crime' accounts, and Harvey's painting of Hindley. The 'true crime' accounts included for this study were *Beyond Belief* (Williams, 1992), *The Trial of the Moors Murders* (Goodman, 1986), *The Lost Boy* (Staff, 2013), *Topping the Autobiography* (Topping, 1989), *Witness* (Smith & Lee, 2011) and *One of Your Own* (Lee, 2010).

Serial Killers, Modernity and Celebrity

The serial killing industry has been focused on producing 'psycho' biographies of serial killers and 'true crime' accounts of their crimes (Haggerty, 2009), often combining lurid detail with a search for the causes of deviant behaviour. There are features of serial killing that set it apart from other forms of murder. The most distinctive feature is the lack of any prior relationship between the killer and the victim. The targeting of groups and selection of potential victims alongside the process of planning the crime is part of the motivation of the killer (Wilson, 2007). These are not, therefore, random acts. The victims become a means to an end for the killer. These factors are clear in the Moors murders case. Brady's notebooks, which contained detailed plans of the crimes, were found by the police after his arrest.

The serial killer is in Foucault's (1990, pp. 42–43) terms 'a new specification of individuals'. Prior to the creation of the term, there were clearly people who carried out multiple murders. The development and usage of the term is a reflection of modern forms of classification—in Foucault's terms, the creation of the case. Alongside these developments, the current use of the term is bound up with new academic and popular discourses—for example psychological profiling—which seek to explain and categorise serial killers whilst unveiling their hidden motivations and the traumas that created them. Psychological profiling makes the claim that by the analysis of crime scenes and a series of other factors, it can provide a detailed psychological portrait of an offender that will assist the police. The overlap between academic discourse and popular culture is readily apparent here. As much as the the serial killer, the psychological profiler is now a fixture in popular culture. In the academic world, offender profiling has become a recognised subsection of forensic psychology—with all that entails in terms of research funding, academic status and prominence. The circle is complete when psychology profilers appear on TV or in the newspaper to provide their explanations of the motivations of killers they have never met or produce programmes 'solving' historical crimes, such as the Whitechapel murders, using modern techniques.

Haggerty (2009) sees serial killing as a by-product of the anonymity of modern life. This can be viewed in two ways. The first is that this anonymity and rootlessness leads to the corrosion of prosocial values in the modern urban *society of strangers*. The second element here is that modern society creates an environment where the serial killer can circulate amongst the population, their seeming normality allowing them to move freely, undetected in this society of strangers, as ordinary people seemingly going about their ordinary lives. This allows them to commit crimes over such a long period (Haggerty, 2009). One common feature of the reporting of serial killers is quotes from those who lived alongside or knew the killer describing them as ordinary (Cummins et al., 2019). However, when they are convicted they are represented as the embodiment of evil. In the case of Brady and Hindley, prior to their arrests, they were clearly seen as an odd or unusual couple in the working class community they inhabited (Lee, 2010). They cultivated an image and dressed in a distinctive fashion and so on. However, we have found no real evidence that they were suspected of any involvement in the abduction and murder of children prior to their arrest (Cummins et al., 2019).

Haggerty (2009) argued that the social atomisation that occurs in late modernity leads to the marginalisation of vulnerable groups. The status of the victim has been a factor in the failure to apprehend serial killers (Wilson, 2007) and the hierarchy of victims constructed in media reporting of serial killing compounds the issue. The victims of serial killers are more likely to come from groups that are regarded as being on the margins of society (Egger, 2002). This, alongside the fact that there is not a personal link between the victim and perpetrator helps to explain why the initial investigation into the first murders that serial killers commit are often not investigated adequately or given high profile media coverage. The police investigation into attacks and murders committed by Peter Sutcliffe highlight this (Wattis, 2018, 2020). Egger (2002) described marginalised victims as the '*less dead*', in the sense that the media create a hierarchy of cultural value. In Sutcliffe's case the distinguishing between his different victims as innocent or somehow deserving, both by the investigating police force and the tabloid media, has been well documented (Smith, 1989; Wattis, 2018). This is an area where there has been a shift from the early 1960s. To the modern reader, one of the startling features of the Moors murders case is how comparatively little attention was paid to the disappearance of the victims. Even allowing for the fact that they took place in areas covered by different police forces, it is surprising that links were not made between the missing children Pauline Reade, John Kilbride, Lesley Ann Downey and

Keith Bennett. In contrast, Greer (2004, p. 113) notes that one of the features of the modern reporting of crime is the *'foregrounding of crime victims'*. This is linked to a wider societal sense of insecurity. One of the features of late modernity is that wider personal freedom is accompanied by increased levels of insecurity (Bauman, 2007). Crime and fear of crime has a particular place in these modern, particularly urban, notions of insecurity. Simon (2007) highlights the way that the media creation of the figure of the serial killer as a modern bogeyman has played a clear role here. These events are, thankfully, very rare indeed. However, media coverage and the dominance of the hunt for serial killers in modern cop dramas and films distort this.

In outlining serial killing as a product of modernity, Haggerty (2009) highlights the creation of the mass media and its symbiotic relationship with popular culture, with particular reference to the latter half of the 20th century. Celebrity and crime are key features here. Serial killing combines these features in one package. Modern celebrity is a bizarrely fluid category. It includes TV presenters, film stars, reality TV contestants and sexual killers like Brady and Hindley. In addition, there is an increasing group of celebrities who are famous for simply being famous. The roots of this fame are lost in the mists of time. However, fame is an ongoing process, that requires the creation and maintenance of an identity or a series of identities. Reinvention or the shedding of a previous skin is at the heart of the celebrity engagement with their public. Celebrity thus becomes a category in and off itself with its own rules and culture.

Cummins et al. (2019) suggest that one way of examining the media responses to the Moors Murders is to see them as the dark side of the swinging sixties, a time when the celebrity culture outlined above was starting to take shape. Early commentators, such as Hansford-Johnson and her husband C.P. Snow, saw the case as the result of the alleged permissive nature of modern Britain and the collapse of traditional values. As noted above, Brady and Hindley became part of the nascent celebrity culture. Rojek (2001, p. 10) defines celebrity as 'the attribution of glamour or notorious status to an individual within the public sphere ... the impact on public consciousness'. He sees celebrity as a cultural fabrication, with mass media representation as the key principle in the formation of celebrity culture. Rojek's (2001) explanation for the emergence of celebrity as a public preoccupation is threefold: the democratisation of society, the decline in organised religion and the commodification of everyday life. Whilst Rojek's (2001) work provides an attempt to explain the rise of celebrity culture in the late twentieth century, the features identified are already recognised as being in play in the 1960s, the period in which Brady and Hindley committed their crimes (Marwick, 1998).

The democratisation of *'swinging'* Sixties celebrity is well documented elsewhere (King, 2013; Sandbrook, 2006). A key feature in this was the rise of the *'ordinary'* man and woman to celebrity status, a world, real or mythical, where the Royals and the great and the good rubbed shoulders with working class actors, pop stars, film makers and photographers (Sandbrook, 2006). David Bailey's *Box of Pinups* (1965) is regarded as a key artefact in documenting this phenomenon, featuring as it does members of the Beatles, the Rolling Stones, Michael Caine, David Hockney, Jean Shrimpton and others, an attempt to document this democratised celebrity. Amongst the others are the Kray Twins, notorious East End gangsters eventually jailed in 1969. Rojek (2001) argues that notoriety is one route into modern day celebrity. He states:

> [...] the figure of notoriety possesses colour, instant cache and may even in some circles be invested with heroism for daring to release the emotions of blocked aggression and sexuality that civilised society seeks to repress. (Rojek, 2001, p. 15)

However, Brady and Hindley's long-term celebrity has been based on public revulsion. The contrast with the Krays is stark. Despite being notorious gangland torturers and killers, they still seem to be regarded, fifty years on with a kind of public benevolence. They have been celebrated in two feature films, the second of which, *Legend* (dir. Helgeland, 2015) focuses on the style and glamour aspect of their 1960s working class hero celebrity status.

The incorporation of serial killers into the modern category of celebrity is part of the transformation of violent crime into a cultural and entertainment product. There is a symbiotic relationship between crime and media. Violent crime is generally newsworthy and receives extensive coverage. The nature of sexual and violent crime and its comparative rarity are factors in these decisions. It is not the case that all violent crime receives the same level of coverage (Jewkes, 2004). For example, femicide is marginalised and often presented in a misogynistic and victim blaming fashion (Wattiss, 2020). This moral economy is often reflected in the media profile that is given to the perpetrator. For example, Kenneth Erskine was convicted of the murder of seven senior citizens in 1988. He was sentenced to be detained under the provisions of the Mental Health Act (MHA, 1983). However, this case has not received the level of coverage of other serial killers in England and Wales (Cummins et al., 2019). One factor in this is the marginalised status of his victims. With this important caveat in mind—that not all serial killing 'makes the news', and the reasons for omission reflect social hierarchies—it is more generally the case that serial killing as a category of crime is more newsworthy than other offences, despite its rarity. Burn (2008, p. 38) coined the term '*murder leisure industry*' to capture the nature of the media/crime relationship, and draw attention to the tendency for media to sensationalise and dramatise murder. It is certainly notable that there are overlaps between the narrative of news reporting and dramatic representations of serial killing, such that it is difficult to discern 'fact' from 'fiction'. From the initial discovery of the crime to the apprehension of the perpetrator, television news and 'true crime' accounts follow a similar arc, albeit that the former tends to be contemporaneous and the latter viewed from a distance. TV 'true crime' accounts use a number of tropes that also occur in film and dramas. The shot of the urban landscape at night to symbolise alienation, the heroic detective and the set piece news conference appear in both genres. Real events are then dramatised or dramatised events given the 'feel' of reality.

Serial killing, and 'true crime' more generally, have become a significant focus for cultural production (Soothill, 1993). Books, films, novels, TV dramas and the news media dominate in these areas. Alongside this, there is a market in serial killer memorabilia and murder mystery tours. The Ripper tours are one of London's biggest tourist attractions. There are tours of Edinburgh and Ystad based on the Rebus and Wallender novels (Cummins & King, 2015). Within this media market, the serial killer has become a dominant figure. The relationship between serial killers and the public has many of the elements of fan culture—for example, the collection of memorabilia and the obsessive poring over details of individual lives. Schmid (2006, p. 297) noted that what he called the trade in '*murderabilia*' was booming, pointing to the selling of a brick from US serial killer Jeffrey Dahmer's apartment building for $300 and a lock of Charles Manson's hair for $995 as examples. The commodification of fame and celebrity creates this market. As with all markets, there is a need to develop new products. In this case, the new products are either new killers or new details and items about an established case.

There is also something of a hierarchy of interest. Brady and Hindley were at the top of this pyramid for fifty years. This is probably still the case despite the passing of time since their arrest and the fact that they are now both dead. The market requires the reproduction of commodity value. This is something that has happened in the Brady and Hindley case at regular intervals since 1965. The death of Brady and Hindley not only led to spikes in interest in the case but further convulsions about the morality of the public and media interest in the case (Cummins et al., 2019). More generally, media coverage is sustained by what Lea (2014, p. 765) calls the 'disturbing attraction-in-repulsion of the transgressive celebrity'. In Rupert Thomson's novel *Death of a Murderer* (2008), Tyler, a prison officer, guards the body of a killer who is clearly Hindley. The Tyler character sums up this attraction-in-repulsion as he addresses the dead Hindley: 'You did something people couldn't bring themselves to think about. You forced them to imagine it. You rubbed their noses in it' (Thomson, 2008, p. 298).

This horror-filled attraction partly accounts for the extraordinary and sustained media attention to the Moors Murders case, including documentaries and films examining virtually all aspects of the case. *See No Evil: The Moors Murders* (dir. Menaul, 2006), a television drama, shown on the fortieth anniversary of the sentencing of Brady and Hindley, is a dramatic reconstruction of the crimes of Brady and Hindley and as such blurs the lines between fact and fiction. At this point, Hindley was dead. In an example of the symbiotic relationship between the media and crime, there was media coverage of Brady's attempt to have the programme blocked (MailOnline, 2005). Brady was clearly aware that these moves would receive significant coverage. Brady objected on the grounds that the mini-series was based on Emlyn Williams' (1992) *Beyond Belief,* which was originally published in 1967 following the conviction of Brady and Hindley. *Beyond Belief* used an approach inspired by Capote's *In Cold Blood,* by including events that the author had invented.

Given the subject matter and its cast (which included Maxine Peake), *See No Evil* (dir. Menaul, 2006) was always likely to attract a large audience. The episodes were originally shown over two nights attracting audiences of over 6 million. The series won a BAFTA at the 2007 awards. The mini-series was a homage to the kitchen sink dramas of the 1960s—such as *Saturday Night and Sunday Morning* and the long running UK soap opera *Coronation Street.* These cultural products had a significant role in the creation of nostalgic images of post war, working class community life. The Moors Murders, in addition to the personal suffering and grief, destroyed this particular vision of community solidarity, so the use of conventions from the original kitchen sink drama in *See no Evil* (dir. Menaul, 2006) was important in illustrating how the Moors Murders fractured this cosy image of working class life. Whilst the series was made in consultation with and with the approval of surviving relatives of the victims it can still be seen as a cultural artefact which is part of the serial killing industry, a further commodification of the case.

Seltzer (1997) argued the public culture of modernity includes a fascination with—almost an addiction to—violence and its representation. Seltzer (1997) coined the term '*wound culture*' to describe this phenomenon. The term encompasses the fascination with a display of defiled and abused bodies. *Wound culture* can be extended from the physical to the psychological, thus it includes a fascination with trauma and its aftermath. Seltzer (1997) argues that a key element of *wound culture* is the public display of distress. This has become entwined with celebrity culture in several ways. Killers such as Brady and Hindley become subject to salacious interest. As with all serial killers, there is both an academic and media interest in excavating their histories, looking for causes rooted in past personal trauma. In the case of the serial killer these traumas have usually remained as private 'wounds', whereas public displays of trauma have become a key feature of the arc of the modern celebrity narrative. One of the key points in the celebrity journey is the confrontation with their own 'personal demons', as they are usually referred to in the press coverage. The repeated examination of 'the wound' is a cornerstone of modern celebrity culture. Hindley herself produced such an explanation for her involvement in the Moors Murders (*The Guardian*, 2000) suggesting that she had been brutalised by Brady and then threatened into participating. For the public, however, this argument held little water and did little to change media representation of public perceptions of Hindley or challenge her 'most evil woman in Britain' status. In many ways Hindley provides the perfect illustration of how Seltzer's (1997) *wound culture* operates, not least because one iconic artefact— 'that photograph'—has come to symbolise the epitome of evil in the eyes of the public, due to a media narrative which was consistent over a number of decades.

That Photograph

Central to the construction of the image of Brady and Hindley have been the photographs taken by the police when they were arrested in 1965. Hindley became the '*most hated woman in Britain*' (see Wilde, 2016 for a discussion of the media use of this term). The case raises fundamental questions about punishment and the potential for reform. Brady never sought parole but Hindley did. In her long campaign for parole, she was never able to escape *that photograph*, taken when she was twenty-three, which was used by the media as a cipher for evil but also as a representation of her continuing threat.

The news of the arrest of Brady, and subsequently Hindley, led to the police search for bodies on the Moors. From that point, there was huge public interest in the case accompanied by ongoing media coverage. This was a period where there was a significant expansion in TV news coverage alongside the print media. It was apparent that the killers were aware of their image and attempted to manage it. Lee (2010) draws attention to their smart attire, clothes cleaned and pressed before each day as part of their performance and public persona. Lee (2010) argues that Hindley in particular was the focus of media attention, adding that:

> How she looked became an obsession; for many the concept of evil had a face and walked into a courtroom. Her freshly bleached blonde hair was tinted lilac and she wore her make-up like a mask. (Lee, 2010, p. 270)

Hindley demonstrated a keen awareness of what Goffman (1967) calls the 'presentation of self'. A letter written to her mother before the trial, for example, reveals her interest in projecting a particular appear-ance:

> Dear mam, as you know the trial begins three weeks on Tuesday [...] could you bring me a bottle of make-up, it's Pond's Angel Face, shade Golden Rose. If you can't get Golden Rose, Tawny will do. (Lee, 2010, p. 219)

Hansford Johnson (1967, p. 22) tells us something about the public reac-tion to Hindley's image, and does so, interestingly, through comparison to the apparently more normal-looking Brady:

> [...] he is a cross between Joseph Goebbels and a bird .... He is dressed in a grey suit, a natty white handkerchief in his breast pocket. On the whole he looks ordinary. Myra Hindley does not[...] she could have served a nineteenth century Academy painter as a model for Clytemnestra: but sometimes she looks more terrible, like one of Fuesli's nightmare women drawn giant sized, elaborately coiffed.

She then goes on to describe Hindley's outfit and hairstyle in some detail. The language is florid and journalistic and the reference points a little obvious, but the concern with the minutiae of appearance is reminiscent of modern-day celebrity-focused magazines or the reporting of Royalty.

Photographers were not allowed into the trial. However, photographs appeared of the couple in *Paris Match*—a magazine that covered news but was more widely known for its fashion and celebrity gossip. Williams (1992) notes how composed both the accused were in the dock. Brady and Hindley's attention to personal grooming and immaculate presen-tation each day was part of a public performance—their last together and the creation of a public image that remained intact until their deaths (Lee, 2010). There was a focus on Hindley partly because of the widespread disbelief that a woman could be involved in such crimes against children (Lee, 2010). In addition, Hindley had presented an aura of calm since the day of her arrest—only becoming distressed when told of the death of her dog (Benfield, 1968).

In his summing up, the judge, whilst not denying Hindley's responsibility in the murders, emphasised Brady's influence. This was in keeping with the dominant children norms at that time concerning female passivity, which were beginning to be challenged by the feminist movement (Ehrenreich, 1983). Brady's Svengali-like influence over Hindley had been a feature of her defence. It was strengthened, not necessarily intentionally, by the judge's comments in his summing up. The judge suggested that away from Brady's influence there was some hope that Hindley would be capable of reform. The judge made it clear that he thought Brady was '*evil beyond belief*' (Winter, 2002, p. 352). These comments took on greater significance in the context of Hindley's quest for parole. Hindley, herself, argued that she had been mesmerised by Brady and coerced into taking part (Lee, 2010).

Hindley, throughout the trial then, was framed as monstrous 'other', a trope that goes back to Gothic fiction. Part of the attraction of the Gothic is that it produces fear (Ingebretsen, 1998). It is the frisson of fear that is the key to audience enjoyment. It can be difficult to distinguish between truth and fiction in this field as the 'myth' of the serial killer overwhelms the reality. For example, the portrayal of the serial killer as some sort of criminal mastermind, plotting, planning and outwitting the authorities is completely at odds with the overwhelming majority of such crimes. Serial killers are often described in the language of Gothic fiction or myth (Halberstam, 1995). They are monsters, vampires. The designation 'Ripper', generally thought to have originated with Jack the Ripper via media reporting of the Whitechapel murders, is a relatively modern addition to this Gothic lexicon. The use of the phrase 'Moors Murderers' establishes a broader cultural link to the Gothic representation of the Moors, given that the Moors is a key trope in Gothic fiction. Gothic fiction seeks to examine a relationship between space and the subject. The process of externalisation is such that the space comes to stand in for the subject. The location and the rugged terrain of the Moors become an ongoing feature, a character in the drama. They are an area of beauty but also they hold terrible secrets—they continue to do so, as the body of Keith Bennett, has never been found.

In Gothic fiction, the external physical appearance of a place can come to imbue evil just as a particular image of a killer can become a representation of the evil of which the individual is capable. There is often a glamour or attraction to this appearance. The modern media use of mugshots—the photographs of Brady and Hindley, taken at the point of their arrest in 1965, being amongst the most used example—alongside the reports of crime are an example of this. The photographs themselves are a standardised format but the audience can project feelings of repulsion and disgust on to them. The images of Brady and Hindley can be used for shock value—they are guaranteed to generate a response. Harvey's painting of Hindley, *Myra* (1995), is a leading example. Harvey's painting is a huge, 11 ft by 9 ft representation of the police mugshot photograph of Hindley. As you get nearer, it becomes clear that the painting consists of handprints of children. Walker (1998) suggests a semiotic analysis would emphasise that the use of the plaster-cast of a child's palm print to make the painting is a way of indicating that Hindley will never escape her crimes—*you may sleep but you will never dream* as the singer Morrissey put it. There is another connection to the Gothic here as there is an uncanniness to the image. From a distance it looks like one thing, on closer inspection it reveals something else, something horrifying. Harvey was seeking to make a comment about the nature of the media representation of Hindley and society's obsessive interest in her. One suspects that, however serious the artistic intent, Harvey knew that the painting would inevitably create a media storm. This it duly did. The painting was vandalised and then withdrawn from exhibition.

This fascination with seeing Hindley and Brady—motivated by an attraction–repulsion discussed above—has continued in various forms over the years. When Brady gave evidence at the Mental Health Review Tribunal (MHRT) hearing in 2013, there was a huge media interest accompanied with the Gothic frisson of the possibility of the sight of Brady fifty years on from his arrest (Cummins et al., 2016). It reflected, perhaps, a desire from the media that he would still look like his original mugshot, Dorian Gray-style, frozen at the point of his evil doings. Brady himself was clearly aware that the MHRT would be a media event. It was shown via a live-feed from Ashworth Special Hospital Media, and tickets were rationed with around 40 members of the Press watching from the media room (Cummins et al., 2016). There were also some tickets for the public in a separate court. Almost all reports of the hearing concentrated on Brady's appearance and his voice as though they would offer some final insight into his crimes. TV and newspaper reports were accompanied by a court artist's sketch alongside his arrest photograph (Cummins et al., 2016).

That arrest—of both Brady and Hindley—must also be amongst the most reproduced images in modern media. Lee (2010, p. 228) makes a similar point in his reconstruction of the photographing of Hindley:

> She was shown into a tiled cell. At one end stood an old-fashioned modern camera on a tripod. Lights glared down from the ceiling. The photographer told her where to stand and, then draped a black cloth over his head and adjusted the focus of the lens. The lights flashed and an image of unparalled British female notoriety was made.

Barthes (2007) argued the beauty of humanity can be read through the face of one woman, Greta Garbo. The opposite is also the case: one image—that of Hindley—came to encapsulate horror. *That photograph* was a symbol of evil and degradation. It is clearly significant that these images are both of women. The picture of Hindley often appeared alongside that of Brady. However, despite Brady's more central role, it is her image that has a more powerful cultural influence, reflective of her transgressive position and the public horror at her multiple transgressions; as a criminal, as a female criminal and as a woman involved in the murder and torture of children. The issue of gender is often discussed in this case. Cummins et al. (2019) note that this obscures the fact that these debates are really focussed on a specific set of gender-related issues—they're about Hindley and women who kill. There is no real discussion about what Brady and other male serial killers might tell us about mas-culinity

Following her arrest, despite spending the rest of her life in prison, Hindley was consistently in the public and media gaze. The fact is that the serial killing industry, like other areas of modern celebrity life, often needs new commodities. Fame is often brief and fleeting, but notoriety is another matter. *That photograph* meant that neither Hindley nor the public were able to escape her crimes. Thompson (2008) in his novel suggests that this continued confrontation with her crimes, generated in part by Hindley's campaigns for parole, was part of the explanation for the vilification of Hindley. *That photograph* appeared in countless newspaper articles. There is something of a subgenre of true crime that is based on the Moors Murder case, and the arrest photographs appear on the cover of most such books. Hindley resented the continued use of the image, arguing that it presented her as cold and callous when, in fact, she was frightened but trying not to show it (Birch, 1994). Any attempts to move the narrative—to present a more complicated picture of Hindley either before her arrest or during her life in prison—usually fell on stony ground. For example, in her Open University degree graduation photograph, taken whilst she was incarcerated, she is smiling and has long brown hair (Stanford, 2006). The major response to this was for some to object to the fact that she had been awarded a Humanities degree. *That photograph* remains dominant. A woman beyond redemption, an image that has become 'synonymous with the idea of feminine evil' (Birch, 1994, p. 42). In his novel, *Alma Cogan*, Gordon Burn (2011) describes the image and the audience relationship with it, thus:

Is it possible to discern evil, as many have supposed, in the cavern-ous upturned eyes, the pasty planes, the heavy bones, the holed head of bleached blonde fringe, the fondant of deep shadow[...] As usual Hindley looks like a composite, an identikit, a media emanation, a hypothetical who never existed in the flesh. (Burn, 2011, pp. 93–94)

Conclusion

Storrs (2004) argues that even though there have been debates about the exact nature of their roles in the commission of the murders, in the public view it is Myra Hindley who has borne the burden of responsibility. If crimes are committed jointly, by men and women, it is the women who become the subject of the wider society's fascination and repulsion (Gavin, 2009). The media and public treatment of Myra Hindley is an extreme example of this, both in the nature of her crimes and the fascination and repulsion that was generated. One factor in this wider fascination is the idea that it is rare for women to be involved in such crimes. An additional factor is that such women are doubly transgressive as they are considered to have offended against the biological essence of women's nature, to love and nurture children. Women who commit such offences challenge deeply entrenched cultural notions of female passivity and nurture (Storrs, 2004). Whatever the truth of Hindley's claims and Brady's counter-claims about the exact role she played in the Moors Murders, her prison letters reveal an intelligent woman (Cummins et al., 2019). She was very aware that she had become a tabloid monster, icon of evil and that '[t]he tabloids have turned me into an industry' (*The Guardian*, 2000). She recognised that stories about her would increase newspaper circulation figures.

Her campaign for parole in effect led to the development of the whole life sentence. It also gave successive Home Secretaries the opportunity to prove that they were 'tough' on crime and violent crime in particular (Schone, 2000). She remained in prison long after she was deemed to pose any threat. Whenever the case was discussed, *that photograph* appeared, reiterating its importance in fixing a particular idea of Hindley and legitimizing the decision to keep her locked up. Here, it said, is a reminder of the face of evil and the things that this woman did in a particular place at a particular time. Public opinion and opposition to her release was a hugely significant factor in Hindley's continued incarceration. It cannot be denied that she was held hostage to public opinion (Stanford, 2006). Brady never showed any remorse. He made it clear that he committed these horrendous crimes for his own personal gratification and would do so again. This, it can be argued, had a knock on effect for Hindley, overriding her attempts to reinvent herself as a reformed character. Clark (2011), argues that the depiction of Hindley as 'evil' was linked to her gender. However, this was further compounded by wider cultural developments. The use of *that photograph* made her the poster girl for two contemporary moral panics. The first is the 'discovery' of the serial killer. As previously noted the term was not in common usage at the time of the Moors Murders but in retrospect Brady and Hindley have been termed as such, perhaps because they were the first serial killers in the modern TV age, and reporting of their crimes provided a template for reporting subsequent cases. Secondly, the 80s and 90s saw a recurrent interest in paedophiles, again rooted in the narrative of the 'evil' and 'predatory' outsider. In stark contrast to the evil, predatory male outsider, she was the evil predatory female insider, able to take children into her confidence because of her gender. The image of Hindley was subsumed into these two distinct but increasingly entwined discourses—serial killer and paedophile. These combined with her gender to cement her extreme deviant status (Clark, 2011). This is a status that *that photograph*—taken at Hyde Police Station in October 1965—has been used to emphasise since its first appearance. The creation of stock categories has been a key feature of the commodification of celebrity, creating a shorthand through which the public can easily recognise types and are aware of their expected reaction to them. *That photograph* is a cultural artefact which provides a perfect illustration of this process.

Study Questions

- What are the connections between modern celebrity culture and the construction of the modern serial killer?
- What role did 'that photograph' play in the construction of Myra Hindley as 'the most hated woman in Britain'?
- What role has gender played in the treatment of Hindley in the media, in terms of public reaction, and by official bodies?
- Cummins and King suggest that the response to the Moors Murders was a product of cultural-historical factors—the 'swinging sixties', as well as successive crises concerning crime and 'law and order'. Summarise their argument and discuss other aspects of the social context that might have influenced the construction and reception of this case.

References

Bailey, D. (1965). *Box of pin ups*. Weidenfield and Nicolson.

Barthes, R. (2007). The Face of Garbo. In S. Redmond & S. Holmes (Eds.), *Stardom and celebrity: A reader*, (pp. 261–262). Sage.

Bauman, Z. (2007). *Liquid modernity. Living in an age of uncertainty.* Cambridge Polity Press.

Benfield, A. (1968). The Moors Murders. *The Police Journal: Theory, Practice and Principles, 41*, 147–159.

Birch, H. (1994). If Looks Could Kill: Myra Hindley and the Iconogra. In H. Birch (Ed.), *Moving targets. Women, murder and representation*. London: Virago Press.

Burn, G. (2008). *Born yesterday*. Faber and Faber.

Burn, G. (2011). *Alma cogan*. Faber and Faber.

Clark, T. (2011). *Why was Myra Hindley evil?* Paper presented to the York Deviancy Conference: Critical Perspectives on crime, deviance, disorder and social harm.

Cummins, I. D., & King, M. (2015). Happy like profilers: Gordon burn, modernity and serial killing. *International Journal of Criminology and Sociological Theory, 7*(3), 1–11.

Cummins, I., Foley, M., & King, M. (2016). The strange case of Ian Stuart Brady and the Mental Health Review Tribunal. *Internet Journal of Criminology and Sociological Theory, 7(3)*, 1–11.

Cummins, I., Foley, M., & King, M. (2019). *Serial killers and the media: The Moors Murders legacy*. Springer.

Egger, S. (2002). *Killers among us*. Prentice Hall Publishing.

Ehrenreich, B. (1983). *The hearts of men*. Pluto Press.

Foucault, M. (1990). *The history of sexuality: An introduction* (Vol. 1). Random House Inc.

Gavin, H. (2009). Mummy wouldn't do that: The perception and construction of the female child sex abuser. In M. Barrett (Ed.), *Grotesque feminities: Evil, women and the feminine*. InterDisciplinary Press.

Goffman, E. (1967). *The presentation of self in everyday life*. Penguin.

Goodman, J. (1986). *The Moors Murders: The Trial of Myra Hindley and Ian Brady*. David and Charles.

Greer, C. (2004). Crime, media and community: Grief and virtual engagement in late modernity. In J. Ferrell, K. Hayward, W. Morrison, & M. Presdee

(Eds.), *Cultural Criminology Unleashed* (pp. 109–120). The Glass House Press.

Haggerty, K. D. (2009). Modern serial killers. *Crime Media Culture, 5*(2), 168–187.

Halberstam, J. (1995). *Skin shows.* Duke University Press.

Hansford Johnson, P. (1967). *On iniquity.* Macmillan.

Helgeland, B (Dir.) (2015). *Legend.* Working Title Films.

Ingebretsen, E. J. (1998). Monster-making: A politics of Persuasion. *Journal of American Culture, 21*(2), 25–34.

Jewkes, Y. (2004). *Crime and media.* Sage.

Lee, C. A. (2010). *One of your own: The life and death of Myra Hindley.* Mainstream Publishing.

King, M. (2013). *Men, Masculinity and The Beatles.* Farnham: Ashgate.

Lea, D. (2014). Trauma, celebrity and killing in the 'contemporary' murder leisure industry. *Textual Practice, 28*(5), 763–781.

Levi-Strauss, C. (1972). *The savage mind* (2nd ed.). Weidenfeld and Nicholson.

Lincoln, Y. (2001). An emerging new bricoleur: Promises and Possibilities, a reaction to Joe Kincheloe's "Describing the bricolge" *Qualitative Inquiry, 7*(6), 693–696.

MailOnline. (2005). *Moors murderer Brady tries to block TV drama.* 8th October 2005.

Marwick, A. (1998). *The Sixties.* Oxford University Press.

Menaul, C. (Dir.) (2006). *See no evil: The Moors Murders.* Granada Television.

Rojek, C. (2001). *Celebrity.* Reaktion.

Sandbrook, D. (2006). *White heat: A history of Britain in the swinging sixties.* Little Brown

Schmid, D. (2006). Idols of destruction: celebrity and the serial killer. In S. Holmes, & S. Redmond (Eds.), *Framing celebrity: New directions in celebrity culture,* (pp. 295–310). Routledge.

Schone, J. M. (2000). The hardest case of all: Myra Hindley, life sentences and the role of law. *International Journal of the Sociology of Law, 28,* 73–289.

Seltzer, M. (1997). Wound culture: Trauma in the pathological public sphere. *October, 80* (Spring), 3–26.

Simon, J. (2007). *Governing through crime: How the war on crime transformed American democracy and created a culture of fear.* OUP.

Smith, D., & Lee, C. A. (2011). *Witness: The story of David Smith, chief prosecution witness in the Moors Murders case.* Mainstream Publishing.

Smith, J. (1989). There's only one Yorkshire Ripper. In J. Smith (Ed.), *Misogynies.* Faber.

Soothill, K. (1993). The serial killer industry. *Journal of Forensic Psychology,* *4*(2), 341–354.

Staff, D. (2013). *The Lost Boy. The definitive story of the Moors murders.* Bantam Books.

Stanford, P. (2006). *Outcasts' Outcast: A biography of Lord Longford.* History Press.

Storrs, E. (2004). 'Our Scapegoat': An exploration of media representations of Myra Hindley and Rosemary West. *Theology & Sexuality, 11*(1), 9–28.

The Guardian. (2000). *Myra Hindley in her own words.* 29th June 2000.

Thomson, R. (2008). *Death of a murderer.* Bloomsbury.

Topping, P. (1989). *Topping, the autobiography of the police chief in the Moors murders case.* W. H. Allen and Co.

Walker, A. (1998). Marcus Harvey's 'sick, disgusting', painting of Myra Hindley: A semiotic analysis. *Marcus Harveye Police Chief in Tate Magazine, 14*(Spring), 56–57.

Wattis, L. (2018). *Revisiting the Yorkshire Ripper murders.* Springer International Publishing.

Wattis, L. (2020). Violence, emotion and place: The case of five murders involving sex workers. *Crime, Media, Culture, 16*(2), 201–219.

Wibberley, C. (2012). Getting to grips with Bricolage : A personal account. *The Qualitative Report, 17*(25), 1–8.

Wilde, N. (2016). *The Monstering of Myra Hindley.* Waterside Press.

Williams, E. (1992). *Beyond belief: A chronicle of murder and its detection.* London Pan.

Wilson, D. (2007). *Serial killers: hunting Britons and their victims, 1960 to 2006.* Hook Waterside Press.

Winter, J. (2002). The truth will out? The role of judicial advocacy and gender in verdict construction. *Social and Legal Studies, 11*(3), 343–367.

10

Real-Life Criminals and Crime Fictions: Adapting the Serial Killer as Gothic Monster in TV Drama

Brigid Cherry

Introduction

In a scene from 2.5 'Episode 5' of the television drama series *Mindhunter* (Netflix, 2017–2019), Bill Tench and Holden Ford, FBI agents in the Behavioural Sciences Unit, remediate the popularised account of Charles Manson and the Family. As they drive away from a prison interview in which Manson has manipulated both men, Ford suggests the accepted history of Manson is 'bullshit'. Arguing his point when Tench asks if that means Ford thinks the DA at Manson's trial lied, Ford says: 'I'm saying he gave it a narrative. He had to explain to a normal, middle-class jury how some normal, middle-class kids brutally murdered seven people'. Specifically, Holden asks: 'What makes more sense? Manson being forced to go along with Tex and Sadie's copycat crime or a race war predicted by the Beatles?' In other words, Holden confronts the profile of

B. Cherry (✉)
St Mary's University, Twickenham, UK

© The Author(s), under exclusive license to Springer Nature
Switzerland AG 2021
M. Mellins and S. Moore (eds.), *Critiquing Violent Crime in the Media*,
https://doi.org/10.1007/978-3-030-83758-7_10

Manson as a Svengali figure widely disseminated in popular discourse. By applying Occam's Razor in this way, the nature of Manson's criminality is opened up to alternate readings. More significantly in the context of the television crime drama, this works as a metatext, one text that describes or discusses another text as in the *Mindhunter* text—through Holden's dialogue—discussing the Manson text as written by the DA, thus commenting on the fact that all such accounts are constructed narratives.

There is nothing out of the ordinary in the idea that accounts of historical incidents are constructed narratives, of course, but this foregrounding of the process in a key scene from *Mindhunter* serves to draw attention to the ways in which contemporary drama remediates the histories of infamous figures such as Manson. Such fictionalised representations of real-life criminals are a feature of several key television drama series of the 2010s. This chapter analyses three examples of this: *Aquarius* (NBC, 2015–2016), *I Am the Night* (TNT, 2019), and the aforementioned *Mindhunter*. *American Horror Story: Hotel* (FX, 2015), which incorporates serial killers in a story focussing on vampirism and hauntings, is also briefly considered.[1] In this chapter, I explore the ways in which these series adapt true-crime stories, and argue that in doing so they are closely related to the Gothic, notably with real-world serial killers encoded in terms of Gothic monstrosity. In particular, and as the scene described above illustrates, these depictions of real-world serial killers in fictional dramas fulfil the function of the Gothic in relation to social morality and the encoding of monstrosity as human evil. By depicting Manson as cult leader ensnaring victims into his belief in a coming race war and manipulating them into committing murder, the DA's narrative draws on the Gothic discourse that 'unnatural acts create monstrosity' (Halberstam, 1995, p. 12). This approach positions these series as hybridised adaptations of non-fiction sources, generically positioned in terms of a Gothic intertext. In this way they form a metatextual commentary on the real-life killers and the milieu in which they operate.

True Crime and Adaptation

Mindhunter, *Aquarius*, *I Am the Night*, and *Hotel* raise an interesting point in relation to adaptation and adaptation studies. Not only are real-world people and events depicted in the narrative, often in central roles, but the series often foreground the non-fiction sources—their antecedent texts—on which the plots are based. These antecedents include popular cultural discourses, as well as published books and media sources dealing with real-world serial killers, their crimes and life histories. In terms of adaptation, the series range from fictionalised dramatisations of non-fiction works to the more general inclusion of real-world figures in original dramas. As a group of recent TV series in the crime genre, these dramas thus represent a suitable case study of a form of adaptation, namely one that fictionalises true-crime texts. In the publicity and press coverage *Mindhunter* and *I Am the Night* overtly draw attention to the fact that they are adaptations of specific non-fiction accounts, *Mindhunter: Inside the FBI's Elite Serial Crime Unit* by criminal profiler John E. Douglass (on whom Holden Ford is based) and Mark Olshaker (1995), and Fauna Hodel's autobiographical account of her search for her birth family in *One Day She'll Darken: The Mysterious Beginnings of Fauna Hodel* (with Briamonte, 2008), respectively. Although these accounts are written from the perspective of investigators (in the case of Hodel, her personal history, and in the case of Douglass, research into the psychology of sequence killers), sensational crimes form central narrative threads within them—and thus to the fictionalised dramas based on them. Several incarcerated killers—including Manson and Family member Tex Watson, Ed Kemper (the Co-Ed Killer), David Berkowitz (Son of Sam), William Henry Hance, and Richard Speck—are the subjects of *Mindhunter*'s study of serial killers, as well as the apprehension of Wayne Williams during the investigation into the Atlanta child murders. Fauna's grandfather George Hodel, a prime suspect in the unsolved Black Dahlia case (the murder and dismemberment of Elizabeth Short), is the main antagonist of *I Am the Night*. *Aquarius*, while it was conceived and written for television, aims for a high degree of historical fidelity to the music, fashions, politics, events and milieu of late 1960s America. It also draws closely on the widely circulated accounts of Charles Manson and the Family, who are central characters in a narrative set in Los Angeles during the year prior to the Tate-LaBianca murders, together with other socio-political issues of the time, notably civil rights, the activities of the Black Panthers, the assassination of Martin Luther King Jr., protests against the war in Vietnam, and the presidential campaign of Richard Nixon. *Hotel* is the looser of these series in terms of not having an overt non-fictional source; however, it incorporates several, albeit disparate, true-crimes. The titular Hotel Cortez is based on the Hotel Cecil in Los Angeles, which saw several murders and suicides on the premises, and is linked to both the serial killer Richard Ramirez (the Night Stalker) and the Black Dahlia, Elizabeth Short. Moreover, the designer of the Cortez in the series is inspired by the killer H.H. Holmes, whose hotel building in Chicago (popularly known as the Murder Castle) was similarly designed with traps, gas chambers, chutes and furnaces used in the murder of his victims and disposal of their bodies. During the series he is shown as the host at a celebratory annual dinner for the ghosts of several serial killers including Eileen Wuornos, Jeffrey Dahmer (the Milwaukee Monster), John Wayne Gacy (Killer Clown), and Ramirez.

The fascination with serial killers in popular culture (as evidenced by the plethora of books, documentaries, media coverage, and online sites) is a context for the ways in which the characters based on these individuals work as intertexts in these series. In other words, the text of the drama series is related to the many other texts—its intertexts—based on the life and crimes of the serial killers. Key here is Thomas Leitch's point that adaptation and intertextuality are closely entwined: 'all adaptations are obviously intertexts, but it is much less obvious that all intertexts are adaptations' (2012, p. 89). The very act of incorporating real-world killers in a drama can be discussed in terms of adaptation then, but it is also useful, especially in the context of Holden's argument in the scene described in the introduction, to consider how these adaptions remediate the accounts for contemporary entertainment media in the digital era. In the sense of Jay David Bolter and Richard Grusin's definition of remediation as 'the formal logic by which new media refashion prior media forms' (1999, p. 273), the fictionalised crime narratives of these drama series draw on a wide range of antecedent texts that include journalistic coverage of crimes and trial reporting, true-crime books and podcasts, and documentary accounts of serial killers, all of which are already remediated in online contexts.

As this indicates, there are numerous accounts (in addition to the primary based on books mentioned above) in many different media that work as intertexts for the series being discussed. In this way too, it can be said that they are intermedial. While Leitch critiques such intermediality as inherently limited since adaptation is not the only form of intermediality (2012, p. 92), the processes of intermedial adaptation are foregrounded in the series being discussed here, as for example with the diegetic positioning of Manson prosecutor Vincent Bugliosi's *Helter Skelter* (with Gentry, 1974)—a copy of which Manson signs for Holden in *Mindhunter* 2.5 'Episode 5', and the Surrealist paintings which are seen from a character's point of view in *I Am the Night* 1.2 'Phenomenon of Interference'—a sequence that intertextually references Mark Nelson and Sarah Hudson Bayliss's account of the Black Dahlia murder in *Exquisite Corpse* (2006). Narratively, these intermedial texts unlock a key enigma for the character, allowing them to see the killer in a new light. Such moments of remediation illustrate the complexities of intermedial adaptation, and also provide a context for discussion of the serial killer as antecedent text in subsequent sections of this chapter, particularly in relation to the Gothic as intertext and metatext.

Crime Fiction and the Gothic

There are then a number of antecedent non-fiction texts that are foregrounded in the narratives of the series under consideration. But other intertexts must also be considered, and—suggested by Jack (writing as Judith) Halberstam's point that there are 'many congruities between Gothic fiction and detective fiction' (1995, p. 2)—of most significance in terms of genre hybridity and intermediality in the Gothic. Catherine Spooner (2010) also reminds us that the Gothic and crime fiction are closely intertwined and it is only critical accounts of canon and matters of taste that have separated the genres. The investigation of crime—in other words, the detective's activities—is to uncover secrets, a common formula of both the crime story and Gothic fiction that 'irrevocably blur[s] the generic boundaries' (Spooner, 2010, p. 248). In terms of their generic intertexts all the series under consideration similarly cross genre boundaries. Not only do they merge non-fiction with fiction, but they draw on the Gothic in their narratives and televisual styles. As might be expected in dramas centred on crime and criminality, the dominant generic tropes are oriented around investigation, although this is not necessarily a criminal one. *Aquarius* is the most straightforward crime drama, with police officers solving crimes and missing persons cases, and *Mindhunter* also relates the Bureau's development of psychological profiling as a crime-solving technique. But the investigative narrative is also organised around personal and family secrets, framed in relation to journalism (Jay Singletary is a reporter seeking a new angle on an old crime story that ruined his career) and family research (Fauna is an adoptee seeking her birth family and discovering the patriarchal killer at its heart) in *I Am the Night*. Furthermore, investigation takes the form of a scientific study into the secrets of the mind that also includes an academic researcher in *Mindhunter*, and forms a personal relationship drama (Hodiak is looking for a teen runaway for an ex-girlfriend) in *Aquarius*. Moreover, *Hotel* is predominantly framed as horror—the series positions itself generically as horror (not least through its main title *American Horror Story*) and overtly incorporates the supernatural (with its ghosts and vampires the hotel is clearly a variant of the 'old dark house'), although the horror itself is also contextualised within a criminal investigation in which detective and serial killer are conflated. Thus while *Hotel* is the only horror series per se, the Gothic must also be considered a notable intertext in all three crime dramas too, and hybridity—or blurring of genre boundaries—is a notable consideration for all the series. As Spooner goes on to state, 'there are traces of Gothic in most crime narratives, just as there are crimes in most Gothic novels' (2010, p. 246).

Crime is an identifying trope of the Gothic, but the Gothic is a trope of the crime drama too. This holds true when considering these drama series as adaptations and remediations of true-crime narratives. Reflecting Holden's point about the DA in the Manson Family trial constructing a narrative, Jeffrey Melnick emphasises that this narrative clearly drew on the Gothic in particular: 'The story Bugliosi told about the Family combined two time-tested American artistic forms—the captivity narrative and the Gothic horror story' (2018, p. 230). Melnick also describes Bugliosi's writing in *Helter Skelter* (1974) as 'purple prose [that] comes from the Nineteenth-Century Gothic, as does the book's sense of untamed, inherent evil and its opposite number, upstanding righteousness' (Melnick, 2018, pp. 459–6). In terms of both style and content then, Gothic crime is a discourse that continues to underpin the true-crime narrative in American popular culture.

It follows therefore that the defining tropes of Gothic crime outlined by Spooner can be identified in the portrayals of the serial killers in the drama series under consideration. As Spooner argues with respect to the 'obvious implications for the relationship of Gothic to crime fiction', crime, which has taken place in the past but has 'continuing and visceral effects within the present', is presented in the context of 'charismatic and powerful men', and has 'peculiar resonances within the family' (2010, p. 245). The representation of the serial killers in the crime drama is clearly framed in terms of the monster of the Gothic novel. In *Mindhunter*, Ed Kemper, for example, is portrayed as extremely charismatic, capturing the interest of the FBI unit; he is a source of particular fascination for agent Holden Ford who gets sucked into his orbit. Similarly, Charles Manson is framed as the charismatic cult leader in *Aquarius*, appealing not just to the young women and men in his Family, but to lawyer Ken Karn who Manson holds in his sphere via illicit sex, murder, and blackmail. In *I Am the Night*, George Hodel is portrayed as a rich and powerful man with the police, the mob, and the city under his influence. Moreover, for Spooner, it is the reminder of past crime that is integral to the Gothic narrative (ibid.). The 'preoccupation with the return of past upon present' (Spooner, 2010, p. 248) is a signifying presence in all of these series too. In *Mindhunter*, the past crimes of the incarcerated serial killers are a key element in exploring the psychology of murder, and this impacts on the present as the agents use what they have learnt to identify the perpetrators of murders in their present day. In *Aquarius*, a flashback to Karn's involvement in the murder of a woman during Manson's earlier activities as a pimp is significant, but the twist in the narrative is the way the future event of the Tate-LaBianca killings is seen in several flashforwards that create an ominous pall over the present just as the past does in the Gothic. In *I Am the Night* crime-scene photos of the Black Dahlia killing, in parallel with Hodel's Surrealist art collection,[2] become a repeated motif that brings Hodel's past into the present. In a gender twist in *Hotel*, it is the Countess (loosely based on the historical figure of Countess Bathory) who holds vampiric power and seduction over the residents of the hotel in which the past is ever present in the form of ghosts, and her own past 'crimes' also return to haunt her both in the form of flashbacks and as returning vampires she once 'made'.

It is also worth noting the locations in which the killers are depicted. Paramount among the list of locales that Robert Mighall suggests are 'threatening reminders or scandalous vestiges of a former time' are prisons and asylums (Mighall, 2003, p. 26). The narrative of *Mindhunter* obviously focuses on these spaces (Vacaville's California Medical Facility, the prison for the criminally insane substituting for both of course in the contemporary Gothicised crime drama). Mighall also includes urban slums, and—while not explicit as such—the haunted art deco hotel in *Hotel*, the Spiral Staircase in Topanga Canyon and the Spahn ranch in *Aquarius* encapsulate the similar run-down or disused qualities of the urban environment and house those who are already dead or reject conformity. All these spaces are representative of past events (the Spiral Staircase was an illicit drinking club for LAs rich and famous during prohibition, the Spahn Ranch a film location when the Western was at its height, the Hotel Cortez represents a past artistic style while it is haunted by the ghosts of its past traumas). Moreover, Hodel's fortress-like Mayan revival Sowden House in *I Am the Night* (the site of debauched parties in the past) was the home of the real-world George Hodel and its use as a location in the series brings historical fidelity into what is otherwise a highly fictionalised adaptation (of both Fauna Hodel's autobiography and Hodel's life story). But more importantly, it is always already a Gothic space. Gary Indiana interprets Steve Hodel's description of the Sowden house, with 'brooding stone archways, long corridors, […] and hidden rooms', and like 'a cave with secret stone tunnels' (2003/2012, p. 69), as something from the Gothic novel: 'a Gothic pile full of secret rooms straight out of Vathek' (2008, p. 19). However, as Mighall goes on to list, the vestiges of the past reside too in 'the bodies, minds, or psyches of criminals' (Mighall, 2003, p. 26). The killers are contained within uncanny architectures, but they also 'contain' the horror. Following Halberstam, they demonstrate that, 'in the Gothic, crime is embodied within a specifically deviant form - the monster - that announces itself (de-monstrates) as the place of corruption' (1995, p. 2). The serial killers depicted in *Mindhunter* illustrate Halberstam's argument. They are literal and figurative embodiments of Gothic/criminal deviancy. Not only are they the worst kind of criminal (psychopathic multiple-murderers), their physical presence itself forms a Gothic architecture with darkness, secrets, and horror within. As Bill says in 1.3 'Episode 3', 'There's nothing behind Kemper's eyes. It's like standing near a black hole.' Richard Speck is an interesting example of this (1.9 'Episode 9'). He is, to use Halberstam's term, a 'skin show'. His very being is a place of corruption as he demonstrates his monstrosity via insulting language, excessive swearing, and the way he has branded himself as a badass (according to Wendy Carr's later comment on the interview) with a tattoo reading 'born to raise hell'. He even resembles the prison itself: the patina of the metal bars and the peeling paintwork find an echo in his greyed skin, lined features, dark bags under his eyes, and yellowish grey hair, while the prison restraints clank like uncanny chains whenever he moves. As Halberstam points out, 'the hide no longer conceals or contains, it offers itself up as text, as body, as monster' (1995, p. 7). The revealing of Speck's inner monstrosity culminates when he dramatically throws an injured bird into the air conditioner fan. These series, then, are examples of the symbiotic relationship between the Gothic and crime drama. In dramatising true-crime stories and the 'careers' of serial killers, Gothic monstrosity is thus a key intertext and it follows that the killers themselves are intertexts of Gothic monsters in their own right.

Gothic Monstrosity and the Serial Killer

Jeffrey Weinstock describes serial killers (who he refers to as psychokillers in the context of the horror genre) as the monsters among us; they 'make

visible the internal lack of humanity obscured by their human facades—
they are monsters on the inside' (2012, p. 280). Given the generic and
narrative connections between crime and the Gothic outlined above,
however, it is not surprising that the invisible/internal monstrosity of
the real-world serial killers in the drama series under consideration is
visibly encoded in terms of Gothic monstrosity. In remediating the non-
fiction accounts of the real-life figures depicted in the aforementioned
series, the killer as human and the associated nature of their internalised
monstrosity is highlighted physically. The study of aberrant serial killer
psychology is the overarching narrative of *Mindhunter* of course, but
it also forms a common theme in all these series. However, the nature
of the Gothic criminal—as a non-supernatural villain—in the Gothic
novel is often remediated in the drama series as akin to the supernatural
monsters of Gothic horror. In fact, the notion of the serial killer as intermedial monstrous entity (already remediated via the slasher movie) was
recognised in *Mindhunter*'s antecedent text:

> Serial murder may, in fact, be a much older phenomenon than we realize.
> The stories and legends that have filtered down about witches and were-
> wolves and vampires may have been a way of explaining outrages so
> hideous that no one in the small and close-knit towns of Europe and
> early America could comprehend the perversities we now take for granted.
> Monsters had to be supernatural creatures. They couldn't be just like us.
> (Douglass & Olshaker, 1995, p. 13)

Accordingly, the supernatural Gothic monster is a clearly identifiable
intertext in *Mindhunter*. Useful case studies in this respect are the
representations of Kemper and Manson (other serial killers are similarly
Gothicised in terms of low intelligence, multiple deprivations due to class
and poverty, and assumptions around race, though Kemper and Manson
are the most fetishised figures in the series). Both are closely based on
their real-life appearance and descriptions from Douglass and Olshaker's
text—in terms of adaptation there is a high degree of historical fidelity
via the casting, make-up, and performance. Holden describes Kemper's
value for the FBI's research project in terms of volubility—'a killer who
can't stop talking is a gift', and his lines of dialogue taken from the book

bring authenticity to the character on screen (displaced even though it sometimes is from arrest records rather than FBI interviews). However, when he first appears on screen in 1.2 'Episode 2' it is to emphasise him as grotesque, with Holden, and the viewer, primed for Kemper's monstrous physicality. Kemper is summed up by Detective Molina: 'You can't miss the guy. He's like six foot nine, 285 pounds.' Holden is impressed, 'Whoa,' he says, 'King size.' 'Super king', is Molina's correction. This creates an expectation of a hulking giant, or in terms of the Gothic intertext, a Frankenstein's Creature. Holden is first shown walking through the jail in medium close-up shots against an out of focus background. Together with the sound of his footsteps loud against the indistinct hubbub of the prison, this isolates him from his surroundings. He looks apprehensively to the side as he walks, a lone hero walking into the monster's lair. There is a similar camera and sound aesthetic employed as Kemper is led to the meeting with Holden, but this time Kemper dwarfs the guard. The camera has to adopt a low angle to take in his whole frame, like shots of a brutish creature in a Gothic horror film. However, and this significantly draws on the Creature in the novel, Kemper—proving to be more than simply talkative—is a disconcertingly eloquent monster, uncannily so in fact; the Netflix summary of the episode describes him as 'eerily articulate'.[3] He speaks in a very cultured manner, discussing his serial killing in terms of a vocation, which he also describes as his 'oeuvre'. 'You can spell it, can't you?' he asks Holden in an attempt to display his intellectual superiority. But at the same time, his gestures and movements are conversely threatening, foregrounding the duality he expresses to Holden:

> I was a thoughtful, educated, well brought up young person. […] But… at the same time… I was living a vile depraved, entirely parallel other life filled with debased violence and mayhem… and fear… and death.

So it is no surprise during Holden's second visit when Kemper grasps Holden's throat in a choking grip, all the while talking about the muscles and cartilage of the neck's anatomy. As Holden begins to choke, Kemper touches his arm in a deliberately reassuring manner and then sits back down. This demonstration of his duality is repeated in 1.3 'Episode 3':

he runs his finger across Holden's neck to demonstrate cutting someone's throat ear to ear, and then touches him on the shoulder as he talks about the 'fantastic passion' when he killed his victims. Particularly with the reassuring touches, Kemper's behaviour here suggests the vampire as much as the Creature.

When Holden visits Kemper after a (faked and manipulative) suicide attempt in 1.10 'Episode 10', Kemper completes this transformation into the vampiric monster snaring their victim. The scenario is no longer one of anonymous killer and victim but takes on qualities of seduction and familiarity. Kemper uncovers the wound on his wrist and thrusts it towards Holden, inviting him to 'take a closer look', much like the vampire opening a vein to turn his victim as Dracula does Mina in various cinematic versions. In fact, Kemper calls his victims his 'spirit wives', alluding to the brides of Dracula. Looming threateningly over Holden, he says Holden can be with him in spirit too, becoming (or at least suggesting) a Dracula and Harker relationship. Again, there is the touch on the shoulder, but as Kemper looms over Holden he then seizes him in an embrace which continues the connection to the vampire. Although Holden fights his way out of Kemper's prison hospital room physically unharmed, he experiences a series of haunting voices (discussed further in the next section) during a panic attack in the corridor. Significantly Kemper's 'Are we friends, Holden?' is the only one reinforced by a shot of the killer, back in the hospital room.

In contrast to Kemper's representation as Creature/vampire, the representation of Manson encodes him as an impish or devilish Trickster figure in both *Mindhunter* and *Aquarius*. From the start in *Mindhunter*, Manson is spoken of not just in terms of criminal insanity (Bill calls him an 'crazy motherfucker' in 1.2 'Episode 2'), but as a mythical or fantasy being—in the same episode Molina refers to him being treated 'like a fucking unicorn' and Bill, after Manson has taunted him, calls him a 'fucking midget' and says 'the guru of Munchkinland can fuck off straight to hell' (2.5 'Episode 5'). As the latter two examples suggest, Manson's stature is a feature of his monstrosity; as Kemper says, 'Manson is really small. Like really small'. Kemper also warns Holden and Bill that Manson is a charlatan but also 'a talker', raising further expectations of Manson as the devil—a liar, a smooth talker, and a tempter (or the Tempter). Manson's devilish qualities are then encoded in the way he sits and speaks during his interview with Holden and Bill, climbing up and perching on the chair back with his feet on the seat. Again, this authentic detail is taken from the antecedent text (Douglass & Olshaker, 1995, p. 83) and designed to create a superiority his lack of height denies him, but this action also draws attention to the Gothic inter-text as Manson thus comes to resemble the demonic creature sitting on the dreamer's chest in Henry Fuselli's Gothic painting *The Night-mare*, said to have inspired both Mary Shelley and Edgar Allen Poe, and also an image recreated many times in popular culture including Ken Russell's *Gothic* (1986) and the Japanese horror film *Ju-on: The Grudge* (2002). Manson is very animated–at one point, he stands up on the chair making extravagant gestures as though he is preaching, and speaks with an assertive drawl, becoming loud at points, using unconventional language (hippie slang), and speaking with emotion and passion (in this way he is the complete opposite of Kemper). His words are sociopathic—avoiding blame while blaming others, making himself out to be a victim, and manipulative (using counterculture discourses to paint himself as a revolutionary, and stirring Bill to anger). He talks in terms of his truth (love, acceptance) and society's lies (hate, violence, pressure to conform), deflecting—and denying—culpability for any crimes he was charged with. He thus remediates his own biography (as written by Bugliosi in *Helter Skelter* and resulting in Holden's question discussed in the introduction) and this representation of Manson forms a metatextual commentary on the real-life Manson.

This signification of Manson as a devil is in keeping with the grotesque figures of Southern Gothic fiction, not least the false preacher Asa in Flannery O'Connor's *Wise Blood*. This is further extended by his sly laughter at the mayhem he creates (and desires)—depicted in *Mind-hunter* when he taunts Bill until Bill cracks, and in *Aquarius* in his response to the assassination of Martin Luther King. In *Aquarius* this is particularly notable. In 2.4 'Revolution 1', Charlie appears to the Family to be praying as they watch the news on TV, but this masks his whispered prayer, 'die, die'. This is just moments before the announcement on the news, creating an almost supernatural connection between Charlie's prayer and King's death. He also celebrates what he predicts is the coming mayhem by saying it is 'far out'. This is re-emphasised when Charlie is seen in the TV coverage of the memorial march for King, again with his praying hands held in front of his face to hide a devilish grin. This depiction of his joy at what he sees as the coming race war underscores his position as a Trickster figure.

Hauntings and Spectrality

These remediations of the serial killer emphasise their monstrous qualities by televisually signalling their aberrant or dangerous psychologies. They are encoded as liminal, and accordingly as spectral presences. The characters based on serial killers in *Hotel* are literal spectres, of course, returning on one night of the year to dine with James March (who haunts his own hotel). But significantly, *Mindhunter*, *I Am the Night* and *Aquarius* all contain scenes which create figurative hauntings or the killers becoming spectral presences. In one sense, the recordings of interviews taken by the agents in *Mindhunter* (though the primary effect is to create a metatextual commentary as the team discuss what the tapes reveal about the mental state of sequence killers) imbue the killers with a spectral presence as they are played during meetings at Quantico. The *Mindhunter* titles reinforce such a reading. Extreme closeups (which also fetishise the technology) on the recording equipment foreground the capture of disembodied voices, while the largely monochrome textures—coldly blue tinged with hints of warmer red, orange, and flesh tones—along with the minimalist music - slow piano, violin, and cello played tremolo—create a spectral atmosphere. The flash frames of crime scene photos add to the horror atmosphere. The narrative is punctuated by sequences of crime scene photographs in *I Am the Night* too, for example with the point-of-view montage in the art gallery in 1.2 'Phenomenon of Interference' when Jay has a moment of insight and realises the crime scene photos of the Black Dahlia and the similarly dismembered corpse he photographed in the morgue exactly match the details of Hodel's surrealist art collection displayed on the gallery walls. In addition, when Fauna is forced to change into a slip in Hodel's basement studio/operating theatre/murder site so she can sit for a portrait before he kills her (1.6 'Queen's Gambit, Accepted') the crime scene photos on the wall underscore the slasher film scenario being played out. The linking of crime scene photographs and surrealist art is not without its own antecedent texts, not least the book by Mark Nelson and Sarah Hudson Bayliss claiming that 'the Black Dahlia murder bears a Surrealist imprint' (2006, p. 105), but also when Maurice Heine incorporated crime scene and autopsy photographs of Jack the Ripper victims Mary Kelly and Catherine Eddows in his play Regards sur l'enfer anthropoclasique (A Look at Anthropoclassic Hell) in issue 8 of the Surrealist journal *Minotaure*. Linda Steer (2008, p. 110) refers to this as a form of appropriation, a common strategy of Surrealist artists. Similarly, the actuality stills at the end of each episode of *I Am the Night* reinforce the realism—the true crime—that the narrative adapts, but at the same time they appropriate the true-crime narrative, drawing attention to the very lack of fidelity in the series.[4]

More overtly still, the killers become spectral presences via point-of-view sequences during hallucinations. When Hodiak's drink is spiked with LSD in *Aquarius* (1.10), the hallucinatory experience which follows incorporates psychedelic imagery through camera lens flare, Dutch angles, and music (Donovan's *Hurdy Gurdy Man*). Hodiak also 'hears' (perhaps imagines or recalls) Manson's words echoing around him. Rather than a hurdy gurdy man singing songs of love on the extra-diegetic soundtrack, Manson's words form a tone poem speaking of death:

Killer man, killer man, open your eyes. ... You have killed, killer man. ... You've drowned the light of life. Who do you kill, killer man? ... Did you eat the old man and spit him out? You have swallowed death. You live on death. Death lives in you.

The televisual aesthetics of the hallucinatory experience thus create a haunting focussed on Manson's spectral presence. Hallucinatory sequences like this one engender moments of horror imagery. Holden's panic attack after Kemper has threatened him is another, but Hodel's visions of the Minotaur remediate his predatory, patriarchal masculinity.

It is pertinent to this that Susan Squier equates chimeric monsters (of which the Minotaur is a significant masculine example) with 'the conflicting significations attached to reproductive technology' (1995, p. 118). In Surrealist art, female bodies were configured to resemble the Minotaur, as are both the bodies of the Black Dahlia and the victim Jay photographs in the morgue in 1.1 'Pilot'. The mythical creature that so enamoured the Surrealist art that Hodel collects is both his spirit animal (he wears a bull mask during his parties) and his nemesis (it haunts his house and his childhood memories, and its persona is taken on by Fauna when she attacks him). The climax of the narrative in 1.6 'Queen's Gambit, Accepted' sees Fauna taking on the role of final girl from the slasher film, injuring Hodel's leg and arm with a weapon improvised from a handkerchief and a spherical *objet d'art*. When she also takes his gun and turns it on him the soundtrack repeats the animal growl motif that has been heard to signify the Minotaur's—and thus Hodel's— monstrosity. Here the camera zooms into an extreme closeup of Fauna's eye showing the bull head reflected in it. In this moment Fauna trans- forms into the Minotaur, appropriating Hodel's totem animal. He is further diminished by this transference, cowering on the floor in pain. Thus, in the final sequence after he has fled the country he is shown to be a broken man, unshaven, leaning on a cane, his face tired and lined, drinking. Fauna's voiceover (from her letter to Jay) emphasises her trans- formation from victim to Minotaur slayer: 'We know what monsters are. We know what makes 'em. And I know what unmakes 'em'. The pan down to Hodel's bull statue—no longer a chimeric monster of myth and Surrealist art—reinforces the point.

The opening up of spectrality in this way also emphasises the duali- ties of identity embodied in the monster. A further example in *Aquarius* 1.4 'Home is Where You're Happy' is when Grace goes to the Spiral Staircase to take Emma home. Emma has taken LSD and her point of view shows Grace's face distorting. The eye sockets become deeper so that her eyes are dark pools ringed by black shadow, like a death's head makeup, her eyebrows pointing Satanically upwards. The chin and cheekbones distort, lengthening and pointing her chin, the nostrils flare, one enlarged into a wide, dark hole. Emma backs away from this vision in horror, and later calls Grace 'the devil'. The hallucination not only distorts Grace's bourgeoise demeanour, but exposes the horror at the heart of the bourgeoise family. The family (the mother here literally, but the father figuratively too via Ken's sexual relationship with Charlie) becomes a source of demonic influence, if not demonic in its own right. Moreover, the skull-like distortion of Grace's face can be read as suggesting a make-up in the style of the Voodoo figure of Baron Samedi. Anne Schroder's argument that Voodoo is 'tied to the categories of power, agency and possession' (2016, p. 431) in relation to the legacy of slavery is pertinent here. Emma taking on the appearance of death, along with Charlie's ex-cell mate Ralph Church returning after his assumed death (the African-American Ralph was the subject of Charlie's racism and was fed a meal of poisonous mushrooms on Charlie's instruction in a murder attempt)—thus becoming a figurative Voodoo zombie, are examples of 'the past in the present and the dead among the living' in Schroder's account of Gothic realism (ibid.). This also links to Charlie's racism and suggests that the 'witchy words' he asks the Family to paint on the Cielo Drive house—intended to blame Black activists—link back to Voodoo witchcraft. The spectral sequences do, then, draw attention to monstrosity and horror but it remains rooted in the true-crime antecedent text. This draws attention to the African-American Gothic intertext and the intersectionality of identity, with race significant in all the series being considered.

Duality and Race

In this context, it is worth noting that in addition to Fauna adapting the role of final girl in defeating the monster in *I Am the Night*, the character is also an adaptation of the fairy tale heroine. In 1.1 'Pilot' Billie Ray (Fauna's adoptive mother) remarks that Fauna is a fairy tale name. This is no longer an incidental detail as it is in Fauna Hodel's account (2008), and her story is framed in the TV series as a variant of the archetype where an orphan girl learns she is a princess. Accordingly, Hodel is transformed into aristocracy (in reality he was—like the fictional Hodiak—of Ashkenazi Jewish descent) when Hodel's ex-wife Corinna tells Fauna that her grandfather's family 'came from the Russian nobility', that they were White Russians who 'hunted wild boar with the Tsar' before fleeing the Revolution (2. 'Phenomenon of Interference'). This fanciful tale serves to highlight the fairy tale theme, though Hodel is in fact the monstrous figure of the fairy tale intertext—he hunts (stalks) Fauna, he is Blue-beard in his castle with its murder chamber, and the incestuous King who would marry his daughter from The Donkey Skin—as opposed to any hero-figure who will bring enlightenment to Fauna (she desires knowl-edge of her roots in order to construct her identity, 'I just want to know where I come from and who I am'). This also locates the story in the Gothic tradition via themes linked to class-based notions of identity (see Bernstein, 1991, p. 165) including rightful inheritance (several charac-ters remark on Fauna now having access to wealth) and the 'merger of classes' (Fauna having been raised in a relatively poor Black community). Moreover, Hodel as Gothic villain problematises any straightforward rendering of family. As Fred Botting points out, the Gothic discourse around familial identity articulates the idea of the sins of the father being visited on the children (1996, p. 49). And certainly, Hodel is a monstrous threat at the heart of Fauna's birth family; 'He's a very, very dangerous man', Corinna warns her, 'Stay away. Stay away from him. Far, far away'.

Building on these approaches to Gothic identity, Justin D. Edwards argues that accounts of American Gothic must also take 'the instability of the "color line"' into account (2003, p. xxv). Certainly, in the context of the television crime Gothic, *I Am the Night* draws attention to such ideas about racial purity and contamination of blood lines when Terrence talks with Fauna at the party in 1.2 'Phenomenon of Interference': 'So your father is Black? That's all it takes, huh? Just that one drop will hold you down forever?' But the concept of purity is further complicated by how George Hodel's life is adapted for the series. With his Jewishness erased, his Whiteness-as-racial-purity is privileged in the narrative. Whiteness is further problematised since Fauna is raised Black and believes herself to be Black (or rather mixed-race), but others do not see her this way. Her Black identity is questioned and undermined when a new White student tries to sit with Fauna and the other White girls tell her not to sit at the 'negro table', she is taunted by another Black student who says 'Light skinned bitch think you all that, and you ain't, Ima see if that light skin scratch off, Ima see if that blood is black'. Thus Fauna with her green eyes and light skin invites disbelief, the motif repeated when the cops assume she is a White girl being harassed by a 'coloured' boy (her boyfriend), and also by Nero, a friend of her cousin Tina. The revelation by Corrine that Fauna is wholly White is not unexpected, but is nonetheless a crisis of identity and can be considered in terms of the American Gothic's 'anxious necessity' of establishing pure bloodlines (Edwards, 2003, p. xxv). In these terms, Jay's Whiteness is problematically constructed too, the character established as the wrong kind of White in his first scene when he is heckled by surfers (a version of privileged White American masculinity) who call him 'Snow White' and say he is 'burning [their] eyes' because, ironically, he is not tanned (that is, dark) enough. He and Fauna are both too white, they are culturally liminal, especially in comparison to Hodel's monstrously elite Whiteness conveyed (in flash-back) via his authoritative presiding over the orgiastic party at his Gothic fortress home in the opening of 1.3 'Dark Flower'.

These dualities of identity, when considered in relation to race, engage with the concept of double consciousness. In *Aquarius* 1.10 'It's Alright Ma (I'm Only Bleeding)', when a journalist threatens to 'out' the Cuban detective (born José Morán) who is passing as the Irish cop Joe Moran, a job he would never have been able to access as a Cuban, Hodiak reveals that his own all-American persona conceals the fact he is of Jewish descent. Hodiak is thus equally liminal, a position that he takes up in opposing the White supremacist position of Manson, J. Edgar Hoover, and the FBI. This revelation is significant in terms of Hodiak's relationship with the Black Panther leader Bunchy Carter who he has developed a cautious friendship with over the course of the narrative. After Bunchy is assassinated, he discusses W.E.B. Du Bois' concept of Black double consciousness with Kristin Shafe (2.10 'Blackbird'). 'Is that how you feel?' he asks Kristin, 'Is that how Bunchy felt?' Shafe, his inter-racial relationship with Kristin already troubled, interjects with what can be perceived as White privilege demoting the way Black people feel: 'Doesn't everybody feel that way sometimes?' Hodiak's response that 'sometimes ain't all the time' reminds us of his own duality as American and Jew, and more importantly that he gets it because he feels it too. The lengthy quote as he reads aloud from The Souls of Black Folk (Du Bois,

2007/1903, p. xiii) forms a significant metatextual commentary at this point:

> It is a peculiar sensation, this double-consciousness, this sense of always looking at oneself through the eyes of others, of measuring one's soul by the tape of a world that looks on in amused contempt and pity. One ever feels his two-ness... An American, a negro. Two souls, two thoughts, two unreconciled strivings, two warring ideals in one dark body, whose dogged strength alone keeps it from being torn asunder.

Employing Du Bois as an intertext at this point allows the narrative to metatextually comment on the racial tensions, not only those depicted in the historical setting of the narrative, but backwards to the history of slavery (Du Bois's seminal Black scholarship being written only 40 years after abolition), and forwards to the contemporary milieu in which the series was made, not least Black Lives Matter which formed in 2013 after the killer of Treyvon Martin was acquitted. This metatext is established in *I Am the Night* too, with a line of 'sampled' (or appropriated) dialogue spoken by a party guest in 1.2 'Phenomenon of Interference'. This functions in a very similar way to the Du Bois quote in *Aquarius*, this time drawing on the words of James Baldwin (1969):

> [When the Israelis pick up guns or the Poles or the Irish] or any White man in the world says 'Give me liberty, or give me death', the entire White world applauds. When a Black man says exactly the same thing, word for word, he is judged a criminal and treated like one.

Moreover, this frames both series as examples of African-American Gothic. The remediations of the shooting of King in both series, and of Carter in *Aquarius*, are a reminder of the traumas inflicted on Black communities, and the extent to which the Othering of African-Americans, particularly in terms of criminality, is still entrenched in American culture. Bunchy is a complex, liminal character in the series, earning the respect of Hodiak (in the maverick cop role) but suspect solely by dint of his colour to the FBI and Hoover. Although not a serial killer or, strictly, a criminal of any kind, Bunchy is criminalised just because he is Black.

As Maisha Wester argues, it is not the ghosts and spirits of African-American Gothic fiction that are terrifying; rather, it is 'the unarticulated stories of trauma they represent and the repeated disruptions to black family that are the sources of horror' (2012, p. 255). Even the arrest of Wayne Williams for the murder of two men in *Mindhunter* 2.9 'Episode 9' cannot erase the horror of loss for the mothers of the child victims or failure to see the killer of their children named as such. The caption at the end of the sequence stating that 'As of 2019, none of the remaining 27 cases have been prosecuted' draws attention to the same horror Wester identifies in the African-American Gothic novel. This lack of resolution for the Black families is also used to point the finger of accusation outside of the text to provide a metatextual comment on policing and race in America: 'Wayne Williams didn't kill my boy. I know that in my bones. You've gone and found yourselves a Black man. Wayne might just be Atlanta's thirtieth victim.' The real horror here is 'the rupture in their family and the uncertainty and loss that haunts the surviving members' (ibid.), not only for the mothers of the murdered boys but potentially Williams' family too. Wester's point that the disruption in the Black family is connected to 'the tragedy of racial violence and communal segregation' (ibid.) can be read as further problematising the Behavioural Sciences Unit assertion that serial killers do not cross racial boundaries. While such racial profiling makes explicit Schroder's point about Gothic realism, it creates contradictions in the adaptation of real-world criminality—and particularly the encoding of infamous serial killers as Gothic monsters—in these series.

Conclusion

As these examples of the adaptation of true-crime non-fiction texts for television drama illustrate, remediation is not (or not necessarily) a straightforward process. As the quote discussed in the introduction makes explicit, both the narrative of the true-crime text and the narrative of the crime drama illustrate the multidirectional and metatextual nature of adaptation. It is important then, as Leitch proposes, to problematise adaptation, especially where this takes the form of heterogenous and hybridised intertexts and metatextual commentaries on real-world killers. As the main points suggest (encoding serial killers as horror monsters, the foregrounding of Gothic spaces and identities, spectrality), the Gothic unreal forms a symbiotic partnership with crime in these series, but as discussed in terms of the African-American Gothic they are also rooted in Gothic realism. Nonetheless, aspects of Gothic identity as embodied in the representation, remediation, and adaptation of real-life serial killers are connected with important considerations of monstrosity in the American Gothic tradition.

Study Questions

- In what ways are the Gothic and crime genres interconnected?
- How are televisual aesthetics employed in the crime drama to create a Gothic atmosphere?
- What does the crime series have to say about monstrosity?
- Why might representations of race and ethnicity in the crime drama be considered Gothic?
- Are the representations of other aspects of identity (e.g. sex, sexuality, gender) significant in the hybrid Gothic/crime genre?

Notes

1. Quentin Tarantino's inclusion of the Cielo Drive murders in *Once Upon a Time… in Hollywood* (2019) is a cinematic example, though Charles Manson and the Family are not the primary focus. Also, with an alt-history narrative (the intervention by Tarantino's fictional characters and prevention of the murders), it takes a different approach towards the depiction of real-world events.
2. The Gothic and crime overlap in the detective fiction of Edgar Allan Poe of course, and it is not insignificant that Poe, who also interested the Surrealists, is quoted by Hodel (with lines from 'A Dream Within

a Dream') during the flashback to his party in 1945 at the start of 1.3 'Dark Flower'.

3. Episodes: *Mindhunter*. Accessed 22 December 2020. https://www.net flix.com/gb/title/80114855.

4. Although Steve Hodel believes his father was the killer, other hypotheses have been made about other individuals including Orson Welles. And in reality, Hodel was no longer in the USA when Fauna was searching for her birth mother (she was already a grown woman with a daughter of her own).

References

Baldwin, J. (1969). The Dick Cavett Show, 16 May. https://www.youtube.com/watch?v=WWwOi17WHpE. Accessed 14 Dec 2020.

Bernstein, S. (1991). Form and ideology in the Gothic novel. *Essays in Literature, 18*(2), 151–165.

Bolter, J. D., & Grusin, R. (1999). *Remediation: Understanding new media*. MIT Press.

Botting, F. (1996). *Gothic*. Routledge.

Bugliosi, V., & Gentry, C. (1974). *Helter Skelter: The true story of the manson murders*. W. W. Norton.

Douglass, J. E., & Olshaker, M. (1995). *Mindhunter: Inside the FBI's Elite serial crime unit*. Scribner.

Du Bois, W. E. B. (2007/1903). *The Souls of Black Folk*. Oxford University Press.

Edwards, J. D. (2003). *Gothic passages: Racial ambiguity and the American Gothic*. University of Iowa Press.

Halberstam, J. (1995). *Skin shows: Gothic Horror and the technology of monsters*. Duke University Press.

Hodel, F., & Briamonte, J. R. (2008). *One day she'll darken: The mysterious beginnings of Fauna Hodel*. Outskirts Press.

Hodel, S. (2003/2012). *Black Dahlia Avenger*. Arcade Publishing.

Indiana, G. (2008). *Utopia's Debris: Selected essays*. Basic Books.

Leitch, T. (2012) Adaptation and intertextuality, or, what isn't an adaptation, and what does it matter? In D. Cartmell (Eds.), *A companion to literature, film, and adaptation*. Wiley-Blackwell.

Melnick, J. (2018). *Creepy crawling: Charles Manson and the many lives of America's most infamous family*. Arcade Publishing.

Mighall, R. (2003). *A geography of Victorian Gothic fiction: Mapping history's nightmares*. Oxford University Press

Nelson, M., & Hudson Bayliss, S. (2006). *Exquisite Corpse: Surrealism and the Black Dahlia Murder*. Bullfinch Press.

Schroder, A. (2016). Voodoo and Conjure as Gothic Realism. In S. Castillo Street, & C. L. Crow (Eds.), *The Palgrave Handbook of the Southern Gothic*. Palgrave Macmillan.

Spooner, C. (2010). Crime and the Gothic. In C. Rzepka, & L. Horsley (Eds.), *A Companion to Crime Fiction*. Wiley-Blackwell.

Squier, S. M. (1995). Reproducing the Posthuman body: Ectogenic foetus, surrogate mother, pregnant man. In J. Halberstam, & I. Livingston (Eds.), *Posthuman bodies*. Indiana University Press.

Steer, L. (2008). Surreal encounters: Science, surrealism and the re-circulation of a crime-scene photograph. *History of Photography, 32*(2), 110–122. https://doi.org/10.1080/03087290801895647

Weinstock, J. A. (2012). Invisible monsters: Vision, horror, and contemporary culture. In A. Simon Mittman, & P. J. Dendle (Eds.), *The Ashgate Research Companion to Monsters and the Monstrous*. Ashgate.

Wester, M. L. (2012). *African American Gothic: Screams from shadowed places*. Palgrave Macmillan.

11

Gender, True Crime and the Violent Subject

Louise Wattis

Introduction

True crime is enjoying something of a moment in terms of renewed popularity and cultural kudos. Up until recently, true crime, defined as crime narratives recounting actual real-life events usually involving violent and grisly 'murder narratives' (Murley, 2008, p. 5), was regarded as a low brow and gratuitous cultural form in text and visual culture, despite pioneering literary work sitting at the high end of the genre such as Truman Capote's (2000) *In Cold Blood* and Norman Mailer's (1989) *The Executioner's Song*. More recently however, true crime has developed in terms of quality and ethical imperatives, reaching larger audiences as new platforms for consumption and different formats have emerged which vary in content, structure and production values. Historically, true crime television relied on melodramatic reconstructions of

L. Wattis (✉)
Teesside University, Middlesbrough, UK
e-mail: l.wattis@tees.ac.uk

© The Author(s), under exclusive license to Springer Nature Switzerland AG 2021
M. Mellins and S. Moore (eds.), *Critiquing Violent Crime in the Media*,
https://doi.org/10.1007/978-3-030-83758-7_11

grisly crimes in standalone episodes. The emergence of new genres, formats and platforms has reignited interest in true crime with a more sophisticated type of true crime television, distinct from its low brow predecessors, emerging in the 2000s, provoking a reassessment of the format. In the context of a genre which encompasses a range of sub genres but tends to be understood mostly in terms of the 'murder event' (Murley, 2008), the new breed of true crime often adopts a documentary and serialised format, with a key concern being to interrogate truth and guilt, and to expose flawed police investigations and justice processes. As such, it differs from its low brow predecessors which generally took a voyeuristic and sensationalist approach, centring on lurid reconstructions of grisly and macabre murders (Murley, 2008, pp. 118–122). In contrast, the more recent true crime documentaries adopt higher quality production values and aesthetics, and lay claim to ethical concerns and a higher purpose via scrutiny of corrupt policing and justice systems, inviting audiences to act as juries and question the guilt of the convicted (Bruzzi, 2016, p. 280). Some of the most successful and well-known of the recent true crime documentaries include *The Staircase* (2008) and *Making a Murderer* (2013). True crime of this type has also enjoyed ratings success and critical acclaim in the podcast format. Indeed, one of the most popular shows *Serial* (2014) is a further example of the 'jurification' subgenre, where the true crime documentary revisits and scrutinises a case, casting doubt upon the guilt of the convicted and questioning the original investigation and prosecution (Bruzzi, 2016). Yardley et al. (2018) argue that 'the internet and technological innovation has provided the catalyst for popular criminological output' (p. 504), transforming how we access and consume broadcast content in the network society with the internet now replete with mediated narratives and images of crime and violence. Indeed, audiences now watch and listen at their convenience with podcasts offering a more intimate medium which transforms how listeners respond to the retelling of murder events (Greer, 2018, p. 154).

Debates about the cultural work and impact of true crime invite similar criticisms to those levelled at news media representations of crime, relating to distortion and selective framing of particular crimes, offenders and victims (Murley, 2008), which in turn promotes conservative ideology and penal populism (Linnemann, 2015, p. 518). Moreover, much true crime dwells on extreme violence and salacious detail, often elevating violent male protagonists and objectifying female victims, which sets templates for specific offender and victim types with wider ramifications for ideologies of masculinity and femininity (Downing, 2013, p. 92; Wattis, 2018, p. 59). Indeed, the theme of gender and representational violence also relates to the popularity of true crime among female audiences with media and academic commentaries offering up a range of explanations for the popularity of true crime amongst women, linked to vicarious fear and risk, empathy, identification and its potential therapeutic function.

However, the focus on female audiences excludes any consideration of men as consumers of true crime and ignores diversity within the genre, which arguably perpetuates an archetype of the figure of the murderer as the sexually motivated, psycho/sociopathic serial killer (Downing, 2013; Murley, 2008; Schmid, 2005). The remainder of the discussion in this chapter takes up these themes and will explore them in the following ways. Firstly, it considers the relationship between serial murder and the true crime genre, which has reinforced the characteristics of the serial killer. Secondly, and relatedly, the discussion will go on to examine ideas around the serial killer in culture as a figure of fascination, identification and as late modern celebrity (Schmid, 2005).

Thirdly, the discussion will expand definitions of true crime and in so doing, will draw attention to previously overlooked subgenres such as the memoirs and biographies/autobiographies of well-known violent criminals involved in organised crime. Drawing on examples, I argue that the figure of the gangster is as equally captivating as the serial killer, and may present as a more acceptable violent masculine subject who appeals to male audiences. The conclusion will consider the argument that the murderer occupies a venerated place in popular culture as a transcendent and exceptional subject (Cameron & Frazer, 1987; Downing, 2013). In doing so, the concluding analysis will contrast the figure of the serial killer with that of the gangster to flesh out the appeal of the latter and the different meanings afforded to the 'subject of murder' (Downing, 2013).

The analysis within this chapter is underpinned by a growing recognition of the value of popular criminology to enrich academic criminological knowledge (Brown & Rafter, 2011; Wakeman, 2013; Wattis, 2018). As Brown and Rafter (2011) note, popular criminological texts permit emotional and psychological engagement with matters of crime which academic texts do not have the capacity for. Taking my cue from the criminologist Brown (2003), who argues for a sociological analysis of crime fiction, I offer sociological (or indeed criminological) readings of the figure of the serial killer and the gangster as represented in popular culture to think through what they can tell us about the place of the violent masculine subject. In addition, to support my analysis of the figure of the gangster in popular culture, I explored online sites such as Amazon to assess the popularity of true crime texts and other products featuring this type of violent subject.

Women and True Crime

Changes in technology and media consumption are a key factor linked to true crime's current appeal, with the rise of streaming platforms, and particularly Netflix, propelling its popularity. *Making a Murderer* aired on Netflix in December 2015 and became a phenomenon as audiences responded to the purported miscarriage of justice presented across ten episodes. Netflix is now replete with true crime titles and crime dramas, often with some basis in fact, which viewers can now curate and consume at their own convenience, often in large quantities. Indeed, the instant gratification of picking and choosing content to binge watch adds a further ethical dimension to how we engage with the suffering of others (Sontag, 2004, p. 35). The fact that we now choose when and how much we consume real life violence is certainly something that requires interrogation. The intimacy of the podcast format and its accessibility and portability certainly has psychosocial implications for our relationship to violence. For instance, do the format and conventions of the true crime podcast offer more progressive takes on mediated violence which allows us to question issues of truth, justice and the representations of victim and offender (Buozis, 2017, p. 254; Greer, 2018)? Or do new technologies and formats raise further ethical concerns about the consumption of mediated violence as we consume in new ways?

The podcast phenomenon has spawned the female-led true crime podcast which differs from serialised documentaries in that they revisit the types of violent crime which have historically been the stuff of older true crime books and documentaries—namely, grisly murder narratives. Appealing to a largely female audience, the shows are presented by women, who discuss past cases, but combine this with a range of tangential topics. The most popular and well-known of the female-led true crime podcasts is the US show *My Favorite Murder*. Comedians Karen Kilgariff and Georgina Hardstark present, discussing historical cases and victims, alongside fashion and relationships, as well as disclosing their own struggles with mental health and trauma. The presenters build a rapport and sense of community with the mainly female audience who are invited to email the show with their own stories of local murders and how they and other women they know have encountered and escaped from potential attackers. Respect for, and remembrance of victims and disregard for male perpetrators lends the show a transgressive and empowering element which stands in contrast to the longstanding veneration of male murderers across the history of popular criminology (Downing, 2013; Wattis, 2018). The success of *My Favorite Murder* has inspired numerous shows based on a similar premise: a group of usually female friends getting together to discuss historic violent crimes, usually murder.

The current popularity of true crime, the advent of the female-led podcast and the publication of audience ratings and academic research which shows women make up the majority of consumers and readers of true crime, as well as crime fiction (Murley, 2008; Vicary & Fraley, 2010), has sparked media and academic interest in gender and the consumption of popular criminology. A flurry of broadsheet media commentaries and academic studies have sought to explain the popularity of true crime and crime fiction, which frequently feature serial killers and graphic portrayals of violence and murders involving women as victims, with female audiences. A number of broadsheet articles have mused on women, true crime and crime fiction, contending that women's attraction to factual and fictional popular criminology relates to the vicarious enjoyment of fear and risk in a safe space, identification and empathy with victims, and the need to understand motivation and solve the crime puzzle (Coslett, 2014; Williams, 2018). In terms of academic work, evolutionary psychologists Vicary and Fraley argue that women read true crime as a survival tactic—to pick up clues regarding dangerous individuals and escape strategies if they find themselves in dangerous situations. In contrast, Browder's (2006) research on women who read true crime argues that these texts may perform a therapeutic function, whereby women who themselves have been victims of male violence may draw comfort and reassurance from reading about female victims who have been through similar experiences.

Serial Murder and Popular Criminology

True crime texts do not focus exclusively on profligate serial killers and those who fit the popular archetype of the serial killer. When we drill down and think about what type of work that counts as true crime, it is clear this is a fallacy. The more recent true crime documentaries such as *Making a Murderer* (2013), *The Staircase* (2008) and *Jinx* (2015) focus, at least in the first instance, on a single murder event (Murley, 2008), from which point they re-evaluate the guilt of the protagonist rather than reconstructing solved cases where the guilt of the perpetrator is more certain.

It is fair to say however, that the true crime genre has become synonymous with serial killers. The history of true crime from the late Twentieth Century onwards, and the history of the cultural life of the serial murder, reveals something of a symbiotic relationship between true crime and the figure of the serial killer. The White Chapel murders of 1888, involving the murder of five impoverished women linked to prostitution in London's East End, arguably gave rise to the figure of the serial murderer as sexually motivated killer in culture (Downing, 2013), and generated a raft of popular cultural texts ranging from 'Ripperology' to fiction and drama which adopted the familiar template set by the murders. The term serial killer would not emerge until the FBI named the problem in the 1970s, but as Linnemann (2015) contends, the serialised reporting in the newly established modern print media, 'cast the shadowy outline of Jack the Ripper on London thereby animating the "lust" or "serial killer" who haunts us still (see Warwick, 2006; Downing, 2013)' (2015, p. 517).

Murley's (2008) exploration of the history of true crime in popular culture identifies the serial killer as the dominant criminal type within these texts. Writing about more recent iterations of true crime in the 1980s, Murley (2008) contends that as its popularity increased across different formats, true crime invoked the serial killer as the popular cultural figure, with whom we are now all too familiar.

> True crime has created and brought to life an important pop culture icon, the socio-psychopath [...] True crime was instrumental in securing for such people a place in an American celebrity culture of infamy, which, while not explicitly glorifying serial murder itself, fetishizes, romanticises, and traffics in the "careers" of such killers. (2008, pp. 4–5)

Likewise, Jenkins (1994), writing about the divergence between the actuality of the serial killer, and his cultural realisation as a captivating figure, implicates true crime as pivotal within this history. Jenkins highlights how the 'facts' of serial homicide converged with news media reporting on a number of high-profile cases which became the focus of the nascent modern true crime industry. This relates to how news media and popular culture responded to increases in homicide and serial murder in the 1970s with sensational reporting of cases such as Ted Bundy, Son of Sam and The Hillside Strangler. Murley (2008) also notes how true crime's popularity grew as US murder rates increased and it 'became the dominant form of non-fiction murder narration' (2008, p. 4). Biressi (2001) observes a similar phenomenon in the British context, whereby a set of notorious and macabre cases captured the public's imagination and generated a surfeit of crime texts which encouraged 'the public appetite for true crime and fictional crime stories' (2001, p. 169) which embedded the serial murder within British culture, as well as inscribing atrocity onto specific locations (Cummins et al., 2018; Linnemann, 2015; Wattis, 2019).

The figure of the serial killer in culture also illuminates the complex relationship between crime 'facts', supposedly contained within texts based on 'actual' events, and fictional crime narratives. For instance, Jenkins highlights how Thomas Harris' fiction drew on the 'real-life' cases of Ed Gein and Ted Bundy, and how he sought advice from the FBI's Behavioural Sciences Unit, the infamous 'Mindhunters'—supposedly exceptional individuals with the sole capability and intuition to understand and apprehend the serial killer, who have been portrayed in this way by popular culture (see also Schmid, 2005). Jenkins (1994) also draws attention to the way true crime 'borrowed' from fiction to create the serial killer as a recognisable and familiar figure:

> The overlap between fact and fiction is especially blatant (and problematic) in the true crime literature, where case studies of serial killers frequently refer to Harris's work as if it were the definitive account of the true-life phenomenon. The fictional Hannibal became a villain as well-known as any authentic offender, and was even cited in journalistic accounts as if he were a real figure. (Jenkins, 1994, p. 89)

Furthermore, according to Jenkins, a key feature of Harris' serial killer fiction was his rendering of the protagonist as an evil and charismatic genius as opposed to a hapless inadequate, which was reinforced in the screen versions of his books—most notably *Silence of the Lambs*. Schmid (2005) extends the idea of the serial killer as a charismatic and attractive subject, contending that this figure now occupies the status of 'exemplary modern celebrity' within late modern contemporary culture. Schmid argues that the dominance of the visual image, combined with the cult of celebrity and a late modern fascination and enjoyment of violence have brought forth this figure, who both captivates and repels us. What Hamilton (2011) refers to as a glamorous terror (2011, p. 116).

More recently, Cummins et al. (2018) have applied the lens of celebrity to the earlier UK case of the Moors Murders—a case which predates the serial killer definition. In 1967 Ian Brady and Myra Hindley were sentenced to life imprisonment for the murder of Lesley Ann

Downey and Edward Evans, with Brady also convicted of the murder of John Kilbride. In the 1980s Brady also confessed to the murders of Keith Bennett and Pauline Reade. For the writers, the case, which occurred amid 1960s optimism when the power of the visual image and the cult of modern celebrity culture was really taking hold, the case was one of the first to become a modern media event whereby the public become intimately involved with a case as they are fed every detail by the media. Drawing upon Rojek's (2001) definition of celebrity as 'the attribution of glamour or notorious status to an individual within the public sphere' (Rojek, 2001, cited in Cummins et al., 2018, p. 39), Cummins, Foley and King contend that with their attention to style and image, Brady and Hindley exuded the air of the quintessential 1960s celebrity couple. Moreover, the ascendance of the image within 1960s culture is also central to the long shadow cast by this case. In this mediation of the serial killer and celebrity, the authors also draw on the work of the writer Gordon Burn who predicted the baseless nature of the cult of celebrity across his writing, combining fact, fiction, celebrity and the Moors Murders in *Alma Cogan*, a fictional reimagining of the life of Alma Cogan, the British singer who dominated in the 1950s and early 1960s.

It is also well-documented that Ian Brady actively sought celebrity status. Influenced by Nietzsche and the Marquis de Sade, Brady embraced notions of masculine transcendence and exceptionality, and following imprisonment published his own manifesto *The Gates of Janus* (Downing, 2013). And of course, the case spawned numerous true crime texts across varying formats, part of the collection of UK cases which Biressi (2001) argues provoked the public's appetite for true crime.

Serial Killers: Attraction, Captivation, Identification

The purported celebrity status of the serial killer has become synonymous with the idea that large numbers of people now look upon the serial killer as a compelling object of fascination. Indeed, cultural fascination with serial killers and the idea that this figure now occupies some sort of 'hero' or celebrity status now presents as a given across media and academic commentaries. The following section will consider how this has been understood and offer some examples of the 'attractive serial killer' within popular culture.

Arguably the high point in our captivation with this type of violence peaked in the 1990s with a number of genre defining films, most notably *Silence of the Lambs (1991)*, which augmented the idea of the serial killer as attractive and intelligent, and crucially someone with whom we could identify (Donnelly, 2012). However, there are numerous examples from across fact and fiction which attest to the appeal of the serial killer, and the role of cultural production in encouraging this widespread fascination.

As Schmid (2005) contends, serial killers as figures of notoriety both repel and compel (Schmid, 2005). Several writers have addressed the wider ramifications of the cultural standing and visibility of the serial killer. For instance, Donnelly (2012) argues that when we regard the dangerous and violent criminal, we differentiate and distance them from ourselves which acts as a source of resolution and reassurance. However, Donnelly also contends that during the Reagan era, the serial killer detracted from diffuse and latent anxieties related to this period. The oft-cited Seltzer (1998) identifies the appeal of the serial killer as symptomatic of a more general fascination with representational violence and troubled and violent individuals. For Seltzer (1998), our attraction to the imagined psychological and violent extremities of the serial killer typifies his notion of wound culture. On the other hand, Smith (2011) argues that in the US context, post-911, when individuals come across state violence which is more diffuse, ubiquitous and disquieting, the serial killer presents as a strangely reassuring figure (see Schmid for similar).

Examples of 'real-life' and fictional serial killers as attractive and identifiable are commonplace in popular culture. However, as a number of writers on crime and culture note, 'real-life' and fiction/drama often cross over in media representations (Brown, 2003). Likewise, there is often 'truth' within fiction as fiction and drama frequently draw upon real-life events and, as Murley (2008) contends, fictional texts 'have furthered or enriched the conventions of true crime' (2008, p. 14). For instance, true crime often reads like fiction, with facts often altered to embellish the story. Jenkins' (1994) analysis of how popular culture has created the serial killer as a particular 'type' highlights the interplay between film, crime fiction and true crime in this construction.

There are numerous examples of portrayals of the serial killer as a compelling figure with whom we may identify and seek to understand. For instance, in episode three of the Netflix documentary series *Dark Tourist* (2018), the journalist David Farrier visits Milwaukee, the home of serial killer Jeffrey Dahmer. The case is macabre and distressing—Dahmer was convicted of murdering 17 young men, which involved necrophilia and cannibalism. True crime portrays Dahmer as an unappealing character; however, in the show Farrier interviews female Dahmer enthusiasts who organise and participate in 'Dahmer tours' of Milwaukee. They explain their identification with and attraction to Dahmer because he is a 'bad boy' and they seek to understand his psyche and motivation. This is in spite of outrage at the tours from media and victims' families. Indeed, the recent historical proximity of the murders renders the tours ethically questionable in a way not considered for older cases such as the White Chapel murders.

To take another example. In 2019 *Extremely Wicked, Shockingly Evil and Vile*, another piece of popular criminology focusing on the serial killer Ted Bundy, was released. Bundy, who was convicted of the kidnap, rape and murder of 30 women (possibly more) in the US in the 1970s, was renowned for his good looks. Zac Efron, also renowned for his good looks and heart throb status, played the killer in the film, winning critical plaudits for the role. This was however, amidst criticism that the film and his performance glamourised Bundy and the murders. Writing about the film's release, Bennett (2017) laments the cultural excitement surrounding the film, citing an interview with Efron in *Teen Vogue* where the rape and murder of young women is minimised alongside yet another portrayal of Bundy as a 'dashing and personable man'.

The most recent television iteration of Hannibal Lector offers a strong fictional example of the attractive serial killer. The portrayal of an 'intelligent and articulate' offender (Jenkins, 1994, p. 89) across Thomas Harris' oeuvre and especially in the film adaptation of *The Silence of the Lambs* (1991), presents a murderer who is attractive, charismatic and relatable (Clover, 1993; Jenkins, 1994; Schmid, 2005). In the NBC television series *Hannibal* (2013–2015), the role is reprised by Mads

Mikkelsen, whose physicality and otherworldly good looks, combined with the character's style, intellect and sophistication, culminates in a character of unquestioning appeal and glamour (Cain, 2015). Moreover, the presentation of extreme violence as ornate tableau reinforces its aesthetic nature. Likewise, Showtime's *Dexter* (2006–2013), again adapted from fiction, portrays a likeable serial killer protagonist which has attracted academic attention due to the show's 'ethical ambiguity' (Gregoriou, 2012, p. 284): he may kill those who kill others, but he nevertheless tortures and mutilates his victims. Donnelly (2012) argues that Dexter's appeal lies in his vigilantism which reflects Smith's (2011) contention that Dexter offers the attractive traits of the serial killer: 'In short, because of these traits, Dexter represents a kind of mythic American hero; problematically, however, he is one who pathologically enjoys murdering his victims, exposing America's deep desire for, and ambivalence about, violence' (2011, p. 391).

Moreover, it is not merely the work of cultural production which renders the serial killer an object of special interest. Individual killers may also self-consciously view themselves as above ordinary humanity—as somehow exceptional (Downing, 2013). Narcissism is a commonly assumed trait of the serial killer (Hickey, 2013). For instance, a note found in the cab of Peter Sutcliffe's lorry read: 'In this truck is a man whose latent genius if unleashed would rock the nation, whose dynamic energy would overpower those around him. Better let him sleep'. Likewise, Ian Brady viewed himself as superior to those around him. Influenced by Nazism, the Marquis de Sade and Nietzsche, Brady viewed human beings as disposable which justified his own pursuit of pleasure, exceptionality and notoriety via murder and torture. Arguably, Brady was successful in achieving notoriety, albeit alongside public revulsion (Cummins et al., 2018), as the following extract from an article written by Bennett (2017), following Brady's death, demonstrates:

> While by no means a eulogy, a BBC obituary can't but establish Brady as a notch above the common run of murderer, which appears to be precisely how he viewed himself. Only the very greatest of the celebrities whose premature deaths punctuated 2016 enjoyed comparably extensive

memorialising, both red-top and broadsheet, featuring extended analysis of his alleged influence on the national consciousness. (Bennett, 2017)

Indeed, the relationship between the media and the serial killer is not necessarily passive on the part of the offender; there are a number of examples where serial killers have actively engaged with the media in a process of identity construction and the acquisition fame and notoriety (Haggerty, 2009). Other examples include Denis Nielsen's collaboration with Brian Masters in the writing of his biography (Downing, 2013; Masters, 2020). Several killers have also engaged in cultural work themselves. For instance, Denis Nielsen and Ian Brady wrote and painted, and the murderer John Wayne Gacy is also well-known for his artwork with a dedicated website johnwaynegacyart.com, dedicated to his paintings. Indeed, there is clearly a market for the creative output of serial murderers as the murderabilia phenomenon illustrates. Murderabilia refers to artefacts with a direct link to perpetrators such as possessions, clothing, drawings and paintings, as well as serial killer merchandise. Items with direct provenance are sold for substantial sums and a brief internet search using murderabilia as the search term offers up numerous sites such as Dark Crime Collectables UK and Artem Mortis. The murderabilia phenomenon lends further support to the dubious position of the serial killer in culture and the cultural industry which sustains it (Seltzer, 1998).

The popular appeal and iconic status of the serial killer in late modern Western culture is now the subject of numerous academic texts and media commentaries which attempt to get to the bottom of the cultural draw of who we believe the serial killer to be. Popular criminology, and especially the true crime genre, is held responsible for creating the template for the serial killer. However, there is a tendency in both popular and academic criminology, and other disciplines such as cultural studies, to frame attraction to the serial killer in something of a uniform way which overlooks the varied ways in which specific individuals are regarded. The serial killer is cast as a charismatic celebrity, superhero and object of fascination, and although revulsion at the monstrous Other is often conceded alongside this fascination (Houwen, 2015; Murley, 2008; Schmid, 2005), this type of dominant academic framing belies differing responses to these individuals who often demonstrate quite divergent qualities. As Houwen (2015) contends, the way in which we respond to the serial killer via the interface of popular culture may not necessarily result in full scale identification, despite our fascination and inability to look away. Pathetic characters such as Denis Nielsen and Jeffrey Dahmer, who purportedly killed and dismembered victims out of the loneliness, diminished and dull men such as Peter Sutcliffe, Steve Wright, Levi Bellfield and Christopher Halliwell or the squalid and macabre world of Fred and Rose West, may inspire fascination, much less identification and admiration.

In addition, fixating on the serial killer precludes any consideration of variety within the true crime genre and how subgenres might appeal to differing audiences with an interest in a different type of violent masculine subject, which would open up exploration of men's engagement with true crime. For instance, true crime's emphasis on 'real life' events means that organised crime, stories of war, espionage, prison memoirs also fit the genre. I now turn to focus on a subgenre of true crime which focuses on a different type of murdering subject, which has received limited academic attention—the biographies, memoirs or autobiographies of violent men frequently involved in organised crime, who I argue, cut a more identifiable and glamorous figure than that of the serial killer.

The Figure of the Gangster and the Gangster Biography as a Subgenre of True Crime

Mayr (2012) refers to the life stories of notorious violent criminals, often involved in organised crime, which generally appear in book format, but may also take the form of films and television dramas, as 'hardman biographies'. Examples of the criminal life story include Fraser (1994) and Richardson (2014), but there are numerous others, often written by criminals who have achieved widespread notoriety, while others stay within the realms of local folklore. These texts often include some detail on the early life of the central protagonist, alongside their involvement in organised crime and violent exploits. A tour of the Amazon website offers up numerous titles written by and about key criminal figures, as well as autobiographies written in collaboration (Kray et al., 2015). Frankie

Fraser is a prolific contributor to the 'hard man' genre, having written a number books recalling violent criminal exploits and prison life (Fraser, 1994, 2019), as well as a guide to London 'gangland' (Fraser, 2019). The extract below from the back matter of *Mad Frank's Diary* (Fraser, 2019) offers a sense of the celebratory tone often found within this type of true crime:

> Mad Frankie Fraser has become a household name, known to millions as one of London's most notorious gangsters. His stories of his life of crime have become the stuff of legend and Mad Frank's Diary delves into areas he has never chosen or never dared to talk about before. Taking the form of a diary, the book chronicles Frank's memories from each day of the year, recalling incidents from throughout Frank's colourful and eventful life in a way that makes his stories highly accessible and hugely entertaining.

Before his death in 2014, Fraser courted the media and his status as celebrity 'hardman', participating in book launches, 'performing' in his own one man show, 'An Evening With …' and taking part in guided tours of 'gangland London'. The fact that the exploits of a man, who spent 40 years in prison, was as an 'enforcer' for the notorious Richardson gang, and was said to have murdered in excess of 40 people, and tortured others by removing their teeth with pliers, are deemed 'colourful' and 'entertaining', with no attempt to hide behind an interest in motivation and concern for victims, brings the ethical questions posed by true crime into sharp focus. In an article reflecting on the celebrity status of Fraser, Blacker (2013) notes how 'old school' villains 'are treated with a strange amount of indulgence by the press and public, their public appearances 'playing to amused well-heeled audiences in the West End'. Blacker further remarks that their acts of extreme violence become removed from their affable, celebrity personas so they appear to be 'almost fictional'. There is a clear contrast between these 'loveable' villains endeared within the national psyche if famous enough, and the purported celebrity status of serial killers. Schmid (2005) also considers the divergent positions occupied by different types of violent protagonist, comparing the vilified outsider status of the terrorist Other post 9–11, with that of the serial killer, who to varying degrees, is accepted by the dominant culture. Schmid (2005) argues that the serial killer is accepted by the wider culture and retains insider status, referring to the serial killer as violence with an 'American face' (2006, p. 254). In the context of British culture, the cultural work and mythology which surrounds the familiar figure of the gangland villain is a further example of the violent subject who resides firmly within culture. Moreover, both figures reflect how masculinity, crime and violence enjoy a level of acceptance which would be unheard of for violent women (Jewkes, 2011). Ruth Penfold Mounce (2010) writes about the relationship between celebrity, criminality and the media and the way in which, in an era of mass media, the details of infamous criminal subjects are followed and portrayed positively within news and popular culture so that the public become intimately acquainted with particular individuals as 'mediated criminal hero' (2010, p. 88). She offers examples of individuals who, due to criminal exploits, and some stories of redemption, have garnered significant media attention. Examples of the 'mediated criminal hero' include John McVicar, famous for prison escapes, who went on to reform and gain a PhD in sociology, and Ronnie Biggs, who took part in the infamous 1963 great train robbery, and whose attempts to avoid extradition to the UK in first Brazil, and then Spain, were frequent featured in the British tabloid press.

Penfold Mounce (2010) differentiates between the aforementioned 'mediated criminal hero' and the 'underworld exhibitionist' who she argues, 'actively manufacture a celebrity career from their past activities' (2009, p. 86). The villain who writes their life story and self-consciously constructs a celebrity criminal persona falls into the latter category. She further contends that the celebrity lifespan of the underworld exhibitionist is short-lived, and many remain unknown beyond specialist audiences, while others such as the Kray twins retain celebrity status into the mainstream and become part of the collective cultural memory. However, this underestimates the attention and standing such figures have among the readership of this subgenre of true crime, which is so often ignored when academics examine true crime, as well as the appeal of the generic figure of the underworld villain or 'hard man' for specialist audiences interested in this true crime subgenre.

To return to the Krays, the identical twins whose violence and involvement in organised crime in London in the 1960s is the stuff of legend, their fame as 'underworld celebrities' extends far beyond niche true crime enthusiasts with an interest in 'hard men', and well into mainstream culture and collective cultural memory. The back matter of John Pearson's (1995) *The Profession of Violence: The Rise and Fall of the Kray Twins* described them in the following way:

> Reggie and Ronnie Kray ruled London's 1960s gangland with a ruthlessness and viciousness that shocks, even today. Building an empire of organised crime on a scale never done before or since, the brothers swindled, extorted, terrorised and brutally murdered.

The Kray twins have inspired and collaborated on numerous true crime texts. A brief search on Amazon revealed 16 books written about the Krays with several collaborations with the twins themselves. As Pearson (1995) notes, following imprisonment, their 'crimes became big business. With books, films and non-stop journalism produced about them, large amounts of money were involved' (1995, p. 317). Arguably, even more interesting are the stylish black and white prints on canvas that are also on sale on the site. The 39 images on canvas are the epitome of the classy black and white 1960s iconic photographic image. The brothers were acquaintances of the acclaimed photographer David Bailey, who also grew up in the impoverished East End of London, and whose pictures chronicle the 1960s, the icons of the era and the development of celebrity culture. Bailey photographed the brothers, alongside the likes of Twiggy, The Beatles and The Rolling Stones, as quintessential 1960s icons. As Cummins et al. (2018) have observed, celebrity status became democratised in the 1960s when anyone could now become a celebrity, including violent criminals.

Hickey (2013) has argued that the definition of serial killers should be broad, including those who kill more than three times. This definition would cover a much wider and varied range of offenders such as terrorists, gang members and state-sponsored assassinations. And yet, the fixation with the serial killer as a particular type prevails: a psychopath and sadist motivated to violence as gratification (often sexual) rather than for instrumental gain. However, the difference between violent subjects is often blurred. In *The Profession of Violence*, Pearson (1995) recounts the early life of the Kray twins through their dominance of London's underworld in the 1960s, ending with their imprisonment for two murders in 1968. Pearson documents gratification as the main motivation for violence, as opposed to an end in itself. Their taste for violence, especially in the case of Ronnie, is well-documented which also challenges the idea that gangsters' motivation to violence is purely instrumental driven by business incentives. Pearson (2015) puts pay to this assumption, drawing attention to the visceral pleasure and expressive nature of violence in the case of the Krays. This also highlights the false distinctions made between serial killers and other violent subjects, given the assumption that only serial killers derive pleasure from inflicting pain for its own sake (Hickey, 2013):

> In all their fights one thing distinguished them once they began; the way they would 'go the limit', carried away by an orgy of violence as if blood and brutality satisfied a need the shared in secret. Even their allies could be frightened by their fury and the pleasure they obviously derived from giving pain. (Pearson, 2015, p. 44)

Ronnie, renowned for being the more unpredictable and sadistic of the brothers, was certified insane in 1958 and upon imprisonment for murder in 1968, was sent to Broadmoor high security psychiatric hospital. Pearson's book gives a sense of his paranoia, fascination with the macabre and 'private dreams of violence' (1995, p. 320), as well as his pursuit of violence beyond instrumental gain which was ultimately the Kray's downfall. The stylish film adaptation of the book, *Legend* (2015) with both brothers played to critical acclaim by Tom Hardy, plays to a choreographed aesthetic of violence, as well as to the iconography and glamour of the Kray brothers. As Pearson notes in the postscript to *The Profession of Violence*, the brothers pursued notoriety and fame from an early age, self-consciously aware of their 'story' and how it might be told. Pearson also touches on the slippage between reality and fiction, common within much true crime writing, in Ronnie's realisation of the twins' story:

What was so scary about these murders was their unreality; the victims being killed like extras in a gangster movie [...] Gangster movies need at least a few dead gangsters and a lot of blood. As if with the plot of the Krays firmly in his mind, Ronnie set about providing them. He was acting out this mental movie till the day he was arrested. (p. 320)

What the above discussion highlights is that the categorisation of violent subjects as distinct types is far from clear-cut. In scientific terms, this would require rigorous psychological assessment to determine the categorisation of certain offenders. My concern here is the way in which popular culture codifies certain violent individuals and the general assumptions which circulate about them within the wider culture. When subject to scrutiny, broad assumptions about the appeal of the serial killer appear as more complex and nuanced when contrasted with other violent types. Schmid's (2005) observation about the Muslim terrorist Other as complete outsider is a case in point here. Moreover, the figure of the gangster across fact and fiction arguably fits the notion of the attractive violent subject more effectively. The serial killer may be the outsider who is permitted to reside *within* the dominant culture and is frequently fetishised; however, the gangster presents as a more acceptable icon of violent masculinity, who to varying degrees, is admired and in some cases, occupies a place within collective cultural memory.

Conclusion

This chapter began by pointing to the enduring popularity of true crime and renewed interest in the genre due to the emergence of new platforms and formats. As a result, true crime is now attracting interest due to its diversification and the way audiences are accessing programmes in new ways and on new formats. One of the biggest questions to emerge from the growing media and academic interest in the true crime phenomenon is why, historically and contemporaneously, true crime across formats is so much more popular with female audiences (bbc.co.uk, 2019; Browder, 2006; Hess, 2018; Murley, 2008; Vicary & Fraley, 2010). Crime writers, journalists and academics alike, offer assorted explanations from the way true crime allows women to engage with vicarious fear, identify with victims, understand psyche and motivation, as well as offering therapy and resolution.

However, I have argued that the preoccupation with female audiences adopts a narrow view of true crime which belies its diversity. The central tenet of true crime is its claim to recount actual events. If this is the case, the scope of true crime can be broadened considerably. For instance, prison memoirs, organised crime, wartime histories, state crime, can also be classified as true crime. This in turn demands a reassessment of audience demographic, preference and motivation. Recognising true crime's assorted and overlooked subgenres has been the key aim of this article. My latter focus has been on the life stories of violent individuals connected to organised crime or 'hard men'. Texts which are not generally invoked when we interrogate true crime narratives. I argue that this relates to dominant assumptions about what constitutes true crime and a preoccupation with the figure of the murderer or more precisely, the serial killer. Drawing upon Murley (2008) earlier on in the chapter, I highlight the symbiotic relationship between true crime (or a particular type of true crime) and the psycho/sociopathic killer where Murley contends that the genre actually brought this familiar popular cultural figure to life, which in turn reinforced what we understand to be true crime. Moreover, given the crosscutting of genres and the borrowing and slippage between fact and fiction, discerning true crime from fictional and dramatized texts is not straightforward (Brown, 2003; Downing, 2013). This has been especially marked in the 'making of' the serial killer in popular culture (Jenkins, 1994; Schmid, 2005).

A further consequence of cultural production around the serial killer has been the ascendance of this figure as object of fascination, admiration and as a late modern celebrity (Cummins et al., 2018; Murley, 2008; Schmid, 2005). Again, a set of preoccupations, often presents the serial killer as a single type and precludes any consideration of the 'appeal' of violent subjects within the context of what Lisa Downing (2013) argues is a culture which worships murderers. The gangster or hardman figure, who has been neglected in academic analyses of violent subjects and popular culture is a further example to support Downing's contention regarding the veneration of the murderer figure. Moreover, the gangster aesthetic and the presentation of violence within 'hard man stories' is done in such a way as to appeal to a male audience who may be attracted to the violent masculine subject portrayed therein (Mayr, 2012).

I focus on the Kray twins in my discussion, whose celebrity and mythology stretches beyond niche true crime and into the mainstream culture and collective memory as part of 1960s iconography. The glamour attached to the Krays and the way in which they have been portrayed in popular culture—especially the film *Legend*—as stylish and attractive villains indicates a public acceptance and admiration relating to wider notions of gangster 'cool' directed at so-called 'honourable' villains. There are numerous other examples of violent protagonists who do similar cultural work. For instance, the recent popularity of *Peaky Blinders*, the BBC drama which depicts the travails of a violent crime family in industrial Birmingham following the First World War features a similar concern with stylish violence and flawed yet appealing subjects.

In her discussion of the 'subject of murder', Downing (2013) argues that the murderer retains a place as 'a paradigmatic modern figure of exception—the subject of murder—has found a place in postmodern global culture' (2013, p. 194). Downing further argues that for men, the act of murder is a route to masculine exceptionality and transcendence via transgression. Often the figure alluded to is the serial killer—Ian Brady's self-conscious quest for exceptionality is well-documented. The pursuit of exceptionality is not available to women because they are denied such complex subjectivity. Furthermore, there is no acceptance of women who kill who, as Downing (2013) notes, present as 'an epistemological and ontological problem' (2013, p. 197) maligned by the media while criminology fails to get to grips with the female murderer beyond the psychological (Morrissey, 2003). Downing also contends that the culture which worships the murderer is misogynist. This relates to the former point, as well as the manner in which culture revels in the masculine murderer while female victims are either ignored or objectified (Strega et al., 2014; Wattis, 2018) and dead women become a lazy and well-worn trope across popular culture (Bolin, 2019; Clark Dillman, 2014). However, as this chapter has shown, the figure of the murderer within culture is complex and requires further interrogation. Likewise, true crime requires more unpacking; its narrow focus distorts and disavows how many experience violence and trauma in the context of late capitalist societies where we obsess about the subjective violence of the 'wound culture', and turn away from structural violence and inequality.

Study Questions

- What might explain the popularity of true crime among female audiences?
- How do you think technology has transformed the way we listen to and view crime-related content? What are the implications of this?
- Is true crime ethical?
- How can we explain the popularity and appeal of the figure of the serial killer in popular culture?
- What differences do you see in cultural representations of the serial killer and the figure of the gangster in popular culture?
- What do representations of violent masculine subjects tell us about gender and crime?

References

BBC.co.uk. (2019). True crime: Five reasons women love it, N.D. https://www.bbc.co.uk/programmes/articles/5BQCFMQd3mPqj7YT4hlvdCL/true-crime-five-reasons-why-women-love-it. Accessed 18 Dec 2019.

Bennett, C. (2017, May 21). 'We Learn Nothing from Ian Brady, We're Just Fetishising Him.' *The Guardian.*

Biressi, A. (2001). *Crime, fear and the law in trial crime stories*, Palgrave Macmillan.

Blacker, T. (2013, June 13). Frankie Fraser: We just can't seem to stop ourselves falling for these old villains. The Independent.

Bolin, A. (2019). *Dead girls: Essays on surviving an American obsession.* New York: William Morrow Paperbacks.

Browder, L. (2006). Dystopian romance: True crime and the female reader. *The Journal of Popular Culture, 39*(6), 928–953.

Brown, S. (2003). *Crime and law in media culture*. Buckingham: Open University Press.

Brown, M., & Rafter, N. (2011). *Criminology goes to the movies: Crime, theory and popular culture*. New York: New York University Press.

Bruzzi, S. (2016). Making a genre: The case of the contemporary true crime documentary. *Law and Humanities, 10*(2), 249–280.

Buozis, M. (2017). Giving voice to the accused: Serial and the critical potential of true crime. *Communication and Critical/Cultural Studies, 14*(3), 254–270.

Cain, S. (2015, August 27). Hannibal: Farewell to the Best Bloody Show on TV. *The Guardian*.

Cameron, D., & Frazer, E. (1987). *The lust to kill*. Polity.

Capote, T. (2000). *In cold blood: An account of a multiple murder and its consequences*. Penguin.

Clark Dillman, J. (2014). *Women and death in television news: Dead but not gone*. New York: Palgrave Macmillan.

Clover, C. J. (1993). *Men, women and chainsaws: Gender in the modern horror film*. Princeton University Press.

Coslett, L. (2014, May 21). Why Women are Hooked on Violent Crime Fiction. *The Guardian*.

Cummins, I., Foley, M., & King, M. (2018). *Serial killers and the media: The Moors murders legacy*. Palgrave.

Donnelly, A. M. (2012). The New American Hero: Dexter, serial killer for the masses. *The Journal of Popular Culture, 45*(1), 15–26.

Downing, L. (2013). *The subject of murder: Gender, exceptionality and the modern killer*. University of Chicago Press.

Fraser, F. (1994). *Mad Frank: Memoirs of a life of crime*. London: Little Brown and Company.

Fraser, F. (2019). *Mad Frank's Diary: The confessions of Britain's most notorious villain*. London: Virgin Digital.

Greer, A. (2018). Murder, she spoke: The female voice's ethics evocation and spatialisation in the true crime podcast. *Sound Studies, 3*(2), 152–164.

Gregoriou, C. (2012). 'Times like these I wish there was a real Dexter': Unpacking serial killer ideologies and metaphors from TV's Dexter Internet Forum. *Language and Literature, 21*(3), 274–285.

Haggerty, K. (2009). Modern serial killers. *Crime, Media, Culture, 5*, 168.

Hamilton, G. (2011). American studies in review: Killer apps. *Canadian Review of American Studies, 41*(1), 115–122.

Hess, A. (2018, February 16). The transgressive appeal of the comedy murder podcast. *New York Times*.

Hickey, E. W. (2013). *Serial murders and their victims* (6th ed.). Wadsworth Publishing.

Houwen, J. (2015). Identifying with Dexter. *American, British and Canadian Studies, 24*, 24–43.

Jenkins, P. (1994). *Using murder: The social construction of serial homicide*. Aldine de Guyter.

Jewkes, Y. (2011). *Media and crime*. London: Sage.

Kray, R., Kray, R., & Dineage, F. (2015). *Our Story: Reg and Ron Kray*. Pan.

Linnemann, T. (2015). Capote's ghosts: Violence, murder and the spectre of suspicion. *British Journal of Criminology, 55*, 514–533.

Mailer, N. (1989). *The Executioner's Song*. Random House.

Masters, B. (2020). *Killing for company: The case of Dennis Nilsen*. Arrow.

Mayr, A . (2012). Chopper: From the inside: Discourses of the 'celebrity' criminal Mark Brandon Read. *Language and Literature, 21*(3), 260–273.

Morrissey, B. (2003). *When women kill: Questions of agency and subjectivity*. Routledge.

Murley, J. (2008). *The rise of true crime: 20th century murder and American popular culture*. Praeger.

Pearson, J. (1995, 2015). *The profession of violence: The rise and fall of the Kray Twins*. London: William Collins.

Penfold Mounce, R. (2010). *Celebrity culture and crime: The joy of transgression*. London: Palgrave.

Richardson, C. (2014). *The last gangster: My final confession*. Arrow.

Rojek, C. (2001). Celebrity. London: Reaktion.

Schmid, D. (2005). *Natural BORN CELEBRITIES: Serial killers in American culture*. University of Chicago Press.

Seltzer, M. (1998). *Serial killers: Death and life in America's Wound Culture*. New York: Routledge.

Smith, V. L. (2011). Our serial killers, our superheroes, and ourselves: Showtime's Dexter. *Quarterly Review of Film and Video, 28*(5), 390–400.

Sontag, S. (2004). *Regarding the pain of others*. Penguin.

Strega, S., Janzen, C., Morgan, J., Brown, M., Thomas, R., & Carriere, J. (2014). Never innocent victims: Street sex workers in Canadian print media. *Violence against Women, 20*(1), 6–25.

Vicary, A. M., & Fraley, C. R. (2010). Captured by true crime: Why are women drawn to tales of rape, murder and serial killers? *Social Psychological and Personality Science, 1*(1), 81–86.

Wakeman, S. (2013). No one wins. One side just loses more slowly: The Wire and drug policy. *Theoretical Criminology, 18*(2), 224–240.

Wattis, L. (2018). *Revisiting the Yorkshire Ripper murders: Histories of Gender, Violence and Victimhood*. Palgrave Macmillan.

Wattis, L. (2019). Violence, emotion and place: The case of five murders involving sex workers. *Crime, Media, Culture, 16*(2), 201–219.

Williams, Z. (2018, May 1). Are women responsible for all the sexual violence on screen? *The Guardian.*

Yardley, L., Kelly, E., & Robinson Edwards, S. (2018). Forever trapped in the imaginary of late capitalism? The serialised true crime podcast as a wake-up call in times of criminological slumber. *Crime, Media Culture, 15*(3), 303–521.

Part IV

True Crime Spaces

12

Feeding the Fascination: Crime-Related Tourism and the True Crime Museum

Hannah Thurston

Introduction

Stories about 'true' crime continue to fascinate, titillate, and captivate on a global scale. However, there is an inherent distortion involved within these spaces of non-fictional narrativity. True crime stories are frequently about the most horrific of crimes. Not content with minor delinquency or deviance, media producers seek out the most brutal of crime-scenes, the wickedest of motives, the most violent of violations. The desire to feed a fascination for the macabre appears somehow intrinsic to human nature. As historians, penologists, sociologists we can be critical of the commercialisation of pain and suffering, of the commodification of these crime stories but ultimately, we too find them interesting. Otherwise why am I sat at my computer writing this chapter and why are you there,

H. Thurston (✉)
University of Brighton, Brighton, UK
e-mail: h.thurston@brighton.ac.uk

M. Mellins and S. Moore (eds.), *Critiquing Violent Crime in the Media*,
https://doi.org/10.1007/978-3-030-83758-7_12

reading it? Whether we like it or not stories about true crime continue to fascinate many of us.

The result of this human interest is an ever-increasing and ever-changing true crime mediascape. For example, developments in technology or travel can impact the modes and methods by which we tell and consume these true crime narratives. From magazines to movies, museums to podcasts, (auto)biographies to documentaries the so-called 'truth' about crime is a lucrative—if not illusive—truth indeed. This dynamic context means we are continually presented with new political, moral, and cultural questions. Moreover, these questions become ever more pertinent when the story is experienced with the body and when the storyteller has a perceived legitimacy or authority. Here I am referring to the growing popularity of museums and other tourist sites associated with policing, punishment, and crime.

Often understood as a form of 'dark' tourism these storied spaces are significant sites in which meanings are made and opinions are formed. When we visit a museum associated with prison or policing, when we seek out sites linked to infamous killings and killers, or when we tour a defunct jail cell, we are—in effect—consuming true crime narratives. Much like other mediated crime narratives they are no doubt partial and limited, forgetting as much as they remember, but this is unlikely to diminish their power or potency. This chapter then, will introduce the reader to some of the issues involved in crime-related tourism. It will begin by offering a typography of crime-related sites to expose the diversity within and between these tourist experiences. It will then move on to consider one such site in more detail: the *True Crime Museum* in Hastings, England.[1] I have written about the methodology I use in museum spaces elsewhere (please see Thurston, 2017a) so the second part of the chapter will instead focus on the exhibits themselves.

---

[1] Please be advised this chapter refers to criminal acts including sexual assault, dismemberment, cannibalism, and other forms of violence. The second half of the chapter in particular includes images of (and written extracts from) the *True Crime Museum* which some readers may find distressing.

Crime Related Tourism: Introducing a Typology

Broll (2020, p. 792) reminds us that humankind has always had a 'deep and persistent cultural fascination with the macabre'. It is maybe not surprising then, that tourist sites associated with death and suffering are a global phenomenon. Often referred to as 'dark' sites, these storied spaces, as Stone (2006) points out, exist along a fluid and dynamic spectrum of intensity. In other words, some sites provide a much 'darker' experience than others. Crime related sites tend to sit somewhere in the middle of this spectrum, although there are no doubt examples to be found at either end too. For example, holocaust tourism would be on the 'darker' end of Stone's (2006) spectrum while 'dark fun factories' such as the London Dungeons are much 'lighter' in relative terms.

As storied spaces then, these specifically *crime*-related dark tourist sites are highly diverse. They include for example 25 Cromwell Street, the now infamous home of Fred and Rose West; The Angola Prison Rodeo hosted by Louisiana State Penitentiary and the 9/11 Memorial and Museum in New York City. More generally, the list might also include narco-related tourism in Latin America; attending the site of an assassination or mass murder; and some forms of gravestone tourism. Even a ghost-walk might be considered a form of crime-related tourism if it includes a story in which a person was killed unlawfully. Similarly, decommissioned cells and former prisons are also being repurposed to perform more touristic functions. To give you some examples, you might be enjoying the theatre in Valparaiso, attending a wedding in Somerset, staying at the Four Seasons in Istanbul, or drinking a cocktail in Canterbury while also being in a former cell. Former sites of imprisonment such as these have been given a new (commercial) purpose in recent years. Add to this every memorial, museum or tour dedicated to crime, punishment, or policing and we begin to see that from Auschwitz to Alcatraz, crime-related tourism is big business. What at first glance might appear to be a rather niche interest is—on closer inspection—a huge part of the tourism industry (Carrabine, 2017).

To help manage, plot, and explore this diversity further I have suggested six categories of 'true' crime-related tourism. It is worth noting though, that these categories are not mutually exclusive and many sites fit into multiple categories at once. Moreover, the list of categories is not exhaustive because the tourism industry is dynamic and ever-changing. Finally, for ease I have excluded sites associated with fictional crime and criminals such as film set locations. In short then, I offer this typography both as a way of distinguishing between different types of (true) crime tourism and as a starting point for further discussion.

- Tourist sites about specific crimes or criminals

These sites tend to be focused on a particular event or series of events offering an often-chronological account of a crime or a criminal's life. The sites which concentrate on a crime (or crime scene) as opposed to a criminal tend to be 'unsolved mysteries', otherwise the narrative focus shifts to the perpetrator. An example of this type of tourist site would be the highly controversial *Jack the Ripper Museum* in London (England). The website suggests that 'As you explore the museum you will discover everything there is to know about the lives of the victims, the main suspects in the murders, the police investigation and the daily life of those living in the east end of London in 1888'.[2] Another good example of this more focussed site would be *The Bonnie and Clyde Ambush Museum* in Gibsland, Louisiana (USA). The museum is in the place where the couple shared their last meal before they were surrounded by police. Other examples include the *Billy the Kid Museum* in Fort Summer (USA)[3] and *The Ned Kelly Museum* in Glenrowan (Australia).[4]

- General tourist sites about crime-related processes

These more general sites are often pitched as 'national' museums which tell a story about the development of large-scale processes. They are less inclined to give nuanced or thorough accounts of a specific

---

[2] Jack the Ripper Museum https://www.jacktherippermuseum.com/about-the-museum.html.

[3] Billy the Kid Museum: http://www.billythekidmuseumfortsumner.com/index.html.

[4] Ned Kelly Musuem (Trip Advisor): https://www.tripadvisor.co.uk/Attraction_Review-g552175-d1233736-Reviews-Ned_Kelly_Museum-Glenrowan_Victoria.html.

crime or an infamous criminal, preferring instead to offer a more over-arching explanation of how a country developed the systems it did. These are often advertised as educational (as opposed to 'entertainment' focused) and market themselves as places to 'learn' about the history of crime and justice. A good example of this type of site would be the *National Justice Museum* (Nottingham, England). The website suggests the museum can facilitate 'curriculum-linked educational visits' which 'use authentic courtrooms, museum spaces, objects and archives to help pupils gain a practical understanding of the law and justice system'.[5] Another example might be the *Medieval Crime and Justice Museum in Rothenberg* (Germany). According to their promotional materials the site displays early modern torture instruments, including instruments that were used to carry out corporal punishment. The collection also includes 'many historical law books, dating from the 13th Century'.[6]

- Tourist sites about the detection of crime and pursuit of criminals

Another category of tourist sites which will likely include a true crime narrative are, more accurately, about methods of crime detection/prevention. Here we find stories of (usually) successful investigations, pursuits, and arrests. While the focus of these sites is generally policing, they nevertheless provide accounts of non-fictional crime and criminals. Much like the museums which position themselves as national museums, the policing sites often express an overt pedagogical or educational function. Examples include the *Federal Police Interactive Museum* in Mexico City (Mexico), which is marketed online as a 'learning place which presents playfully and interactively, the job of Federal Police'.[7] Similarly, *The Beijing Police Museum Beijing Police Museum* (China) promotes itself online as a place in which 'people from all walks of life

---

5 National Justice Museum: https://www.nationaljusticemuseum.org.uk/education/.
6 Medieval Crime and Justice Museum: https://www.kriminalmuseum.eu/?lang=en.
7 Federal Police Interactive Museum: https://sic.cultura.gob.mx/ficha.php?table=museo&table_id=1578.

can know about capital polices' adding that the site is 'also an important base of education in patriotism for teenagers'.[8]

- Tourist sites about the punishment of criminals

Much like policing museums, punishment museums and jail cell tours also tell their true crime stories through the frame of an institution. Many have an historical focus, and many are housed within or around former sites of incarceration giving them a locational authenticity. Examples include the *Eastern State Penitentiary* (Philadelphia, USA). Built in 1829, this former prison was designated a National Historic Landmark in the 1970s and as a museum, the site includes displays about infamous inmates such as mob boss Al Capone.[9] A further example is the *Clink Prison Museum* (London, England). The website tells us the museum is built on the original site and presents the 'scandalous truth' of Old Bankside. Visitors can 'experience the sights, sounds and smells of the prison, handle torture devices, and hear all about the tales of torment and many misfortunes of the inmates of the infamous Clink Prison'.[10] Similarly, *The Abashiri Prison Museum* (Hokkaido, Japan) is promoted as an outdoor museum 'where buildings of the original Abashiri Prison are conserved and exhibited'. The site is described as a collection of 'nationally important cultural properties'.[11]

- Tourist sites which originate from personal collections

These sites vary massively in size and in the level of expertise of staff/curators. Most begin with an enthusiast collecting objects of interest or a criminal justice professional (such as a police or prison officer) saving items in the course of their jobs. These collections are then gifted or loaned, so they can be displayed for public consumption. *The Beaumont Police Museum* in Texas (USA) is an example of this type of site.

[8] Beijing Police Museum: https://www.chinatravel.com/beijing/attractions/beijing-police-museum/.
[9] Eastern State Penitentiary: https://www.easternstate.org/.
[10] Clink Museum: https://www.clink.co.uk/.
[11] The Abashiri Prison Museum: https://www.kangoku.jp/multilingual_english/.

It was set up by a serving officer after he secured a collection of weapons and mug shots which were due to be destroyed.[12] *The Old Police Cells Museum* in Brighton, England is another example. The website includes a blog written by one of the museum's creators. In it he explains that he 'requested any police items people didn't want anymore' and that gradually they collected enough items to display. In his words, 'it is fair to say we didn't have too much idea about setting up a museum'.[13] *The True Crime Museum* (Hastings, England) discussed later in this chapter also began as a private collection but is now a considerable museum set in over 3000 square feet of caves on Hastings seafront.[14]

- Tourist sites about atrocities and mass loss of life

Finally, there are those sites which are associated with mass suffering and loss of life. These are usually the darkest of sites and include for example, *Auschwitz-Birkenau Museum and Memorial*[15] in Oświęcim, Poland. The museum is set in the grounds of a Nazi concentration camp where over one million men, women and children were killed. Another example would be *The Tuol Sleng Genocide Museum*[16] in Phnom Penh, Cambodia. This museum is housed in a former school which was used by the Khmer Rouge regime to imprison and interrogate people in the late 1970s. The number of people kept here is not known, but it is estimated to exceed 20,000. Unlike some of the other crime-related sites (such as *The True Crime Museum* discussed shorty) these sites usually seek to establish a sombre tone often acting as both official and unofficial memorials as well as museums.

In summary, this first section of the chapter has sought to establish how diverse true crime-related tourism really is. It is also worth noting the examples above are mainly museums. If we were to include other types of sites associated with non-fictional crime and victims, we could

---

[12] Beaumont Police Museum: https://police.beaumonttexas.gov/police-community-relations/police-museum/.

[13] Old Police Cells: https://www.oldpolicecellsmuseum.org.uk/.

[14] True Crime Museum: https://www.truecrimemuseum.co.uk/.

[15] Auschwitz-Birkenau Museum and Memorial: http://auschwitz.org/en/.

[16] The Tuol Sleng Genocide Museum: https://tuolsleng.gov.kh/.

include for example: graveyard tourism (the resting places of Lee Harvey Oswald and Malcolm X are particularly popular); walking tours (such as those associated with Pablo Escobar[17] or the 'Gangsters, Brothels and Lolly Shops tour' in Melbourne[18]); decommissioned cells which have been repurposed (such as hotels, restaurants and cocktail bars); and any sites associated with state crimes, war crimes, and victimless crimes. This is a substantial section of the tourism industry; it appears that crime really does pay! Having established the sheer size of this specific part of the tourism industry, I would now like to turn our attention to one such site: *The True Crime Museum* in Hastings, England.

The *True Crime Museum* Hastings, England

Located in a series of caves near Hastings seafront, the *True Crime Museum* is probably the largest collection of crime memorabilia in England. What began as a privately owned family collection is now a substantial museum and giftshop which opened to the public in 2014. The exhibits are housed in a series of connected rooms and caves, meaning that visitors move through the space in a specific way. In this section of the chapter I will discuss a selection of exhibits under three connected headings. First, we will examine how the museum seeks to entertain its patrons by explicitly blurring the line between fact and fiction. Second, we will discuss where the museum manages to capitalise on the creepy, making familiar objects somehow obscene. Finally, we will explore how the site uses humour, mocking and gamification to encourage a specific tone, one which ultimately trivialises the plight of both offenders and victims alike.

---

[17] Pablo Escobar Tours: https://theboutiqueadventurer.com/pablo-escobar-tour-medellin/.

[18] Gangsters, Brothels & Lolly Shops tour: https://www.melbournehistoricalcrimetours.com/book-now.html.

Blurring the Line Between Fact and Fiction

Having paid my entry fee of £8.50 I enter the *True Crime Museum* through the gift shop.[19] The experience begins with a corridor called *Ripper Alley* (Fig. 12.1). This is a reference to 'Jack the Ripper', an unknown assailant who killed and mutilated women in Whitechapel during the late 1880s. In Ripper Alley we find among other things, a series of poster boards, each one dedicated to a different serial killer. For example, we learn about the crimes of John Reginald Christie who was a Special Constable and respected 'family man'. The poster goes on:

> *"But nice Mr Christie at 10 RILLINGTON PLACE, was a SERIAL KILLER, driven by his unquenchable LUST to gas and strangle his pretty victims, then RAPE them as they lay dying on his floor". (emphasis in original)*

We also meet Ed Gein who 'liked to make things out of DEAD PEOPLE [...] Nimble-fingered Ed made a BELT to hold severed nipples against his chest while he worked the farm'. If that was not visceral enough, we also learn that 'He slept wearing a sliced off face'. Then there is Stephen Griffiths: 'He abducted, tortured, murdered, cut up and ATE three Bradford Sex workers'. And Aileen Wuornos who is quoted as saying: 'I robbed them all & I killed them, cold as ice, and I'd do it again cos I've been HATING HUMANS for a long time'.

Other than their status as killers there is nothing that explicitly connects the people selected for the display. Instead this is more of a 'who's-who' of the most gruesome or gory or unusual killers and killings. However, with closer inspection there is a narrative theme running between the posters: the blurring of reality and a very specific form of fiction. Here I am referring to the tropes and characters we commonly associate with the genre of supernatural (often urban) fiction and fantasy. The first poster in Ripper Alley (Fig. 12.2) makes this connection clear:

---

[19] The *True Crime Museum* has given permission for the author to use photographs taken within the museum.

Fig. 12.1 Ripper Alley

Fig. 12.2 Serial Killer Poster in Ripper Alley

"More victims than The Werewolf, more bloodthirsty than Dracula and more relentless than a legion of Zombies."

This attempt to depict real-life criminals as more terrifying than fictional monsters is not uncommon in other mediated narratives. After undertaking a qualitative analysis of news stories in both the UK and the

USA, Wiest (2016) found they differed in terms of content and tone. Referring specifically to articles about serial killers she concludes that 'U.K. articles include more monster imagery and U.S. articles include more celebrity imagery' (p. 327). This divergence may be at least in part because of the language which surrounded the Whitechapel Murders in 1880. Sensationalised accounts of these brutal crimes perpetrated by the aforementioned 'Jack the Ripper' became commonplace in newspapers of the time. Vronsky (2004) suggests it was here that we began to see the development of a character-type which is now common in many media formats: the monstrous (or 'monsterised') criminal with evil or demonic desires. Similarly, Epstein (1994) found that films about serial killers also tended to depict the criminals using the fictional monster frame, comparing the perpetrators' desires to those of mythic beasts such as vampires and werewolves. That said, while the *True Crime Museum* did clearly reference these fictional beasts, the display was also keen to remind visitors these killers are human.

> ... *don't look for fangs or claws on the MONSTERS shown here in Ripper Alley, for these BEASTS hide behind faces just like ours. They will greet you with a smile, not a snarl. Their charming words and helpful acts will mask their twisted desires until it is too late to save you.*

In many ways it is not surprising to find this dual identity of both 'human' and 'monster' because the representation of serial killers in recent years has shifted (Haggerty, 2009). Rather than deranged, scary, or unhinged, modern cultural products tend to portray killers (both real and imagined) using altogether more positive character traits (Fox et al., 2019). We find ourselves being drawn into these stories precisely because the protagonists do not fit the mould of 'monster' so readily. The modern serial killer can be intelligent, handsome, even charming; he has (and is) an 'appealing monstrosity' (Green, 2012). These individuals are no doubt capable of monstrous deeds but they need not look like monsters and they need not always act like them either. This more nuanced portrayal of a serial killer will likely provoke feelings of fear, as fictional monsters can, but this sense of insecurity is somehow more 'real' (Altheide, 2003). Unlike vampires and werewolves, these killers have lived alongside you;

they could be a regular in your local pub, they could serve you in a super-market, they could drive the bus that takes your child to school every day. These are people in the 'real' world, which leads to an unnerving question—how do you spot a monster if they look like a human? A question the museum leaves unanswered.

The poster boards in the *True Crime Museum* which are dedicated to the individual killers make this uncertainty (and associated insecurity) very clear. We learn that Stephen Griffiths was writing a PhD and Harold Shipman was a doctor—not so monstrous on the surface. In addition, we find out that Ed Gein's victims included 'the woman who ran the local tavern' and 'Bernice who ran the hardware shop', decidedly 'normal' acquaintances by all accounts. These references to what we assume are ideal victims also help to cast the criminals as an ideal type. As Jewkes (2004, p. 44) suggests, when a crime story is presented as a simplistic binary of good and evil the audience are encouraged to 'suspend their skills of critical interpretation and respond in unambiguous accord'. Consequently 'a complex reality is substituted for a simple, preferably bite-sized message' (p. 45). In this case the message is clear: *Be afraid, human monsters walk amongst us.* Toward the end of the first poster in Ripper Alley (Fig. 12.2) these politics of fear are most overt:

> *"MURDER. TORTURE. MUTILATION. RAPE. IMPRISONMENT. NECROPHILIA. EVEN CANNIBALISM.*
> *And ONCE is never enough. The HORRORSHOW must be repeated. Over and over again."*

Moreover, these poster boards are just one part of a much bigger museum story in which the killer is regularly compared to fictional beasts while at the same time being presented as 'human' and thus undetectable. A further example of the contrasting character—both monster and human—is a pair of displays in adjacent rooms found further inside the *True Crime Museum*. First visitors walk through a room called *The Art of Murder*. This is a large collection of paintings, sketches, sculptures, and poems all created by offenders (Fig. 12.3). The first time we see these objects they stand as a testament to human creativity even in the darkest of places. Maybe the best illustration of this is a sculpture made by Antony McKenzie while he was imprisoned in Rykers Island. It is constructed from toilet paper, wood, and acrylic and is named 'Untitled Crucifiction' (irregular spelling in original, see Fig. 12.4). No further explanation is given.

From this room filled with artwork, we make our way through an arch into a small cinema (Fig. 12.5). As the museum is housed within a series of caves the cinema is naturally cold and dark, adding to the intensity of the experience and atmosphere. A film entitled *'Voices of Death: The minds of murders in their own words'* plays on a loop. The film is a collection of clips taken from different documentaries in which killers speak about their crimes. To give you some indication of tone and content, one murderer speaks dispassionately about raping the corpse of his victims, another recounts how he would wait before dismembering the corpses to ensure the least mess, and another still speaks about the moments directly after his kills when he would think 'here I am, sitting with a severed head in my hands, looking at it and talking to it'.

On completion of the film we walk back through the room of artwork pictured in Fig. 12.3, but the exhibits take on a new meaning. Rather than a testament to human creativity these sculptures, paintings, and poems are now tainted. Having been reminded of the artists' monstrous deeds their creativity becomes somehow ugly. This new juxtaposition

Fig. 12.3 The Art of Murder

Fig. 12.4 Untitled Crucifixion

places the identity of 'killer' alongside that of 'artist'. *The Art of Murder* is (re)constructed as even more captivating because the film has made celebrities of the artists6. Presented as the protagonist of their own life story, the artwork takes on new value as a result. This type of tension, or polysemy—seeing the killer as both artist and beast—is not uncommon in other stories told about specific murderers. For example, Broll (2020) discusses how different groups, including those which identify as 'dark fandoms', create and negotiate conflicting character traits when discussing Eric Harris and Dylan Klebold (the perpetrators of the shooting at Columbine High School). Moreover Sarat (2001) has likewise examined the layered and at times contradictory media portrayal

Fig. 12.5 Cinema Showing 'Voices of Death'

of Timothy McVeigh, an ex-soldier/veteran who was responsible for the terrorist bombing of a federal building in Oklahoma.

In summary then, the oscillation between humanising offenders and portraying them as grotesque blurs the lines between fact and fiction. Not quite monster, but not quite human, these people seem to exist in the space between. A constructed reality where monsters hide in plain sight will be compelling to many. There is obvious allure for the true crime enthusiast, but the displays also capture the imagination of those who prefer tales of fictional beasts and mythical monsters. The museum actively encourages us to make these connections between the genres, to summon other mediated stories that can loop and spiral as we tour the space (Ferrell et al., 2008). A patchwork of memories lend moral meaning to our experience of the museum. Together then, the displays clearly offer a distorted depiction of *who* and *what* we should fear. Somewhat disconcertingly though, once we leave the museum and return to our daily lives, this distortion will likely remain. We will continue to look over our shoulder when walking home at night. We will continue to fear the monstrous or depraved stranger lurking in the shadows. And all of this means we can avoid confronting the arguably darker reality that many assaults take place in the home and many are victimised by those they love, or once loved.

Capitalizing on the Creepy and the Bizarre

After viewing the posters about serial killers in Ripper Alley, patrons walk past a 'suspects wall' (see Fig. 12.6). The criminal characters on either side of the wall—or more precisely the mocking tone used to describe them—will be discussed later in this chapter, but for now let us consider the wall itself. Visitors are encouraged to hold up a chalk board and write their name and (a fictional) offence on it. They can then stand in front of the wall to have their photograph taken. This is a common element of crime-related tourism, with many former sites of incarceration and many police museums providing similar backdrops. Interestingly though, the *True Crime Museum* has 'branded' their suspect wall with their logo and included reference to specific criminals. Branding the backdrop with the logo allows the site to be instantly identifiable to anyone scrolling social media posts of friends and family. Moreover, as we shall see later, the descriptions of the crimes/criminals chosen to adorn the suspect wall make clear to potential patrons just how weird and wonderful 'true-crime' can be.

Leaving the suspects wall behind, visitors are next confronted with a life-size electric chair (Fig. 12.7). They are encouraged to climb the steps, take a seat, and place the helmet on their head. There is plenty of space around the electric chair to get another photograph, ready for that all important social media update. In many ways both the chair and the suspects wall are implicit invitations to become part of the museum story. They encourage the tourist to advertise the site but also offer an opportunity to display one's enjoyment of 'true crime'. Moreover, considering social media posts are, at least in part, a way of constructing an 'online-self' these photo-opportunities act as a kind of identifier. Taking a 'selfie' and *posting* that image will (however inadvertently) align the online-self with the true crime genre, but also more broadly with the ethos of the museum.

Back to the life-size electric chair, the poster next to the chair (beneath the *True Crime Museum* branding) details what happens to the condemned during electrocution. Here our attention is drawn to the 'melted zips and buttons' on the prisoners' clothing. We also learn that their 'eyeballs would burst' and their 'bones would fuse' into a seated

Fig. 12.6 Suspects Wall

position meaning their corpse would need to be strengthened in preparation before burial. I have only seen one other electric chair on display, in the Texas Prison Museum in Huntsville, USA (Fig. 12.8). It is not within the scope of this chapter to discuss this alternative display in detail. However, it is worth noting the Texan story did not include the more gruesome elements of an execution. Instead, the explanatory poster in Texas was nostalgic in tone referring to the chair as 'Old Sparky' and describing electrocution as 'riding the thunderbolt' (for more discussion please see Thurston, 2017b). In addition, the aesthetics of the chair are very different in each of the sites. In Texas, the chair sits in a mock death house and is protected by security glass and rope. In Hastings, visitors climb into the chair and mimic electrocution for that all-important photograph. The *True Crime Museum* also shrouds the chair in theatrical lighting compared to the more intuitional lighting in Texas. A further invitation to identify the experience (and any image of that experience) with the true crime genre.

There are three possible explanations for this marked difference in the way the chair is displayed. Firstly, in Texas the chair was used in the execution of over 200 people; in Hastings the chair is a replica. As Smith (2008) suggests, authenticity gives the Texan chair a kind of legitimacy; it is a unique object worthy of protection. Secondly, in Texas the curator (Jim Willet) is also an ex-warden who has overseen many executions by electrocution; in Hastings, the curator (Joel Griggs) is a true crime enthusiast who has opened the museum to share his collection. Witnessing hundreds of executions means Jim Willet has a personal connection to the chair's heritage and this may go some way to explaining both the nostalgic tone of the poster and the respect the object commands aesthetically. Lastly, and maybe most importantly, executions are still

Fig. 12.7   Electric Chair (True Crime Museum)

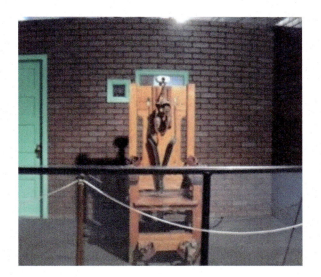

Fig. 12.8 Electric Chair (Texas Prison Museum)

performed in Texas albeit by lethal injection and support for execution is still relatively high compared to other states (see Thurston, 2016). The Texan chair then is an important part of an educational story about the modernisation of execution. Rather than drawing attention to the gruesome reality (zips melting, eyeballs bursting, and bones fusing) the Texan display makes the chair the beginning of a less sensational narrative about developments in corrections. In contrast, the Hastings chair is a one-off object. It is a foreign object from another land, making the theatrics which surround it culturally more permissible. In addition though, the chair in Hastings is surrounded by numerous, arguably more authentic and more disturbing objects.

It is worth noting that not all the objects on display in *the True Crime Museum* create such a formidable image as the electric chair. Quite the reverse in fact. Some objects appear disconcertingly average on first inspection. Take the bathtub pictured in Fig. 12.9 for example. This object is far less striking than the electric chair but reading the text accompanying the bath we learn it has an altogether more sinister story. The text reads:

Fig. 12.9	Bathtub Exhibit

"*This is the bathtub from Flat 13 Dolphin House, Poplar, London, E14 in which contract killer John Childs dismembered at least four and probably all his victims. [...] Childs cut the bodies into small pieces using a saw and burnt them in his fireplace. It took three days to reduce each victim to ashes which he scattered from the window of his car on the A13 road. No trace was ever found*".

While the electric chair is a replica this bath is—for want of a better phrase—'an original'. Much like Old Sparky in the *Texas Prison Museum* this bath has been touched by death. Smith (2008, p. 162) suggests that certain objects seem to possess 'an auratic quality [...] bestowed by death'. The bathtub has this same quality. Holding captive some essence of Child's victims, death clings to the air around this object. Yet it is the familiarity of the object which is also important here. A crime which is peculiar will always be newsworthy but 'paradoxically, a part of what makes [...] murder into entertainment is the shock of ordinariness invaded by the brutal' (Peelo, 2006, p. 164). As Peelo (2006) suggests, consuming crime stories often includes the process of 'defamiliarization'. This is where something we think we know is offered back to us in a new or extraordinary way; the bathtub exhibit is a good illustration of this process. The ordinary becomes extraordinary because of its connection to violence and murder. The mundanity of a bathtub also reminds us that while his deeds were monstrous, John Child was nevertheless still human. A household object used to clean and purify is juxtaposed in stark contrast to the (imagined) scene of filth and depravity. Having learned of the object's gruesome past the image of it likewise becomes obscene; a terrifying reminder that such wickedness exists within humanity. While the electric chair will always be initially confronting, to be in the same space as this bathtub is maybe even more disconcerting.

In summary then, the *True Crime Museum* is a 'horrid spectacle' of crime and punishment but it does not exist in a narrative vacuum (Huey & Broll, 2017). For a tourist site like this to survive, an understanding of user driven photography is vital (Shin & Ju, 2013). The electric chair will always make for a formidable image, so it is not surprising the *True Crime Museum* offers an opportunity to have a photo taken in it. Why not capitalise on the inherent creepiness of an object we associate so readily with death? Moreover, the chair and the suspect wall are essentially part of the *True Crime* brand; staged sets where we (the visitor) can take the lead role of criminal, capture that moment on film and share it with our friends, family and followers. By providing opportunities to take selfies next to dark objects such as the bathtub, the museum increases the likelihood these exhibits will be shared on social media and thus reach a wider audience. The museum has successfully capitalised on the macabre, creating creepy sets for staged selfies and making the familiar seem somehow obscene.

Tourist Tone: Gamification, Mockery, and Humour

The primary goal of the museum has shifted in recent years. Once buildings devoted to educating the public and preserving cultural and collective memories, successful museums now need to be customer-focused public spaces, in which the visitor experience is of utmost importance (Van Aalst & Boogaarts, 2002). In other words, museums are under increasing pressure to create engaging experiences for their patrons. Concerned with how visitors perceive and experience their sites, curators are exploring new ways to engage visitors using social media, smart-technology and interactive exhibits. While education is still a goal, there has been a distinct move toward 'gamification' within museums, which now need to also amuse, delight and fascinate their audiences (López-Martínez et al., 2020). This final section of the chapter then, will discuss the overall 'tone' of the *True Crime Museum*, examining how the museum uses gamification, humour and mockery to entertain and thrill its visitors.

One of the most overt illustrations of gamification comes in the form of a quiz, found in 'Ripper Alley' discussed earlier. In the bottom right of the posters about serial killers, there is an associated question which reads like a pub quiz question. I have provided three examples below:

> *In the 1971 true crime classic "10 Rillington Place" which famous actor plays Richie? A) John Hurt B) Antony Hopkins C) Richard Attenborough D) Bob Hoskins.*
>
> *Sentenced to death, Aileen Wuornos turned to the jury, what did she say? A) Thank you for showing your duty; God be with you all. B) Shows over ya vultures! Back to your boring little lives. C) I was raped! I'm innocent. You should be raped. Scumbags of America. D) Please go to Hell. I'll be waiting there for ya.*
>
> *Which of these movie madmen was not based on Ed Gein? A) Leatherface: Texas Chainsaw Masace. B) Freddie Krueger - A Nightmatre on Elm Street. C) Norman Bates – Pycho. D) Buffalo Bill - The Silence of the Lambs.*

First, it is worth noting the questions refer to other cultural products within the true crime genre, which for the enthusiast will likely situate the museum experience within the wider true crime mediascape. The quiz also draws attention to crime movies, further widening its appeal. This explicit reference to fictional films and characters is present in other exhibits too, specifically about 'Gangs and Gangsters'. For example, in one display which attempts a rather comical tone we learn about Joe Bananas, the Mafia boss who provided inspiration for the character of Don Vito Corleone (The Godfather trilogy). The poster about 'Joe Bananas and the Casket Crew' reads:

> *"When the corpses of his rival started to clog the Hudson River, practical Joe invented the DOUBLE DECKER BURIAL. He Brought a Brooklyn funeral home and sent every sadly missed grandma to the cemetery resting on one of his lead-filled enemies."*

Much like the posters which referenced vampires and werewolves, these quiz questions and accounts of fictional crime movies again shift the narrative away from the reality of crime and into entirely different storied spaces. The answers to the quiz can be found as you exit Ripper Alley, and in case you are curious: Richard Attenborough played the part of John Reginald Christie; Ed Gein was the inspiration for Leatherface, Freddie Krueger and Norman Bates; and Aileen Wuornos reacted to her sentencing by saying: 'I was raped! I'm innocent. You should be raped. Scumbags of America'.

A further example of how the site seeks to gamify crime can be found towards the middle of the museum. Directly after the electric chair and suspects wall discussed earlier, we are confronted with a darkened living room fireplace above which hangs a slightly creepy framed picture of three children (Fig. 12.10). As we get closer to the fireplace a text board reveals the display is about luminol, the chemical used by forensic officers to detect traces of blood at a crime scene. As visitors we are invited to pick up a torch, shine a light on the domestic scene and reveal the bloody handprints hidden from the naked eye (Fig. 12.11). While there are no overt references to police procedurals such as *Silent Witness* or *CSI* in the exhibit, the scene will likely resonate with anybody who has even a passing interest in these (fictional) shows. The more factual account of how luminal is used meets the rather more sensationalised example of a full handprint on a portrait which would not be out of place in a budget horror movie. Again, we find genres combining to create an entertaining experience. Moreover, while this is not a game per se it does rather encourage children and adults alike to 'play' detective, using the clues to speculate about what might have happened to disrupt this domestic scene. It is also worth noting that even though this exhibit is deliberately crafted to replicate a family setting there is no mention of child abuse, domestic violence, or intimate partner violence. Clearly this type of crime narrative—while arguably more 'true' than many of those selected for display—would not fit the tone of the *True Crime Museum*.

A further element which adds to the tone of this site, are the instances in which humour is used to mock and ridicule criminals and their inadequacies. I return your attention back to the suspect wall discussed earlier (please see Fig. 12.6). You may remember the images of people on either side. These pictures depict real-life offenders of varying heights. Three of those depicted on the wall are Louis Lefèvre, Edmund Kemper, and Grady Stiles. The text accompanying each of their pictures reads as follows (see Fig. 12.12 for a closeup of the suspect wall):

Fig. 12.10 Livingroom Scene (No Blood)

Fig. 12.11 Livingroom Scene with Torch

Louis Lefèvre, 5ft 9. (Murder/Rape):	*Lefèvre started 16 April 1916 at a healthy 6ft 9. He ended it nine inches shorter, courtesy of the guillotine at Tours. See those nine inches he lost at the death chamber, here in the True Crime Museum.*
Edmund Kemper, 6ft 9. (Multiple Murder):	*American serial killer Kemper was a physical giant.... However in 1973 he decapitated his mother, raped her headless body and used her head as a dartboard, suggesting he was a moral midget.*
Grady 'Lobster Boy' Stiles, 3ft 2. (Murder):	*The US sideshow performer suffered from ectrodactyly, a limb deformity. It didn't stop him shooting his daughter's fiancé to death in 1978. Fourteen years later though, Stiles was himself murdered by a hitman hired by his wife for $1500.*

Further examples of this mocking tone can be found in the posters on Ripper Alley. The poster about Ed Gein—who made the belt of nipples and wore a face to bed—includes a quote from his neighbour: 'Ed was a

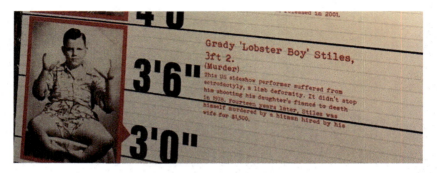

Fig. 12.12 Close up of Suspect Wall

simpleton, he'd ask his Mama's OK to go pee-pee'. And Stephen Griffiths, who murdered the sex workers, is referred to as a 'narcissistic nerd — a woman hater with body odour'. And apparently for Aileen Wuornos, the serial killer who 'hated humans', it was 'her loud mouth and an inability to hold her drink that led to her arrests'. The poster about Aileen also ends by insinuating her defence (that she was raped) should not be believed: 'with a voracious love of attention and the TV camera, Aileen said A LOT. Rarely the same story twice' (emphasis in original).

So we have identified examples where the museum displays use comedy or shaming techniques to undermine the criminal identity, and others where the tone is more akin to ridiculing or mocking. Neither of these are unique to the *True Crime Museum*. They can be found in other crime-related tourist sites as well. When analysing the Angola Prison Rodeo (in which inmates perform rodeo games for the tourist gaze) both Schrift (2004) and Adams (2001) identify a similar tone at play. Most of the prisoners that participate have little or no familiarity with livestock or rodeo. This inexperience makes participation a dangerous decision and gives the event a kind of gladiatorial atmosphere. The audience desire to see a criminal body flail and flounder in the rodeo ring may seem somewhat vindictive, even vengeful, yet the atmosphere of the rodeo is one of excitement and celebration. Much like the audience, the inmates view it as a 'day out' (Adams, 2001). Yet the rodeo promotional materials mock and ridicule the inmate. One leaflet reads: 'More often than not, these convict cowboys are from the city, as foreign to the rodeo as a country boy in a three-piece suit' (cited by Schrift, 2004, p. 339). This comical, mocking tone is also expressed in the juxtaposition of two different identities. As a cultural symbol the cowboy is a folk hero; courageous, brave, stoic but above all else, he is free. This image is in sharp contrast to the inmate identity. He is 'captive, stripped of his freedom and individuality, and more often than not, a symbol of social filth' (Schrift, 2004, p. 337). The label 'convict cowboy' is a form of mockery in and of itself.

In summary then, on the one hand this museum seeks to instil a sense of fear by suggesting that killers should be viewed as human monsters who walk among us. But on the other hand, we are encouraged to mock these people and laugh at their failings. The mocking/comical tone serves an important function then; it has the potential to restore the balance and (re)establish the status quo. Rather than leave the museum scared of crime and of criminals, patrons are encouraged to leave with a far more positive outlook. Yes, these monsters exist but we—the law abiding—are somehow better, superior, so we can laugh at these creatures we are supposed to fear. In the context of crime tourism, mocking the monsters becomes a way of fighting back against the indescribable fear we have of the dangerous criminal 'other' (Greer & Jewkes, 2005; Thurston, 2020).

Conclusion

The aim of this chapter has been two-fold. First, I wanted to illustrate the diversity which exists within crime-related tourism. I hope this chapter has offered at the very least some food for thought to media scholars and students alike. My second aim was to introduce you to some of the exhibits in one such site. This second section was not an in-depth analysis of the *True Crime Museum*, rather an attempt to show the richness of data which is there for the taking. Moreover, it has not been within the scope of this chapter to explore the ethical questions associated with crime-related tourism, and there are many. I was left feeling quite uneasy as I left the *True Crime Museum*. Should these sites display personal items—including body parts—without permission? What are the implications of having souvenirs for sale in a gift shop? Can it ever be ethical to make a profit from the suffering of others? How would the family of a murder victim experience these exhibits? What do the displays teach us about gender or race? These critical questions are important if we are to fully understand the crime media relationship and unpack the allure of the true crime genre. These sites may profit from the public desire to consume stories of violence, but they alone do not create it. And lest we forget, we too seek to feed that fascination to some degree, otherwise I would not be writing this chapter and you would not be reading it. Are we really so far from taking a seat on that electric chair or standing against the suspect wall for that perfect selfie? My *True Crime Museum* magnet and keyring suggests maybe not.

Indeed, it is easy for me to be critical of these types of sites. They clearly distort crime as a social issue, undermine the pains of imprisonment, sensationalise violence, blame individuals not structures, trivialise gendered violence—I could go on. Yet such a critique begs the question of what I believe a 'good' crime museum would look like. What stories would it tell and how? And if such a thing does not exist, then what are the consequences of *not* telling those stories? Of marginalising those narratives? Maybe these are the more critical questions for us to consider. Open to the public, these sites are important spaces of narrativity, which have for the most part remained at the periphery of criminological academic debate about the media–crime relationship. Maybe it is time that we—as academics—get involved in the stories and advise the storytellers. The transmission of memory is all about power and these types of collaborations present powerful opportunities for us to reach different audiences, big and small. By understanding the needs of other storytellers—in this case the museum curator—we have the potential to shape rather than just critique crime in the media.

Study Questions

- Take a look again at the six categories of 'true' crime-related tourism outlined in the first part of this chapter. How might we account for the breadth and appeal of these tourist sites?

- How does the true crime museum analysed above blur the line between fact and fiction?
- How does the museum capitalise on the macabre?
- What do you think a 'good' crime museum would look like? (What stories would it tell and how?)

Bibliography

Adams, J. (2001). "The wildest show in the South": Tourism and incarceration at angola. *The Drama Review, 45,* 94–108.

Altheide, D. L. (2003). Toward a politics of fear. *Crime, Conflict and the Media, 1*(1), 37–54.

Broll, R. (2020). Dark fandoms: An introduction and case study. *Deviant Behavior, 41*(6), 792–804. https://doi.org/10.1080/01639625.2019.159 6453

Carrabine, E. (2017). Iconic power, dark tourism, and the spectacle of suffering. In J. Z. Wilson, S. Hodgkinson, J. Piché, & K. Walby (Eds.), *The Palgrave handbook of prison tourism* (pp. 13–36). Palgrave Macmillan. https://doi.org/10.1057/978-1-137-56135-0_2

Epstein, S. C. (1994). Characters amok: The representation of serial killers in American film, a Doctoral Dissertations. https://opencommons.uconn.edu/dissertations/AAI9503659. Accessed 14 August 2020.

Ferrell, J., Hayward, K. J., & Young, J. (2008). *Cultural criminology: An invitation.* Sage.

Fox, J., Friel, E., & Levin, J. (2019). *Extreme killing: Understanding serial and mass murder.* Sage.

Green, S. (2012). Desiring *Dexter*: The pains and pleasures of serial killer body technique. *Continuum: Journal of Media and Cultural Studies, 26*(4), 579–588. https://doi.org/10.1080/10304312.2012.698037

Greer, C., & Jewkes, J. (2005). Extremes of otherness: Media images of social exclusion. *Social Justice, 32*(1), 20–31.

Haggerty, K. D. (2009). Modern serial killers. *Crime, Media, Culture, 5*(2), 168–187.

Huey, L., & Broll, R. (2017). Punishment as sublime edutainment: "Horrid Spectacles" at the Prison Museum. In J. Z. Wilson, S. Hodgkinson, J. Piché, & K. Walby (Eds.), *The Palgrave handbook of prison tourism* (pp. 517–539). Palgrave Macmillan.

Jewkes, Y. (2004). *Media and crime.* Sage.

López-Martínez, A., Carrera, Á., & Iglesias, C. A. (2020). Empowering museum experiences applying gamification techniques based on linked data and smart objects. *Applied Sciences, 10*(16), 5419.

Peelo, M. (2006). Framing homicide narratives in newspapers: Mediated witness and the construction of virtual victimhood. *Crime Media Culture, 2*(2), 159–175.

Sarat, A. (2001). *When the state kills: Capital punishment and the American condition.* Princeton University Press.

Schrift, M. (2004). The Angola prison rodeo: Inmates, cowboys and institutional tourism. *Ethnology, 43*(4), 331–344.

Shin, M., & Ju, D. Y. (2013). Online advertising as a new story: Effects of user-driven photo advertisement in social media. Conference paper. https://doi.org/10.1007/978-3-642-39253-5_12 https://doi.org/10.1007/978-3-642-39253-5_12

Smith, P. (2008). *Punishment and culture.* University of Chicago Press.

Stone, P. (2006). A dark tourism spectrum: Towards a typology of death and macabre related tourist sites, attractions and exhibitions. *Tourism: An Interdisciplinary International Journal, 54*(2), 145–160.

Thurston, H. (2016). *Prisons and punishment in Texas: Culture, history and museological representation.* Palgrave Macmillan.

Thurston, H. (2017a). Museum ethnography: Researching punishment museums as environments of narrativity. *Methodological Innovations.* https://doi.org/10.1177/2059799117720615

Thurston, H. (2017b). Don't mess with Texas: Stories of punishment from lone star museums. In J. Z. Wilson, S. Hodgkinson, J. Piché, & K. Walby (Eds.), *The Palgrave handbook of prison tourism* (pp. 583–606). Palgrave Macmillan. https://doi.org/10.1057/978-1-137-56135-0_2

Thurston, H. (2020). Popular and visual narratives of punishment in museum settings. In M. Althoff, B. Dollinger, & H. Schmidt (Eds.), *Conflicting narratives of crime and punishment* (pp. 113–137). Palgrave Macmillan.

van Aalst, I., & Boogaarts, I. (2002). From museum to mass entertainment: The evolution of the role of museums in cities. *European Urban and Regional Studies, 9*(3), 195–209.

Vronsky, P. (2004). *Serial killer: The method and madness of Monsters.* The Berkley Publishing Group.

Wiest, J. (2016). Casting cultural Monsters: Representations of serial killers in U.S. and U.K. News Media. *Howard Journal of Communications, 27*(4), 327–346.

13

Exploring the Presence of the Digital Detective within the True-Crime Genre and its Online Spaces

Farhana Irshad

Introduction

In *Don't Fuck with Cats: Hunting an Internet Killer* (Netflix, 2019), we join two digital detectives' investigation who are key subjects within this documentary series. What is noteworthy in *Don't Fuck with Cats* is not only the use of these sleuths as key subjects, but also their focus on the journey that these digital investigators undertake to catch a killer. It is a documentation of their extensive efforts and commitment to digital detection as *netizens* (citizens of the net). Although Deanna Thompson and John Green's investigation may be much more fully fledged than the majority of true crime audience members, those watching the show identify with these detectives and their desire to 'solve' the crime. Current audiences of the true crime genre are now exploring newer avenues to fully satiate this need but as Tanya Horeck articulates, the amateur/couch

F. Irshad (✉)
St Mary's University Twickenham, London, UK
e-mail: farhana.irshad@stmarys.ac.uk

M. Mellins and S. Moore (eds.), *Critiquing Violent Crime in the Media*,
https://doi.org/10.1007/978-3-030-83758-7_13

detective is not a new phenomenon. 'If armchair detection has long been a central part of the appeal of true crime, a genre that has its roots in the nineteenth century and even earlier, then the internet has thoroughly rebooted the notion of audience's interactive engagement with crime for the contemporary era' (Horeck, 2019, p. 7). The term digital detective is now frequently used in regard to the online audience who seek more knowledge about the case they are observing, but also to any person who may contribute to an investigation.

One of the most popular and frequently occurring methods of audience 'self-integration' into a true crime case is through taking part in discussions. Katz et al.(1973) during their uses and gratifications model that examined why audiences choose to consume media, referred to this as the need to *socialise*. For example, office watercooler discussions about last night's show can and still do occur in certain circles, particularly with unavoidably significant pop-culture television shows such as *Game of Thrones* (HBO 2011–2019). Within the true crime genre however, these discussions often occur online, as that is the space that true crime inhabits and holds its territory for audiences. Another appealing quality of the genre is that whilst watching a true crime documentary series or film, audiences may search for further opinions and discussions regarding the show, not just from news outlets and media broadcasters, but also from 'regular' people who offer their thoughts on the investigations, and their own research, providing a 'gate-way' into true crime spaces.

In these spaces, audiences of the genre and the public can immerse themselves in investigations, particularly if the case is unsolved or awaiting verdict. For instance, a viewer of a Netflix true-crime documentary series may be intrigued with the 'narrative' of the case that is unfolding in front of them. Perhaps they begin with Googling a surviving victim's name, or the current whereabouts of a romantic partner of the perpetrator who refuses all interview requests, or to sneak a look at the progress of the legal proceedings surrounding the verdict. From there, the viewer may venture into exploring online articles, discussion forums, Twitter conversations, YouTube videos and podcasts.

This chapter considers the impact of video-on-demand services, as well as the accessibility of platform mobility that enables further discussions and integration into true crime spaces. With a focus on the amateur sleuth, and their role as an internet citizen, this discussion observes our narrative transportation as we follow the digital detective journey through media with opportunities to partake in dark tourism, fulfil roles such as the amateur sleuth, digital-detective and even juror (Bruzzi, 2016).

True Crime On-Demand

Our level of media consumption, in terms of technology such as the internet, social media and other apps, plays a huge factor in the appeal of true crime. Current audiences of film and television are able to multitask and fit television into their own schedule, particularly when using a video-on-demand service (VOD) such as Netflix. Chuck Tryon, in his book *On Demand Culture* (2013), discusses the concept of 'platform mobility', which he described as 'the ongoing shift toward ubiquitous, mobile access to a wide range of entertainment choices' (Tryon, 2013, p. 4). The shift towards platform mobility allows the audiences to pick and choose their viewing schedule, such as when they watch and how they consume. Chuck Tryon further asserts that:

> Within this culture of platform mobility, we also encounter the individualized consumer, one who is ostensibly capable of controlling his or her viewing experience, whether that entails starting a movie on one platform and continuing it on another, watching a movie on a mobile device, or accessing digital libraries through various streaming platforms and digital downloads from anywhere an internet connection is available. (Tryon, 2013, p. 4)

We now can, with the assistance of modern technology, continue our consumption of our chosen media across various devices, and are even encouraged to do so. Whether for a long commute to work, whilst cooking, or being active, the ability to multitask and to continue our consumption of media offline (by way of downloading) has changed the way we consume film and television and has had a particular effect on the true-crime genre. This platform mobility, combined with the rise of video-on-demand services, correlates with the increase of binge-watching in audience. Whilst binge-watching certainly predates video-on-demand, as audiences previously consumed DVDs and VHS television series box sets, Netflix and other subscription services have made this much more accessible. 'Netflix's delivery makes the process easier to both commence and continue, either in one sitting, or in consecutive sittings, with the ease of picking up where we left off across multiple media platforms' (Barker & Wiatrowski, 2017, p. 38).

Crime stories have a long history of appeal. In his book, *Complex TV: the poetics of the contemporary television storytelling*, Jason Mittell (2015) states that crime stories have always appealed to audiences as they are 'drawn into a compelling diegesis (as with all effective stories) and focused on the discursive processes of storytelling needed to achieve each program's complexity and mystery' (Mittell, 2015, p. 52). Additionally, Tanya Horeck, in her book *Justice on Demand* (2019), comments that 'its enduring popularity as a genre derives from its importance as a vehicle for articulating sociocultural issues of the time' (Horeck, 2019, p. 7) However, the appeal of the genre is also heavily sustained by the 'way in which it lends itself to the operations of Google search culture and the circulation of information, judgements, and effects that govern interactions on Facebook and other forms of social media' (Horeck, 2019, p. 11). The genre's transferability to the Google search culture, and the narrative appeal to audiences through its 'complexity and mystery', are key to understanding the role of the digital detective and its presence within the true-crime space. Mittell calls this model of audience engagement with the television genre, 'forensic fandom' (Mittell, 2015, p. 52), which speaks to the increasing popularity of the genre and the conversion of audiences from passive viewer to an engaged and committed digital detective.

The Role of the 'Digital Detective'

There are investigations that may have been paused, or unsolved, and justice may not have been served. Digital detectives, amateur sleuths, or whatever term you would like to call these unskilled investigators, have been shown to have a significant contribution to cases, and even solve them. *The Keepers* (Netflix, 2017) follows the investigations of the murder of Sister Cathy Cesnik in 1969. Without amateur sleuths investigating into this old case, inviting people to come forward to give their statements, it would not have been reopened.

In the first episode we are introduced to Gemma Hoskins and Abbie Schaub, who were both students of Sister Cathy at the Keough School in Baltimore before her disappearance. We first see Abbie Schaub visiting what appears to be a library of archives where she asks a librarian to provide some assistance regarding a search warrant that was found during their research into Sister Cathy's murder. The two ex-students, now approximately in their 60s, begin by sharing their thoughts about Sister Cathy, who was their favourite teacher, and their efforts in researching her disappearance and the recovery of her body two months later. Gemma Hoskins interviews people and gathers their stories and accounts of the time around the disappearance of Sister Cathy and tries to piece together a timeline. Meanwhile, Abbie Schaub takes the role of a researcher and examines online and physical archives, as well as her own personal collections of evidence and paperwork within her home filing system—all related to their research in the murder of Sister Cathy.

The online spaces these two women have created for their investigation are extensive. They include a Facebook page called *Justice for Cathy Cesnik and Joyce Malecki*, where people who were in the area at the time, or colleagues, students, friends or acquaintances of the two women, could contribute to any of the research or related questions that both Gemma and Abbie share on the page or can provide their own accounts of events related to the murders. Additionally, they also set up a website (WhoKilledCathy.org) where interested parties can find all the supporting news articles and materials, and volunteer support for this research, as well as submit anonymous information that may benefit the investigation. At the time of writing this chapter all updates to the site have been paused due to the mass of submissions and support received in response to the release of the series on Netflix.

Another example of a physical online space that contributes to the discussions within the true-crime spaces is the BuzzFeed YouTube channel, *BuzzFeed Unsolved Network*. What is remarkable about this

YouTube channel, and others like it, is the physical true-crime space below the video itself. In an almost video-essay format, the hosts use their audio as a narrative that is aided by images related to the case, such as the victims, suspects, locations, including stock images to further support their audio narration of their true-crime case. Their videos follow popular trend topics within the true-crime genre such as serial killers, (e.g. Bundy, Jack the Ripper and the Zodiac killer), but also include videos about mobsters and gangsters, and a 'how they were caught' series (for both gangsters and serial killers). Unlike podcasts, where audiences may be persuaded into taking on the host's opinion and investigation, YouTube offers an additional voice to the true-crime space: other audiences. Viewers of the video can comment below with their additional thoughts and theories to the case, as well as their reviews of the video, such as praise for the unique perspectives, or that they thought the conspiracy theories were 'far-fetched'. The structure of the *Unsolved Network*'s channel also further allows the exploration of this true-crime space. With curated video playlists, they have provided their audience with easy access to the various themes they cover, such as true-crime, the supernatural and conspiracy theories—allowing them to explore the areas that interests them. Audiences can watch a video on YouTube, join and read discussions, debate within the comment section and then continue to consume more content from the same creator by browsing their playlists. This allows the audience their required social interaction but also aids in their participation to a level of digital sleuthing.

It could be suggested that both Gemma and Abbie from *The Keepers* are, essentially, digital detectives. As far as we know, they are not fans of the true-crime genre, and are not drawn into an investigation by watching a documentary film/series or hearing about the news. Instead, they are motivated by their passion to find justice and uncover the truth of what happened to Sister Cathy. Gemma and Abbie also note their evidence has surpassed the initial police investigation. The pair hold official paperwork from the time of Sister Cathy's murder, such as warrants, case reports, witness accounts, in addition to their collection of statements from family members. What *The Keepers* have successfully shown within their series is the ability of these amateur digital detectives who have also supported their community through their commitment in researching a forty-year-old closed murder investigation. It was clear that without their research, support and continuous pressure on law enforcement, that the case may not have reopened. The 'interference' by these amateur sleuths, and the spaces they built, which permitted others to come forward with their stories, really shaped their investigation. It also enabled them to support 'Jane Doe's' public statement declaring that she had been sexually abused by Father E. Magnus and Father Joseph Maskell at Keough School and that Maskell had been involved in the murder of Sister Cathy. The online and local anonymous submissions to the investigations and victims of the events at Keough and Baltimore led to building a supportive survivor network, and the Archdiocese of Baltimore has provided a monetary settlement to a number of the victims. However, both Magnus and Maskell, now deceased, have not been charged at the time of the documentary, or the writing of this chapter.

Another Netflix true-crime documentary series that demonstrates the role and effects of a digital detective, and the spaces they create, is *Don't Fuck with Cats: Hunting an Internet Killer* (Netflix, 2019). In this example, *Don't Fuck with Cats* (DFWC) follows a group of self-proclaimed 'internet nerds', or netizens, who instigate a *digital* man-hunt to find the anonymous person posting videos of themselves torturing and killing kittens. The short, but intense, three-part 'limited-series', *Don't Fuck with Cats* begins with an interview of Deanna Thompson (who works under the online alias of Baudi Moovan). Deanna takes us through her experience of first coming across a video in 2010, which reveals a person killing two kittens by placing them in a vacuum sealable bag. Deanna describes feelings of anger, disgust and outrage that were also shared across her Facebook network. However, unlike views expressed in the comments section of the video that revealed a desire to report the kitten-killer to the authorities, Deanna retorted to the documentary interviewers that this was unlikely to happen. Deanna then found a link to a Facebook group called '*Find the Kitten Vacuumer...For great justice*', which contained posts from people who actively wanted to find the kitten-killer. Deanna virtually met John Green in the group and the two digital sleuths began to dissect the first video of the kitten-killer and share their findings with the group.

In this three-part documentary series, we are taken on a journey with the sleuths as they navigate their way through cities such as Toronto, New York and London by using Google maps and export thousands of video frames into images. The dedication and attention to every minuscule detail throughout their painstaking investigation allowed them to create a portfolio of supporting materials to move their investigation forward. An example of this is at the beginning of their investigation where John created a schematic of the bedroom layout which was featured within the killer's video. From there, Deanna investigated the wolf bedspread, finding out the origins of the blanket on eBay, but realising the online store delivers world-wide. Similarly, the team investigates the video's audio, which appears to be background noise, only to find out that it is a segment from a Russian sitcom. The group now realise that after weeks of investigating, the kitten-killer was perhaps a step ahead of them. Meanwhile, another video appears on YouTube which was then shared on Facebook. Featuring the same room, the video now shows the kitten-killer playing with dead cats whilst releasing pictures of the deceased kittens to the Facebook page. Deanna, now more desperate to find the killer as another photo of a blurred face is submitted to the group, and wary that he has now infiltrated their Facebook group, turns her attention to the yellow vacuum visible within the second video. She enters an internet forum that discusses vacuum repairs and asks if anyone knows the make and model of the vacuum. It was identified immediately by forum participants, who were also able to advise Deanna where it can be purchased, allowing her to pinpoint the U.S., Canada and South America as potential locations.

This allows us to feel that we are journeying with Deanna and John as we venture through their online spaces hunting for the kitten-killer. Both pairs of our digital detectives, act as our 'on-screen surrogates' (Horeck, 2019, p. 169), leading the investigation in a relatable way across platforms. The more the audiences 'travel' between the platforms, the further they explore the case and its narrative. For example, in DFWC, as we follow Deanna and John's investigation, it becomes clear that there is a pressing need to hunt for the kitten-killer as their crimes are escalating. Confirming their fears, Deanna and John came across a video of a man, later identified to be student, Jun Lin, being sadistically murdered.

Due to his filming style and references to his earlier videos, they strongly believed the maker of the video to be Luka Magnotta. Deanna and John determined that Luka was currently situated in Montreal, Canada, and they consistently contacted the local police. Although initially ignored, Deanna and John's web-sleuthing greatly supported the police's investigation as the police came to discover a human torso hidden in a suitcase outside an apartment building in Montreal. John, towards the end of Episode 2, reflects that if the police had listened to them (the digital sleuths) then 'maybe Jun Lin wouldn't be dead today'. Luka Magnotta was caught and imprisoned after being listed on Interpol's wanted list.

The impact of digital sleuths is noteworthy, particularly as 'criminologists are beginning to explore the significance of digital web-sleuthing as a more diverse and varied activity than previously imagined, with web-sleuths investigating a "wide variety of cases, including homicide, missing persons, terrorism, property offences and sexual offences"' (Horeck, 2019, p. 177). However, as the digital-detective/web-sleuths are creating spaces to investigate perpetrators of crime, they are also creating safe spaces for victims and supporters to inhabit. These spaces build communities that provide support to those affected by the crimes featured in the investigation. *The Keepers'* Gemma and Abbie are examples of this. They have created safe, online spaces where people could submit their tips and anonymous submissions, and a link to a page of dedicated resources for victims of sexual assault (https://thekeepersimpact.com/). This support site, created after the launch of the seven-part documentary series, includes supportive material for victims, but also resources to train families, parents and friends of victims on how to appropriately respond to disclosures of sexual violence, build techniques on bystander intervention and how to recognise child grooming.

In addition to providing safe spaces and building a supportive community for victims of crime and their families, true-crime spaces also allow audiences to not only indulge in investigatory techniques, but to take up the role of the courtroom jury. They can study the evidence provided to them and decide whether the alleged perpetrator is innocent or guilty. In spaces such as Twitter or Facebook, users can share their thoughts and opinions regarding a case that is in the news and offer advice on how to achieve justice. Stella Bruzzi suggests that as audiences we 'find ourselves "jurified" and being asked to adopt the juror perspective in relation to the evidence unravelled before us' (Bruzzi, 2016, p. 274). This also plays on our 'desire for truth' (Horeck, 2019, p. 10). This 'desire' and act of becoming 'jurified' is part of our modern-day way of living, as Stella Bruzzi states,

> In one way this is a very contemporary attitude as we live in an era when factual television is forever asking us to decide, vote, make up our minds on whether someone is a good singer, which celebrity should leave the jungle. Conversely, this format recalls much older courtroom narrative conventions in which cases are brought before juries made up of members of the public. (Bruzzi, 2016, p. 274)

In an interview with *Real Crime Profile* and the hosts, Liza Zambetti, Laura Richards and Jim Clemente (Episode 275 & 276), Deanna reflects on her actions as a digital detective. The hosts asked Deanna if she calls herself an 'internet activist' or 'sleuthers', and Deanna responds that she prefers not to use these terms but instead refers to herself as a person who cares, she is a '*netizen*'. John Green agrees with Deanna and also identifies with the term *netizen* rather than 'internet sleuth'. The use of the term *netizen* reflects their selfless commitment to the digital hunt and cements their actions as that of a good citizen. This sense of citizenship is mirrored by Gemma and Abbie's actions who donated significant time and resources to uncover the truth about what happened to Sister Cathy's murder, delivering a victim support network, as well as uncovering the corruption within the Archdiocese of Baltimore who had ignored and denied the actions of Maskell.

True-Crime Podcast: Dark Tourism and Narrative Transportation

The preference for podcasts, in comparison to documentary series, is subjective to the flexibility of its use. Although television and films can be downloaded to be watched offline anywhere, at any time, it does not provide the screen-less entertainment, narrative transportation and dark tourism that can be found within podcasts.

The fascination and exploration of these crime scenes within podcasts suggests a link to 'dark tourism'. 'Tourist interest in recent death, disaster and atrocity is a growing phenomenon in the late twentieth and early twenty-first centuries and that theorists have both noticed and attempted to understand it' (Lennon & Foley, 2000, p. 3). While podcasts are not necessarily 'tourism', they do incorporate the same need of 'exploration' of a new environment. In this case this would be the 'online environment' or space in which the investigation and the digital detectives dwell. As Sharpley and Stone state in their 2009 book, *The Darker Side of Travel: The theory and practise of dark tourism*, that 'if physically going to witness an execution may be labelled dark tourism, may not turning on a computer or a mobile phone to witness the same execution be similarly labelled?' (Sharpley & Stone, 2009, p. 44). It can be suggested that dark tourism is present within true-crime podcasts due to the nature of the shared information in these spaces and the morbid nature of many of the crimes discussed. Podcasts are able to take audiences to the crime scene, provide 'tours' of the last known activity of the victim, or missing perpetrator. There is an attraction to this 'transportation' and to explore the scenes of death and partake in what appears to be a form of voyeuristic reflection of mortality and human nature. It illustrates an audience interest in 'morbidity-related tourism' (Sharpley & Stone, 2009, p. 13).

These podcasts within the true-crime genre are often hosted by amateurs, whom may have little to no knowledge or experience in matters of law enforcement and investigations. These amateurs are dedicated to creating content to discuss a range of topics such as the 'classic' serial murderers and unsolved cold cases. These podcast hosts may consider themselves digital detectives, whilst others may lean towards being a reporter, or 'content creators' of the 'space' due to their narrative style. Audiences of the genre can listen to podcasts to discover more about a case they are following, and it can be way of continuing the 'narrative' of a case. However, some audiences may not just consume podcasts as a secondary source of information to support their current research, or use them to feed their curiosity after seeing the case in the news. Podcasts are, in their own right, a true-crime space—a primary source of information, as well as a gateway and narrative transportation into the true-crime space.

Podcasts 'thrive on niche global audiences' (Spinelli & Dann, 2019, p. 8), and are 'interwoven into social media and as such have a heightened capacity to enhance with, and activate, an audience' (Spinelli & Dann, 2019, p. 8). This makes the possibility to join in on conversations, and become an amateur sleuth, incredibly accessible. It also depends on narrative transportation, which is 'the extent that individuals are absorbed into a story or transported into a narrative world, they may show effects of the story on their real-world beliefs' (Green & Brock, 2000, p. 701). Although this can be achieved whilst watching a true-crime Netflix documentary series, it does not quite have the same effect as a podcast. Podcasts are able to fulfil the need of social interaction, however, it achieves this in a different way to television and their traditional watercooler discussions. Instead, podcasts provide an invitation to a structured discussion, that includes facts and opinions, as well as personality—which is not always present within true-crime documentary films or series.

The personality derives from the podcast's hosts, who are often ordinary people showcasing their detective skills, which allows their listeners to feel as if they are a part of their research team. The personal nature of these podcast hosts supports audiences to transport themselves into the case's narrative, but to also integrate themselves into the investigation, and create their own opinion and even research. This results in more 'conversational, informal, personal, even supportive, atmospheres. Podcasting also exemplifies the maxim that "the specific is universal" by creating spaces for niche and cult content that caters for the more idiosyncratic cultures of interest' (Llinares et al., 2018, p. 2).

For example, *Morbid: A True Crime Podcast*, hosted by Ash and Alaina, has a strong focus on personalisation. In each episode, the hosts introduce themselves and lead in with background information on what the serial killer did, who the victims were, as well as details of the police investigation. All of this is explained by the two hosts who chat to the audiences as life-long friends. They include interruptions to their scripted true-crime presentation, such as jokes, personal thoughts, as well as referencing relatable and ordinary things in their lives—all embellished with many curse-words. *Morbid*, with its relatable discussions, full break-down of true cases, along with the hosts' additional research, allows audiences to hear a discussion and debate and feel as if they have been interacting socially with friends about a crime investigation. However, *Morbid* is a podcast that is focused on the retelling of solved cases and although this may contribute to the true-crime spaces, where audiences may engage in post-investigation analysis, such as the dissection of a serial killer's childhood, there isn't a need for any further investigation to the case by the audience or the host/s.

On the other hand, *Missing and Murdered: (S2) Finding Cleo*, a podcast by CBC and hosted by Connie Walker, follows the investigation of a woman trying to locate her missing sister. In this true-crime podcast we are introduced to Christine, who was separated from her biological family when she and her siblings were adopted. When Christine reunited with her family at age 19, she found out that her eldest sister, Cleo, had been killed. We are told that Cleo was hitch-hiking from her adopted home in the U.S. to return to her biological family in Saskatchewan, Canada. It was assumed that Cleo was kidnapped on her journey, raped and murdered.

Finding Cleo takes us through Christine and Connie's journey to find the truth about Cleo's short life after the adoption. One of the most powerful features within *Finding Cleo* is the inclusion of original audio that was recorded during the initial investigation. For example, in the first episode we hear Christine's phone call with social services at the Saskatchewan government. During the phone call Christine attempts to request access to her sister's files, only to discover that the little information she has (that Cleo was adopted and moved to Arkansas, U.S) is incorrect. Christine discovers that social services are withholding information about Cleo and begins to cry, stating 'It's my sister. Do you have a sister?' (Episode 1: Stolen. Missing. Murdered). The inclusion of this raw, emotional moment between Christine and the social services, as well as others throughout the series, distinguishes the audience's narrative journey to that of *Don't Fuck with Cats*. Although *Don't Fuck with Cats* follows Deanna and John's investigative journey, it is mainly through interviews recollecting their investigation which is aided by re-enactments. Instead, *Finding Cleo* transports the audience back to the precise moment that the investigation was taking place. We experience the same emotions of disappointment, sadness and satisfaction as we discover the answers to the investigation and the 'life-long mysteries' (Episode 1), that the family had suffered when we find out the cause of death and the final resting place of Cleo.

Although the audience is taken on a narrative journey, they are unable to contribute to its investigation. However, one podcast that does requests its listeners to become active investigators and contribute their knowledge to the case, is *Down the Hill: The Delphi Murders* podcast (2020). This podcast demonstrates a high-level of narrative transportation and signals elements of dark tourism. Containing eight episodes, each averaging around 45 minute, *Down the Hill* revisits the unsolved murder case of Abby Williams and Libby German in Delphi, Indiana. The podcast hosts speak directly to the listener and introduces them to the case. With phrases such as, 'we're going to take you there, to Delphi, across the next eight chapters' (Chapter 1: A Walk on The Bridge), informing the listener of the journey and narrative transportation they can expect to be taken on. The hosts also mentions that they will 'introduce the people that have lived this', as well as 'unfold the story', by 'walk(ing) those key locations' (Chapter 1), and for us (the audience) to 'come along', with them on this journey to discover the case. The hosts take us on a journey where we can visit the scene of the crimes, witness interviews and even be provided a 'tour' of the last known activity of the victims.

Furthermore, the hosts introduce the listeners to all key police investigators, as well as the family and friends of Abby and Libby to establish their personal network as the whole town rallies together to try and find the girls. This enables the audience to build a connection to the victims as we hear how good-hearted the two teenagers were and build up their image as the ideal victim (Christie, 1986). One week after the bodies were found, the police find a recording on Libby's phone of a man walking towards them on the bridge, as well as the audio of the man's voice saying, 'down the hill'. The local townsfolk used the public materials available to them, the three spoken words, the physical description and composite sketch that had been provided by the police, to search for the murderer and continued to hunt and contribute to the investigation.

Consequently, the people of Delphi were voluntarily surrendering themselves to the police with statements and their alibis during the time of Libby and Abby's disappearance and murder. The town were eager to provide tips of who the murderer might be as they continued to assess their neighbours for any suspicious behaviour—as requested by the police. Additionally, *Down the Hill* listeners, are spurred on by the hosts who continually invite the audience to use the evidence (the video, audio and physical description) to further investigate and even hunt for the identity of 'Bridge Guy' (the name provided for the unknown subject in the video). Our desire for truth (Bruzzi, 2016), is what is fuelling the town, the police, as well as the audience, to continue to investigate the case years after the murder. We are transported back to Delphi as we watch the video repeatedly in order to identify Bridge Guy. This level of dark tourism, where audiences can re-visit the scene of the crime whilst being continually motivated to identify the perpetrator, speaks to the level of narrative transportation present within the *Down the Hill* podcast and its attraction for audiences to continually regenerate their interest and motivate their investigations.

Conclusion

The online spaces within the true-crime genre provides an arena to share discussions regarding open or closed cases or investigations under trial proceedings. The unravelling of the allegations and cases in these online spaces creates platforms that are 'an arena for cultural trauma' (Moore, 2014, p. 147), which in turn allows 'the event in question to be narrated as a story' (Moore, 2014, p. 147). As the case and investigation unfolds, media in the genre such as documentaries and podcasts are able to adapt those events into narratives for audiences to follow, primarily for entertainment. However, entertainment within the true crime genre can also include the act of becoming a digital detective.

Whilst scrutinising the case and evidence, audiences create and take part in online discussions, forums, and participate in online true-crime spaces to assist in their cases. Those true-crime spaces are not just for the online watercooler discussions, but instead provide an area where amateur investigations can occur. Consequently, audiences are exploring new avenues to satisfy their unique needs in this current climate of platform mobility. By building these spaces online to discuss and investigate cases, there is an added appeal to the genre that coincides with audiences' need for online social integration and participation to which both true-crime podcasts and documentaries have been shown to cater for.

Study Questions

- Why might audiences watch true-crime? Consider the appeal of watching true-crime documentary series on video-on-demand services, such as Netflix, and why audiences might binge-watch.
- What is a digital detective? What are the differences between a person initiating an independent investigation and audiences integrating themselves into an investigation after consuming a documentary or podcast?
- What is a true-crime space? How can people create, access and make use of these spaces?
- Why might audiences listen to true-crime podcasts? How is the narrative transportation in podcasts different to the narrative in a documentaries/series?

Bibliography

Barker, C. & Wiatrowski, M. (2017). *The age of Netflix*. 1st ed. USA: McFarland & Company, Inc.

Bruzzi, S. (2016). *Making a genre: The case of the contemporary true crime documentary*. Taylor and Francis Online. https://doi.org/10.1080/17521483. 2016.1233741

Christie, N. (1986). *The ideal victim: From crime policy to victim policy.* Macmillan.

Green, M. C., & Brock, T. C. (2000). The role of transportation in the persuasiveness of public narratives. *Journal of Personality and Social Psychology, 79*(5).

Horeck, T. (2019). *Justice on demand.* Wayne University Press.

Katz, E., Blumler, J., & Gurevitch, M. (1973). Uses and gratifications research. *The Public Opinion Quarterly, 37.* Retrieved August 23, 2020, from http://www.jstor.org/stable/2747854

Lennon, J. J., & Foley, M. (2000). *Dark tourism.* Continuum.

Llinares, D., Berry, R., & Fox, N. (2018). *Podcasting: New aural cultures and digital media.* Palgrave Macmillan.

Mittell, J. (2015). *Complex TV: The poetics of contemporary television storytelling.* NYU Press.

Moore, S. (2014). *Crime and the media.* Red Globe, Springer Nature.

Sharpley, R., & Stone, P. R. (2009). *The darker side of travel: The theory and practise of dark tourism.* Channel View Publications.

Spinelli, M., & Dann, L. (2019). *Podcasting: The audio media revolution.* Bloomsbury.

Tryon, C. (2013). *On demand culture: Digital delivery and the future of movies.* Rutgers University Press.

Websites and Other Resources

Buzzfeed Unsolved Network, YouTube channel. Accessed 6 December 2020. https://www.youtube.com/c/BuzzFeedUnsolvedNetwork/featured

Don't Fuck with Cats: Hunting an Internet Killer. Netflix, 2019. Accessed 5 December 2020. https://www.netflix.com/watch/81031766?trackId=200257859

Iden, A., Macdonald, B., & Szematowicz, D. Episodes 1–9 in *Down the Hill: The Delphi Murders.* February 5, 2020–March 25, 2020. Podcasts. Accessed 6 December. https://podcasts.apple.com/ie/podcast/down-the-hill-the-delphi-murders/id1494167201

Jeffrey Epstein: Filthy Rich. Netflix, 2020. Accessed 6 December 2020. https://www.netflix.com/search?q=jeff&jbv=80224905

The Keepers. Netflix, 2017. Accessed 6 December 2020. https://www.netflix.com/search?q=the%20keeprs&jbv=80122179

Walker, C. S2, Episodes 1–10 in *Missing and Murdered: Finding Cleo* March 6, 2018–April 2, 2018. Podcasts. Accessed 6 December 2020. https://pod casts.apple.com/gb/podcast/missing-murdered-finding-cleo/id1166556648

Zambetti, L., Richards, L., & Clement, J. Episodes 275 & 276 in *Real Crime Profile*. September 28 and 30, 2020. Podcasts, 44:10 & 52:33. Accessed 6 December 2020. https://podcasts.apple.com/gb/podcast/dont-f-ck-with-cats-with-deanna-thompson-and-john-green/id1081244497?i=100049277 8825

14

Live Streaming of Murder: Regulatory Responses and Challenges

Gregor Urbas

Introduction

The advent of live-streaming functionality on social media around a decade ago enabled users to broadcast to the world in real time any event that could be filmed using a webcam or smart phone. Though mostly used to capture sporting, entertainment and celebratory spectacles, this technology has also predictably been misused by antisocial and criminal elements to film their unlawful exploits. These include assaults, rapes, child molestation, terrorist attacks and even homicides. In many cases, it is undeniable that a major part of the motivation behind live-streaming is the instant gratification and notoriety that this adds to the commission of the crime. In cases involving terrorist violence, it also facilitates the communication of a political message to a global audience.

G. Urbas (✉)
Australian National University, Canberra, Australia
e-mail: gregor.urbas@anu.edu.au

M. Mellins and S. Moore (eds.), *Critiquing Violent Crime in the Media*,
https://doi.org/10.1007/978-3-030-83758-7_14

355

Live-streamed murders have included the random killing of a 74-year-old man in Cleveland, Ohio on Easter Sunday in 2017, viewed by over 1.6 million in the hours that followed; terrorist attacks in 2019 on a synagogue in Halle, Germany and two mosques in Christchurch, New Zealand, both streamed via helmet cams to give a shooter perspective; and a shopping mall shooting spree in Thailand, with live video posted via Facebook, in February 2020. In these cases, the social media platforms acted within hours to remove the offending videos, the public was implored to stop sharing the material, and regulators explored measures that might prevent similar episodes.

Arguably the most substantial regulatory response to date has been legislation enacted in Australia in response to the Christchurch attacks, which were carried out by an Australian citizen. The *Criminal Code Amendment (Sharing of Abhorrent Violent Material) Act 2019* (Cth), which received assent on 5 April 2019, created offences that apply to social media and other internet services where they do not act expeditiously to remove content falling within the definition of 'abhorrent violent material'. This was defined to include self-produced video or streaming of terrorist acts, murder, attempted murder, torture, rape or kidnapping. Penalties of imprisonment and very substantial fines apply to failure to comply with the statutory requirements. Defences include law enforcement investigations, genuine research, media reporting that is in the public interest, advocacy for law reform and good faith artistic works.

Despite a general level of acceptance of these legal reforms from social media platforms such as Facebook, and ongoing co-operation with agencies such as the police and e-Safety Commissioner, there is still uncertainty as to what threshold must be reached before reporting and removal obligations arise, and what constitutes expeditious removal. The fact that the Christchurch shooter video was removed only after complaints and urgent police requests indicates that social media can adopt a largely reactive posture, relying on the ongoing argument that they serve as a conduit for user-generated content rather than as a publisher with editorial and monitoring responsibilities. However, with further legislative reform in progress both in Australia and other countries, the burden of responsibility will continue to shift to online providers to remove offensive content. Whether this will stem the flow of live streaming of murder in the future is still to be seen.

Live-Streamed Murder

Live-streaming of murder and similar acts of violence can be viewed as a 'performative crime' (Bender, 2017). The motivation is not only to engage in the criminal act itself, but to use this as a performance or communication to an audience, which can be an individual, group or wider society. Often this involves the ventilation of some personal or political grievance, including those of terrorist groups (Conway & Dillon, 2019). For some, it may simply be a means to attain online notoriety, an extreme version of the narcissistic world of online celebrity and influencers (Fietkiewicz et al., 2018).

Arguably, part of the motivation and attraction of live-streaming is the direct control that the killer has over the messaging, unmediated and unedited by traditional gatekeepers such as the media. As Cooper (2018) observes:

> Livestreaming, by ordinary people using apps such as Facebook Live or Periscope, symbolises the current biggest challenge to journalism. It encapsulates the collapsing of boundaries around what a journalist is or what journalism does. It has a direct effect on what journalists themselves see as the key challenges to their profession — the failure of the traditional economic model and the rise of fake news. It allows use of more graphic imagery.

While there have been many instances of killings and other violent acts committed deliberately in front of media cameras, such as in hostage situations, with live-streaming there are no filters or editors involved. The journalistic buffer of warnings to viewers or excising of content deemed too graphic to screen on television is lacking. The killer who live-streams his or her acts is also his or her own broadcaster. This poses new challenges to those who control the flow of information to the public, from public regulators and traditional media, to social media services such as Facebook, Periscope and Twitch. The following three events illustrate, and frame the discussion of legislative responses that follows.

The 'Facebook Killer'

On Easter Sunday in 2017, a man in Cleveland, Ohio fatally shot a random stranger and posted video of the killing on Facebook Live under the title 'Easter Day slaughter'. The victim was 74-year old Robert Goodwin Sr, and the video records the shooter, Steve Stephens, saying 'Found me somebody I'm going to kill … This guy right here — this old dude'. Before shooting him at point blank range in the head, the perpetrator demanded that the victim say the name of his girlfriend, Joy Lane, and after the shooting said to his phone camera, 'That motherf–ker dead because of you, Joy'.[1]

Afterwards, the perpetrator shot himself at a McDonald's drive through when confronted by police.[2] Responding to criticism that the video posted by Stevens was not removed from Facebook until three hours later, during which time it had been viewed 1.6 million times, the CEO of Facebook expressed his sympathies to the victim's family at the company's conference, adding that 'we have a lot more work and we will keep doing all we can to prevent tragedies like this from happening'.[3]

The Christchurch Mosque Shootings

In mid-March 2019, Australian man Brenton Tarrant with extremist political views perpetrated a 30-minute attack on two mosques in Christchurch, New Zealand, during which 51 people were fatally shot. He posted prior to the attack, filmed himself driving to the mosques

---

[1] Joe Tacopino, 'Man wanted for posting murder on Facebook' (*New York Post*, 16 April 2017).
[2] Sonam Sheth, '"Facebook killer" Steve Stephens found dead' (*Business Insider*, 19 April 2017).
[3] Kif Leswing, 'Mark Zuckerberg talks about the "Facebook killer": We will keep doing all we can to prevent tragedies like this' (*Business Insider*, 19 April 2017).

and live-streamed the shootings using a helmet-mounted camera with the images appearing on Facebook Live. The live stream lasted nearly 17 minute, and the offending video was removed only after some 40 minute had elapsed from the first complaint to Facebook by a user (Valcic, 2021). The use of other platforms also ensured that the video went 'viral' in a short time, as noted by Macklin (2019):

> In filming his rampage and posting it online, Tarrant grasped intu-itively that digital technology could and would amplify his murderous message, ensuring its projection far beyond the cloistered confines of the 8chan sub-thread on which it originated. Under 200 people watched the ongoing carnage as it unfolded during Tarrant's live broadcast. None of these individuals reported the video to Facebook, which received its first user report 29 minutes after the video started, and 12 minutes after the live broadcast ended. Including the views the live broadcast received, the video was viewed approximately 4,000 times before Face-book removed it from its site. The video quickly went viral, however. Indeed, as one commentator noted, "the New Zealand massacre was live-streamed on Facebook, announced on 8chan, reposted on YouTube, commentated about on Reddit, and mirrored around the world before the tech companies could even react."

After the attacks and the suspect's arrest by New Zealand authorities, legal proceedings commenced and after a few months a guilty plea was entered to murder charges, leaving only sentencing to be finalised.[4] Tarrant was sentenced to life imprisonment without parole in August 2020.[5] However, despite the resolution of the criminal charges, the events sparked continuing public disquiet about the ease with which such violent acts can be live-streamed, and some sections of the online community's willingness to share the material. In New Zealand, a

---

[4] Barbara Miller, 'Christchurch mosque attacker Brenton Tarrant changes plea to guilty, to be sentenced for 51 murders' (*ABC News*, 26 March 2020).

[5] Mazoe Ford and Barbara Miller, 'Christchurch shooting: Mosque attack gunman Brenton Tarrant jailed for life without parole' (*ABC News*, 27 August 2020).

number of such sharers have been prosecuted, while in Australia a significant legislative response eventuated (discussed further below).[6]

The Halle Synagogue Shooter

In early October 2019, a gunman filmed himself using a helmet cam which was live-streamed using Twitch, as he shot dead two people in Halle, Germany, and unsuccessfully sought to enter a Jewish synagogue to find more victims. Using the first-person shooter perspective familiar to online gamers, the assailant included an anti-Semitic rant in his performance. The social media service stated:[7]

> Twitch has a zero-tolerance policy against hateful conduct, and any act of violence is taken extremely seriously. We are working with urgency to remove this content and permanently suspend any accounts found to be posting or reposting content of this abhorrent act.

By contrast with the Christchurch attack, the live-streaming of the Halle attack appears to have been viewed in real time by only a handful of people, and about 2200 viewed it in the 30 minute during which it was still available on Twitch before being flagged and removed.[8] Subsequent investigation by the company indicated that the Twitch account used had been created about two months prior to the attack and had only attempted to live-stream once before, and that the sharing of the video was done by individuals using messaging services rather than the sharing features of the Twitch site.[9]

---

[6] Radio New Zealand, 'Charges laid in 35 cases over sharing of video of Christchurch terror attacks' (Radio New Zealand, 2 September 2019). Interestingly, New Zealand did not follow Australia's lead in introducing new legislation aimed at social media platforms, but instead concentrated on reform of its gun laws: *ABC News*, 'New Zealand gun laws pass 119–1 after Christchurch mosque shootings' (10 April 2019).

[7] Donie O'Sullivan, 'Germany shooting suspect appears to have livestreamed attack online' (*CNN Business*, 10 October 2019).

[8] Charlotte Gee, 'Germany's synagogue shooting was live-streamed on Twitch—But almost no one saw it' (*MIT Technology Review*, 10 October 2019).

[9] Catherine Thorbecke, 'Video of synagogue shooting in Germany viewed more than 2000 times on Twitch' (*ABC News*, 11 October 2019).

Although each of these three events shows a degree of responsiveness by the social media platforms involved, public criticism of the availability of live-streamed murder content and the behaviour of users who shared it prompted a reaction at governmental levels. The following discussion will focus on the Australian response, as this was the first to result in significant legislative reforms.[10]

The Australian Legislative Response

The Criminal Code Amendment (Sharing of Abhorrent Violent Material) Bill 2019 was introduced into the Australian Parliament on 3 April 2019. Its direct impetus was the Christchurch shootings by an Australian citizen only three weeks earlier, as was made clear by the Attorney-General[11]:

> I might commence by starting this speech by paying tribute to all those who suffered and lost their lives and lost loved ones as a result of the Christchurch terrorist attack on Friday, 15 March 2019. The victims, their families and their loved ones; the Muslim community in New Zealand and Australia and around the world; and New Zealanders, who have been shocked and saddened by that vile act, know, of course, that Australia stands with them. The horror of that act was brought to the world in real time and the platforms that were used to connect with the world were turned against us to amplify the shooter's message of hate and intolerance.
>
> The relevant footage was broadcast for 17 minutes without interruption and it was another 12 minutes after that point in time that the first user report on the original video was received by Facebook. The material

---

[10] However, it should be noted that Germany enacted somewhat similar restrictions on social media providers in 2017, as an extension of its longstanding prohibitions on pro-Nazi and other 'hate speech': *BBC News*, 'Germany starts enforcing hate speech law' (1 January 2018).

[11] Attorney-General Christian Porter, 2nd Reading Speech, Criminal Code Amendment (Sharing of Abhorrent Violent Material) Bill 2019 (Cth), 4 April 2019. The *Criminal Code Act 1995* (Cth) is the Commonwealth's main criminal legislation, including on cybercrime and telecommunications offences: see generally Urbas (2020).

was live-streamed on Facebook and available on that platform for almost an hour and 10 minutes until the first attempts were made to take it down. Simply put, we find that unacceptable.

The Australian government expects that internet platforms should take responsibility for preventing the spread of abhorrent violent material online. The internet is not an ungoverned space. Together, we must act to ensure that perpetrators and their accomplices cannot leverage online platforms for the purposes of spreading their violent and extreme fanatical propaganda. These platforms should not be weaponised for evil purposes.

The Criminal Code Amendment (Sharing of Abhorrent Violent Material) Bill represents an important step in this process. It will ensure that hosting and content services expeditiously remove abhorrent violent material and notify the Australian Federal Police when it appears on their platforms. Internet platforms must take the risks posed by the spread of abhorrent violent material online seriously. The new offences will therefore be accompanied by criminal penalties.

The Bill was passed into law without amendments on the following day, as the *Criminal Code Amendment (Sharing of Abhorrent Violent Material) Act 2019* (Cth). The following statutory definitions are found in new Subdivision H of Division 474—Telecommunications Offences:

474.30 Definitions
In this Subdivision:
abhorrent violent conduct has the meaning given by section 474.32.
abhorrent violent material has the meaning given by section 474.31.
consent means free and voluntary agreement.
content service means:

(a) a social media service (within the meaning of the *Enhancing Online Safety Act 2015*); or
(b) a designated internet service (within the meaning of the *Enhancing Online Safety Act 2015*).

hosting service has the same meaning as in the *Enhancing Online Safety Act 2015*. For this purpose, disregard subparagraphs 9C(a)(ii) and (b)(ii) of that Act.

474.31 Abhorrent violent material

(1) For the purposes of this Subdivision, *abhorrent violent material* means material that:

(a) is:
(i) audio material; or
(ii) visual material; or
(iii) audio-visual material;

that records or streams abhorrent violent conduct engaged in by one or more persons; and.

(b) is material that reasonable persons would regard as being, in all the circumstances, offensive; and
(c) is produced by a person who is, or by 2 or more persons each of whom is:

(i) a person who engaged in the abhorrent violent conduct; or
(ii) a person who conspired to engage in the abhorrent violent conduct; or
(iii) a person who aided, abetted, counselled or procured, or was in any way knowingly concerned in, the abhorrent violent conduct; or
(iv) a person who attempted to engage in the abhorrent violent conduct.

(2) For the purposes of this section, it is immaterial whether the material has been altered.
(3) For the purposes of this section, it is immaterial whether the abhorrent violent conduct was engaged in within or outside Australia.

474.32 Abhorrent violent conduct

(1) For the purposes of this Subdivision, a person engages in *abhorrent violent conduct* if the person:

(a) engages in a terrorist act; or
(b) murders another person; or
(c) attempts to murder another person; or

(d) tortures another person; or
(e) rapes another person; or
(f) kidnaps another person.

Murder

(2) For the purposes of this section, a person (the *first person*) murders another person if:

(a) the first person's conduct causes the death of the other person; and
(b) the conduct constitutes an offence.

[Subsections 474.32(3)—(7) explain the meaning of the other conduct listed in paragraph (1)].

Under these definitions, a 'social media service' is defined in the other legislation referred to as having the following main features[12]:

(i) the sole or primary purpose of the service is to enable online social interaction between 2 or more end-users;
(ii) the service allows end-users to link to, or interact with, some or all of the other end-users;
(iii) the service allows end-users to post material on the service.

Social media platforms allowing live-streaming, such as Facebook Live discussed above, clearly fall within the relevant definitions of 'social media service' and thus 'content service' as well as 'hosting service' as defined in the legislation.[13]

Turning to the definition of 'abhorrent violent material', however, the scope of key terms is somewhat less clear.

Abhorrent Violent Material

---

[12] *Enhancing Online Safety Act 2015* (Cth), s 9. Note that this legislation establishes the Office of the eSafety Commissioner, with primary responsibility for responding to complaints of cyberbullying and similar online abuse, with powers to order removal of offending content by the social media and other services involved.

[13] *Enhancing Online Safety Act 2015* (Cth), ss 4, 9, 9A and 9C.

According to s 474.31(1), 'abhorrent violent material' is audio, visual or audio-visual material produced by one or more persons participating in 'abhorrent violent conduct', where the material records or streams that conduct, and that reasonable persons would regard as being, in all the circumstances, offensive. In turn, 'abhorrent violent conduct' is defined to include such acts as murder and attempted murder, though the related definition of these offences in subsection (2) does not reference the murder and attempt provisions of the Commonwealth Criminal Code, but is stated in broader terms of unlawfully causing the death of another person, which would arguably encompass murder, manslaughter and a number of other acts causing death.[14] This approach is meant to facilitate decision-making by service providers in a non-legalistic manner[15]:

It is not necessary for a prosecution to prove that conduct under one or more of these categories constitutes an offence. It is enough that the conduct has met the definitions under s 474.32 of engaging in a terrorist act, murder, torture, rape or kidnapping. This is to ensure that internet service providers, hosting service providers and content service providers have clarity as to the threshold for reporting abhorrent violent material to the AFP, or in the case of hosting service and content providers, have clarity as to the threshold for when abhorrent violent material should be removed from or cease to be hosted on their services.

The offensiveness criterion in s 474.31(b) is familiar from provisions in the Commonwealth Criminal Code dealing with child abuse material, defined in part using the same wording, and with the following additional exposition of offensiveness[16]:

473.4 Determining whether material is offensive

---

[14] See *Criminal Code Act 1995* (Cth), ss 11.1, 71.2, 71.3, 115.1, 115.2, 268.8 and 268.70.

[15] Explanatory Memorandum, Criminal Code Amendment (Sharing of Abhorrent Violent Material) Bill 2019 (Cth) at [25].

[16] *Criminal Code Act 1995* (Cth), s 473.4 to which definitions in ss 473.1 and related offences refer. Note that subsection 474.3(2) provides an additional explanation of offensiveness in the context of intimate images.

(1) The matters to be taken into account in deciding for the purposes of this Part whether reasonable persons would regard particular material, or a particular use of a carriage service, as being, in all the circumstances, offensive, include:

(a) the standards of morality, decency and propriety generally accepted by reasonable adults; and
(b) the literary, artistic or educational merit (if any) of the material; and
(c) the general character of the material (including whether it is of a medical, legal or scientific character).

As the abhorrent violent material provisions have been added to Part 10.6 of the Commonwealth Criminal Code, s 473.4 applies to them ('for the purposes of this Part') and thus the standards of morality, decency and propriety generally accepted by reasonable adults, as well as the other considerations mentioned, are to be applied to assessing material as falling within the definition.[17]

Offences

Turning to the offences, the interesting feature of the offence provisions under the legislation is that the streaming of abhorrent violent material by the perpetrator is not the law's target, but the failure of a service provider to notify authorities and expeditiously remove it.[18]

474.33 Notification obligations of internet service providers, content service providers and hosting service providers

(1) A person commits an offence if:

(a) the person:
(i) is an internet service provider; or
(ii) provides a content service; or

---

[17] Explanatory Memorandum (cited above) at [15].

[18] Of course, conduct such as murder is already a criminal offence in all Australian jurisdictions, noting that the definition of 'murder' in s 474.32(2) takes a non-legalistic approach; and the use of a telecommunications service to send or distribute offensive material is also an offence under s 474.17 of the *Criminal Code Act 1995* (Cth), which since amendments in 2017 extends also to non-consensual sharing of intimate images.

(iii) provides a hosting service; and

(b) the person is aware that the service provided by the person can be used to access particular material that the person has reasonable grounds to believe is abhorrent violent material that records or streams abhorrent violent conduct that has occurred, or is occurring, in Australia; and

(c) the person does not refer details of the material to the Australian Federal Police within a reasonable time after becoming aware of the existence of the material.

Penalty: 800 penalty units.

(2) For the purposes of this section:

(a) it is immaterial whether the content service is provided within or outside Australia; and

(b) it is immaterial whether the hosting service is provided within or outside Australia.

(3) Subsection (1) does not apply if the person reasonably believes that details of the material are already known to the Australian Federal Police.

Note: A defendant bears an evidential burden in relation to the matters in this subsection: see subsection 13.3(3).

474.34 Removing, or ceasing to host, abhorrent violent material
Content service

(1) A person commits an offence if:

(a) the person provides a content service; and

(b) the content service can be used to access material; and

(c) the material is abhorrent violent material; and

(d) the person does not ensure the expeditious removal of the material from the content service.

(2) For the purposes of subsection (1), it is immaterial whether the content service is provided within or outside Australia.

(3) Subsection (1) does not apply to material unless the material is reasonably capable of being accessed within Australia.

(4) The fault element for paragraphs (1)(b) and (c) is recklessness.

Hosting service

(5) A person commits an offence if:

    (a) the person provides a hosting service; and
    (b) material is hosted on the hosting service; and
    (c) the material is abhorrent violent material; and
    (d) the person does not expeditiously cease hosting the material.

(6) For the purposes of subsection (5), it is immaterial whether the hosting service is provided within or outside Australia.

(7) Subsection (5) does not apply to material unless the material is reasonably capable of being accessed within Australia.

(8) The fault element for paragraphs (5)(b) and (c) is recklessness.

Penalty for individual

(9) An offence against subsection (1) or (5) committed by an individual is punishable on conviction by imprisonment for a period of not more than 3 years or a fine of not more than 10,000 penalty units, or both.

Penalty for body corporate

(10) An offence against subsection (1) or (5) committed by a body corporate is punishable on conviction by a fine of not more than the greater of the following:

    (a) 50,000 penalty units;

(b) 10% of the annual turnover of the body corporate during the period (the **turnover period**) of 12 months ending at the end of the month in which the conduct constituting the offence occurred.

(11) For the purposes of this section, the **annual turnover** of a body corporate, during the turnover period, is the sum of the values of all the supplies that the body corporate, and any body corporate related to the body corporate, have made, or are likely to make, during that period, other than the following supplies:

(a) supplies made from any of those bodies corporate to any other of those bodies corporate;
(b) supplies that are input taxed;
(c) supplies that are not for consideration (and are not taxable supplies under section 14.72–14.5 of the A New Tax System [Goods and Services Tax] Act 1999);
(d) supplies that are not made in connection with an enterprise that the body corporate carries on.

(12) For the purposes of subsection (11), it is immaterial whether the supplies were made, or are likely to be made, within or outside Australia.

(13) Expressions used in subsections (11) and (12) that are also used in the *A New Tax System (Goods and Services Tax) Act 1999* have the same meaning in those subsections as they have in that Act.

(14) The question whether 2 bodies corporate are related to each other is to be determined for the purposes of this section in the same way as for the purposes of the *Corporations Act 2001*.

When material is removed from a content service

(15) For the purposes of this section, material is **removed** from a content service if the material is not accessible to any of the end-users using the service.

Note that one penalty unit equates to $210 as per the *Crimes Act 1914*
(Cth), s 4AA, so that a fine of 50,000 penalty units or 10% of annual
turnover under s 474.34(10) will amount to over $1 million.

Notification Requirements
Notification requirements for specified categories of material apply to
online service providers under a range of existing laws. For example, in
relation to child abuse material (which includes child sexual exploitation
material), the Commonwealth Criminal Code provides[19]:

**474.25 Obligations of internet service providers and internet content
hosts**
   A person commits an offence if the person:

(a) is an internet service provider or an internet content host; and
(b) is aware that the service provided by the person can be used to access
    particular material that the person has reasonable grounds to believe
    is child abuse material; and
(c) does not refer details of the material to the Australian Federal Police
    within a reasonable time after becoming aware of the existence of the
    material.

Penalty: 800 penalty units.
It is clear that the new s 474.33(1) offence is based on this pre-existing
provision, and the two sections share the same penalty unit amount.
However, an interesting difference is that s 474.25 does not specify
that the relevant material must have some territorial connection with
Australia (i.e. the material may have been made and become available online in a foreign jurisdiction), whereas s 474.33(1) is restricted
to 'abhorrent violent conduct that has occurred, or is occurring, in
Australia'. It is unclear why this territorial limitation has been added, as
arguably the Commonwealth has constitutional jurisdiction with respect

---

[19] *Criminal Code Act 1995* (Cth), s 474.25, as amended by the *Criminal Code Amendment
(Sharing of Abhorrent Violent Material) Act 2019* (Cth) which introduced ss 474.33 with the
same 800 penalty unit amount; under the *Crimes Act 1914* (Cth), s 4AA, this equates to $
176,000, but there is a multiplier of 5 times the stated penalty for bodies corporate under s
4B, so that this is instead 4000 penalty units or $840,000 for corporations. T.

to telecommunications generally, not requiring that these originate in or are sent to or within Australia. However, in practical terms, the limitation may be explained in that there is little point in referring details of material to the Australian Federal Police unless they have some basis for further investigation, of either the activity depicted or the streaming or posting of the material so that it is available to the Australian public[20]:

> The purpose of the new offence under subsection 474.33(1) is to ensure that the AFP is notified by providers of both the existence of the underlying abhorrent violent conduct (for example, a terrorist act that is being live-streamed) as well as the existence and accessibility of the abhorrent violent material itself online.

As a consequence, despite the explicit references to the Christchurch shootings in the introduction of this legislation, it appears that the notification offence in s 474.33(1) would not apply (or have applied if then in force) to that live-streamed or shared video footage, as it did not depict 'abhorrent violent conduct that has occurred, or is occurring, in Australia'. It occurred in New Zealand.

Subsection 474.33(2) takes a more expansive approach to the location of the content service or hosting service, as it provides that it is 'immaterial whether the content service [or hosting service] is provided within or outside Australia'. This means that both domestic and foreign providers are subject to the notification requirements of the legislation.[21]

Subsection 474.33(3) provides another practical dispensation, as the offence in subsection (1) does not apply if the provider 'reasonably believes that details of the material are already known to the Australian Federal Police' (AFP). In particular circumstances, it may be a reasonable assumption that police are already aware of the material, or that it has been reported by someone else, but the onus of establishing this as a defence carries an evidential burden, as per the note to subsection (3)[22]:

---

[20] Explanatory Memorandum, Criminal Code Amendment (Sharing of Abhorrent Violent Material) Bill 2019 (Cth) at [37]. Note, however, that the definitions of 'internet service provider', 'content service' and 'hosting service' refer to other legislation that may limit their meaning to services available within Australia.

[21] Explanatory Memorandum (cited above) at [44].

[22] Explanatory Memorandum (cited above) at [47]–[48].

Subsection @474.33(3) would provide a defence for a person who failed to report abhorrent violent material to the AFP because they reasonably believed that the AFP was already aware of the material. This has been expressed as a defence rather than as an element of the offence as the defendant's beliefs are peculiarly within the knowledge of the defendant.

The note under subsection @474.33 clarifies that the evidential burden falls on the defendant if they wish to rely on the defence in subsection @474.33(2).

Two aspects of the legislation continue to be the subject of criticism from online service providers, as well as some commentators. The first is the qualification to the notification offence in s 474.33(1) of 'reasonable grounds to believe' that material is in fact abhorrent violent material, as this seems to be applicable when particular material is examined, either because of a complaint or referral from an outside source, or because it has been identified by the provider in its own self-auditing capacity. However, internet service providers and other intermediaries are historically resistant to general obligations to systematically monitor the content of their customers' online postings, taking the position that they are 'conduits' rather than 'publishers' of information (Urbas, 2018). Neither s 474.33(1) nor its child abuse material counterpart in s 474.25 imposes an explicit obligation to monitor content, so that it would appear that this general approach is not necessarily undermined by the new provision. However, it is arguable that the 'reasonable grounds to believe' test in s 474.33(1)(b) imposes an objective standard of the 'reasonable' service provider, such that liability will more likely be found if the provider simply failed to consider and deal with the accessibility of objectionable material i.e. wilful blindness will not be an acceptable position for a service provider to take (discussed further below in relation to the 'recklessness' fault elements applying to s 474.34).

The second matter is the stipulation that the AFP must be notified within a 'reasonable time after becoming aware of the existence of the material' (same wording as in s 474.25). What constitutes a 'reasonable time' is not further elaborated, but a practical approach should be applied[23]:

---

[23] Explanatory Memorandum (cited above) at [39].

A 'reasonable time' is not defined. A number of factors and circumstances could indicate whether a person had referred details of abhorrent violent material within a reasonable time after becoming aware of the existence of the material. For example, the type and volume of the material, and the capabilities of and resourcing available to the provider may be relevant factors. In a prosecution for an offence against section @474.33, the determination of whether material was referred within a reasonable time will be a matter for the trier of fact.

Similar considerations apply to the use of 'expeditiously remove' in s 474.34 (discussed below).

Removal Requirements

Under s 474.34(1), a content service that can be used to access material which is abhorrent violent material commits an offence if it does not ensure the expeditious removal of the material. However, unlike the requirement of awareness of the material as in s 474.33(1), this provision imposes a fault element of 'recklessness' in relation to the fact that material can be accessed through the service, and that the material is abhorrent violent material, as per subsection (4).

Recklessness is defined in the Commonwealth Criminal Code as follows[24]:

5.4 Recklessness

(1) A person is reckless with respect to a circumstance if:

    (a) he or she is aware of a substantial risk that the circumstance exists or will exist; and

    (b) having regard to the circumstances known to him or her, it is unjustifiable to take the risk.

(2) A person is reckless with respect to a result if:

---

[24] Under s 5.6, recklessness is the 'default' fault element for any physical element of circumstance or result.

(a) he or she is aware of a substantial risk that the result will occur; and

(b) having regard to the circumstances known to him or her, it is unjustifiable to take the risk.

(3) The question whether taking a risk is unjustifiable is one of fact.

(4) If recklessness is a fault element for a physical element of an offence, proof of intention, knowledge or recklessness will satisfy that fault element.

Applied to the elements of the offence in s 474.34(1) and (5), this means that a service provider or hosting provider will be liable if the physical elements of the offence are satisfied, and the provider is aware of a substantial but unjustifiable risk that the service can be used to access material which is abhorrent violent material. This does not equate to a requirement of awareness, or knowledge, as this would encourage willful blindness[25]:

> Subsection @474.34(4) provides that the fault element for new paragraphs @474.34(1)(b) and (c) is recklessness. As paragraphs @474.34(1)(b), and (c) both refer to a circumstance rather than conduct, recklessness is the appropriate fault element. This is consistent with the default fault elements that would otherwise apply per section 5.6 of the Criminal Code. It would not be appropriate to restrict the fault element to knowledge, as this could incentivise content service providers to be wilfully blind to the content provided on their service, rather than proactively engage with the removal of abhorrent violent material.

In other words, service providers and hosting providers must take a proactive rather than reactive position. It is not enough simply to avoid monitoring of accessible content in order to avoid liability and potentially very substantial penalties. Rather, the legislative intent is to impose a positive obligation to detect and expeditiously remove abhorrent violent material.

---

[25] Explanatory Memorandum (cited above) at [56].

The meaning of 'expeditious' is also contested and unclear, which arguably puts providers in a difficult position in terms of complying with the legislation[26]:

> 'Expeditious' is not defined and would be determined by the trier of fact taking account of all of the circumstances in each case. A number of factors and circumstances could indicate whether a person had ensured the expeditious removal of the material. For example, the type and volume of the abhorrent violent material, or the capabilities of and resourcing available to the provider may be relevant factors.

This explanation overlooks the fact that capabilities and resourcing are the result of business forces and decisions that in part react to the regulatory landscape i.e. if there is a risk of criminal liability and substantial fines for not proactively detecting and expeditiously removing abhorrent violent material, then a rational service provider will allocate greater resources to ensuring compliance.

Currently, social media providers such as Facebook and YouTube employ a mix of detection methods to identify offensive content for possible removal (Smith & Urbas, 2021; Valcic, 2021):

- Automated matching by machine—where content is matched against a library of known images or video files e.g. containing child exploitation or terrorist recruitment material;
- Automated flagging by machine—where content is identified by artificial intelligence programmes trained to identify and flag material in prohibited categories;
- Human flagging—where content is identified by employees of the platform or through user complaints and notifications.[27]

Role of the eSafety Commissioner and Defences

---

[26] Explanatory Memorandum (cited above) at [51] and [60].

[27] Facebook's Help Center has easily understood instructions on how to report objectionable content including videos; while Youtube videos on reporting offensive YouTube videos can readily be found by searching.

Additional provisions provide a role for the Australian eSafety Commissioner in relation to abhorrent violent material. Sections 474.35 and 474.36 allow the Commissioner to issue notices and provide for certain presumptions to apply, respectively, in relation to content services and hosting services. In particular, a notice may state that a specified service can be used to access specified material, and that the specified material is abhorrent violent material. Such a notice must be based on reasonable grounds, and must be provided to the relevant service. Presumptions then apply, to the effect that the service provider is reckless as to whether the service can be used to access specified material, and as to whether the specified material is abhorrent violent material. Thus, in a prosecution under ss 474.33 or 474.34, the prosecution is facilitated by these presumptions, unless the provider can adduce or point to evidence that suggests as a reasonable possibility that it was not reckless.[28]

The purpose of a notice from the eSafety Commissioner may be to expedite the removal of content considered to be abhorrent violent material, so that prosecution is not necessary[29]:

> This notice would put the content service provider on notice that their service is being used to access abhorrent violent material. In effect, the notice would also put the provider on notice that they may commit an offence if they have not removed or do not remove it expeditiously.
> … In most circumstances, if the content service provider were to ensure the expeditious removal of the material after receiving the notice, a prosecution would be unlikely. However in some circumstances, such as where the content had been available for a significant period prior to the Commissioner issuing the notice, a prosecution may be appropriate notwithstanding the expeditious removal of the abhorrent violent material after receipt of the notice.

Additional statutory defences are provided under s 474.37 in a range of specified circumstances, summarised as follows (Dawson, 2019)[30]:

---

[28] Subsections (5) and (6) of ss 434.35 and 474.36 set out these presumptions.

[29] Explanatory Memorandum (cited above) at [74] and [85].

[30] The operation of these defences is meant to negate liability for the use of video of abhorrent violent acts such as terrorist or other attacks, which may have been self-produced by the

- the material relates to a news report, or a current affairs report that is in the public interest and is by a person working in a professional capacity as a journalist;
- the accessibility of the material relates to the development, performance, exhibition or distribution, in good faith, of an artistic work;
- the accessibility of the material is for the purpose of advocating the lawful procurement of a change to any matter established by law, policy or practice in an Australian or foreign jurisdiction and the accessibility of the material is reasonable in the circumstances for that purpose;
- the accessibility of the material is necessary for law enforcement purposes, or for monitoring compliance with, or investigating a contravention of a law;
- the accessibility of the material is for a court proceeding;
- the accessibility of the material is necessary and reasonable for scientific, medical, academic or historical research; or
- the accessibility of the material is in connection with and reasonable for the purpose of an individual assisting a public official in relation to the public official's duties or functions.

Section 474.38 preserves the constitutionally implied freedom of political communication, while s 474.39 provides a form of 'safe harbour' protection for carriage service providers and billing services, stating that they are not content service providers for the purpose of the offence provisions merely by operating their respective capacities.

Finally, the Attorney-General's consent is required under s 474.42 for the prosecution of a foreign entity under s 474.33, or generally under s 474.34. The interpolation of the Attorney-General in the decision-making process culminating in any prosecution is a safeguard measure, which finds expression in a number of other situations under the Commonwealth Criminal Code.[31] This itself raises interesting questions

---

perpetrators, in e.g. a legitimate news broadcast which is in the public interest. No further guidance on what is in the public interest is given.

[31] See e.g. *Criminal Code Act 1995* (Cth), ss 16.1, 70.5, 71.20, 72.7, 73.5, 82.13, 83.15, 93.1, 115.6, 119.11, 123.5, 268.121, 270.3B, 272.31, 273.21, 274.3, 474.24C and 490.6. While

of discretionary choice, such as who might be appropriate to charge. Valcic (2021) explains:

> However, the issue raised is if the content is shared across so many platforms, who should or would the Government be charging first, or at all? If the Attorney-General decides to charge all platforms in breach for the singular incident, it would likely be a significant drain on public funds. Further, the court system would become inundated with prosecutions under the [Act]. There are many lines of reasoning the Attorney-General could take in deciding who to prosecute, for example, the platform which the content was first accessible, or the largest platform, or the platform with the highest number of views of the content. Overall, the Attorney-General would have to determine the best platform to prosecute for a breach, if the Act is going to be enforced.

At the time of writing, there have been no reported prosecutions under these provisions. Indeed, this may be a desirable outcome, indicating that social media platforms have responded to the changing regulatory landscape by exercising greater diligence over their hosted content.

Conclusion

The attractiveness of services such as Facebook lies in the ability of users to post material, without editorial approval or intervention, so that it can be shared with other users in an interactive way. There are, of course, many restrictions on some types of material, as set out in terms and conditions posted by service providers, including that distribution of the material is prohibited by law.[32] However, unless material falls within the scope of a prohibition, the operational default setting is that it may be posted and shared with others. To err on the side of notification and removal just in case material might be classified as abhorrent violent

---

most of these provisions relate to extra-territorial considerations, some also relate to prosecutions of persons under the age of 18 years.

[32] See e.g. Facebook's 'Community Standards' which include restrictions on violence and criminal behaviour.

material runs against the very purpose of social media and other online services. In order to comply with legal requirements without unduly compromising the freedom of expression that underpins online interactions, clarity is needed.[33] However, some features of the new provisions discussed above show that clarity is elusive.

Whether material depicts an act of murder or attempted murder, potentially falling within the definition of 'abhorrent violent conduct', is a matter of judgement taking into account the content and context of the material. Not everything that is posted on social media sites is clearly and accurately labelled, indicating its provenance. How is a service provider to ascertain whether the material has been posted or streamed by a participant in the conduct depicted, as opposed to a third party such as a bystander? How can a service provider accurately distinguish between a depiction of an actual murder and a realistically staged but fictitious murder, of the kind portrayed countless times in movies and television series? How can it be discerned whether footage of a violent altercation amounts to attempted murder, as opposed to mere thuggery? In what circumstances will such material be judged to be contrary to the standards of morality, decency and propriety generally accepted by reasonable adults?

These decisions are to an extent outsourced under the legislation to the eSafety Commissioner, through the use of notices under which various presumptions apply, including as to recklessness. This is a very unusual feature of the provisions, as establishing a fault element for a criminal offence is traditionally done by reference to the evidence of what was intended, known, foreseen or believed by the defendant. It may be scant consolation to a service provider that the presumption is rebuttable by the defence, again casting an operational onus on providers to proactively monitor content made accessible or hosted by them, so as to avoid the risk of liability for users' content. Especially given the very significant monetary penalties that apply to failure to remove such content which is found to constitute abhorrent violent material.

---

[33] Note that one of the provisions added by the *Criminal Code Amendment (Sharing of Abhorrent Violent Material) Act 2019* (Cth) is s 474.38, preserving the implied freedom of political communication.

At the time of writing, there have been no reported prosecutions under these provisions. However, it can be expected that the next time an act of murder or attempted murder is live-streamed, cautious social media and other online service providers will act swiftly to respond. Whether this will deter any offenders who seek fame or infamy through filming their criminal acts, remains to be seen.

Study Questions

- Why do social media providers tend to be reactive, rather than proactive, in responding to the live streaming of murder?
- What might be the motivation for live streaming murder?
- According to Urbas, live streamed murder 'poses new challenges to those who control the flow of information to the public'. What are these challenges, and how do you think they might be overcome?
- What problems does Urbas identify in the legal restrictions and obligations concerning 'abhorent violent material'?

Bibliography

Bender, S. M. (2017). Performing murder on live television and social media. In *Legacies of the degraded image in violent digital media* (pp. 35–58). Springer.

Conway, M., & Dillon, J. (2019). *Future trends: Live-streaming terrorist attacks?* VoxPol. Dublin City University. http://www.voxpol.eu/download/vox-pol_publication/Live-streaming_FINAL.pdf

Cooper, G. (2018). Why livestreaming symbolises journalism's current challenges. *Journalism, 20*(1), 162–172.

Dawson, S. (2019). The concerns and competing interests surrounding Australia's new social media legislation. *Communications Law Bulletin, 38*(2), 1–3.

Fietkiewicz, K. J., Dorsch, I., Scheibe, K., Zimmer, F., & Stock, W. G. (2018). Dreaming of stardom and money: Micro-celebrities and influencers on live streaming services. In G. Meiselwitz (Eds.), Social computing and social media: User experience and behavior. *Lecture Notes in Computer Science*, vol. 10913. Springer. https://doi.org/10.1007/978-3-319-91521-0_18

Macklin, G. (2019, July). The Christchurch Attacks: Livestream Terror in the Viral Video Age. Combatting Terrorism Center (CTC) Sentinel, 12(6).

Smith, M., & Urbas, G. (2021). *Technology law—Australian and international perspectives*. Cambridge University Press.

Urbas, G. (2018). Old wine, opaque bottles? Assessing the role of Internet intermediaries in the detection of cybercrime. In L. Chang & R. Brewer (Eds.), *Criminal justice and regulation revisited: Essays in honour of Peter Grabosky*. Routledge.

Urbas, G. (2020). *Cybercrime: Legislation, cases and commentary* (2nd ed.). LexisNexis.

Valcic, J. (2021). The sharing of Abhorrent Violent Materials Act: The realities and implications of Australia's new laws regulating social media companies. *Bond Law Review, 33*(1), Article 2.

15

Conclusions: Exercises in Critiquing Violent Crime in the Media

Maria Mellins and Sarah Moore

Introduction

Through the consideration of the press, documentaries, films, podcasts and other forms of popular culture, this collection has interrogated and critiqued representations of twenty-first century violent crime in the media. From the research contained in these pages important emergent themes can be identified that both contribute to existing debates in contemporary culture, but also prompt recommendations for future research. The authors of this collection have highlighted media examples

M. Mellins (✉)
St Mary's University, Twickenham, UK
e-mail: maria.mellins@stmarys.ac.uk

S. Moore
University of Bath, Bath, UK
e-mail: sm2315@bath.ac.uk

that include problematic depictions of crime, in terms of victims, perpetrators and investigators, aligned with intersectional factors of gender, race, ethnicity, class, sexuality and disability that contribute to misunderstandings and obscurity about 'real' crime. It has found that in some cases, such representations perpetuate myths and confusion and actually delay the public's understanding and identification of certain crimes, and fail to signpost much needed avenues of support. Conversely, contributors have also pointed out examples where the media has fostered information gathering, education, activism and progress. And this book has found a multitude of cases where these two tendencies—to mystify and demystify, impede and spread awareness—have stood in tension with one another, or been negotiated in a particular media treatment. Invariably, media representations are pluralistic. We should not be looking for representations that are all good or all bad, but unpicking the complexities of variation. This book has said a lot about media and crime, but in order to draw the collection together the following discussion reframes the work contained within this volume and explores how this research unpacks central themes in twenty-first century media treatments of violent crime that we can take forward. Themes can be broadly organised into four areas: the historical and contemporary predisposition for the media to submit cases to a public 'trial' that is linked to the commodification of victims; digital space that functions as transportive, immersive, intimate, but also a consideration of how we can contribute to discussions of ethics and online harms; the nostalgic criminal as gothic character and the role of the media in education, awareness raising and activism.

Media 'Trial' and Commodification of Victims

The first theme that has emerged throughout this collection is concerned with crime narratives, complete with 'characters' that are constructed by media representations of real crime, which invite audiences, readers and listeners to attend a type of 'trial' whereby they consider evidence and testimony, in what Stella Bruzzi (2016) in her article that marks out the genre of true crime, calls jurification. For instance, texts may be 'injustice narratives' aimed at establishing the accused/convicted's innocence, and may even offer up a new suspect. Or conversely, we are invited to consider the guilt of those who have evaded justice by some means (by a not-guilty verdict or by being deceased in the case of Jimmy Savile). In her chapter on *Making a Murderer*, Larke Walsh critiques the injustice narratives at work in this case study, and states that characterisation is a natural part of all storytelling, but outlines that this is even more central to true crime. In *Making a Murderer* the documentary invites emotional engagement on the part of the audience so we may 'get to know' the accused/convicted, in this case Steven Avery and—perhaps even more so—his nephew Brendan Dassey. We are asked to scrutinize these characters as people, to get to know them and to 'judge'. Alexa Neale demonstrates through her presentation of the historical case of Gay Gibson in 1947, whilst media 'trials' may have become even more identifiable with the development of digital, interconnected, participatory media platforms, it is certainly not a new theme in the remediation of crime stories. Neale draws on newspapers of the 1940s that invite readers to 'consider your verdict', even after James Camb had been convicted and hanged for the murder of Gay Gibson.

During a case study of Jimmy Savile documentaries, Susanna Menis also addresses the theme of media trials, but does so by explaining the complex relationship between victims, the media and the deceased-accused. With the perpetrator dying two years before the first documentary aired, and consequent possibilities of criminal justice thwarted, the 'trial' was instead played out through the media. In order to understand the way this representation constructed the 'characters' within this trial, Menis turns to Nils Christie and the 'Ideal Victim' (1986) category, which is explained as a term allocated to those who are framed as more deserving of social empathy and recognition. Menis links the nature of society's attachment to 'victims' to a sense of fear, risk and a perceived threat to our security that encourages a collective fascination with victimhood. In this way, Menis moves on to mark out the victims in the mediation of the trial of Jimmy Savile, after his death, as having been commodified as part of an aggressive media campaign that is fuelled by commercial targets. The representation of Savile's victims was mostly one-dimensional and consequently their experience was, in many instances, not explored in a meaningful and supportive way. Menis asserts that whilst the media did play a role in revealing these sex crimes and raised awareness amongst the public, the victims in these documentaries were recruited as 'extras', marginalised to the peripheries of the narratives, with Jimmy Savile cast as the central role. Menis views this trial as locating the problem as institutional rather than social, allowing us, as audience-members, to collectively experience being victims of 'the system' too, as opposed to considering how we—and society more broadly—are implicated in the problem of sexual violence.

In a similar vein, Larke Walsh engages with Horeck's (2019) work to point out the treatment of Teresa Halbach in *Making a Murderer*, who is merely footnoted in the series. The narrative here, is entirely focused on the injustices of the state's treatment of Steven and Brendan, who were convicted of her murder. Sarah Moore, during her discussion of repetition and re-enactment in *The Staircase* and *Serial*, also finds that these texts join others from the true crime genre, as they construct a narrative arc that focuses on a male protagonist and his claim to be innocent, a victim even, but in doing so *lose* the women who have died and therefore any real sense of understanding of them as people. By constantly re-enacting the death of Kathleen Peterson and Hae Min Lee, and circling around the scene of the crime in an attempt to recover memories, there is often an evacuation of meaning and value. These examples and countless others that have emerged throughout this book, expose the media positioning of perpetrators at the centre of such crime stories, often using monikers to describe them such as the 'Yorkshire Ripper' or the 'Night Stalker', which contribute to their mythical, celebrity status, whilst the victims-survivors and their families are often relegated to the periphery, if included at all (readers are encouraged to consider the work of David Schmid [2006] here on celebrity and serial killers). As Louise Wattis points out in her chapter, there is a need to establish the overlooked subgenres of true crime, and broaden the scope of examples that moves away from the dominant academic framing of attractive and fascinating perpetrators.

Even when victims are represented through a close-up lens this doesn't necessarily equate to a meaningful memorialising of the victim's experience. Media representations foreground certain victim qualities, whilst decisively excluding others. Cummins, Foley and King's chapter about the Moors Murders underlines that there is disproportionate representation of victims of crime that is closely linked to a person's status. Cummins, Foley and King draw on Egger (2002) as they discuss that victims of homicide who are at the margins of society are often not investigated adequately and are not afforded high-profile media coverage. As Egger describes, marginalised victims are often not prioritised and appear 'less dead'. This exposes biases around the media and society's favouring of certain types of victims over others that links to intersecting factors such as race , gender , sexuality, disability and mental health. We know, too, that these can also have direct impacts on the justice system. As Cummins, Foley and King suggest, the lack of media coverage of people who fall outside the 'ideal' victim category can have a direct result on the investigation and be a barrier to apprehending the perpetrator. Cummins, Foley and King link this to their own case study of Ian Brady and Myra Hindley, but also apply this to the serial killer Peter Sutcliffe, who was found guilty of murdering 13 women and attempting to murder a further seven women in West Yorkshire and Manchester 1975–1980. The police investigation into these murders was severely hindered by its preoccupation with the perceived lifestyle of the women victims and centralising whether or not they were involved in sex work.

As a number of author contributions have outlined, future research that continues to underline the representations of victims in the media—both those that are included, but also those who are excluded from media attention—is vital to hold the media to account and to develop content that has social responsibility and is victim-survivor focused. Continuing to research and critique these media representations can uncover the structural prejudices within our society that often glamorize, favour and even make celebrities of 'rock star' proportions out of male perpetrators, in contrast to the treatment of victims who may be commodified, blamed, constructed as culpable or left out altogether. This is too often the case in terms of women victims in media representations of domestic abuse, sexual assault and murder, as well as victims who are LGBT+, not white, male victims of domestic abuse and sexual assault, those who have current or historic drug or alcohol addictions, have mental or physical health concerns, are disadvantaged in terms of class/income.

Important changes and developments are occurring in this field. The involvement of academic researchers, experts and specialists in projects that address representation can inform the language and depiction of news reports, documentaries and wider media. For instance, the recent Level Up 'Dignity for Dead Women. Media Guidelines for Reporting Domestic Violence Death' (2018) was informed by key professionals in the field, such as criminologists, domestic violence experts and victims' families/advocates, in collaboration with journalist to provide vital guidance so that reports are accurate and sensitive.[1] This guidance supports journalists to avoid referring to domestic abuse as isolated 'incidents' and instead include language that acknowledges the pattern of behaviour, which may include coercive control. Reports should avoid narratives of romantic love and crimes of passion, ensuring accountability and responsibility on the perpetrator of the violence and not blame the victim. Naming the crime as domestic abuse as opposed to 'tragedy' or 'horror' is key when writing headlines and language, as well as a consideration of the victim's dignity, cultural and religious beliefs and concern for the deceased person's family. Similarly important guidance has been written in other areas and it is hoped that these relationships continue to grow.

Critique Task

Consider an example of a crime 'trial' that has played out in the media (e.g. an example from a true crime documentary or a news item that considers the guilt/innocence of a subject in some way) and reflect on the following:

- How is the perpetrator represented in the text? Are we being invited to 'get to know' them and make our own decisions about their guilt?

---

[1] Professionals include Dr. Liz Kelly CBE, Dr. Jane Monckton-Smith, Prof Rebecca Emerson Dobash, Luke and Ryan Hart, Frank Mullane (Advocacy After Fatal Domestic Abuse), Rossalyn Warren, Aviah Day (Against Violence and Abuse), Leah Cowan (Imkaan), Megha Mohan, Sharan Dhaliwal, Nadine White, Jannat Hossain and Huda Jawad.

- What about the victim and their family? How are they represented? Are they included in a meaningful way?
- Can you note any other 'characters' within this case?
- Now consider the representation of the crime itself. If it is a murder case how is the murder examined in the text? Is there a sense of re-enactment? Does the text repeatedly return to 'scene of the crime' in an attempt to recover new evidence or memories?

Crime Transportation, Tourism and Digital Harms

The second theme that has emerged in this book is directly related to the media construction of crime trials, but specifically considers the role of developing digital technologies in expanding true crime's transportive capacities. Digital crime platforms allow for increased immersion in crime texts, that further encourage consumers to experience crime from the vantage point of those who are directly involved, from the detectives who try to 'solve' the case, to the juries who listen, draw inferences and decide. Participation in crime stories is not new. Thurston, in her chapter that presents a typology of crime-related tourism, points out how spaces such as 'true crime' museums have a long history and are yet another way we can consume crime. From historical public beheadings, to Grand Guignol theatre displays, to the crowds that arrive to attend the gallery in high-profile murder cases, to dark tourist sites such as State Penitentiary's or 25 Cromwell Street (the home of Fred and Rose West)—the public are drawn to moments of trauma and violence. Thurston draws on Broll (2020, p. 792) to remind us that humankind has a 'deep and persistent cultural fascination with the macabre'.

However, what is *reasonably* new, in terms of twenty-first century developments, is the way that we are now engaging with these texts. Irshad's chapter demonstrates the varied ways that texts take us on a transportive journey and propel us into locations of crime, as we attend intimate audio scenes, like a 'guest at wedding' (Spinelli & Dann, 2019). For Irshad, the podcast host becomes a disembodied voice in the listener's head, accompanying us wherever we go, encouraging us to join their investigative journey as they relive the victim's last moments. This preoccupation with solving crimes and deciding guilt and innocence is also a dominant narrative within the texts themselves. Irshad adds to Larke Walsh's examples of injustice narratives as she identifies *Don't Fuck With Cats*, *The Keepers* and *Serial*, as texts that include the theme of the digital 'everyday' detective or netizen that is motivated to solve the mystery.

Irshad outlines the intimate relationship established with podcast listeners and wider true crime consumers, as they are transported across crime geographies. Irshad notes how, in *Down the Hill*, listeners are transported to Delphi, USA, where they hear from close family members about their trauma and loss after the bodies of thirteen-year-old Abigail Williams, and fourteen-year-old Liberty German were discovered in 2017 after they went hiking on Monon High Bridge. This dark, dilapidated narrow bridge is in the centre of a vast expanse of dense woodland—a landscape that has been foregrounded in the representation of this case—akin to the gothic geographies described in chapters by Cherry, as well as Cummins, Foley and King (a theme we return to below). Listeners travel virtually to these woods whilst detectives search for the missing girls, they attend town hall meetings and receive briefings from law enforcement. They migrate across digital platforms to access information about 'Bridge Guy' and actively try to discover leads that may help to find the perpetrator. This provides an emotionally deepened listener experience, as we discover the awful truth, sometimes, as *Finding Cleo* demonstrates, in perceived synchronicity with the family. The digital cross-platform consumption of true crime encourages consumers to participate in immersive crime experiences that have opened up collective communities of listeners who feel engaged in activism and social justice. This level of absorption within the true crime space correlates with the success and 'bingeability' of the content, but does raise questions about the role of the media in prescribing justice. As Bruzzi points out, this transportation and 'jurification' of audiences may lead to an eliding of documentary and law which may affect the stability or instability of truth (2016, p. 39).

This ability to transport viewers and listeners to the scene of the crime is also examined by Gregor Urbas, but in his chapter the discussion moves away from examples of true crime narratives that are essentially a retelling of past events by a producer or investigative journalist, to an *actual* crime scene that is being live streamed by the perpetrator of violence. Urbas notes that live-streaming of murder and similar acts of violence can be viewed as a 'performative crime' (Bender, 2017) and the motivation behind this form of streaming violence stems not only from committing the crime itself, but also the communication of this to an audience. This type of crime is often linked to a personal or political grievance and is used by the perpetrator to have ultimate control over the message they broadcast. Urbas draws on global crime cases including the 'Facebook Killer' in the USA, the 'Halle Synagogue Shooter' in Germany and the mass killing at two mosques in Christchurch, New Zealand as he considers the regulatory responses and challenges to identification, removal and prosecution of such illegal and offensive content. This chapter joins wider research of online harms and digital abuse—including the use of deep fakes, image-based abuse, exploitation, cyber stalking, privacy and surveillance—that calls for a reconsideration of the roles and responsibilities of the technology companies that provide social media and networked technologies so that they can play a more active role in the prevention of this increasingly pervasive phenomenon.

Critique Task

Consider an example of crime media that has transported you to another space and/or time in some way.

- What type of media was it? For instance was it a podcast or a documentary? Perhaps it was a crime tour? What specific appeal does this type of media have?
- Can you think of an example of a recent crime that spurred you to find out more information about the case? What case was it and what did you find out?
- Conduct a brief online search of tourist attractions related to real crime. Are there any ethical issues related to these spaces?
- What are the challenges of addressing the live streaming of murder? What is the role of tech companies here?

Nostalgic Aesthetics, Gothic Criminals

The book's third core theme is related to the representation of perpetrators, and how this links to the gothic reimagining of real crime. Cummins, Foley and King's work on the appeals of serial killer narratives identifies gothic tropes within the narratives. Cummins, Foley and King make use of Seltzer's work on society's preoccupation with 'wound culture' which underlines a persistent fascination with violence, and the public and private experience of trauma in media representation. Drawing on the case of Ian Brady and—in particular—Myra Hindley, their chapter examines the media construction of 'evil', and considers the role of gender norms in how female perpetrators of murder and violent sex crimes are depicted. Cummins, Foley and King draw on Hansford Johnson's account of Hindley's trial to illustrate the way that Hindley, like other female offenders of serious crime, is framed in media and society as Other. Media representations have consistently been concerned with Hindley's appearance, captured and historically set by what Cummins, Foley and King call 'that photograph'—the mug shot of Hindley taken at Hyde Police Station in 1966—and, as part of that, the gendered fascination, shock and repulsion that she could be involved in crimes against children.

Cummins, Foley and King's chapter aligns with Cherry's work when they consider the gothic tropes utilised in media depictions of crime. For instance, Cummins, Foley and King spend time examining the ways that the media photographs of Brady and Hindley are often linked to stylised appearances of gothic bodies. Perhaps even more identifiable though, is the depiction of gothic geographies within this case, which is exemplified through the use of the term 'Moors Murders' that underlines a link with gothic representations of crime. The construction and foregrounding of the 'Moors' setting in Manchester, England, conjures associations of vast, unwieldy gothic landscapes, which hold within them 'terrible secrets' of their rugged terrain.

Cherry's work examines fictionalised representations of real-life serial killers and spree murderers in the television dramas *Mindhunter* (2017–19), *Aquarius* (2015–16), *I Am the Night* (2019), and *American Horror Story* (2011–19). Similar to the gothic representations discussed by

Cummins, Foley and King, Cherry also identifies how these texts reimagine gothic bodies. Using examples of Ed Kemper, whose size and structure is reminiscent of Frankenstein's 'eerily articulate' Creature, and Charles Manson, who is contrastingly encoded as mythically impish or devilish Trickster, crouching on the back of his seat akin to Henry Fuseli's painting *The Nightmare* (1781), Cherry outlines how media texts encode monstrosity. For Cherry, these are constructed monstrous structures and settings in their own right. Like the Saddleworth Moor, their bodies themselves serve as gothic environments that attract viewers to watch and observe them as they house secret atrocities. Audiences look for signs and clues of what lies within, searching for displays of guilt and glimmers of the acts of which they may be capable. This once again reveals our culture's fascination with perpetrators and their mediation as monstrous characters.

Critique Task

Consider an example of serial killer narratives in either a documentary series or film. How does this link to gothic fiction? Can you think of any examples of the following?

- The presence of gothic characters
- The use of gothic settings and/or landscapes
- The use of gothic imagery in the title sequence and any other visual features used in the series?
- If this is a historical case (e.g. from the 1970s) does the text include features that might be considered nostalgic of this time? (for instance music or footage from that decade)

Media's Role in Education, Awareness Raising and Victim-Survivor Activism

Whilst a great deal of the research contained within these pages does critique and problematize the media representation of crimes, this collection has also examined the ways that critiquing crime in the media can positively contribute to raising the profile of inconsistencies and social injustices of crime. For instance, Cherry's work outlines how *Mindhunter* draws attention to the discrimination and marginalisation experienced by the black families of the Atlanta child murders during the late 1970s and early 1980s. At the end of the second season the series acknowledges the horror, loss and lack of resolution experienced by the families of the child victims. The final caption states that '[a]s of 2019, none of the remaining 27 cases have been prosecuted'. Cherry underlines that this moment is used to 'point the finger of accusation outside of the text to provide a metatextual comment on policing and race in America'.

Using varied case studies of contemporary media, this book has also considered the media's potential for awareness raising and its ability to influence and positively inform public health and society's awareness of crime. Hoffman and Hobbs' chapter demonstrates examples of true crime media, post #MeToo, which locate the victim at the centre of their narrative. They demonstrate how docuseries like Amazon's *Ted Bundy: Falling for a Killer*, and BBC's *The Yorkshire Ripper Files: A Very British Crime Story* have potential to *both* reframe women's voices in ways that challenge and reject the problematic conventions of the true crime genre, but also continue to uphold patriarchal structures that fall foul of acknowledging the range of experience of female victims-survivors. Mellins' chapter draws on media coverage of the case of Alice Ruggles, who was stalked and murdered in 2016, to highlight the importance of media representations of stalking. Drawing on media texts including the podcast *Real Crime Profile* and VICE's 'Unfollow Me' campaign, Mellins demonstrates how media exposure can raise the profile of stalking and coercive control and that dissemination of information about stalking motivations, behaviours and long-term impacts, which directly tackle myths and minimisations of this crime, has the potential to effect a shift in public perspectives and attitudes.

Similarly, Murphy's work on coercive control within human trafficking and intimate partner violence calls for more realistic and nuanced examples of human trafficking to be incorporated within media representations, which reveal the diversity of experiences. Murphy's consideration of the film *Taken* (2008) demonstrates that the perpetuation of unhelpful tropes and clichés align, once again, with Christie's concept of the ideal victim (1986). Murphy argues that these more extreme examples of stereotypical human trafficking representations are damaging as they lead to misunderstanding about trafficking and particularly the methods of recruitment. Much more expanded considerations, informed by knowledge from services, researchers and experts that include the psychological acts of coercion and control are required. Similar to encouraging media representations of stalking that unpack the variation in behaviours of this crime and include signposting for how to access support, Murphy identifies a need to move beyond news and screen media images of modern slavery of the 'shackled victim' in favour of content that reflects fuller experiences of victims-survivors.

The media is an incredibly powerful institution at the heart of our society. We hope that it is not too idealistic that further research that brings together collaboration between researchers and experts working in the field of crime and justice with media professionals will result in more fully developed experiences of crime being represented. Through embracing the current public appetite for true crime, the media can raise the profile of insidious crimes and disseminate important information which will result in earlier recognition and a more effective response. In this way, media awareness campaigns can join the formal education system to raise awareness amongst young people so they have a better understanding of dangers and lead to positive and much needed shifts in our culture.

Critique Task

Choose either (a) stalking (b) modern slavery (c) sexual violence with education environments. Conduct brief online research to find examples of campaigns that raise awareness of this crime.

- What examples of videos, posters, podcast or documentaries can you find?
- What are the specific aims of the media you have found? (what awareness is it trying to raise?)
- If you were employed by a charity that was working to raise awareness of this crime, can you think of a campaign that you might develop? (This could be a simple poster or infographic that can be shared on social media, or a more detailed video or documentary)

Bibliography

Bender, S. M. (2017). Performing murder on live television and social media. In *Legacies of the degraded image in violent digital media* (pp. 35–58). Springer.

Broll, R. (2020). Dark fandoms: An introduction and case study. *Deviant Behavior, 41*(6), 792–804. https://doi.org/10.1080/01639625.2019.1596453

Bruzzi, S. (2016). Making a genre: The case of the contemporary true crime documentary. *Law and Humanities, 10*, 249–280.

Christie, N. (1986). The ideal victim. In E. A. Fattah (Ed.), *From crime policy to victim policy* (pp. 15–30, 18). MacMillan.

Egger, S. (2002). *Killers among us*. Prentice Hall Publishing.

Hansford Johnson, P. (1967). *On iniquity*. MacMillan.

Horeck, T. (2019). *Justice on demand: True crime in the digital streaming era.* Wayne State University Press.

Schmid, D. (2006). *Idols of destruction: Celebrity and the serial killer.* In S. Holmes & S. Redmond (Eds.), *Framing celebrity: New directions in celebrity culture* (pp. 295–310). Routledge.

Seltzer, M. (1998). *Serial killers: Death and life in America's wound culture.* Routledge.

Spinelli, M., & Dann, L. (2019). *Podcasting: The audio media revolution.* Bloomsbury.

Starling, J. (2018). *Dignity for dead women: Media guidelines for reporting domestic violence death.* Level Up Feminist Community.

Index

© The Editor(s) (if applicable) and The Author(s), under exclusive
license to Springer Nature Switzerland AG 2021
M. Mellins and S. Moore (eds.), *Critiquing Violent Crime in the Media*,
https://doi.org/10.1007/978-3-030-83758-7

Printed by Printforce, United Kingdom